THE STATE
AND LABOR
IN MODERN
AMERICA

THE STATE & LABOR

IN MODERN AMERICA

MELVYN DUBOFSKY

The University of North Carolina Press

Chapel Hill & London

Publication of this work was made possible in part through
a grant from the Division of Research Programs of the
National Endowment for the Humanities, an independent
federal agency whose mission is to award grants to support
education, scholarship, media programming, libraries, and
museums, in order to bring the results of cultural activities
to a broad, general public.

The paper in this book meets the guidelines for
permanence and durability of the Committee on Production
Guidelines for Book Longevity of the Council on Library
Resources.

Library of Congress Cataloging-in-Publication Data
Dubofsky, Melvyn, 1934–
    The state and labor in modern America / by Melvyn
Dubofsky.
        p.   cm.
    Includes bibliographical references and index.
    ISBN 0-8078-2125-X (alk. paper).
—ISBN 0-8078-4436-5 (pbk. : alk. paper)
    1. Labor policy — United States — History — 20th
century.   2. Trade unions — United States — History —
20th century.   3. Labor movement — United States —
History — 20th century.   I. Title.
HD8072.D848   1994
331'.0973 — dc20   93-21404
                                                    CIP

98 97 96 95 94   5 4 3 2 1

In Memory of C.E.F.

Contents

ix   Acknowledgments

xi   Introduction: State and Society
in Modern United States History

Chapter 1   Laissez-Faire and the Origins of
1   Federal Intervention, 1873–1900

Chapter 2   The Progressive Approach: From
37   Theodore Roosevelt to Woodrow
Wilson, 1900–1916

Chapter 3   World War and the Positive State,
61   1917–1920

Chapter 4   Interregnum: The State as "Neutral,"
83   1921–1932

Chapter 5   The New Deal Labor Revolution,
107   Part 1, 1933–1936

Chapter 6   The New Deal Labor Revolution,
137   Part 2, 1937–1941

Chapter 7   War and the Creation of a New
169   Industrial State, 1940–1946

Chapter 8   An Almost Perfect Machine:
197   Industrial Relations Policy in an
Age of Affluence, 1947–1973

233   Conclusion
239   Notes
275   Cases Cited
279   Bibliography
305   Index

Acknowledgments

Any book as long in the making as this one owes debts to so many individuals and institutions that it is nearly impossible to acknowledge each and every one properly. The following acknowledgments represent, at best, a partial repayment of my many debts.

A summer fellowship from the National Endowment for the Humanities provided financial support at a crucial stage of the project. Binghamton University generously offered sabbatical and research leaves that enabled me to complete the book. A small grant from Binghamton University's Graduate School funded the final stage.

So many librarians and archivists offered assistance along the way that I cannot thank each one separately. Yet this book could not have been written without the aid of the staffs at the Herbert Hoover, Franklin D. Roosevelt, Harry S. Truman, and Dwight D. Eisenhower presidential libraries; the National Archives and its branch in Suitland, Maryland; the State Historical Society of Wisconsin, the Labor-Management Documentation Center at the Catherwood Library, New York State School of Industrial and Labor Relations, Cornell University, Ithaca; the Archives of Labor and Urban Affairs, Walter P. Reuther Library, Wayne State University; and last, but certainly not least, those responsible for operating the interlibrary loan services at the Binghamton University library. I must also thank my colleague at University Publications of America, Randy Boehm, who worked with me at many of the libraries and archives cited above to microfilm trade union and government records that reveal much of the history of the state and labor in modern America.

From start to finish, numerous colleagues and graduate students have shared their own research and ideas with me. Readers will see immediately my enormous debt to Joseph McCartin and Colin Davis, who completed dissertations under my supervision on aspects of state-labor relations. Such other graduate students as Steven Burwood, Taylor Hollander, Patrizia Sione, Sandra Spingarn, Paul Street, Peter Friedlander, and Bryan Palmer, to name only a few, taught me a great deal about how to do history. During the summer of 1992, Sam White served as my research assistant, tutored me in the complexities of E-mail and other computer functions, and, most important, helped me finish the book. Robert Harris conceived the baseball metaphor that I used in the conclusion. At scholarly conferences and in personal conversations and correspondence, Christopher Tomlins, William Forbath, Staughton Lynd, Karl Klare, John Laslett, Robin Einhorn, Judith Stein, Howell John Harris, Paul Krause, and many others subjected my work and theories to scathing yet constructive criticism. My colleague Tom Dublin and my friend Steve Fraser read an earlier version of the manuscript. For more than twenty years, David Montgomery has taught me how to be a better historian. My colleagues in the Research Working Group on World Labor at the Fernand Braudel Center — Giovanni Arrighi, John Casparis, Donald Quataert, Mark Selden, Beverly Silver, and Immanuel Wallerstein — made me think in terms of a larger world-historical system. My former student, coauthor, and good friend Warren Van Tine has helped me in more ways than I can mention. David Brody, Robert Zieger, and Kenneth Straus, good friends all, read the entire manuscript and saved me from numerous errors (those that remain expose my own limitations as a scholar). Lewis Bateman, executive editor of the University of North Carolina Press, has been a nurturing editor. Jan McInroy did an absolutely superb job of copyediting. My final debt of gratitude goes to my late colleague to whom the book is dedicated, Charles E. Freedeman, a bon vivant, fly fisherman extraordinaire, and sterling scholar, who, through thirty years of close and good friendship, taught me how to become a good historian and a better person.

Introduction:

State and Society in

Modern United States

History

"More than ever before," the British political scientist Ralph Miliband wrote in 1969, "men now live in the shadow of the state. . . . It is for the state's attention, or for its control, that men compete; and it is against the state that beat the waves of social conflict."[1] Since Miliband wrote those lines, many social scientists, though perhaps historians least of all, have been busily engaged in "bringing the state back in" to scholarship.[2] For almost two decades, however, the dominant tradition in the writing of labor history in the United States neglected the realm of politics and policy-making. Instead historians, influenced largely by the cultural approach to working-class history pioneered by E. P. Thompson in England and Herbert Gutman in the United States, focused on how sturdy ethnic subcultures enabled workers to resist their employers and to establish a measure of autonomy in their lives. Other historians, strongly influenced by David Montgomery, stressed that workers' shop-floor culture enabled them to exercise real power (workers' control) at the point of production. Still other historians, most notably Sean Wilentz in his study of New York City artisans and Leon Fink in his treatment of the Knights of Labor, integrated culture with the political ideology of "republicanism," which they used to explain the most salient aspects of working-class behavior.[3] And more recently yet, the claims of gender and discourse theory have come to the fore.[4]

Unfortunately, the tendency of historians to emphasize ethnicity, gender, race, shop-floor traditions, and discursive ideologies has led them to slight, in the words of Elizabeth Fox-Genovese and Eugene Genovese, "who rides whom" (or who rules whom).[5] Indeed, all too often, the "new" labor history exaggerated the power of working people and sentimentalized their subcultures.[6] The stress on the private rather than the public, the cultural rather than the political, the discursive rather than the policy-making aspects of the past has made it more difficult for us to understand two central themes of labor history: (1) patterns of trade union growth and decline and (2) the persistent dominance of capital in its relations with labor.

Ever since the late 1950s when I began my dissertation on New York City workers during the Progressive era, I have been intrigued by the relationship between the power of the state and the growth and evolution of the labor movement in the United States. Subsequently, whether I studied the radicalized workers who joined the Industrial Workers of the World (IWW) or that prototypical "business unionist" John L. Lewis, I discovered that the policies and actions of the state substantially shaped the history of working people and the movements that they built.

Not only has the state had an exceptional influence on the history of workers and their movements in the United States; a history of that relationship also discloses much about the basic dynamics and dilemmas of democratic politics in the modern era. In examining the relationship between the state and labor, one encounters an economic system that creates gross material inequalities within a regime of universal citizenship and mass democratic voting rights. For the beneficiaries of economic inequality, legitimacy sometimes seemed problematic. How could large property-holders and successful entrepreneurs protect their rights and prerogatives from an aroused and vengeful mass democracy? Equally important and problematic, how could a republican democracy built on the participation of economically independent freeholders and artisans endure in a society composed in the main of dependent wage earners? In broader terms, how could social order and civil peace be maintained in a democratic order that failed to shower its benefits equally on all citizens? Indeed, could the concept of "republicanism," which has done so much to enrich our comprehension of revolutionary and early national history and which became a leitmotif in the writings of many younger labor historians, explain much about the world of modern working people and their movements?[7]

As the twentieth century draws to its close, we confront a reality that compels us to reexamine the historical relationship between the state and labor in the United States. By the end of the 1980s, the United States had a smaller proportion of its labor force unionized than any other advanced industrial nation. From a post–World War II high of nearly 36 percent of the nonagricultural labor force being represented by unions, the level fell to 16 percent, a decline that now seems irreversible. Between 1983 and 1988, trade unions in the United States lost more than five million members, a decline that persisted despite an extensive economic expansion after 1983 that lasted until the end of the decade.

Not only did unions lose members; they also signed concessionary contracts that surrendered several of labor's most cherished gains. Official statistics from the Department of Labor show that most new union contracts negotiated during the 1980s granted wage increases that were less than the inflation rate and less than the raises typically received by nonunion workers. The same statistics reveal, moreover, that the number of strikes declined to a level not experienced since the balmy days of the late 1920s. All the indicators point to a labor movement in full retreat.[8]

It is no coincidence that the precipitate decline of the American labor movement coincided with the presidency of Ronald Reagan. When Reagan entered the White House in January 1981, trade unions were already in disarray. The president's brutal treatment of the Professional Air Traffic Controllers' Organization (PATCO) strikers in 1981 sent employers and workers an unmistakable message: hereafter, the federal government would not tolerate militant action by trade unions. To make sure that this message would not be misread, the man Reagan appointed as chair of the National Labor Relations Board, Donald Dotson, emphasized: "The scheme of unionized labor relations in the United States bears no resemblance to what was intended by the framers of our basic law." Dotson added: "Collective bargaining frequently means labor monopoly, the destruction of individual freedom, and the destruction of the marketplace as the mechanism for determining the value of labor."[9]

What makes developments in the United States during the 1980s more perplexing is the contrast with what happened among workers to the north in Canada. Faced with the same global economic crisis, a new conservative government in power, and an even less expansive job market, Canadian workers neither deserted their unions, whose membership actually rose, nor agreed to employer demands for contractual concessions.

Two primary explanations have been offered to account for the contrasts between the trajectories of late-twentieth-century trade unionism in the United States and Canada. Paul Weiler, a Canadian and a professor of labor law at Harvard Law School, suggested that the variations in the growth patterns of the U.S. and the Canadian labor movements are best explained by the differences in the industrial relations codes of the two nations.[10] By contrast, American sociologist Seymour Martin Lipset asserted that the cause for the difference in trade union growth can be found in the dissimilar American and Canadian value systems, the former stressing individualism and mobility, the latter sanctioning more cooperative modes of behavior and a stronger corporate sense of community.[11]

Like Weiler, I prefer to look to the state and its tangible labor policies rather than to such abstract concepts as national character or value systems in order to understand patterns in trade union development. That development is precisely what I intend to examine in this book, tracing the relationship between the American labor movement and the shifting labor policies of the national state from the 1870s to the present.

Recently, as I noted above, political scientists and sociologists have refocused our attention on the role of the state. Such scholars as Ralph Miliband and Nikos

Poulantzas in Europe and Theda Skocpol, Stephen Skowronek, and Fred Block in the United States have brought a new sophistication to the study of the state in modern capitalist societies. Their theories and hypotheses offer us one way to begin to write the sort of political history that William E. Leuchtenberg demanded in his recent presidential address to the Organization of American Historians.[12] And it is precisely the sort of political history that this book intends to narrate.

In seeking to understand how the state intervenes in the sphere of labor-capital relations, we must evaluate several theories that explain the bases for state action. In North America, the pluralist model of public policy implementation has normally been the dominant one. In that model, public officials, freely and openly elected to office under democratic rules, serve the interests of those who vote for them. Because no single group of voters dominates the society and economy, contending blocs, or interest groups, compete for public favor. Public officials, in turn, act as honest brokers, mediating among the competing power blocs on behalf of the larger public interest. The reverse image of the pluralist model is the crude, or vulgar, Marxist one, in which the state serves as the slugging agency of the ruling class, instrumentally ensuring that the interests of capital prevail whenever and wherever challenged.

Because the history of most industrial societies in the twentieth century shows manifold examples of the state acting against the immediate interests of capitalists, some younger leftist scholars have revised the crudely instrumental Marxist model. At first, beginning in the 1960s, a small coterie of young American historians who identified with the "New Left" politically and for whom the historian William Appleman Williams served as scholarly godfather, developed the so-called corporate liberal interpretation of history. In their analyses, exceptionally class-conscious corporate leaders, aware that reform served their self-interest better than repression did, replaced the policeman's club with the soft glove of a more socially conscious welfare capitalism. To thwart the rise of a militant working-class movement, these corporate reformers welcomed negotiations with "responsible" antisocialist labor leaders and urged the state to enact welfare measures that would ensure a minimum level of health and decency for all citizens.[13]

Unfortunately for the advocates of the corporate liberal interpretation, most corporate reformers deemed the only good unions to be those that represented someone else's employees and the only good welfare law to be one that failed to affect their enterprise. Since the original contributions of the corporate liberal school, however, labor historians have been largely silent in the debates raging about the role of the state and the relationship between state and society.[14]

As political scientists, sociologists, and even legal scholars came to dominate scholarship about the state's role in modern society, a more sophisticated body of largely neo-Marxist theory emerged to suggest that the state acts autonomously, that it is not the agency of a ruling class, competing blocs, or sophisticated "corporate liberals." Fred Block even titled one of his more argumentative essays "The Ruling Class Does Not Rule."[15] In this version, the state does not serve the direct interests of any particular set of capitalists, reactionary or progressive, myopic or farsighted. Instead, the state, acting autonomously, promotes the vital interests of capital by subordinating the sectoral and selfish concerns of individual capitalists to the general welfare, a process that creates the social peace necessary for the expanded reproduction of capital. The real battles that determine the fate of society and the economy are fought between and among bureaucrats who respond as much to the imperatives of their administrative agencies as to the imprecations of their external constituents. What Theda Skocpol and Stephen Skowronek, among others, define as state administrative capacity determines which reforms and legislative initiatives prevail. Bureaucracies that have ample treasuries, experienced administrators, and a history of administering programs successfully prove most adept at molding state policy. Thus the state becomes a battleground on which conflicting classes and contending bureaucrats simultaneously compete for power.[16]

The notion that the state, whether or not it serves ruling classes and capitalists directly, actually succeeds in stilling social conflict and even in winning the consent of working people to their subaltern role has gained enormous currency among scholars who have examined the impact of the law on labor in North America. With the exception of historian Christopher Tomlins, whose detailed study of federal labor relations policy in the United States from the Wagner Act to the Taft-Hartley Act asserts that the only thing labor can expect to win from the state is a "counterfeit liberty," most of this scholarship has been the product of law school faculty and political scientists. Tomlins himself drew heavily from the theoretical work of Karl Klare, Katherine Stone, and other members of the school of critical legal history, most of whom concede that the modern state has promoted trade unionism and collective bargaining. Yet they suggest that legal doctrines legitimated post–New Deal industrial relations practices because, in Klare's words, trade unionism and especially "collective bargaining is a system for inducing workers to participate in their own domination by managers and those whom managers serve."[17]

This interpretation has also had echoes on the Canadian side of the border. Canada's Industrial Relations Act of 1948 (a northern variation of the Wagner Act) was, assert Leo Panitch and Donald Swartz, "an adjustment devised not to undermine but to secure and maintain under new conditions capital's long run . . . dominant position. . . . What before had taken the appearance of the Mounties' charge, now increasingly took the form of the rule of law by which unions policed themselves in most instances." So Canadian workers, too, found themselves bequeathed a "counterfeit liberty" by their state, one in which, according to Panitch and Swartz, "trade unionism . . . bore all the signs of the web of legalistic restrictions which enveloped it. Its practices and consciousness were highly legalistic and bureaucratic, and its collective strength accordingly limited."[18]

Thus, among various scholars of different nationalities, we see an interpretation that contends, first, that the state has acted to suppress rank-and-file militancy, trade union autonomy, and trade union democracy in the interest of social stability and capital accumulation and, second, that the law has rendered trade unions the servants of capital and the state. Even among scholars who see the impact of the state and the law on labor as perhaps more ambiguous, there has been a tendency to explain the failure of the American labor movement to act more militantly and to pursue a course of independent radical politics as a logical (if not necessary) response to the repressive function of the law. Both William Forbath and Victoria Hattam assert that the community-based "populist" politics exemplified by the Knights of Labor and its predecessor movements succumbed to the sectoral craft unionism and political voluntarism expressed by the American Federation of Labor (AFL) because of the impact of judicial decisions on workers' collective rights. They answer the "Sombart question" by suggesting that the state through its legal doctrines shaped the American labor movement into an exceptional nonsocialist and even apolitical form.[19] In contrast to this emerging interpretation of the repressive role of the state, I would like to suggest that the relationship between the state and labor is far more ambiguous and that workers and their unions have gained from positive state intervention at particular junctures in American history.[20]

Of course, in writing a more balanced narrative of state intervention, I would not want to suggest to readers a monocausal explanation of the past. Business cycles certainly affected the dynamics of union growth. The New Deal years aside, before the 1980s trade unionism in the United States rose and fell in harmony with the expansion and contraction of the national economy and such exogenous factors as wars and global economic competition. Nevertheless, I would still like to insist upon the salience of the state in the history of the modern United States labor movement. Let me elaborate.

A good place to begin might be with a quick glance at those moments when trade unionism in the United States advanced most rapidly and broadly. My reading of history and statistics reveals that there were six especially significant periods of union growth: the years at the turn of the twentieth century, roughly from 1898 to 1903, when the organized labor movement more than quintupled in size; the World War I years, 1916–20, when trade unions nearly doubled their membership; the New Deal years, when organizers rebuilt a theretofore moribund labor movement; the World War II years, when mass-production unionism and the so-called modern industrial relations system matured; the Korean War period, 1950–53, when unionism reached the upper limits of its historical penetration among American workers; and, finally, the years of Lyndon B. Johnson's "Great Society," 1964–68, the last time trade unionism experienced an absolute increase in membership. At each of those historical moments, workers, their unions, and the state constructed an amicable relationship. They were eras when, in varying combinations, popular politics, administrative policy formation, and union influence on the legislative and executive branches of the state operated to promote stability by furthering the interests of workers and their organizations.

Here I should also proffer a few caveats. First, I have consciously chosen to omit the separate state and local governments from the narrative, not because such political units were unimportant (indeed, before the era of the New Deal, state and local governments probably had a greater impact on workers and unions than the federal government did) but because a single scholar can do only so much. Second, even within the national state, it is difficult to identify a single locus of power or policy-making, owing to the constitutional separation of powers. At different times and in different ways, the legislative, judicial, and executive branches intruded on the relations between labor and capital. Third, I have intentionally focused on just one set of state policies or actions, those that impinged most directly on the relations between capital and labor, management and unions, employers and workers. I have thus chosen to neglect the history of the evolution and devolution of the twentieth-century welfare state and those state initiatives that set minimum levels of health and welfare for citizens. I have done so because the struggles over such welfare reforms in the electoral arena, the legislative chambers, the state bureaucracies, and the courtrooms failed before the 1960s to expose the society's and polity's fissures as lucidly as did the often simultaneous battles between the advocates of capital and labor over their respective organizational, economic, and juridical prerogatives. It was the latter struggles that bared most clearly what David Brody has referred to as the great issue in labor history, the question of power, "the efforts of laboring people to assert some control over their working lives, and . . . the equal determination of American business to conserve the prerogatives of management," as well as the reality "that power and interest can be issues of deadly conflict even in a system in which men agree on fundamentals."[21] That reality was clearly grasped by the historical actors themselves. In the aftermath of the violent railroad strikes of 1877, a Southern newspaper observed that "the Southern question was dead," to be superseded by "the question of labor and capital, work and wages."[22] Or, as a representative of coal operators in the state of Illinois observed in 1901: "By the side of the labor problem all other worldly problems are secondary. . . . Here it seems everything in the industrial world begins and ends."[23] Indeed, for the time period on which I plan to focus, the years from the late nineteenth century through the passage of the Taft-Hartley Act, the relations between labor and capital exposed the single most contentious issue of public policy in a mass democracy — the proper division of the national income and wealth.

A final admonition before the story commences. Although my concern with the subject is partly theoretical, partly analytical, and partly interpretive, I have chosen to pursue a narrative strategy. I follow the history of the interaction between the state and labor in the United States chronologically, sometimes breaking from the narrative to analyze or to interpret the story but most often embedding the analysis and interpretation in the narrative. Theory, too, will remain more implicit than explicit, more embedded in the ongoing narrative than isolated from the story and thrust forward for the reader's attention. In a conclusion, I will attempt to describe succinctly where the preceding narrative fits into the contending theories concerning the relationship between the state and society and to suggest my own interpretation of that relationship in the case of the United States. Beyond that, I leave it to the sociologists and political scientists on whose work and theories I have grown so dependent to use my historical narrative to enrich their scholarship as they have mine.

A word is probably also in order concerning my research strategy. Any work of scholarship treating a subject as large as this and over such a long sweep of time must necessarily rely on the published contributions of numerous fellow tillers in the fields of history. Part synthesis and part original research, this book draws on several generations of published history as well as my own research in published public records (legislative journals, legislative hearings and reports, judicial reports, presidential papers) and numerous unpublished public and private archival collections. For the period from the 1870s through the end of World War II, I rely as heavily on unpublished and published sources as I do on the contributions of other scholars to construct my synthesis. The concluding chapter on the years from 1947 to the present, however, depends preponderantly on the writings of journalists and a legion of social scientists and legal scholars. Finally, the narrative that follows aims to open, not to close, to research and discussion the subject of the historical relationship between the state and society in the modern United States.

THE STATE
AND LABOR
IN MODERN
AMERICA

Laissez-Faire and the Origins of Federal Intervention, 1873–1900

During the late nineteenth century, the labor question first became a national issue. The growing centralization of the economy and a swelling wave of strikes prompted federal officials, most especially the president and district and circuit judges, to act during industrial disputes. More often than not, the intrusion of the executive and judicial branches into "private conflicts" between workers and employers favored business interests. Time and again, judges issued injunctions that crippled strikes, and presidents used federal troops and marshals to similar effect, either to enforce judicial injunctions or to establish martial law. Over the course of the three decades between the 1870s and the turn of the century, however, presidents, members of Congress, and even some judges began to rethink the use of federal power to regulate labor conflicts. As the century ended, the federal authorities seemed poised to adopt policies that would abet the emergence of responsible unionism and peaceful collective bargaining as alternatives to violent conflicts between workers and employers.

A National Economy

By 1900 the relations between labor and capital, workers and their employers had been largely reshaped by more than fifty years of technological and organizational innovations. At the end of the Civil War, only the railroads and some of the larger textile firms operated as modern business corporations. They obtained their capital from myriad private investors in impersonal credit markets, hired professional managers to use other people's money for operations, supervised work forces that came to number in the hundreds and thousands, and competed in national markets. At the same time, the more typical enterprises remained small family proprietorships or simple partnerships. In such businesses, the owners raised their capital largely from among family members or close associates, managed their firms themselves, employed relatively small work forces with whom they maintained personal relations, and competed mostly in local or regional markets.

A half century of sweeping economic change did not totally obliterate the structure of the American economy as it had appeared in 1865. But as Alfred D. Chandler, Jr., has shown, the large, hierarchically structured and professionally managed corporation became characteristic of the most dynamic sectors of the economy. The type of modern management pioneered by railroads between 1850 and 1870 spread by 1900 first to other transport and communications firms, then to the iron and steel industry, meatpacking, agricultural implements, and other key sectors of the economy.[1] These firms, with their large professionally managed labor forces, became involved in the most contentious labor-capital conflicts of the late nineteenth century, those that commanded national attention and the concern, on occasion, of the federal government. At the other pole of the economy, particularly in sectors where local market competition prevailed, the family firm or private partnership remained predominant. There too, to be sure, labor conflict increasingly roiled employer-employee relations. But those conflicts, which were more numerous and persistent than the struggles in the corporate sector of the economy and perhaps more important to the history of trade unionism in the late nineteenth century, rarely commanded national attention. Neither the president nor Congress bothered themselves with disputes between local noncorporate employers and their workers, although federal courts sometimes intervened through the issuance of restraining orders and injunctions.

For both businesspeople and workers, the economy and society of late-nineteenth-century America proved unsettling. As the "transport-communications revolution" intensified competition among firms, business enterprises rose and fell. Some entrepreneurs and managers adapted successfully to new forms of national, and even international, competition; others failed. In the best of circumstances, economic change would have wrought hardship on many employers and workers. But the late nineteenth century was scarcely the best of times. Known to economic historians as the era of the "great depression," the years from 1873 to 1897 in the United States and elsewhere in the world were marked by steadily falling prices, repeated depressions or recessions (1873–77, 1883–85, 1893–97), high rates of business failure, and substantial levels of periodic unemployment. For the period as a whole, the total number of years of economic contraction exceeded those of expansion.

Nevertheless, the American economy continued to grow absolutely, becoming by the 1890s the world's most productive nation, far surpassing the former leader, Great Britain. Much of that economic growth resulted from two developments that exacted a heavy price from workers. In order to survive in a business environment marked by intensive competition and falling prices, entrepreneurs struggled ceaselessly to reduce their costs of production. On the one hand, they applied new forms of technology where its introduction could lower unit costs of production. Technological innovations in the steel, meatpacking, and tobacco industries, among others, greatly expanded the rate of production and lessened its cost per unit of input.[2] On the other hand, even in the absence of significant technological innovation, many firms experimented with new methods of routing the flow of work, controlling their sources of supply and inventories, and supervising their labor forces. These changes added up to what Daniel Nelson has characterized as a managerial revolution.[3]

Whether victims of technological innovation or managerial reform, workers faced a turbulent new world of toil. Some skilled workers saw machines obliterate their dearly acquired skills or tighter forms of supervision diminish their on-the-job autonomy. The less skilled found themselves subject to stricter forms of work discipline and fewer breaks from the exhausting sorts of physical labor in which they were concentrated.[4] Had such changes in work methods and discipline occurred in a time of general economic expansion and stability, most workers might have adapted with a minimum of stress. Coming at a time of recurrent depression, repeated cyclical reductions in the total labor force, and general economic insecurity, the innovations exacted a heavy material and psychological price from many workers.

Just as employers reacted to a changing situation by experimenting with new methods of production and combining into larger enterprises, so, too, did workers seek to adapt to their new environment. Whereas before the Civil War the typical workers' organization was a local trade union or at best a citywide coalition of such local unions, in the postbellum decades union builders struggled to create national organizations. They had no choice. In sectors of the economy untouched by national product competition, workers competed with each other for jobs. The tramping artisan or the displaced transient worker was a characteristic figure in late-nineteenth-century America. Only an effective national union that maintained uniform wages and conditions of work could protect the standards of all. In sectors where the primary competition was among products, the situation was no different. To protect the wages and conditions of one group of workers, the union had to insist upon uniform national standards, else lower-wage, lower-cost firms could displace higher-wage union enterprises. Thus, from the 1870s through the 1890s union builders sought first to create effective national trade unions and then to consolidate them into an equally effective national federation of unions.[5]

In the late nineteenth century workers and their trade unions also pioneered modern methods of industrial warfare. The strike and the boycott, the latter of which was particularly effective at the local level against employers dependent on working-class patronage, became the most common modes of working-class action. We have no reliable statistics before 1881 (fragmentary data from Massachusetts and New York, however, suggest that workers in those states increasingly turned to the strike), but between that year and 1885, the number of both strikes and the workers involved in them rose irregularly. Then, a year later, the total number of strikes more than doubled from the preceding year (695 to 1572), as did the number of workers involved (258,000 to 610,000). For the remainder of the late nineteenth century, the number of strikes remained well above pre-1886 levels, though only in 1894 did the total number of strikers surpass that of 1886. In fact, after 1886, the number of strikes annually never fell below twice as much as the initial level in 1881. By the 1890s, then, the strike had become the workers' chosen weapon in their ongoing struggle against capital.[6]

Even more important than the total number of strikes and workers involved, however, was the changing character of such disputes. At the start of the period, strikes were often as spontaneous as planned (that is, lacked formal union control), more commonly defensive than offensive (usually in protest against a wage cut), and less likely to succeed. By the end of the 1890s, most strikes were union-initiated and planned; offensive in objective (to seek higher wages, a union shop, or a formal contract); and more likely to succeed.[7] It was the strike, especially those that affected the nation as a whole, that initially impelled the federal government to intervene in labor-capital relations and to grope somewhat blindly toward a national labor policy.

The National State and Labor

As presidents, members of Congress, and federal judges navigated through the maze of labor-capital conflict, they reacted to the new social-economic order with ideas and values inherited from a simpler agrarian and republican heritage. Basic to that heritage were two beliefs that, while in theory affirming the rights of the common person and the dignity of labor, in practice protected the prerogatives of capital. First was the concept of equality under the law, stated so forcefully in Andrew Jackson's bank veto message in which the president proclaimed that if government "would confine itself to equal protection, and, as Heaven does its rains, shower its favors alike on the high and the low, the rich and the poor, it would be an unqualified blessing." That government was best not which governed least but rather which enacted no class legislation. Second was the often stated belief that labor was, in the words of Abraham Lincoln, "prior to, and independent of capital. . . . Labor is the superior of capital, and deserves much higher consideration." Such sentiments led Lincoln to state in a public speech in March 1860, "I am glad to see that a system prevails in New England under which laborers can strike when they want to." But such paeans of praise for the worthy laborer signified no hostility to capital or sympathy for industrial warfare. The same Lincoln who extolled the respectable toiler insisted, "Capital has its rights, which are as worthy of protection as any other rights." Rather than envision a society in which labor warred upon capital, Lincoln favored one in which equality under the law and the absence of class legislation allowed "the humblest man an equal chance . . . with everybody else," in which the laborer of today became the capitalist of tomorrow.[8]

By the end of the Civil War, an amalgam of the Jacksonian Democratic commitment to equality before the law and the Lincolnian Republican praise for the dignity of labor (what Eric Foner in a different context has called the ideology of "free soil, free men, and free labor") had become the common currency of popular belief and national politics. For a time, as David Montgomery has shown in his study of labor and the Radical Republicans, some labor radicals demanded that state policy go "beyond equality," that the government should enact laws that lifted the humble and restrained the mighty, that promoted equality of condition as well as equality of opportunity. Such demands may have split Radical Republicanism, as Montgomery suggests, but they scarcely dented the ideology of legal equality, free labor, and individual opportunity.[9] The tenacity of that ideology was well illustrated in the speech of a congressman from Ohio, who in June 1874 introduced on the floor of the House a bill to incorporate the Iron Molders' International Union. Capital and labor are not enemies, proclaimed the congressman, for "in this free land of ours the laborer of to-day is the capitalist of to-morrow, while the capitalist in turn may become the laborer."[10]

Lincoln could not have said it better. Nor did the Iron Molders' president disagree, for in his own petition he assured members of Congress that the molders' union believed in harmony between capital and labor and that the respectable worker repudiated all subversive influences. On the one hand, the union president pledged to respect fully the rights of capital, yet on the other hand, he asserted that he and his union were "unalterably fixed in our determination to resist by all lawful means any and every effort made to deprive the molder of his right to demand and receive a fair equivalent for his labor, or to abridge his right to fix a price for that labor."[11]

The contradiction between the union leader's pledge to respect the rights of capital and his insistence on the worker's right to fix his own price for labor (skilled workers at this time preferred to speak in terms of prices rather than wages, for the latter suggested dependence and servility in contrast to the former's signification of independence and manhood) was not the only paradox inherent in the free labor ideology. More important, it was a structure of belief that had emerged in an era when independent, landowning farmers remained the largest single segment of the productive population and also when self-employed crafts-people were still a substantial proportion of the urban work force. In antebellum America, the structure of society remained sufficiently decentralized and open to the ambitious to sustain the myth.

By the 1870s, however, the full-time, dependent wage earner had become more characteristic of the economy than the self-employed artisan, and independent farmers saw their relative influence shrink. With each passing year the proportion of dependent wage earners rose as that of independent farmers fell. Thus, in a society and economy that experienced increasing centralization and concentration of material resources, the myth of free labor and equal opportunity lost its luster. Still, if citizens at the end of the nineteenth century were no longer equal in the economic arena, each man remained both free and equal in the realm of politics, where the votes of the masses far outweighed those of the fortunate few who built the Gilded Age's mammoth corporations and amassed its great fortunes. Indeed, time and again, when labor found itself locked in conflict with capital or the masses struggled against the plutocrats, they trumpeted the virtues of a people's, or democratic, republic. And time and again, when the representatives and agencies of the national state involved themselves in labor-capital struggles, their commitment to equality before the law conflicted with their responsibilities as trustees for a people's republic. In theory, federal officials maintained that legal equality guaranteed individual opportunity and preserved popular sovereignty, while in practice, the law in its impartial majesty protected the property of the blessed few from the onslaughts of the angry many.

Before the 1870s, however, the relationship between labor and capital had rarely, if ever, intruded on the consciousness, policies, or actions of federal officials. Ritualistic defenses of the protective tariff as the guarantor of high wages and an American standard of living for workers and equally ritualistic critiques of the tariff as a device to rob the productive masses for the benefit of the rapacious few served as the bread and wine of Democratic and Republican politicians. Republicans, by and large, lauded protection as the source of national prosperity that best promoted harmony between workers and their employers. Democrats, by contrast, damned tariffs as a device that impoverished working people and hence intensified social, economic, and even racial conflict. Yet both Republicans and Democrats preferred to believe that the market, not public policy, should determine the level of employment and the rate of wages. During Ulysses S. Grant's second term, when the depression of the 1870s led to demands for public works projects to employ the jobless, associates convinced the president that "it is no part of the business of government to find employment for people."[12] Nor was government obligated to secure for people a decent income or to protect workers against their employers. As long as individual opportunity remained untrammeled and all citizens were equal under the law, the law of supply and demand operating through Adam Smith's "invisible hand" would shower its favors alike on the high and the low, the rich and the poor.

But the federal government did have a responsibility to intervene when conflict between labor and capital threatened republican government or disrupted law and order, as Andrew Jackson had done in 1834 when he sent federal troops into Maryland to end rioting among Irish immigrant canal workers. Yet between the time of Jackson's use of troops to quell a labor disturbance in the 1830s and 1877, the federal government distanced itself from the arena of labor-capital relations.[13]

This policy was so for several reasons. First, and most obviously, no branch or department of the federal government existed to deal with the subject. Second, as the lawmaking branch of the state, Congress was restrained both by constitutional imperatives and by the dominant ideology of free labor from passing laws to govern the relations between workers and employers. Under prevailing constitutional interpretations, the everyday relationships between workers and employers fell within the sphere of the separate states and not that of the national government. Congress, of course, could and did enact legislation granting federal employees first the ten- and then the eight-hour day. But these laws actually covered few employees, since private firms did much government contract work, and were also not always observed for employees hired directly by the federal government. Third, the same constitutional restraints that narrowed Congress's responsibility in the sphere of labor-capital policy ensured that labor cases rarely reached the federal judiciary. Before the 1870s, judicial decisions concerning workers' rights, the status of trade unions, and the legality of strikes and other forms of union action were resolved at the state level. And if the diversity of state court decisions could be said to show any consistency on the subject, it is that the rulings suggested that unions were legal entities for whose members the right to withhold their labor (that is, to strike) was theoretically inviolable. Yet the same set of diverse rulings in one instance or another declared almost every tactic used by trade unions to accomplish their aims to be unlawful as a common law conspiracy in restraint of trade.[14] Those judicial precedents rarely impinged on the rulings of federal judges, however, until the railroad labor wars of the late nineteenth century. Fourth, and finally, in the years since Jackson, no chief executive had found himself called upon to police a labor upheaval. Time and again between the 1830s and the early 1870s presidents dispatched U.S. marshals and troops to maintain law and order in the western territories and in the Reconstruction South — but not to quell industrial violence.

All of that changed during the depression of the 1870s. Not only did the spread of mass unemployment lead to demands for public works projects, but laborers increasingly engaged in bitter and sometimes violent industrial conflicts. Whether in such railroad shop towns as Susquehanna Depot, Pennsylvania, or Waverly, New York, in the anthracite district of northeast Pennsylvania or the soft-coal mining community of Braidwood, Illinois, or in the iron mills of Johnstown, Pennsylvania, workers fought their bosses with a militancy and tenacity rarely before seen in American history. Direct assaults on employers' property and "riotous" behavior in which strikers were joined by sympathetic community members led the better sort of citizens to demand more vigorous enforcement of law and order. Where local police forces could not contain strike disorder, governors rarely hesitated to send in the state militia. As the first wave of such disturbances swept the nation in 1873 and 1874, the federal government appeared to hold itself aloof from the raging conflicts.[15]

The Great Railroad Strikes of 1877

Less than four years later, the executive and judicial branches of the federal government found themselves mired in labor-capital conflict. Between 1874 and 1877 the depression had deepened, unemployment had worsened, workers had grown more restive, and violent strikes had imperiled the nation's transportation network. The local disturbances and riots of 1873 and 1874 had simply been rehearsals for the more tumultuous and destructive happenings of 1877. When several major railroads cut wages repeatedly and also intensified work loads for already aggrieved employees, they precipitated a series of strikes that spread from West Virginia, to Maryland, to Pennsylvania, and on into Indiana and Illinois, and then eddied back into New York and parts of New England. Initially a battle between railroad workers and operators over wages and work loads, the struggles intensified into incipient civil, or class, war, in such cities as Baltimore, Pittsburgh, and St. Louis. The year 1877 was, as Robert Bruce proclaimed in the title of his book, a "year of violence." So much violence that John Hay, Abraham Lincoln's former private secretary, demanded federal military repression of the rioters. Hay privately confided that "the prospects of labor and capital both seem gloomy enough. The very devil seems to have entered into the lower classes of working men."[16]

The Devil did his work first in West Virginia. When in July the Baltimore and Ohio Railroad cut wages for a third time, its trainmen resisted. By the middle of the month, railroad workers had effectively paralyzed freight traffic in the state, cutting the flow of commerce between Baltimore and the Midwest. Strikers obstructed every effort by the B&O to move its cars. Railroad executives and the governor of West Virginia agreed that the state lacked police power sufficient to resume train traffic. They cooperated with each other to inveigle federal military intervention. The railroad executives used their influence in Washington to lobby federal officials for assistance, while on July 18, Governor H. M. Mathews wired President Rutherford B. Hayes that he lacked the force to execute the laws of his state and therefore sought federal military assistance "to protect the law abiding people of the State against domestic violence, and to maintain supremacy of the law." Personally, Hayes had little knowledge or understanding of the sources of railroad labor conflict. Nor over the next tumultuous weeks did he evince antipathy toward strikers or sympathy for their employers. Still, he firmly believed that it was the president's responsibility to ensure the blessings of republican government for all citizens and also that it was his constitutional obligation to maintain public order when state authorities proved unable to do so. As long as the governors of the separate states adhered to proper constitutional procedures, confessed their inability to enforce legal process, swore that law and order had collapsed, and declared that masses of their citizens were engaged in domestic insurrection, Hayes was prepared to act. Thus, upon receipt of Governor Mathews's wire of July 18, the president ordered federal troops to West Virginia to preserve law and order.[17]

West Virginia proved only the beginning of federal military intervention in the labor conflicts of 1877. Events in the Mountain State seemed orderly compared to what was to follow in the cities of Baltimore, Pittsburgh, and St. Louis. On Friday evening, July 20, strikers, local factory workers, and their sympathizers clashed with state militia on the streets of Baltimore. Fearful that the mob, estimated at 15,000 or more, would cause untold damage to the city, the governor of Maryland confessed his inability to maintain law and order. The next day, 500 federal troops were on duty in Baltimore at President Hayes's order. As the fires of "rebellion" burned out in Baltimore, they reignited the following day, Saturday, July 21, in Pittsburgh. There, an equally large and angry mob of working people clashed on the city's streets with militia sent from Philadelphia. The bloody battle with state troops failed to slake the anger of the city's workers, who promptly released their resentment on the property of the Pennsylvania Railroad. By Saturday night, mobs had put the Union Depot and much of the railroad's rolling stock to the torch. For a day and a half Pittsburgh merited its appellation of the "smoky city." On Monday morning, as federal troops arrived in the city, quiet returned. And well it should, for by then twenty-four people lay dead, the Union Depot appeared to be a smoldering shell, 79 other railroad buildings lay in ashes, and 104 locomotives and 2,152 railroad cars had been destroyed. Over that week and the next, the "riot" spread west to the cities of Cincinnati, Chicago, and St. Louis.[18] Small wonder that the *St. Louis Republic* shrieked, "It is wrong to call this a strike, it is labor revolution."[19]

In a sense, President Hayes acted as if it were a revolution. Even when state governors failed to follow constitutional niceties in requesting troops or, indeed, made no such requests, the president found reason to dispatch troops. In some cases the military arrived to enforce the orders of federal courts; in other instances, to protect federal property. Whatever the reason for their presence, U.S. troops saw duty not only in West Virginia, Maryland, and Pennsylvania (in Philadelphia and the anthracite region, as well as Pittsburgh) but also in Indiana, Illinois, and Missouri. Not only did troops assist in reopening railroad traffic, they also policed striking coal miners and canal workers. Hayes ceded his field commanders relatively free rein because he honestly believed that the strikers and "rioters" were illegally and violently seizing the private property of others, destroying both life and property, and interfering with the right of free laborers (strikebreakers) to do their jobs. Army officers had few qualms about what they were doing. For most of them, capital represented law and order, and the rights of property commanded the greatest respect. Labor, by contrast, appeared to be a lawless mob, seeking chaos and the destruction of stability. As one army captain remarked, his obligation was as "the conservator of law and order and of the rights of the people to peacefully change the law." He added, "The army is the supporter of no classes and of no party. It stands for the united nation."[20]

Precisely how the army ended the upheaval of 1877 is less than clear. For one thing, the army lacked sufficient numbers of troops to patrol and repress a national uprising. A majority of the most experienced veterans in a total force of 25,000 remained on Indian duty west of the Mississippi, and everywhere strikers and their sympathizers far outnumbered federal forces. For another thing, by the time troops arrived in Baltimore and Pittsburgh, the scenes of the worst rioting, peace had returned. As the commanding general, Winfield S. Hancock, observed: "It was the moral force of the United States government that was displayed — not its physical force . . . not a drop of blood has been shed — nor as far as I know, has a shot been fired by our troops."[21] Apparently, the presence of federal troops as symbols of law and the moral force of government was sufficient to enable railroads to use strikebreakers and run their lines without interference. It was also sufficient to cow striking coal miners and canal workers in West Virginia, Maryland, and northeastern Pennsylvania, where troops remained on duty into the middle of August. As the historian of those events has written, "federal troops . . . served not as a force to restore order but as a threat to compel strikers to return to work."[22]

That troops dispatched initially and solely to restore law and order could subsequently remain on duty to break even peaceful strikes resulted from Hayes's failure to define General Hancock's mission strictly. Although the president and his cabinet met several times to discuss the matter — discussions during which Hayes evinced sympathy for the strikers and some disdain for autocratic railroad executives — they apparently never discussed or resolved basic questions raised by General Hancock.[23] On July 24, Hancock had wired the secretary of war the following advice concerning the mission and chain of command for federal troops: "When state governments declare their inability to suppress domestic insurrection . . . and call upon the President . . . to intervene . . . he should not do it through the civil powers of the States which have already failed, but that it should be done by . . . the President exercising the controls."[24] Instead, however, Hayes ordered the field commanders to serve under the direction of state governors, who, as often as not, cooperated closely with the dominant railroad and mine operators in their respective states. With the line of command and mission of the federal troops thus defined, it was only natural that they then served the interests of private businessmen and, in the case of Pennsylvania anthracite, remained on duty through October, long after the reasons for their original assignment had diminished.[25]

Hayes and the executive branch were not alone in assisting private capital, whether inadvertently or consciously. As a result of the depression, a large number of railroads had fallen into receivership and come under the protection of federal courts. When labor trouble inflicted those roads, the concerned judges viewed the disputes not as conflicts between labor and capital but as a war between citizens and the state. Hence federal judges in Indiana, Illinois, and Wisconsin used their equity power to enjoin railroad workers from striking. In Illinois, Judge Thomas Drummond declared: "A strike or other unlawful interference with the trains will be a violation of the United States law, and the court will be bound to take notice of it and enforce the penalty."[26] A receiver for one of the railroads in St. Louis informed Secretary of the Interior Carl Schurz: "I am managing property now in the custody of U.S. courts and I shall certainly not permit my employees to fix their own rate of wages, nor dictate to me in any manner what my policy shall be."[27] It was to enforce just such injunctions that Hayes sent troops into states whose governors had not requested federal intervention. Over the next twenty years federal judges would refine and expand their equity power as a device to quell labor discontent.[28]

The actions of the executive and judicial branches of government in 1877 lent credence to the words of one writer who in the 1870s condemned the state's treatment of workers. "All the machinery of the state stands ready," he wrote, "to protect and further the interests of capital, while labor is left absolutely without law, a law unto itself, save when it commits some act, to be dealt with as a criminal."[29] And for doing precisely that, President Hayes earned the praise of his countrymen, expressed in scores of letters and telegrams.[30] Other advocates of stern action, though satisfied with the outcome of events in 1877, nevertheless showed disquiet. One of the injunction judges, Walter Gresham, wrote to a friend, "Our revolutionary fathers . . . went too far with their notions of popular government. . . . Democracy is now the enemy of law & order & society itself & as such should be denounced." To which a future U.S. senator from Missouri added, "Universal suffrage is a standing menace to all stable and good government. Its twin sister is the commune with its labor unions, etc."[31] The hosts of labor had been defeated in the summer of 1877. Their right to vote remained, as ever, a potential threat to wealthy property owners.

Faint echoes of working-class voting power were heard in October, when Congress convened in special session to consider increased appropriations for the military. A few representatives from districts with overwhelmingly working-class constituents, especially one from northeastern Pennsylvania, rose on the floor to condemn the use of federal troops as a police force to repress discontented laborers. Far more voices, however, praised the army for defending the American people and their frontiers from the depredations of Indians and Mexicans.[32] Beyond that, Congress said nothing about Hayes's policies and actions during the previous summer, nor did it offer solace to its laborer constituents.

The Blair Committee

The return of prosperity in 1878 not only stilled discontent and eased fears among conservatives about a democratic franchise; it also enabled workers to rebuild their shattered trade unions and to fight their employers in more favorable circumstances. As a consequence, strikes grew more numerous, though none elicited a federal response. In this interim between violent national labor upheavals, some members of Congress sought to define and establish a more reasoned federal policy. Lacking a constitutional mandate to enact laws governing relations between private employers and employees and hesitant to violate the laws of supply and demand, Congress resorted to its power to investigate. On June 15, 1882 Democratic senator John T. Morgan of Alabama moved that the Senate appoint a select committee of seven to investigate strikes and to recommend measures to modify or eliminate their causes. Two weeks later, the Republican chair of the Senate Committee on Education and Labor, Henry W. Blair of New Hampshire, recommended that the Senate approve an expanded version of Morgan's resolution, which called for a complete investigation of the relations between labor and capital. Blair's version also stressed the need to investigate the causes of strikes and to recommend legislation to remove such causes and to promote harmonious relations between labor and capital, especially by improving the condition of the industrial classes. On August 7, the Senate passed Blair's revised resolution, and soon thereafter the Blair Committee, or the Senate Committee upon the Relations between Labor and Capital took up its charge.[33] For two years the committee traveled to diverse parts of the country and took testimony from ordinary laborers, trade union leaders, social reformers, fiery radicals, and corporate tycoons.[34] From their travels and their witnesses, the senators undoubtedly learned much about the realities of social conflict in Gilded Age America, yet not enough to motivate them to introduce any legislation on the subject. Such a pattern became characteristic of the congressional response to labor conflict. In reaction to the pained cries of defeated strikers or the demands of middle-class citizens outraged by the costs of industrial conflict, Congress investigated. Because any legislative solution might anger influential constituents, stir constitutional controversies, or contravene ideological verities, Congress declined to enact legislation.

The end of the Blair Committee's assignment coincided with a new moment of labor-capital conflict — the "great upheaval of 1885–86" — and another round of federal intervention. This time the federal judiciary and Congress would seize the initiative, and the president would play a lesser role. For strikers and their unions, however, the results would be largely the same.

Labor Reform versus Judicial Activism

In the early 1880s, as trade unions rebuilt their strength and renewed their battles with employers, the "labor issue" reemerged as a federal question. Throughout the last quarter of the nineteenth century, no line demarcated working-class political action and economic action. The two forms of labor action remained inextricably interrelated. Thus, as trade unions flexed their economic muscles through direct action in shops and factories, their members used the ballot to influence the major parties or to build independent local labor parties. The political influence of workers manifested itself most directly at the municipal and state levels, where legislators and officeholders competed to win the support of working-class constituents. In the 1870s and 1880s many of the industrial states enacted laws regulating factory conditions and the hours of labor for women and children. Those states in which the coal-mining and hard-rock-mining industries were significant sectors of the economy adopted safety and hours regulations for adult men employed in what were defined as the dangerous trades. And many states also established bureaus of labor, or bureaus of labor statistics, both to give unions a voice in government and to compile hard data on the "labor question."

Similar political pressures made themselves felt in Congress. In the spring and summer of 1884 Republican congressional leaders, preparing for the fall's presidential election, maneuvered legislation through Congress to establish a Bureau of Labor in the Interior Department. After perfunctory debate, in which some Southerners ritualistically warned against federal encroachment, the legislation passed both houses with large majorities and was signed by President Chester A. Arthur on June 27. The new law created a fact-finding agency patterned on those already in operation in several of the states, and its first director, Carroll Wright, was recruited directly from such a state bureau in Massachusetts. As had been true among the states, so also at the national level the establishment of a bureau for labor enabled congressmen to proclaim their devotion to the common people by offering labor a voice in the federal government.[35]

Political gestures, however, failed to resolve the labor question or silence the demands of trade unionists. Instead trade unionists grew ever more assertive in 1885 and 1886. The number of strikes rose substantially and in 1886 reached a new peak. Not only that, but once again, as labor militancy spread to workers on the interstate railroads, federal officials became directly involved in the upheaval. And once again the upheaval took political as well as economic form. Local labor parties challenged for power in Chicago, Milwaukee, Cincinnati, New York, Kansas City, Richmond, Virginia, Rutland, Vermont, and Leadville, Colorado, to name only a few cities where in 1886 workers reached for local power.[36] As the Knights of Labor grew in just over a year from a little more than 100,000 members to an estimated 750,000, its leaders appeared to many disconcerted political conservatives and businesspeople to be a conspiratorial private government with the power to paralyze the national economy. One editorialist warned that the Knights was "an organization in whose hands now rests the destinies of the republic." And another suggested of its executive board: "It is doubtful whether any other five men in America have the power for weal or woe among the working class that this quintet has."[37]

The increasing discontent of working people echoed through the halls of Congress. During Senate debate in February 1885 over a bill to outlaw the importation of foreign contract labor, the Republican senator from Kansas stressed the gravity of a situation in which "in the midst of copious abundance there is haggard wretchedness and starvation." It was a situation, he added, in which socialism and anarchism, violence and revolution flourished, in which people openly proclaimed that "property is robbery." Something had to be done, he and his colleagues agreed, to assuage the discontent of American workers and to restore social stability. What the senators in fact chose to do was partly rhetorical and partly substantive. On the one hand, Republican senators such as John Blair of New Hampshire extolled the virtues of the American laborer, the foundation of our civilization and whatever is of worth in American "spiritual, intellectual, and aesthetic culture." On the other hand, an overwhelming majority of senators (50–9) voted to protect the dignity of labor by banning the importation of foreign contract laborers.[38]

In reality, because few immigrant workers entered the country under contract, Congress had accomplished little of substance. Working-class discontent was neither allayed nor unrest diminished. Quite the reverse. No sooner had politicians demonstrated their solicitude for labor than railroad workers became involved in a wave of strikes reminiscent of 1877. It began in the spring and summer of 1885 when shopmen and operating trainmen on the Wabash Railroad acted collectively to resist wage cuts. Their job action rapidly spread to other parts of Jay Gould's railroad network in the Southwest and paralyzed freight traffic on his lines in Missouri, Kansas, and Texas. It also conjured up fears about domestic insurrection, as strikers and their working-class neighbors in railroad shop towns united to intimidate nonunion members, strikebreakers, and potential strikebreakers. In this instance, Gould settled the dispute on terms favorable to the strikers before their unrest flamed into violence.

Despite this victory for the strikers and the Knights of Labor, several federal judges had intervened in the strike and set precedents that boded ill for the future of railroad labor. In one case, brought by the receivers of the Wabash Railroad in the circuit court for the Western District of Missouri, the judge ruled, in effect, that workers employed on a line in federal receivership could not take job action without the court's permission. He conceded the right of employees to cease working as they chose or to combine peacefully to forward their interests, but his concession involved several caveats that made the theoretical right to do so meaningless. First, all such collective action had to be lawful as defined by the court. Second, strikers could violate no contract or federal court responsibility. Third, in the case of a railroad in receivership, when employees and receivers failed to settle their differences by compromise, the dispute had to be resolved by law and the courts. Fourth, private labor disputes could not be allowed to inflict harm on outside and innocent members of the community. In the case before him, that of shopmen employed by the Wabash in Moberly, Missouri, he found that the strike interfered unlawfully with the management of the railroad by its court-appointed receivers and hence was in contempt of court. "Such a thing as taking the law into their own hands," he scolded the local union leaders, "will not be tolerated." He sentenced both defendants to terms in the county jail as well as one-year peace bonds.[39]

The judge's recital of the facts in this case and his interpretation of the law illustrated what was rapidly becoming the judicial perspective on industrial conflict. Committed above all to orderly procedures and social stability, federal judges viewed strikes as disorderly by definition and as threats to the social order. Action, which in theory was permissible and lawful, became in practice unlawful. By treating business organizations and labor unions identically, federal judges used common law rules and precedents concerning combinations in restraint of trade to exact a heavy price from labor leaders and strikers. Under the common law, it was not illegal for businesses to regulate markets and set prices or for unions to regulate wages and hours. Such private agreements in restraint of trade were simply unenforceable. Any party to a business association could breach that body's trade rules without penalty, while nonmembers could not be coerced to adhere to association rules. Likewise, workers were free to breach union discipline — for example, to cross picket lines during strikes — without penalty, and nonunion workers could not be required to join the union in order to obtain work or lose work because of a strike. Because union rules demanded obedience and strike success depended on solidarity and the ability to keep nonmembers from filling strikers' jobs, workers and their unions ran afoul of judges' interpretation of the common law. Once strikes infringed the rights of nonunion workers or affected detrimentally the welfare of the community, for example, denying citizens essential services or impairing the businesses of parties not directly involved in the dispute, judges declared such labor action in violation of the common law. Also, partly because the vast majority of workers did not belong to unions, partly because the working class was fragmented ethnically, racially, and religiously, and partly because a substantial number of workers believed in the inviolability of the private market and freedom of contract, strikes commonly created conflict between unionists who sought to shut an enterprise down and workers who were eager to step in and replace the strikers.

Since most judges deemed that strikes to enforce the closed shop or picketing to bar replacement workers was illegal, they also used the law of conspiracy to preempt union action. Under the law of conspiracy, it was illegal to conspire to participate in such a labor action even if the strike never occurred. In the words of a legal historian, courts "could punish people who had not actually performed an illegal act, but who had been part of a conspiracy to commit one." Indeed, in some instances, judges would come close to legitimating forms of involuntary servitude.[40]

To be sure, federal judges could not enforce their antiunion and antistrike rulings without the cooperation of the executive branch, which held a monopoly of coercive power. And judges received such cooperation because their rulings resonated with older national traditions concerning republicanism, civic virtue, antipathy toward group violations of the free market, and equality before the law.

Less than a year later, industrial conflict returned to Gould's southwestern railroads. This time the financier-entrepreneur refused to concede or compromise. Gould determined to defeat the Knights of Labor once and for all. Consequently, this second strike caused substantial turmoil and violence. It also erupted at a more sensitive moment, on the eve of the national movement for an eight-hour day and the Haymarket tragedy of May 1886. If judges and conservatives had reason to fear for the stability of society in 1885, a year later they had a firmer foundation for their anxieties.

The great labor upheaval of 1886 was not long in making itself felt in Congress and the White House. On April 10, a Republican member of the House introduced a bill to create a system for the arbitration of strikes, which, he argued, "is the only method that seems to be open for the peaceful and speedy and just settlement of such disputes."[41] In the midst of debate over an arbitration system, congressional attention turned to the conflict on Gould's railroads. At the behest of assemblies of the Knights of Labor, several members of the House introduced a resolution calling for the appointment of a committee to investigate the causes of the conflict on the western railroads. Almost immediately Southern Democratic members rose to oppose the intrusion of federal power into the domain of the states. Not only did the Southerners turn to their traditional constitutional argument for state rights. They also turned the free labor ideology against their Republican foes. "Let these men [the Knights] . . . understand that they are at liberty either to work or to refuse to work," said a representative from Mississippi, "or to go and take farms and be good citizens." Beliefs that Republicans had originally formulated to woo northern workers to the antislavery cause were increasingly being used to deny the federal government a role in labor-capital relations.[42] This led a congressman from the Scranton, Pennsylvania district to reply that a House investigating committee would only determine if railroad workers had been wronged by their corporate employers and denied "life, liberty, and the pursuit of happiness." "If there is no power in this Congress under the Constitution to redress such a wrong," the Pennsylvania Republican averred, "God knows our 'Constitution is a rope of sand' and is of no avail for the protection of the people."[43] On this issue Southern Democrats spoke only for themselves. The House went ahead and appointed a select committee to investigate labor troubles on the railroads of the Southwest.

In the meantime, President Cleveland moved personally on the issue of labor-capital relations. By 1886 the Supreme Court had ruled decisively that the operation of interstate railroads fell within federal responsibility under the Constitution's commerce clause. And while the House was debating strike arbitration procedures and an investigation of the Gould conflict, the Senate was itself in the midst of a debate over passage of a bill to establish an interstate commerce commission. At precisely that moment, on April 22, Cleveland sent a special message to Congress recommending the establishment of a three-person federal voluntary arbitration commission housed within the Bureau of Labor and charged with the responsibility of averting strike troubles. The president filled his message with paeans to the noble American laborer and the virtues of a democratic republic that eliminated all vestiges of class. He equally condemned irresponsible labor and oppressive capital. Cleveland, moreover, appealed to Southern sentiments by deferring to constitutional restrictions on federal power and proposing an arbitration commission whose role would be primarily investigatory and whose recommendations would be nonbinding.[44]

During this session and the next, Congress continued to debate Cleveland's

proposal for a railroad arbitration commission. The debate touched all the traditional themes as both the opponents and the advocates of federal intervention used
the free labor ideology and the ideal of equal opportunity to press their respective
cases. "I protest in the name of liberty against class legislation," remarked a
Southern Democrat in opposition to his own president's bill. "Every boy born
under the Star-Spangled Banner is born to glorious opportunity. He is not born to
real poverty, although the winds of heaven may come through the crevices of his
humble cabin, and there may be but little blanket on his limbs. He is born to
boundless opportunity."[45] Using almost the same vocabulary, a Northern Republican insisted that Congress must do something to ensure harmony between capital
and labor. "We have no classes here," he proclaimed, "and the great prizes of life
are open to them [laborers] as to other citizens . . . and with their welfare is linked
the welfare of all the citizens of this country." Because laborers are now discontent
and their relations with employers have become the central national problem,
Congress must act to ensure that American workers remain, as always, "the
happiest, most content, and most prosperous in the world."[46]

Congress, however, proved as committed to social stability as the federal
judiciary was. For example, the House committee that investigated the conflict on
railroads in the Southwest chose to stress the disorder and violence associated with
the strike rather than its proximate causes. After traveling 4,880 miles and examining 578 witnesses, the committee's majority condemned one man, Martin Irons,
the strike leader, as "a dangerous if not poisonous man," whose agitation protracted the strike and precipitated most of the violence. The committee's report
stressed the need to protect the general community from the damage caused by
strikes, which the federal government could do under its power to regulate
interstate commerce. It also recognized the right of workers to combine into
unions because the single workman was powerless against the corporation. The
report insisted that unions must equally recognize the rights of workers who
choose to remain outside the organization and continue to work during strikes, for
all citizens may "dispose of their labor with perfect individual freedom." In the
end, the committee majority equally condemned corporate capitalists who combined to exploit the public and trade unionists who allied to coerce the nonunion
laborer.[47]

How to avert strikes, simultaneously protect the right of workers to join unions
and to remain outside them, and also defend the community against industrial
conflict remained an insoluble dilemma for members of Congress. Both the critics
of trade unionism and its advocates opposed Cleveland's arbitration bill — but
from contradictory perspectives. Republican senator Henry M. Teller of Colorado,
for example, played all the variations on the free labor theme. "It is the laborer
alone that creates wealth . . . and makes it possible for him who has capital to live

in ease and safety." Hence neither the state, nor the employer, nor fellow workers (unionists) should interfere with the individual worker's freedom to dispose of his labor as he chooses. "The difference between a slave and a freeman consists mainly in the fact that the freeman may freely dispose of his labor . . . on the terms fixed by himself." What the American worker wants, Teller concluded, was freedom from control by others, the ability to care for himself untrammeled. Under such a system, "To-day an employee, to-morrow an employer."[48] Paradoxically, an advocate of trade unionism could oppose federal arbitration in almost the same language. Congressman Martin Foran of Ohio, a former trade union official, asserted that effective arbitration (meaning compulsory) would place the liberties of citizens at the discretion of federal judges. It would suggest that workers and employers were unable to manage their own affairs. Then Foran turned to Democratic advocates of free trade and Republican enthusiasts of the free labor doctrine and said, "*Laissez faire, laissez passez.* . . . Let the workingmen and the capitalists of this country alone and they will work out their own salvation." Admitting that strikes were a great evil and a source of harm to the community, Foran nevertheless concluded, "Both workingmen and employers purchase experience by strikes." As early as 1888 he had clearly expressed what twenty years later would coagulate as the American Federation of Labor's doctrine of "voluntarism," the concept that unionism flourished in the absence of state intervention.[49]

A majority of Congress, however, believed that something had to be done to protect the public against strikes. That majority condemned capital and labor as irresponsible. Within the majority, critics of Cleveland's proposal stressed its emptiness. Absent the element of compulsion, arbitration could not curb industrial conflict. More effective means were needed, these critics suggested, to inoculate the community against the paralysis of commerce. In response, Democratic supporters of the administration bill countered that compulsion subverted personal liberty. Better to rely on the force of public opinion than the weight of coercive law to resolve disputes peacefully. An arbitration board's impartial report would prompt irresponsible parties to moderate their behavior. As no majority could be built in favor of compulsory arbitration, the advocates of more forceful antistrike legislation joined the proponents of the Cleveland bill, and in September 1888 the federal government enacted its first antistrike legislation in the guise of a voluntary railroad arbitration commission.[50]

At the same time, as a sop to organized labor, which was antipathetic to any form of arbitration, Congress overwhelmingly passed a bill to establish an independent Department of Labor (the successor to the Bureau of Labor) with its own commissioner. Carroll Wright, who remained the commissioner, acquired no further power, but he did obtain more funds, greater bureaucratic autonomy, and a vote of confidence. Although some sponsors of the legislation perceived such a department as offering trade unionism a direct voice in the government, Wright's reappointment insulated it from any direct labor influence.[51]

Even as Congress debated the issue of railroad strike arbitration, the workers and managers of the Chicago, Burlington, and Quincy Railroad waged battle. In this case, the strongest of the operating railroad unions, the Brotherhood of Locomotive Engineers, demanded that management observe the union's work rules and not unilaterally alter existing practices. When the Burlington's management rejected the union's claims, the Brotherhood of Engineers declared a strike, which the railroad immediately broke with nonunion employees. Thwarted by the Burlington, the Brotherhood of Engineers asked its members on other railroads that interchanged freight with the CB&Q to boycott the latter road. Immediately the Burlington went to federal court seeking an injunction requiring other railroads to interchange freight cars and forbidding the union to boycott Burlington traffic. In short order, federal judges issued injunctions against a federal land grant railroad, another in federal receivership,[52] and three solvent ones, enjoining them from refusing to handle Burlington traffic. The same injunctions also forbade the Brotherhood of Engineers to conduct secondary boycotts. The injunctions were so effective that Charles E. Perkins, the chief executive of the railroad, informed his wife that the judge's restraining order "has had a good effect upon people everywhere and the general impression this morning . . . is that the total collapse [of the strike] is not far off." He added that if a second judge proves equally resolute in his ruling, "it may end the whole thing."[53]

The judicial rulings in this instance placed nearly all aspects of labor relations on interstate railroads under federal jurisdiction. Whether under the terms of the Constitution's commerce clause, the Interstate Commerce Commission (ICC) Act of 1887, or common law interdictions of conspiracies in restraint of trade, the federal judges devised a battery of weapons to curtail railroad strikes. Railroads, judges came to rule, were quasi-public enterprises built to serve the common interest, not private profit. Profit, in the purview of many judges, meant not employers' desire to accumulate capital but workers' thirst for higher wages or shorter hours. One judge, for example, referred to the engineers involved in the Burlington strike as a small group of allegedly wronged men seeking their own private profit. "To redress the small wrongs of a few they inflict irreparable injuries upon the many." Although he conceded workers the right to strike, he denied them the right to boycott Burlington traffic or to "intimidate" strikebreakers. "The question," he asked, "is, what shall be obeyed — the law of the land, or the order of the chiefs of the railroad engineers? . . . Is this a power fit to be assumed and wielded by any set of irresponsible men under the sun?"[54]

Only three years later a federal district court in Ohio extended the reach of injunctions against union-sponsored boycotts from the railroads to a small-town newspaper. The court claimed jurisdiction because the newspaper was published in Covington, Kentucky, and the union concerned was located in Cincinnati, hence establishing the diversity of citizenship necessary to bring suit in a federal court. In its ruling, the court referred to the boycott initiated by Cincinnati Typographical Union No. 3 as "an organized conspiracy to force the complainant to yield his right to select his own workmen, and submit himself to the control of the union." It then enjoined members of the union and their sympathizers from engaging in a boycott that aimed to establish a closed shop and hence cede to a union the right to limit a businessman's free use of his own private property.[55] Thus within three years federal courts had deprived both national unions and purely local ones of effective weapons of industrial warfare.

The alacrity of federal judges to rule decisively against strikers and their unions, however, failed to elicit a consensus or to reduce the rising intensity of industrial conflict. While judges indicted labor leaders, President Cleveland in his fourth annual message to Congress in 1888 warned against the danger of common citizens about to be "trampled to death beneath an iron heel." He stressed that "corporations are fast becoming the people's masters." The president pointedly referred to the rapid emergence of contending classes and the widening gulf between employers and employed.[56] Cleveland was not alone in his anxieties. A year later, a member of the House committee investigating labor troubles in the anthracite region asked, in his minority report, how republicanism could be maintained in the face of powerful corporations and masses of necessitous voters. "We must admit," he warned, "that the mere law of supply and demand can not solve the question of the needs of labor. Men as men, have necessities, which can not be foregone." Unlike beasts of burden, whose number determine their value, men are citizens with political rights. Their needs and desires thus "will not be denied, but will in some form or another, in a land of universal suffrage, force [themselves] to favorable solution."[57] Over the next five years such forebodings would prove extremely prophetic.

Homestead and the Coeur d'Alenes

In the spring and summer of 1892, the ongoing war between labor and capital again forced itself into national politics. Once more a president, the U.S. army, the federal judiciary, and the two political parties intervened directly in industrial conflicts. Moreover, in 1892, threats to interstate commerce did not precipitate federal action. The reality of labor violence as well as the potential for it brought a sharp response from national authorities. Two strikes, both of which erupted into violence in July, brought legal injunctions, military intervention, and congressional investigations — and also influenced that year's presidential election.

The more famous of the two conflicts, that waged between steelworkers and the Carnegie Company in Homestead, Pennsylvania, brought both a House and a Senate investigating committee to the Pittsburgh area. It also intruded on the contest between the incumbent Republican president, Benjamin Harrison, and his opponent, Grover Cleveland, although the Pennsylvania state militia proved adequate to the task of restoring "law and order." Ordered to Homestead by the state's Republican governor, the militia disarmed the strikers, replaced local law enforcement officials who were themselves union members, and protected the Carnegie Company's steel mill and the strikebreakers inside. In effect, the presence of state troops ended the strike in favor of the company.[58]

By the time the House and Senate investigating committees arrived in Homestead the struggle was over and their missions irrelevant. Both committees did little more than state the obvious. They warned that the use of Pinkertons, though legal, caused violence. They also doubted that the federal government could intrude on the affairs of private parties and dismissed compulsory arbitration as an affront to the free labor doctrine. The two Republican senators who visited Homestead suggested that congress could do much to temper industrial conflict in the future by repealing all "class legislation" and drastically restricting immigration.[59] The last of these recommendations enunciated the Republican party's labor program and foreshadowed the issues at the heart of the election campaign. Republicans appealed to workers on the basis that a high protective tariff would be the guardian of an American standard of living and immigration restriction would serve as its handmaiden. They promised to protect the American laborer against cheap foreign goods and cheap alien labor. Democrats told workers to look at the reality of Republican policies. What, Democrats asked, had steelworkers gained from high tariffs? Employers only cut wages and caused conflict. When steelworkers struck to protect their American standard of living, a Republican governor sent troops to break their strike and a Republican president did nothing.

Simultaneously, events in the state of Idaho proved that a Republican president could serve the interests of employers as decisively as a governor could. In the northern panhandle district of that state (the Coeur d'Alenes) a dispute between hard-rock miners and their employers necessitated federal intervention. Because the miners controlled most town and county offices in the Coeur d'Alenes, they kept the mines closed and strikebreakers out of the district. From the first, mine owners realized that they could not prevail without external assistance. For them, only federal authorities had the power to break the strike. First they went to the federal district court for Idaho to seek an injunction prohibiting union members from trespassing on company property, interfering in any way with mine operations, or intimidating new employees. This they acquired from a compliant judge who ruled that union actions to enforce a closed shop and a union wage scale were unlawful restraints on the use of an employer's private property.[60] Injunctions alone, however, could not restore the mines to operation. For that the mine owners needed armed protection. This they schemed to obtain through the good offices of Idaho governor Norman Willey, who, in turn, asked President Harrison for federal troops. In the absence of violence in the Coeur d'Alenes, Harrison refused to provide military aid to the mine owners.[61] Then, only five days after Pinkertons and steelworkers clashed violently in Homestead, a mob attacked and seized two mines in the Coeur d'Alenes, on July 11, 1892; during the fray two men were killed, six wounded, and company property destroyed. As at Homestead, so in northern Idaho the violence abated as quickly as it had flared. Yet here, too, it provided mine owners the opportunity to demand and obtain military protection. Almost before anyone really knew what had happened or could evaluate events, Idaho's attorney general wired his state's two U.S. senators that "the mob must be crushed by overwhelming force. We can't retreat now. . . . Gatling guns and small howitzers . . . should be sent. Nothing but overwhelming force will . . . prevent serious fight." And Governor Willey formally requested federal military assistance, swearing that he lacked the means to maintain law and order in the Coeur d'Alenes. President Harrison sent the troops, and the mine owners got what they wanted.[62]

Like Hayes in 1877, Harrison in 1892 turned federal troops over to the command of a governor who, in turn, placed the U.S. army in the service of mine owners. The military authorities immediately arrested more than 600 men, 350 of whom were held in custody for nearly a week. All local union officers were incarcerated and held for trial on civil and criminal charges. Military commanders offered to release their imprisoned suspects only if they admitted to crimes and signed nonunion pledges. As Jerry Cooper, the leading student of the history of the U.S. army's role in late-nineteenth-century strikes, has written: "The state government and army were simply the tools the owners used to combat an increasingly militant and active union movement."[63] In this case, the troops broke the strike although the law acquitted the indicted strike leaders and unionism later returned to the district in an even more militant form.[64]

Certainly, working people now had much evidence that the Republicans, despite their rhetoric, were scarcely the friends of labor. Democrats, of course, were quick to indict their political opponents as the lackeys of corporate capital and the servitors of monopoly. In November in the steelmaking communities of western Pennsylvania and elsewhere in the industrial Northeast, Democrats defeated Republicans at the polls. In the Coeur d'Alenes and other Mountain States mining communities, a Populist-Democratic coalition rode to political power. And nationally Grover Cleveland and the Democrats ousted the Republicans. What part the labor movement and working people played in the results is hard to say, except for such places as Homestead and northern Idaho, where their votes and those of their sympathizers were dominant. Nationally, however, the labor movement numbered too few members to act as an influential political force, and the great masses of workers remained fragmented by race, nationality, and religion. Perhaps Andrew Carnegie had it right when he wrote of Cleveland's victory: "Cleveland! Landslide! Well we have nothing to fear and perhaps it is best. People will now think the Protected Mfrs. will be attended to and quit agitating. Cleveland is a pretty good fellow."[65]

A fellow Democrat and friend of Cleveland's was also right about the significance of the summer of 1892 for labor-capital relations in the United States. "The labor question has come to stay; it cannot be ignored," Walter Q. Gresham, a future U.S. attorney general, wrote to a friend on August 1. "What is an equitable division of the joint product of capital and labor, and who is to decide the question? . . . The laboring men of this country . . . firmly believe that they are oppressed. They are growing stronger daily, and unless capital yields, we will have collisions more serious than the one which occurred at Homestead."[66]

The Judiciary and Labor

As 1892 passed into 1893 and workers increasingly resorted to the strike as the most effective instrument to relieve their "oppression," federal judges attended to the labor question. More and more often, they chose to decide the question that Gresham found so contentious, the equitable division of the fruits of production. How they decided that question evidenced little consistency within the judiciary. Without exception, judges ruled that coercion or unlawful methods were not to be used in the contest between labor and capital. For some judges, however, the strike and the boycott were coercive and unlawful measures. For others, peaceful strikes and primary boycotts remained lawful. Several judges believed that where they had jurisdiction, it was perfectly legitimate for them to set fair wages and decent working conditions. Other judges held with equal sincerity that only managers serving as the duly appointed trustees for investors had the right to make such decisions. If, however, there was any overall pattern to judicial decisions in the area of labor-capital relations, it favored capital.[67]

The fact of the situation was that judges proved most adept at fashioning decisions that served to disarm workers of their most effective weapons of economic warfare. In March 1893, for example, a judge in the federal court for the eastern district of Louisiana found a union of teamsters guilty of violating federal law because their strike against shippers and warehouse operators had succeeded in restraining interstate commerce. In an imaginative ruling, the judge declared that the Sherman Antitrust Act of 1890 applied to the behavior of unions as well as that of corporations. Conceding that the Sherman Act originated in the evils of massed capital, he ruled that the debate in Congress proved that the bill's sponsors intended to cover combinations of labor as well as capital. To him, it was manifest that the act was meant to include "combinations which are composed of laborers acting in the interest of laborers." And he had no doubt that the strike by the teamsters of New Orleans was unlawful because "they endeavored to prevent, and did prevent, everybody from moving the commerce of the country."[68]

Little did the judge in this particular case realize that he had delivered a decision that over the following four decades would sow dissension among trade unionists, judges, congressmen, presidents, and scholars. Did the authors and supporters of the Sherman Act intend it to apply to labor? Senators disagreed about what their real intentions had been. A careful reading of the congressional debate on the bill offers no definitive answer to the question of intent. Still, it is hardly disputable that popular anxieties about business monopolies, not fear of trade unions, caused politicians to satisfy symbolically their constituents' anticorporate sentiments. Thus some scholars conclude that a majority in Congress never intended the Sherman Act to apply to unions.[69] Other equally capable scholars declare to the contrary, finding that Congress intended the law to encompass unions but left it to the courts to determine how to apply it.[70] My own reading of the same evidence suggests that a majority in Congress in 1890 never intended the law to apply to trade unions. They simply lacked the political courage to exclude labor by precise language, a fact pointed to by the small minorities that favored either specific inclusion or exclusion. In 1890, as for the next forty years, most members of Congress preferred to draw the laws on labor-capital relations ambiguously and leave their interpretation and application to the federal courts, a responsibility that, as the Louisiana case of March 1893 revealed, judges refused to shirk.

Only a month later, in April, a federal judge in the western district of Georgia also ruled the Sherman Act applicable to union actions, a ruling he never had to reach because the case in question concerned an interstate railroad and was already covered by the Constitution's commerce clause and the ICC Act. Yet in a decision otherwise quite favorable to labor — he required the Central Railroad of Georgia to sign a contract with the Brotherhood of Locomotive Engineers with respect to wage rates and to implement a form of job seniority to be administered by the court — the judge in an obiter dictum declared that federal laws, including the ICC and Sherman acts, made railroad strikes and boycotts illegal. He reached that decision because of the Locomotive Engineers' union rule (no. 12), which obligated members to strike in sympathy with engineers on other lines. The judge simply declared that such a rule, because it violated the Sherman Act, was inoperative and hence no threat to management's rights.[71]

The Locomotive Engineers' rule no. 12 dominated several other crucial federal cases. In a case that came before William Howard Taft in 1893, when he was sitting as a member of the circuit court for northern Ohio, brought by a railroad involved in a dispute with the Engineers, whose cars were not being interchanged with another line, Taft cited the precedent of the 1888 *Burlington* case. In agreement with the rulings of most other judges, he found railroads to be quasi-public enterprises and also directly subject to federal law. Also in keeping with the mainstream of legal interpretation, Taft declared that workers have a perfect right to threaten to quit work or to quit when not in violation of contract, for man has an inalienable right to his own labor. That right, he stressed, is not absolute and if it is used unlawfully, as, for example, in a sympathetic strike under rule 12 — which is legally a boycott, not a strike — then "Neither law nor morals can give a man the right to labor or withhold his labor for such a purpose." And he warned union president P. M. Arthur that rule 12 "make[s] the whole brotherhood a criminal conspiracy against the laws of their country." Taft thus issued a temporary mandatory injunction ordering engineers on unaffected railroad lines to handle traffic from the struck railroad.[72]

In a companion decision by a judge in the same circuit, the equity power of federal courts received its fullest expression. Citing Supreme Court justice David J. Brewer as his authority, he said, "I believe most thoroughly that the powers of a court of equity are as vast, and its processes and procedures as elastic, as all the changing emergencies of increasingly complex business relations and the protection of rights can demand."[73]

A decision rendered by a federal court in the eastern district of Wisconsin disclosed precisely how vast and elastic were the powers of equity. This case concerned the right of unionized employees of the Northern Pacific Railroad, then in federal receivership, to act collectively against two consecutive unilateral wage reductions. Facing a strike, the receiver went to court for an injunction against such collective action. Without hesitation, the judge granted a preliminary injunction, which was subsequently extended, that banned workers from collective action and denied unions the right to communicate with their members. When the unions went before the judge to have the injunction lifted because they had not and would not engage in unlawful action, the court ruled that the injunction had been needed and remained necessary not because violence had occurred but because the unions had to be restrained before they caused irreparable damage to innocent parties. Referring to the railroad's employees (all 12,000) as officers of the court, the judge declared, "Liberty and license must not be confounded. . . . Rights are not absolute but relative. . . . One has not the right arbitrarily to quit service without regard to the necessities of that service." He then literally compared railroad workers to surgeons in the middle of an operation and, of course, drew the logical conclusion. That was not all he said. He added that strikes were essentially conspiracies to extort, and, failing that, to injure. "It is idle to talk of a peaceable strike. None such ever occurred. The suggestion is impeachment of intelligence . . . force and turbulence, violence and outrage, arson and murder, have been associated with the strike as its natural and inevitable concomitants." He then quoted fulsomely from Justice Brewer's speech before the New York Bar Association in 1893. "The strike has become a serious evil, destructive to property, destructive to individual right, injurious to the conspirators themselves, and subversive of republican institutions. Certainly, no court should give encouragement to any combination thus destructive of the very fabric of our government, tending to the disruption of society, and the obliteration of legal and natural rights."[74]

There were federal judges, however, who dissented from such harsh antiunion reasoning and were not bashful about saying so. In a case much like the above one, the receivers for the Union Pacific Railroad had tried to cut wages without conferring with the affected unions, and when the unions threatened to strike, the receivers sought an injunction. This time, however, the judge for the eastern district of Nebraska refused to issue an injunction to compel workers to stay on the job when the receivers had cut wages without notification and the joint conferences required by the existing contract. "In this country," he ruled, "it is not unlawful for employees to associate, consult, and confer together with a view to maintain or increase the wages, by lawful and peaceful means. . . . What is lawful for one [corporations] to do is lawful for the other [unions]. . . . Both act from the prompting of enlightened selfishness, and the action of both is lawful when no illegal or criminal means are used or threatened." For this judge, "the legality and utility of [unions] . . . can no longer be questioned."[75]

Yet only a month later, William Howard Taft ruled that railroad receivers should be free to set wages at whatever level the law of supply and demand determined to be proper without conferring with unions or facing the threat of strikes. In his Ohio circuit, Taft granted the sort of injunction which the judge in Nebraska had denied.[76] In the future, though judicial critics of antistrike injunctions might voice their opinions, the Taft perspective would prevail.[77]

The Crisis of the 1890s:
The Cleveland Administration and Labor

Judicial rulings probably intensified rather than stilled popular discontent. Although Americans prided themselves on being a society of "laws and not men," it rankled republican sensibilities to watch nonelected federal judges, many of whom had served as corporation attorneys in their prebench careers, rule against the actions of working people. Even more conducive to the rise of popular discontent, however, was the onset of the panic of 1893 and the ensuing economic depression, best known both to contemporaries and to later historians as the "crisis of the nineties." As depression destroyed enterprises, bankrupted indebted farmers, and spread unemployment, popular discontent intensified.

It percolated throughout the society, economy, and polity. Populism excited farmers and workers, and its political manifestation, the People's party, threatened the hegemony of Democrats in the South and Republicans in the West. Workers grew more restless and their organizations more active in politics and industrial conflict. The unemployed, too, were heard from. Organized into so-called industrial armies — Kelley's, Coxey's and others — their members seized railroad cars, rode the rods, and headed toward Washington to petition Congress for relief. Even as events seemed to move out of control, the number of bills and petitions introduced in Congress to provide relief or special benefits for farmers and workers reached unprecedented proportions. For many more-conservative Americans, the warning issued only two years earlier by the House committee investigating the Homestead conflict seemed prescient indeed: "Within the next decade we may reasonably expect a revolution."

The crisis of the 1890s, it appeared, would test Andrew Carnegie's estimation of Grover Cleveland. Was the Democratic president worthy of the trust and respect of corporate America? Would he hold firm in the face of mass discontent, and use the powers at his disposal to maintain law and order?

Answers to these questions were fast in coming. Although at first the Cleveland administration lacked a fully articulated policy concerning labor upheaval, the Justice Department under Attorney General Richard Olney (a former railroad attorney and director) step by step developed such a policy. Susceptible to the fears and counsel of fellow corporation attorneys and businessmen, Olney used his power to break strikes and weaken unions under the pretext of protecting property and maintaining law and order. In the spring of 1893 the attorney general authorized territorial officials to break a strike in Utah, and in the autumn he ordered U.S. marshals to do the same to a transit strike in Minneapolis–St. Paul because it interfered with the movement of the mails.[78] The following spring (1894) the president himself ordered federal troops to remove striking coal miners in Indian Territory from private mines operated under the supervision of the Interior Department. As these examples proved, the Democrats in power were willing to act quickly and decisively to thwart militant workers.[79] They showed equal decisiveness in coping with the industrial armies of the unemployed and in combating a strike by the American Railway Union (ARU) on the Great Northern Railroad. In those two instances, Olney built the precedents that would enable federal courts to issue antistrike injunctions in order to protect the mails and interstate commerce as well as to have the president authorize the use of marshals and troops to enforce court orders.[80]

Carnegie had nothing to fear from Cleveland. The same could not be said for Eugene V. Debs, the leader of the ARU, who was about to involve his members in the most tumultuous and famous industrial conflict of the nineteenth century, the Pullman Boycott of 1894.

When the labor dispute between industrialist George M. Pullman and his workers spilled over into a boycott of Pullman sleeper cars by members of the ARU, affecting almost every major railroad from Chicago west, the federal government was ready to act. Although Debs and his followers intended neither to paralyze interstate commerce nor to interfere with the mails, the policies of the western railroads, as implemented by their General Managers Association (GMA), ensured that the ARU boycott would do both. They also guaranteed a vigorous response from federal authorities. Attorney General Olney, who had been in regular contact with the GMA, appointed as the federal government's special attorney in the situation a lawyer who, in effect, had been chosen by the affected railroads. Cleveland and Olney prepared to act vigorously because they perceived the Pullman Boycott as much more than a dispute between employers and employees. In the hyperbolic language of the attorney general, the ARU boycott in early July 1894 had brought the nation "to the ragged edge of anarchy and it is time to see whether the law is sufficiently strong to prevent this condition of affairs. If not, the sooner we know it the better that it may be changed."[81] As members of the administration, Congress, the courts, and conservative opinion makers saw it, the struggle in Chicago and the West pitted workers against the state, criminal conspirators against the law, anarchy against order, revolution against constitutionalism.

To nip anarchy in the bud, Olney and Cleveland devised an ingenious legal-political strategy. First, they went into federal court to obtain injunctions prohibiting railroad workers from interfering with both interstate commerce and the mails. The judges promptly granted broad-based injunctions that prohibited all officers of the ARU from communicating in any way with their members as well as all unnamed ARU members and railroad workers from furthering in any way the boycott. Whether under the terms of the Sherman Act, the ICC Act, the passage of the mails, or common law conspiracies, the judges restrained the railroad workers from further boycott activity.[82] Judicial attitudes were best reflected in the charge of one judge to an Illinois grand jury about to indict ARU officials for violating the injunctions. Asking the grand jurors to uphold the supremacy of law, he declared that "neither the torch of the incendiary nor the weapon of the insurrectionist, nor the inflamed tongue of him who incites to fire and sword is the instrument to bring about reforms."[83]

Although Debs later claimed that it was the injunctions that broke the boycott and although he served time in prison for civil contempt of an injunction, the truth is that legal process alone did not move freight or free the western railroads from the clutches of the boycotters.

Both Cleveland and Olney knew that. For them the court orders were merely a precondition for using armed force to break the strike. Washington regularly received reports from military officers in the West stressing that local populations sympathized with the strikers, that marshals could not serve legal process, and that railroads could not secure strikebreakers. From Utah, Nevada, and California, officers reported that "along the Union Pacific . . . a general sympathy with the strikers exists at all points." And from Butte, Montana, they learned that "labor unions were so thoroughly organized and embraced so large a proportion of the population . . . that they met with practically no opposition."[84] That is why Cleveland and Olney sent troops to Chicago and throughout the western states before any appreciable violence erupted (in fact, the first real violence occurred only after the arrival of federal troops). And that is why they disregarded Illinois governor John Altgeld's insistence on respect for constitutional traditions concerning federal-state relations and his pledge to uphold the law in Illinois as vigorously as necessary. Only the presence of the army could ensure that legal process would be served and, more important, that the railroads could obtain and use strikebreakers to replace the boycotters. Only the army could break the boycott, and it did so more swiftly than any other means available to federal authorities and the railroads.[85] As Debs later understood, the arrival of the army transformed a conventional industrial dispute between employers and employees "into a conflict in which the organized forces of society and all the powers of the municipal, State, and Federal governments were arraigned against us."[86]

Although a few Populists rose on the floor of Congress to defend the boycotters as rebels against the tyranny of Pullman, their feeble voices were drowned by the large majority, which condemned the strikers as insurrectionaries. "Do not the people realize," asked one member of the majority, "that the Constitution itself is upon trial and that the country itself is in danger?" Thus both houses of Congress passed resolutions endorsing Cleveland's actions.[87] From beyond Capitol Hill Cleveland won even more fulsome encomia. "On every hand, and from old enemies as well as old friends," wrote Richard Gilder, editor of *Century Magazine*, "nothing is now heard but praise and the expression of intense satisfaction at your patriotic and fearless action."[88] A little later, Supreme Court justice Stephen Field declared that "no just man can withhold his full thanks for the bold, straight forward and courageous conduct shown by him in putting down by force the monstrous strikes. No battle of the century will reflect upon the winner greater honor."[89] Finally, a year later, the Supreme Court sanctioned the Cleveland-Olney policies when it unanimously turned down Debs's appeal against his conviction for civil contempt. The court ruled forcefully that the federal government had more than ample power under the commerce clause, the ICC Act, and federal mail statutes to take the action it did. And much to Olney's pleasure, the court declined to rely on the Sherman Act for its ruling. In the attorney general's mind, the court had "decided Debs case in my favor on all points — in fact took my argument and turned it into an opinion."[90]

Reform versus Repression

Having proved that repression restrained labor militancy, federal officials now sought to shape a less radical trade unionism than that which had been personified by Debs and his ARU. To do so, they moved toward reform and accommodation with trade unionism on several fronts simultaneously. As early as October 1894, a decision handed down by John Marshall Harlan, speaking for the Seventh Circuit Federal Court of Appeals, decisively upheld the legality of trade unions and strikes. It also limited the Sherman Act as a basis for enjoining union action. Harlan ruled that to deny workers the right to quit in the absence of a contract to the contrary was to establish a form of involuntary servitude. Strikes as such, he added, cannot be enjoined; only illegal actions in furtherance of union goals may be subject to judicial restraint. Harlan thus found the original injunction issued by a Wisconsin judge against union members on the Northern Pacific Railroad, in which strikes per se were declared to be illegal, without justification and ordered its revision.[91] Simultaneously, Attorney General Olney was straining toward the same end as Judge Harlan was. In the aftermath of Pullman, Olney had decided that "responsible" unions could be tolerated. He had recently seen the railroad brotherhoods assist the railroads in finding workers and the AFL reject Debs's call for a general strike. Having by his actions proved sympathy strikes to be illegal and ineffective, Olney sought contradictorily to sanction the legitimacy of lawful strikes on railroads and also to eliminate them through an arbitration panel. Harlan's ruling served the attorney general's aims perfectly, for in Olney's sense of what the courts should do, it stood as "practical proof" that judges understood and appreciated "the greatest social problem of the day." Such a decision served to repudiate those equity proceedings that had defined all strikes as illegal and hence inflamed workers.[92] The special federal strike commission appointed to investigate the causes of the Pullman Boycott served the same purpose. As chaired by Carroll Wright, it strove to encourage responsible and conservative unionism. In the words of Wright's biographer, the commission report drew public attention away from injunctions and troops and directed it to "malefactors of great wealth, whom no one loved, the potential value of responsible unions, which few appreciated, and the advisability of compulsory arbitration, which no one wanted." Cleveland, however, apparently never read the report that was personally presented to him. For the remainder of his life, the president would defend his policies and actions during the Pullman Boycott and call for no new accommodation with labor.[93]

Congress also joined the rush to mollify labor once it had been adequately disciplined. As early as March 1894, well before the Pullman Boycott, the House had authorized its Judiciary Committee to investigate the behavior of the federal judge in Milwaukee who had issued the injunction against Northern Pacific workers that declared strikes and unions illegal. The committee majority subsequently recommended that Congress limit the power of federal judges both to issue labor injunctions and to punish for contempt. They also recommended that the judge in question be censured for his improper and abusive actions against workers.[94] After Pullman, Congress moved in two other ways to assuage labor's grievances. Immediately after the conflict on the western railroads had ended, Olney began to draft legislation that would sanction railroad unionism of the brotherhood variety and establish voluntary arbitration as an alternative to strikes.[95] On December 6, 1895, Representative Constantine J. Erdman introduced such a bill in the House. After more than a year of desultory debate on the Erdman railroad strike arbitration bill, during which the railroad brotherhoods demanded its passage and one representative speaking for the AFL criticized its provisions as a form of compulsion, involuntary servitude, and surrender of union power, the House passed the bill by a wide margin. But between its initial passage by the House in February 1897 and its final adoption more than a year passed. As enacted by overwhelming majorities of both houses in May 1898, the Erdman Act recognized the legitimacy of trade unions on interstate railroads, banned the "yellow-dog" contract, and established a voluntary federal arbitration board as an alternative to strikes. In the words of one congressman, "it recognizes organized labor and puts them in a position to assert their rights in behalf of their members."[96] On their part, the railroad brotherhoods had recognized that the federal government would tolerate no strike that substantially affected interstate commerce. Rather than confront state power directly, as Debs had done, the union leaders preferred to accommodate reality, glory in congressional recognition of their legitimacy, applaud legislative sanction for collective bargaining on the railroads, and accept voluntary arbitration as a substitute for strikes.

The Industrial Commission:
Prologue to Progressivism

Simultaneously, Congress sought to allay the anxieties of nonrailroad workers. The same sessions, that considered and debated the Erdman Act also discussed the establishment of an industrial commission to probe labor-capital relations in all their complexity. A bill to establish such a commission had easily passed the House in 1895 but had been delayed in the Senate by an influential group of northeastern Republicans who objected to its chimerical nature and argued that it should be tabled in view of the opposition from business and industry. A large majority of senators, however, favored its passage, alluding to the growing political restiveness of labor, the movement of many trade unions to independent radical political action, and the ever-widening breach between capital and labor. To relieve the fears of conservatives in Congress about a commission to be appointed solely by the president on the advice of union, farmer, and business groups, the Senate amended the House bill to provide that the presiding officers of Congress would each appoint five commission members and the president would appoint nine others equally divided among labor, agriculture, and capital. Such a bill finally came to a vote in the Senate on March 3, 1897. Though the Senate remained divided between those eager to mollify labor (a large majority), who, in the words of one senator, "want . . . a recognition of the labor interests," and those few, like Senator Thomas Platt of Connecticut, who railed that "human laws should be like the divine laws. They should apply to all," — the Industrial Commission Bill swept through both houses that same day. President Cleveland nevertheless pocket vetoed the bill.[97] The following year Congress again enacted the Industrial Commission Bill, and in June 1898 President McKinley signed it.

Taken together, the passage of the Erdman Act and the Industrial Commission Bill appeared to be harbingers of a new "progressive era" in federal labor policies. Before the provisions of the Erdman Act could take effect or the commission even reported, however, the old order of repression once more made itself felt. In 1898 a federal judge again demonstrated why trade unionists were so enraged at court rulings. In a case concerning a strike against the American Steel and Wire Company in Cleveland, a circuit court judge first ruled that ex parte preliminary injunctions, such as those issued during the Pullman Boycott, could be used to restrain unincorporated trade unions and that they could be made to encompass unnamed as well as specified parties to a dispute. Second, he ruled peaceful picketing and persuasion unlawful. In this case, both the mayor and the police chief of Cleveland testified that the strikers had used neither intimidation nor violence and had never harmed life, limb, or property. All they had done was to march and demonstrate in the streets near the plant and their homes in protest against strikebreakers. To this the judge responded, "The truth is that most potential and unlawful force or violence may exist without lifting a finger, or uttering a word of threat." Only if evidence had been offered that one strikebreaker had in fact passed the picket line and gone to work would proof have existed that the strikers used peaceful persuasion. The judge then offered a ringing defense of the right of individual contract. Even scabs are guaranteed "the right to work as one pleases, and the right to contract as one chooses. . . . In this country, this right to contract in business is a constitutional freedom, which not even state legislatures can impair, and certainly not strike organizations."[98]

The courts having once again limited the right of a union to strike and picket, a year later, in 1899, federal troops went to the Coeur d'Alenes for a second time to break a miners' strike. McKinley acted in almost the same manner as Harrison had. When the governor of Idaho, Frank Steunenberg, informed the president that strikers in the Coeur d'Alenes had created a state of insurrection that the governor lacked the power to end, McKinley ordered federal troops to northern Idaho to reestablish law and order. Just as they had done seven years earlier, the army officers worked hand in glove with the governor and the mine owners. But this time they were more adept and forceful in their actions. For two years under Steunenberg's declaration of martial law, army officers saw to it that no union members returned to work in the mines and that no union agitation occurred. Again hundreds of miners were arrested and imprisoned in hastily built stockades, and this time the army helped the state purge town and county officials who were sympathetic to the union. As one lieutenant colonel observed, only the presence of federal power assured that the Coeur d'Alenes would be obliterated as a "plague spot of incivism and anarchy."[99] McKinley ignored the questions raised long ago by General Hancock concerning the proper relationship between national and state authorities when the army was used to repress domestic discontent. In Idaho in 1899, as in 1892, U.S. troops served at the pleasure and orders of state officials, not of the commander in chief.

As judges continued to issue antilabor injunctions and troops patrolled the hills of northern Idaho, the Industrial Commission went about its business of investigating the relations between capital and labor. The commission members did yeoman service, compiling a final report that in published form (1902) ran to nineteen fact-filled volumes and covered nearly every sector of the economy and every region of the country. The final summary volume described the plight of workers at the end of the century in language that a radical labor leader would have admired. "The seller of labor," the report observed, "is worse off in several respects than the seller of almost any physical product. His commodity is in the highest degree perishable. That which is not sold to-day disappears absolutely." Thus, the report observed, "the workingman is almost always under grave disadvantage as compared with the employer. . . . Under such conditions the result of free competition is to throw the advantages of the bargain into the hands of the stronger bargainer." Only organization of workers into unions and the achievement of the closed shop could equalize bargaining power between employers and employees and promote democracy in the shop.[100]

After such stirring rhetoric, the commission's actual recommendations for the amelioration of labor-capital relations were anticlimactic. The majority simply proposed that the separate states enact uniform laws to assure decent working conditions; that the power of federal courts to issue injunctions in labor disputes be restricted but not eliminated; that the federal government regulate the wages, conditions, and hours of railroad workers; and that yellow-dog contracts be outlawed without diminishing the right of nonunion workers to labor on their own terms. Even such mild recommendations were too much for three separate commission minorities, however, which worried about the federal government's intruding on state rights, requiring uniformity of laws in a diverse nation, unsettling the minds of businesspeople, and upsetting immutable economic laws.[101]

The commission majority's recommendations, however, formed a national agenda for labor reformers in the succeeding Progressive Era. Called into being in 1898 to find answers to the social chaos of the Gilded Age, the commission provided a program of action for the Progressive presidents, Theodore Roosevelt and Woodrow Wilson, a legislative menu for reformist legislators, and a rationale for critics of the labor injunction. Its members left it to the federal officials of a new century to devise and implement labor policies that would be more responsive to the interests of trade unionists.

The Progressive Approach:

From Theodore Roosevelt to

Woodrow Wilson, 1900–1916

The battle between labor and capital, workers and employers, unions and management dominated the hidden agenda of Progressivism.[1] Of all the issues that roiled reformers and national politics in the early twentieth century, none disclosed as graphically the conflict between private power and the general welfare as the labor question. It proved the most sensitive issue and the one least amenable to lasting compromise. It was so contentious that most politicians preferred evasions, even though it persistently arose as a partisan question in national elections.[2] Presidents Theodore Roosevelt and Woodrow Wilson, both of whom as activist executives refashioned the national state to lodge more power in the executive branch, sought to regulate conflict between workers and employers. But it was unelected federal judges with lifetime tenure who determined national labor policy more often and more decisively than elected public officials did.

The Progressive Ethos and Labor

The labor question proved so divisive politically because trade unionism challenged basic American traditions in two ways. First, socialists and syndicalists were a growing presence among organized workers in the years from 1900 through 1916. Both forms of labor radicalism threatened an economic and political system founded on the sanctity of private property and the prerogatives of wealth. And syndicalism, to boot, derided the virtues of representative parliamentary government. Of course, the radicals represented only a minority of organized workers. Yet even the nonradical majority refused to behave as domesticated citizens in an emerging corporate-liberal system. If the Samuel Gomperses and the John Mitchells (presidents, respectively, of the American Federation of Labor and the United Mine Workers) rhetorically extolled private property and free enterprise, their actual practices — especially the closed shop and collective bargaining — conflicted with established principles of property and circumscribed entrepreneurial liberties. As David Brody has written, "power and interest can be issues of deadly conflict even in a system in which men agree on fundamentals."[3] Such was indeed the case in the early twentieth century, when employers waged bloody battles with even the most "responsible" and "conservative" of trade unions. Let there be no mistake about it, American business *never* willingly conceded any of its prerogatives to workers and unions or to political reformers.

Even more troubling to employers was the fact that at the turn of the century organized labor for the first time in American history built a durable mass movement. Between 1897 and 1903 the unions affiliated with the AFL grew more than sixfold, from 400,000 to almost 3 million members. The independent railroad brotherhoods grew as rapidly and achieved a stable contractual relationship with most of the major interstate railroads. Despite an aggressive employer counterattack beginning in 1903, followed by the economic contraction of 1907–9, trade unionism did not shrivel as it had in similar circumstances in the previous century. On the contrary. After generally holding its own from 1905 through 1910, in the last year of that period the labor movement resumed its momentum, now organizing workers — new immigrants and young women — hitherto deemed unorganizable.

The rapid growth of the labor movement, however, brought industrial conflict as often as mutual accommodation between employers and workers. After a brief labor-capital honeymoon between 1898 and 1903, the war between unions and management resumed with a bitterness reminiscent of 1877 and 1894. For over two years (1903 to 1905) a literal civil war engulfed the mining districts of Colorado, as the governor suspended civil process, declared martial law, and dispatched the militia to crush the Western Federation of Miners (WFM) at the behest of the mine owners. In 1905, in Chicago, teamsters, strikebreakers, and police fought pitched battles in the city's streets. During these years leaders of the Structural Iron Workers' Union operated a dynamiting conspiracy against anti-union employers, which culminated in the 1910 bombing of the Los Angeles Times building and the arrest of union leaders James B. and John J. McNamara. These battles flowed ceaselessly across the industrial landscape, sweeping over the textile, steel, coal, meatpacking, rubber, oil-refining, and garment industries. Graham Adams, Jr., was certainly not wrong in referring to the years 1910 to 1915 as an "age of industrial violence." And not without reason have the years from 1910 to 1922 been called the era of the mass strike.[4]

The growth of the labor movement and the rising intensity of industrial conflict coincided with increased national political participation by workers and their unions. This was almost inevitable, because as unions grew in size and their conflicts spread into a larger national arena, the policies and actions of the federal government proved decisive to the cause of labor. John Mitchell expressed the labor movement's sense of political reality when he wrote in 1903: "The trade union movement in this country can make progress only by identifying itself with the state."[5]

The State and Labor: Theodore Roosevelt

When Mitchell wrote those words he was probably thinking of President Theodore Roosevelt. By 1903 Roosevelt had already made a reputation for himself as an activist chief executive, one not loath to use the "bully pulpit" of the White House to ask the people to join him in a crusade to make the public interest superior to all private interests. Unsparing in his criticisms of "malefactors of wealth" and "irresponsible labor leaders," Roosevelt saw himself as guardian and advocate of the general welfare. He was a true conservative, a firm believer in stability and order, yet also one who understood instinctively and intellectually that order and stability depended on controlled change. For Roosevelt, to conserve was to reform. To preserve the benefits of the private business corporation, to maintain people's respect for private property, including great concentrations of wealth, and to strengthen Americans' faith in popular republican government, he envisaged an intrusive national state that would simultaneously define the limits of corporate power and radical dissent. His state-defined general welfare had a place for corporations and unions, business executives and labor leaders, as long as they played by the president's rules.[6] And it was those rules that John Mitchell asked trade unionists to identify with.

What were Roosevelt's rules of labor-capital relations? How did he apply them to the often unruly and violent world of American industrial relations?

More than any previous president, Theodore Roosevelt dealt with the "labor question" in his public addresses and private correspondence. Beginning with his first annual message to Congress, in which he defined the most vital national and even global problem as "the effort to deal with that tangle of far-reaching questions which we group together when we speak of 'labor,'" Roosevelt yearly reiterated that theme.[7] For him, combinations, whether of capital or labor, were necessary and essential concomitants of modern life. Immorality not organization, badness not bigness, were the salient issues.

While Roosevelt gloried in portraying himself as a "modern man," much of his rhetoric about business and labor echoed the language of Andrew Jackson and

Abraham Lincoln. "We are neither for the rich man as such nor the poor man as such," he proclaimed in his second annual message to Congress. "We are for the upright man rich or poor."[8] And like his nineteenth-century predecessors, nothing troubled him as much as a rise in class feeling. "Every far-sighted patriot," he warned in a special message to Congress in 1906, "should protest first of all against the growth in this country of that evil thing which is called 'class consciousness.' "[9] Simply put, for Roosevelt the worth of an individual came before the interest of a class, and so, although he regularly lauded the virtue of collective action for businesspeople and workers, he simultaneously insisted that government must be based solely on the theory "that each man, rich or poor, is to be treated simply and solely on his worth as a man."[10] In fact, he explicitly warned organized capital and organized labor that each must harmonize its interests with those of the general welfare and in so doing always respect individual freedom.[11]

In theory, then, Roosevelt's concept of labor-capital relations hinted at both promise and peril for trade unionists. On the one hand, he recognized the legitimacy of labor organizations as well as business corporations and encouraged employers to negotiate with representatives of their workers. On the other hand, however, he denigrated class feeling and praised individualism, pledging to defend the individual nonunion laborer from the tyranny of union bosses. And what he gave to labor came more from a blend of Machiavellian politics and Christian charity than from any sympathy for or softness to unions. "The friends of property [of which he obviously defined himself as one] must realize," he wrote to Philander C. Knox, "that the surest way to provoke an explosion of wrong and injustice is to be short-sighted, narrow-minded, greedy and arrogant, and to fail to show that in actual work that here in this republic it is peculiarly incumbent upon the man with whom things have prospered to be in a certain sense the keeper of his brother with whom life has gone hard."[12]

The 1902 Anthracite Strike

Early in his first term Roosevelt had an opportunity to apply his princely politics to the relations between labor and capital. By intervening in a dispute between anthracite coal miners and operators, he could establish both his leadership in the Republican party and the primacy of the public interest over special interests. Although the Republican party was home to those business interests most hostile to trade unionism, Roosevelt's primary competitor for party leadership, Senator Mark A. Hanna of Ohio, was a leading advocate of an accommodation with responsible labor leaders. A former executive in the Ohio coal, iron, and steel industries, Hanna had a history of bargaining with unions and also had already helped compromise a labor dispute in anthracite coal. Moreover, he was not bashful about stating publicly his belief in organized labor and the fact that where able and honest leaders commanded unions "it is much easier for those who represent the employers to come into close contact with the laborer, and, by dealing with fewer persons, to accomplish results quicker and better."[13]

Both Hanna's philosophy of labor relations and Roosevelt's response to it flowed as much from political exigencies and conservative principles as from any love for trade unionism. First of all, both men represented states (Ohio and New York) in which unions were relatively well organized and politically influential. Keeping the labor vote in the Republican party, where much of it had been since 1894, was no mean task.[14] Second, Hanna and Roosevelt feared radical influences and perceived responsible trade unionists as allies in a struggle against socialism. For those reasons Hanna applauded Samuel Gompers, who "took the broad ground that in the interests of labor there was no room for the socialist or the anarchist, no room for men who undertook to disturb the principles of our society and government."[15]

The competition between the two men drove them to seek a political accommodation with labor and to prove that the national state, if not the firm ally of trade unionism, was at least not its foe. They wanted labor leaders to forget the nineteenth-century tradition of executive actions by which Presidents Hayes, Harrison, Cleveland, and McKinley used federal troops to break strikes and smash unions. The dispute between the anthracite coal miners and their employers in 1902 provided an opportunity to practice a new federal approach to labor relations. In fact, for Hanna and Roosevelt, no labor dispute could better have served their purposes. The parties to the conflict, the United Mine Workers on one side and the coal operators on the other, were characters from a morality play. The union and its president, John Mitchell, acted responsibly at all times, disdaining violence, maintaining contractual obligations, and showing due regard for the public interest. By contrast, the operators, led by George Baer, were not only "monopolists"; they also appeared obdurate and cool to the general welfare. On one side, then, we had the honest, humble laborer petitioning his employer for his just rewards. On the other side, we had the arrogant capitalist upholding his divine right to determine what was just for his employees. Onto this stage Roosevelt could stride as the impartial mediator, the trustee for the general welfare.[16]

In many ways the coal dispute should never have occasioned a federal response. It was limited to a small region of the country; despite repeated stories of violence, local and state authorities had no difficulty maintaining order; and, most important, the strike in no way threatened the public interest, for, even with the approach of the winter heating season, an adequate, economical supply of alternative fuel was readily available.[17]

Yet at that time, political and popular perceptions suggested a different reality, one in which the persistence of the strike by hard-coal miners into the fall and perhaps the winter of 1902 threatened Republican electoral prospects in the Northeast and endangered the health of citizens. From the first, Roosevelt acted on just such commonly held perceptions of reality. At the beginning of the dispute he sent Commissioner of Labor Carroll Wright to the anthracite district to seek an accommodation between miners and operators. Wright reported that the United Mine Workers (UMW) was amenable to arbitration but that the operators rejected all negotiations with a union.[18] As the strike dragged on into the summer, Roosevelt called representatives of the union and the operators to the White House to seek an accommodation. Again the operators proved obdurate.[19] Meantime, both public anxiety and political pressures on the Republicans intensified. Working together, Hanna and Roosevelt used their connections in the Wall Street financial community — namely J. P. Morgan, whose investment bank ultimately controlled the anthracite interests — to compel the operators to arbitrate. Yet Baer and his business associates absolutely refused to recognize the legitimacy of trade unionism. When Roosevelt proposed an arbitration commission composed equally of representatives of business, labor, and the public, the operators fought the appointment of a labor leader, insisting that it would be tantamount to union recognition. When Roosevelt finally appointed a union leader, E. E. Clarke of the Order of Railway Conductors, to the Anthracite Coal Strike Commission, he labeled him an "eminent sociologist." Even the president declined to compel businesspeople to accord unionism legitimacy.[20]

Although Roosevelt's actions won him a reputation as a friend of labor and also played well with the general public, the final recommendations of the Anthracite Strike Commission ceded trade unionism far less than a full victory. The commission did mandate higher wages and shorter hours for the miners (the operators to be recompensed by higher prices for their product). It also established an arbitration procedure under which Carroll Wright would rule on workers' grievances. But the UMW suffered two severe setbacks in the final award. The commission failed to require employers to recognize or bargain with union representatives, and, more important, it upheld their right to run open shops.[21] The final resolution to the dispute displayed the virtuosity of Roosevelt's Machiavellian politics. Unlike his nineteenth-century predecessors, he did not use federal power to smash trade unionism; that won him the plaudits of reformers and many workers. Still, the actual results of federal arbitration showed the proclivities of a patrician paternalist rather than the proponent of independent trade unionism.[22] But just as popular perceptions distorted the reality of the anthracite strike, they also credited Roosevelt with accomplishments he never achieved.[23]

Roosevelt wasted little time in proving to those conservatives in his own party and constituency that he harbored little sympathy for workers and unions who declined to play by his rules. As he wrote on one occasion, "I wished the labor people absolutely to understand that I set my face like flint against violence and lawlessness of any kind on their part, just as much as against arrogant greed by the rich."[24] In 1903, a year after the anthracite strike, he demonstrated that commitment by sending federal troops to the territory of Arizona to police a dispute between hard-rock miners and their employers. In this case, the conflict was short-lived and Roosevelt quickly withdrew the troops without incident.[25] And the following year, 1904, he made the same point by refusing to dispatch troops to Colorado where hard-rock miners and mine owners were locked in a deadly conflict. In this instance the union, the WFM, beseeched the president to protect their members' civil rights against the depredations of a governor and a state militia who authorized the arrest, trial, and deportation of strikers without due process. Probably because Roosevelt identified the leaders of the WFM with socialism, anarchism, and violence, he declined to aid their cause. Only two years later, when leaders of the WFM were standing trial in the state of Idaho for conspiracy in the murder of a former governor, Roosevelt publicly condemned them as "undesirable citizens" and demanded their conviction.[26]

Even in the case of the WFM, however, Roosevelt distanced his labor policies from those of previous presidents. He tried hard to make the state a neutral party to labor-capital conflicts. In yet another strike, involving the WFM and the even more radical IWW in Goldfield, Nevada, in 1907, Roosevelt displayed his credentials as a neutral. Acting on the request of the governor of Nevada, Roosevelt dispatched federal troops to Goldfield to maintain public order in the absence of effective state police power. Yet the president emphasized to the commander of the federal troops that the military was not to take sides in the dispute, nor was it to interfere with the activities of any person who behaved in a peaceful and orderly manner. Equally important, he ordered the commander not to make policy on his own or act at the behest of state officials. All military action had to be cleared with the president. "Better twenty-four hours of riot, damage, and disorder," warned Roosevelt, "than illegal use of troops." Still, because the president was convinced that the union leaders involved in the dispute, especially William D. "Big Bill" Haywood, were undesirable citizens and murderers, he kept the troops on duty until March 1908, by which time the strikers had been thoroughly beaten.[27]

Roosevelt established his credentials as a moderate acceptable to more-conservative Republicans and businesspeople through his position on the question of union security. If any single labor demand rankled conservative sensibilities and traditional values, it was the union, or closed, shop, which denied nonunion workers employment.[28] Where such contractual arrangements existed in the private sector by mutual agreement, the state could not intercede to uphold individual rights (in fact, several states by statute specifically legitimated the closed shop). In

1903, when the International Typographical Union demanded that a printer in the Government Printing Office be discharged for not being a union member, Roosevelt acted. Union rules, he proclaimed in tones reminiscent of those federal judges who ruled against the Locomotive Engineers, cannot transcend U.S. laws. The only standard for public employment must be good citizenship and efficient work, not the requirements of a private, voluntary institution. Moreover, Roosevelt's own Anthracite Strike Commission had just decided that mine owners need not contractually close their mines to nonunion miners, that the open shop was the only just hiring principle. What held for private sector employment, the president informed his secretary of commerce, must also hold for the public sector. Roosevelt simply ordered the reinstatement of the discharged nonunion printer.[29] In his commitment to a shop open to nonunion as well as union men, which he promised to "guarantee by every means in my power," Roosevelt may have established his neutrality, but in the real world of the early twentieth century, it was a neutrality that operated in favor of employers and against unions.[30]

The sphere of protective legislation provided broader scope for Roosevelt's paternalistic approach to labor. "The wage-workers," he stressed, "are peculiarly entitled to the protection and the encouragement of the law."[31] In almost every message to Congress, he devoted space to demanding that the states adopt uniform legislation to improve working conditions for men and especially women. He also called for the enactment of employers' liability laws and the abolition of child labor. In a special message to Congress in March 1908, Roosevelt suggested passage of a bill to eliminate child labor in the District of Columbia, where Congress had clear constitutional authority to do so, if it could not be abolished nationally and totally.[32] Already Roosevelt was moving rapidly to promote the rudimentary welfare state which would be embodied in his Progressive party presidential campaign of 1912.

The Judiciary versus Labor

As had been true in the late nineteenth century so, too, in the early twentieth century, the federal judiciary acted more persistently and decisively than any other branch of the national state in dealing with labor-capital relations. Overall, the most important judicial rulings went against workers and their unions. Yet within the pattern of antiunion prejudice, sharp distinctions in judicial attitude emerged. For one thing, many judges approached labor issues with the same split vision as Theodore Roosevelt demonstrated. Paternalist to a degree, they proved more tolerant of legislation and action by the state under its police power to improve the health and welfare of working people than of attempts to increase trade union power. As early as 1898, the Supreme Court had upheld the constitutionality of a

Utah law limiting the working hours of underground miners. Then, despite the infamous *Lochner* decision of 1905, in which the court declared unconstitutional a New York State law restricting the hours of adult male bakery workers,[33] it went ahead to sanction protective legislation for women workers and a mandated eight-hour day for railroad workers.[34] Although a majority of federal judges consistently enjoined unions from using their most effective weapons of industrial warfare (strikes, picketing, and boycotts), a significant minority dissented from judicial conservatism. Many judges agreed with the advice uttered by Chief Justice William Howard Taft in the early 1920s: "Government of the relations between capital and labor by injunction is a solecism. It is an absurdity. Injunctions in labor disputes are merely the emergency brakes for rare use and in case of sudden danger."[35]

Too often in the early twentieth century, however, federal judges saw emergencies and sudden dangers all about them and applied the brakes to labor frequently and hard. The Sherman Act remained a convenient device with which to declare strikes, boycotts, and picketing illegal conspiracies in restraint of trade. Where the Sherman Act could not reach, common law traditions about conspiracies applied. And after 1903, as the employer counterattack against trade unionism gained momentum, business associations increasingly turned to the courts to help their cause. After 1908 the granting of labor injunctions by federal courts grew rapidly. Most of them, moreover, were granted as ex parte restraining orders with neither notice to the defendants nor opportunity to be heard (in fact, only in a minuscule number of such cases did the complainants offer supporting evidence of their allegations concerning illegal union behavior).[36]

A group of crucial cases disclosed first, how judicial rulings crippled trade union power and second, how a minority of judges could interpret the same statutory and common law to legitimate trade union actions. The same cases exposed how the federal courts simultaneously stripped unions of effective weapons of economic warfare and sanctioned the employers' favorite antiunion devices. They also revealed how the Supreme Court, faced repeatedly with contradictory lower court rulings, invariably decided against labor. The cases in question concerned primarily the consumer boycott and the "yellow-dog," or antiunion, individual employment contract.

For trade unions unable to gain their objectives through direct action, most notably the strike, a call upon their members and sympathizers to boycott the products of a recalcitrant employer proved an effective alternative. In the late nineteenth century, citywide consumer boycotts of beer, cigars, and overalls — products heavily consumed by workers — had made unionism an effective and powerful presence in those trades.[37] By 1900 it was thus common for trade unions to call upon their union brothers and sisters to boycott "unfair" employers, and for the AFL to publish in its monthly journal a "We Don't Patronize" list. Prior to the passage of the Sherman Act in 1890, no federal law forbade such boycotts. After the passage of the act, however, firms engaged in interstate commerce increasingly sought to restrain unions from boycotting their products. Two such suits became causes célèbre for organized labor in the early twentieth century.

The first case originated in 1906 and concerned a boycott called by the United Hatters' Union against the Danbury, Connecticut, firm of E. W. Loewe. Loewe went to federal court in order to enjoin the union from pursuing its boycott. The firm alleged that the Hatters' Union's action violated Sherman Act strictures against restraints on interstate commerce. The first federal judge to rule on the question declared in December 1906 that the boycott did not materially restrain interstate commerce. He pointed out that the union did not interfere with the shipment of hats from Danbury to retailers in other states and that, most important, the actual retail sale of hats is not interstate commerce, "nor are the hats themselves during such distribution the subject of interstate commerce." Thus he would grant no injunction.[38]

Loewe appealed the decision to the Supreme Court, which in 1908 ruled that the Sherman Act outlawed precisely such boycotts as restraints of interstate trade. It remanded the case back to the lower courts for trial.[39] There both judges and juries found against the union, levying a fine with treble damages under the Sherman Act and declaring the assets of union members in Danbury subject to seizure. After the case had dragged on for five years (1908–13) as a result of appeals and counter-appeals, an appeals court judge in upholding the conviction declared on December 18, 1913, that the Sherman Act "makes no distinction between classes, employers and employees, corporations and individuals, rich and poor, are alike included in its terms."[40]

The second case proved even more sweeping and crippling to union power. This one arose from a boycott declared by the Iron Molders' International Union against Buck's Stove and Range Company. As part of the boycott, the AFL had placed the firm on its "We Don't Patronize List." The company, whose owner was then one of the leaders in the antiunion movement, promptly sought a federal injunction against the AFL for restraining interstate commerce. A federal court in the nation's capital granted the firm's request in 1907 and ordered Gompers to remove Buck's Stove from the AFL's boycott list. Gompers refused, citing his constitutional right to free speech and free press. The courts disagreed. Three lower court federal judges ruled that no constitutional protection existed for free speech used in the furtherance of criminal actions. Because the AFL boycott was illegal under the Sherman Act, the district court found Gompers and two associates, Frank Morrison and John Mitchell, guilty of contempt, fined them, and sentenced them to jail terms. Gompers immediately appealed to the Supreme

Court. There, a majority also found that the boycott was illegal under the Sherman Act and that Gompers was indeed guilty of contempt for refusing to obey a legitimate injunction to remove Buck's Stove from the list. Because the original cause for the suit had been made moot by an agreement between the firm and the molders' union and the statute of limitations for contempt had expired, the Supreme Court diplomatically stayed the fines and prison sentences. No need to turn Gompers, Morrison, and Mitchell into martyrs for the causes of trade unionism and free speech.[41]

In effect, then, by 1914 the courts had vitiated the economic effectiveness of union boycotts. The only boycotts that remained legal affected solely intrastate business (and many state courts found such action illegal) or workers in interstate commerce who had an immediate, direct relationship to the interdicted firm.

Yet the same judges who declared consumer boycotts violations of the Sherman Act had little difficulty rationalizing and legitimating employer boycotts of union members. The employer counterpart to the union boycott was the yellow-dog contract, which required the worker as a condition of employment to promise never to join a union. In 1898 the federal government through the Erdman Act had outlawed such contracts on the railroads, and subsequently Kansas and several other states had enacted similar bans on the yellow-dog contract. It was not long before challenges to these laws made their way through the federal courts and ultimately to the Supreme Court. In the same year (1908) that the nation's highest court found the Danbury Hatters guilty of violating the Sherman Act, in the case of Adair v. U.S. it declared the anti-yellow-dog clause of the Erdman Act to be an unconstitutional infringement on the individual worker's absolute right of free contract.[42] Seven years later, the Court ruled the Kansas statute unconstitutional, again citing the principle of free contract.[43] Of this latter decision, Felix Frankfurter wrote that it was the product of "arterial sclerosis" among judges "who move in their own small narrow groove which gradually makes for comfort and gradually makes the rest of the world unknown and therefore unnatural."[44]

A year after the Supreme Court ruled in the *Adair* case, federal courts began to use that precedent to enjoin unions from organizing nonunion employees. The most famous of the cases deriving from the Supreme Court's legitimation of the yellow-dog contract, one that occupied the federal judiciary from 1909 through 1917, concerned the efforts of the United Mine Workers to organize the nonunion mines of West Virginia. In September 1910 a federal district judge enjoined the UMW from attempting to recruit miners at the Hitchman Coal and Coke Company, all of whom had signed yellow-dog contracts. Basing his decision on the *Adair* case, the judge ruled that the UMW's organizing campaign was "a conspiracy to destroy others' vested contract rights."[45] Three years later a second district court judge in West Virginia, Alston G. Dayton, further enjoined the UMW and expanded on the previous ruling. In a long opinion filled with references to history, medieval British common law, and the Sherman Act, Judge Dayton declared, "Human nature is the same substantially yesterday, to-day, and forever," and thus neither laws nor unions "can supersede the natural law of supply and demand." He then ruled that the UMW was engaged in a common law criminal conspiracy with northern mine operators to destroy the livelihoods of West Virginia mine owners and miners. For good measure, he added that the conspiracy also violated the Sherman Act. Finally, in the most astounding part of his decision, he observed that any union, such as the UMW, which had rules binding its members and which sought a closed shop, was prima facie in violation of both the U.S. Constitution and the Sherman Act. In effect, he deemed unions to be illegal.[46]

That this judge did not speak for all federal judges and that his opinion was extreme in the utmost became evident in 1914 when a circuit court of appeals overruled his decision on every point of law. Its members rebuked him for misreading history and miscomprehending labor-capital relations in the contemporary world. The struggle between labor and capital, the appeals judges ruled in language Felix Frankfurter would have appreciated, "is a condition and not a theory." They declared that the UMW was legal in its constitution and in its actions, that the closed shop was as legitimate as the open shop, and that equity jurisdiction did not exist to strengthen the powerful at the expense of the weak. "This is an age of co-operation through organization," opined the judges, citing the activity of doctors, lawyers, teachers, bankers, and manufacturers. "Such being the case, it is just as essential and perhaps more important, that the laboring people should organize for their advancement and protection, than it is for any of the vocations we have mentioned."[47]

In the spring of 1917, however, a six-member majority on the Supreme Court established that antilabor sentiment remained the dominant tradition within the federal judiciary. The majority overruled the appeals court's repudiation of Dayton's injunction against the UMW and found the latter's indictment of the union's policies and actions to be valid. The Supreme Court reinstituted the injunction against the UMW's campaign to recruit members at the Hitchman mine because it was an unlawful invasion of individual contractual rights. As Frankfurter commented, "Judges continue to indulge 'the illusion of mathematical certainty' and to think they are, like silkworms, unfolding 'law' from the legal cocoon. In fact they are but translating their own unconscious economic prejudices or assumptions."[48]

Unions Fight Back

What amounted to a declaration of war against organized labor by the federal courts coincided with the employer's antiunion offensive and, in part, aided business to retard labor's advance. Even before the worst of the decisions were handed down, most union leaders realized that federal actions vitally affected the security of their institutions, a lesson railroad union leaders had already learned. Gompers and his associates in the AFL were faced with a condition and not a theory. However much Gompers and other craft union leaders extolled the theory of "voluntarism," the concept that unions were totally private, voluntary institutions which sought nothing from the state and deserved absolute freedom from state regulation, they recognized the reality of the state's involvement in union activities.[49]

However much union leaders also proclaimed organized labor's indifference to partisan politics, they devoted much time to developing a mode of political action most suitable to the needs of unionism. And because they were more realists than theorists, American labor leaders pursued a serendipitous form of politics. For them it was no easy matter to win the loyalty and solidarity of a union rank and file that was split three ways politically among Republicans, Democrats, and Socialists. American labor leaders were also cognizant of overseas political developments. They had seen a series of high court opinions in the United Kingdom drive the British labor movement more deeply into independent politics. The same pressures that drove British labor leaders to form a Labour party seemed to be gathering momentum at home. Not only was socialism making substantial inroads among American workers, especially in such large core unions as the United Mine Workers, the International Association of Machinists (IAM), and the United Brewery Workers, but city centrals and state federations of labor also flooded AFL headquarters with petitions and letters demanding the creation of an American labor party. And most petitioners cited the British precedent.[50]

Gompers and the members of the AFL executive council thus devised a political strategy to mollify rank-and-file demands for independent action while causing the least dissension. Judicial rulings may have shaped the political activities of the trade union movement, as several scholars maintain, but not in quite the manner that has been suggested. True, the AFL's highest political priority was to liberate trade unions from the "iron cage" of judicial injunctions, a goal that appeared to push labor toward a policy of voluntarism, meaning autonomy from state regulation, and nonpartisan politics. In practice, however, labor's new politics, as it manifested itself between 1906 and 1912, drove Gompers and his associates into an ever tighter alliance with the Democratic party and toward a more positive opinion of state regulation of the economy and society.[51] Hence, in 1906, the AFL drew up Labor's Bill of Grievances as a petition to leaders of both parties in Congress. Second, labor leaders established a Labor Representation Committee (patterned after the British model) to seek the election of trade unionists and union sympathizers to Congress. Third, they targeted specific members of the House, all Republicans, for defeat. Fourth, Gompers went to the 1908 Democratic and

Republican conventions, demanding that they incorporate labor's primary goals into their platforms. If the AFL's demands could be reduced to their simplest element, it was that labor wanted relief from the Sherman Act and reforms in the injunction process.[52]

Labor's more aggressive politics quickly made itself felt in the nation's capital. Beginning with his fifth annual message to Congress in December 1905, President Roosevelt on five consecutive occasions asked the legislature for reforms in the equity process. At first, he sought little substantive change. As titular leader of a national party, most of whose prominent spokespeople defended the autonomy and integrity of federal judges, Roosevelt had little room to maneuver. He simply suggested that judges give all parties due notice of equity hearings and that they exercise more forbearance and better judgment in their rulings.[53] Only if judges declined to behave more cautiously might Congress have to act.

As the AFL grew more militant, socialist influence among workers spread, and labor parties arose on the municipal and state levels, Roosevelt, too, demanded substantive reforms. Now, he said, reform was necessary to preserve the sanctity of the courts from judges who had abused equity proceedings. Judges who not only enjoined union members from acting but also convicted them of contempt for violating injunction orders bred class consciousness among workers. "A 'class grievance,' " he warned, "left too long without remedy breeds 'class consciousness' and therefore class resentment." Thus in a special message in 1908, Roosevelt asked Congress to enact his proposal requiring that contempt cases be heard by judges other than the one who issued an injunction.[54] Soon he asked relief from the Sherman Act for unions. Here, too, he drew a fine line, insisting that any reform of antitrust legislation still prohibit boycotts and sympathetic strikes.[55] Repeatedly, he called on fellow Republicans to join him in reforming to preserve judicial authority. Roosevelt reminded congressmen that all too many judges seemed divorced from the real world and used the concept of liberty of contract as an academic exercise that bore no relationship to the actual distribution of power. It was time, said the president, for the courts to enter a universe of modern social and economic jurisprudence. The injunction process had to be reformed; otherwise, the AFL's political campaign might succeed and "mean the enthronement of class privilege in its crudest and most brutal form, and the destruction of one of the most essential functions of the judiciary in all civilized lands." Roosevelt was engaged in a careful balancing act, on the one hand satisfying labor's demands for relief from injunctions and on the other hand mollifying Republican traditionalist defenders of the judiciary.[56]

The president performed a similar balancing act in the arena of electoral politics. He simultaneously called for labor reforms and campaigned personally for candidates targeted for defeat by the AFL in the elections of 1906 and 1908.

Especially in campaigning for Republican members of Congress who had opposed reforms in the Sherman Act and in federal equity procedures, Roosevelt appealed over the heads of labor leaders, directly to the workers as American citizens who recognized that class was an alien concept.[57]

The history of congressional efforts to reform the Sherman Act and to provide labor with relief from injunctions illustrates the fine political line that Roosevelt had to walk as president and Republican party leader. Southern Democrats and their northern comrades from working-class districts led the congressional attempts to reform federal labor law. It was a peculiar political alliance. The northerners were quite obviously appealing to a union and working-class constituency. By contrast, the Southern Democrats defended labor by denying the federal government the power to intrude on the realm of the separate states, which was where most labor disputes should properly be settled.[58]

Because Republicans controlled the key committees and because the chairs represented the more conservative wing of the party, they defeated or buried every move toward reform. In doing that, they made the prophecy of a trade unionist observing the proceedings of the 1901 session of Congress come true: "I warn the Republicans that they and their party will not be able to go on forever posing as the friends of the toilers during elections, then betray them on every appeal for legislation to justly protect them against the greed and oppression of their employers."[59]

The Democrats and Labor

The realities of national politics and the increasing political assertiveness of the AFL coalesced to forge an alliance between organized labor and the Democrats. In 1908 the Democratic party incorporated the AFL's demands for injunction reform into its presidential platform. In return, Gompers and other members of the executive council cooperated with the Democratic National Committee in campaigning for William Jennings Bryan. For their part, the Democrats had good reason to seek union support. As a minority party nationally, they needed new political allies. Moreover, as a party whose strength was concentrated in the rural South and West, Democrats shared part of organized labor's antagonism to business. Political calculation and sentiments increasingly bound Democrats and labor together. In Congress, for example, as we have seen, Democrats reacted more favorably to Labor's Bill of Grievances. The trade unionists actually elected to the House were mostly Democrats (in 1910, of fifteen elected, thirteen were Democrats).[60]

William Howard Taft's accession to the presidency furthered the union-Democratic coalition. Taft had far less interest in the labor question than Roosevelt and was far less the executive activist or reformer. He was also more supportive of the federal judiciary and less amenable to reform of the equity process. As he said in his inaugural address, "Take away from the courts . . . the power to issue injunctions in labor disputes and it would create a privileged class among the laborers and . . . [eliminate] a most needful remedy to all men for the protection of their business against lawless invasion." And as he said in vetoing a congressional bill to deny funds to the Justice Department for prosecuting unions under the antitrust laws: "This provision is class legislation of the most vicious sort."[61] Taft's appointments to the Supreme Court (he made five) solidified the antilabor majority, making the court for the next two decades a firm barrier to reform in labor law and industrial relations. As one of his appointees said, justices should never yield "to the clamor of a temporary majority."[62]

Taft's principles and policies on the labor question encouraged Republican conservatives in Congress to resist every Democratic effort to reform equity procedures or the Sherman Act. After the election of 1910, when Democrats and insurgent Republicans, known as "progressives," took control of the House, Taft and his conservative allies used all their parliamentary wiles to bottle up labor legislation. Conservative Republicans made no secret of their hostility toward trade unions or of their defense of the injunction as an essential instrument to restrain labor's excesses. To limit the power of the courts to enjoin boycotts or sympathy strikes, said one Republican congressman, "is the most dangerous limitation of power that it is possible to conceive." In contrast, Democrats appeared remarkably united on the issue. Big-city representatives defended their working-class constituents. Rural Southern Democrats reached the same position through hostility to intrusive federal power. And even a conservative Democratic representative and attorney, such as John Davis of West Virginia, could lead his party's rebuttal of Republican criticism of injunction reform.[63]

By the summer of 1912, one of the Democrats leading advocates of labor reform in the House, himself a former trade union official, was William B. Wilson of Pennsylvania, who could state on the floor why workers should vote Democratic in November. Citing as the key issue in the presidential campaign the more equitable distribution of production, income, and wealth, Wilson named twenty prolabor bills passed by the Democrat-controlled House, including an eight-hour law for all government work, the establishment of both a cabinet-level Department of Labor and a Children's Bureau, and, most important, an anti-injunction bill.[64]

Woodrow Wilson and Labor

Paradoxically, however, the emergence of Woodrow Wilson as a national political figure at first threatened the Democratic-Labor alliance. Though Southern-born, Wilson was "discovered" and promoted politically by what remained of the old northern Democratic financial community, the "gold bugs." Wilson brought to

Democratic politics a distaste for organized labor. A "Credo" written by the future president in 1907 defended the absolute right to liberty of contract from its union critics, whom he defined as men "who have neither the ideas nor the sentiments needed for the maintenance or the enjoyment of liberty." Only two years later, he declared at an antilabor banquet, "I am a fierce partisan of the Open Shop and of everything that makes for industrial liberty." Not surprisingly, then, when Wilson ran for governor of New Jersey in 1910, the state's labor movement united against him. And thus did political realities begin the reeducation of Woodrow Wilson on the labor question. To quiet the voices of his trade union critics, Wilson sang a different campaign tune. "I have always been the warm friend of organized labor," he assured New Jersey's trade unionists, as he now defended their right to organize independent unions.[65]

Still, at the 1912 Democratic convention, labor held firmly in the anti-Wilson camp, much preferring the candidacy of Missouri's Champ Clark. Once the nomination was his, Wilson had little choice but to further his rapprochement with labor. Nor did Gompers have much choice other than to accept Wilson's overtures, unless he preferred to concede a good part of the labor vote to Debs and the socialists or to Roosevelt and the Progressives. In 1912, the Democrats once again incorporated the AFL's primary demands into their platform. Although Gompers asserted in his 1925 autobiography that he played no active role in the election of 1912 and the public record in fact shows only circumspect labor support for Wilson and the Democrats, the AFL national office served as a clearinghouse for Democratic National Committee efforts to woo the labor vote. The party chairman contacted Gompers about sending AFL organizers to different parts of the country on behalf of the Wilson campaign. John L. Lewis, for example, campaigned for the Democrats in New Mexico and Arizona.[66]

AFL assistance surely did not harm Wilson's election prospects. Both AFL and Democratic party leaders believed that trade union endorsements brought Wilson more votes than he would otherwise have received. Of course, he owed his victory largely to the split in the Republican party. The results nevertheless proved how vital labor was to future Democratic success. The only party among the four major ones that offered nothing to workers and unions, Taft Republicans, received less than 25 percent of the popular vote. Wilson could interpret the returns as well as anyone. They signified that as president he should move even more rapidly to solidify the alliance between organized labor and the Democrats. And he began to do so.[67]

The AFL-Democratic Alliance Tightens

Wilson proved adept at offering organized labor the symbols of influence. He opened his administration wider than any predecessor to the leaders of trade unionism. Cabinet officers, especially the secretary of labor, conferred regularly with the AFL executive council. Gompers corresponded often with the president, who appreciated the labor leader's counsel. Wilson appeared personally at the dedication of the new AFL headquarters building on July 4, 1916, and said the proper ceremonial words. He also sought the AFL's advice on pending judicial appointments up to and including the Supreme Court, a matter of great importance to organized labor. And a year after his reelection in 1917, Wilson became the first president to address an annual convention of the AFL. Surely, American labor now had a friend in the White House.[68]

The Department of Labor aggressively advocated trade unionism's case inside the administration. The secretary, William B. Wilson, an ex-UMW official, considered himself a partisan of trade unionism. As he wrote to Gompers after eight years of service as secretary, the most important of his department's duties was "to have someone as its directing head who can carry the viewpoint of labor into the councils of the President." Wilson dedicated himself to that task. He told the 1914 AFL convention, "If securing justice to those who earn their bread in the sweat of their faces constitutes partisanship, then count me as a partisan of labor." A year earlier he had declaimed to the same audience, much to the consternation of many conservatives, that no absolute right to private property existed. Society, he warned, has a perfect right, indeed an obligation, to modify such rights "whenever in its judgment it deems it for the welfare of society to do it."[69]

Wilson staffed his new department on the basis of prounion principles. Whenever possible he chose appointees sympathetic to the labor movement or drawn directly from the trade unions. The federal conciliation service recruited many of its mediators from the UMW. In their capacity as mediators-conciliators, these Labor Department agents promoted recognition of the AFL and so-called legitimate unions as well as smoothed industrial conflicts. In a real sense, then, the Labor Department acted as organized labor's advocate in Washington.[70]

The field work, public hearings, and final report of the United States Commission on Industrial Relations (CIR) served labor equally effectively. Originally conceived in the waning days of the Taft administration as a federal response to the rising intensity of labor-capital violence, the Wilson-appointed CIR functioned as an advocate for the poor and the powerless. That was largely because of the character of the person Wilson chose to chair the CIR: Frank P. Walsh, a Kansas City attorney and left-wing Democrat. Although Wilson balanced his appointees by choosing representatives of enlightened capital, responsible labor (the AFL and railroad brotherhoods), and the public-at-large, Walsh and his lieutenant, Basil Manly, drove the commission to the left.[71]

For more than two years the CIR held public hearings, at which witnesses from management, labor, and the community testified about industrial conflict, labor relations, and exploitation. Almost invariably, whatever the subject of the public hearings, they offered unions a friendly forum in which to make their case. In dealing with businessmen, however, Walsh played the prosecutor. He pilloried John D. Rockefeller, Jr., for his role in the infamous Ludlow, Colorado, massacre of 1914 and for his part in setting the labor policies of the Colorado Fuel and Iron Company. Walsh, however, publicly and privately extended a comradely hand to radicals — not only such "respectable" ones as the socialist Morris Hillquit but also such notorious Wobblies as Vincent St. John and William D. Haywood. During the public hearings, field investigators were at work probing the social and economic realities and compiling reports that supported organized labor.[72]

Given the CIR's tripartite composition and Walsh's radicalism, the body split three ways in making its final report and recommendations. The representatives of capital favored a middle course. They condemned irresponsible capital and radical labor equally, preferring enlightened businessmen and reasonable trade unionists to bargain moderately. They also defended the open-shop principle and drew no distinction between independent and company unions. The public representatives, John R. Commons and Mrs. J. Borden Harriman, balanced precariously between the representatives of capital and the Walsh majority. More sympathetic to trade unions than to the employers on the CIR, Commons and Mrs. Harriman found Walsh too condemnatory of business, too soft on radicals, and too favorable to intrusive state action. Commons and Harriman preferred to have "experts" chair impartial labor-management boards that would bring law and order to the anarchy of industrial relations. They were the true advocates of "corporate liberalism" in Wilsonian America. The majority report, in contrast, prepared by Manly and signed by Walsh and the three labor unionists, was perhaps the most radical document ever released by a federal commission. It blamed social and economic problems on the gross maldistribution of wealth and income, the ubiquity of unemployment, and corporate denial of workers' human rights. "Relief from these evils cannot be secured by petty reforms," declared the majority. "The action must be drastic." Thus they proposed federal laws to protect the right of workers to organize and bargain collectively through independent trade unions of their own choosing. This was to be the central objective of federal labor policy. They also suggested a panoply of welfare measures to protect workers and their families against unemployment, illness, and indigent old age, as well as to redistribute wealth and income. As Walsh wrote to a UMW leader, the recommendations were "more radical than any report upon industrial subjects ever made by any government agency."[73]

Trade unionists and radicals gloated over the Walsh report. A railroad brotherhood journal proclaimed that the report "will go down in history as the greatest contribution to labor literature of our time." The socialist *Appeal to Reason* described it as peeling the hide off capitalism, and the *Christian Socialist* compared it to the Declaration of Independence and the Emancipation Proclamation. And the *Masses* saw such an official document as "the beginning of an indigenous American revolutionary movement."[74] Indeed so, for the Walsh-Manly recommendations of July 1915 demanded a program of labor and welfare reform more ambitious than anything ever tried in American history. Such ambitious proposals and the three-way split within the CIR ensured that nothing substantial would come immediately from the commission's work.

More peculiar was the Wilson administration's failure during its first three years to stock labor's legislative cupboard. Of no issue was this truer than of the one dearest to labor's heart, relief from legal injunctions and antitrust legislation — and this despite the fact that a majority in Congress favored reform of both equity procedures and antitrust legislation. In fact, reform was stymied by the political cowardice and abstract principles of most congressmen. A small minority of conservative Republicans had the courage of their convictions. They would vote for no "class" legislation that exempted labor from judicial scrutiny and declared that "the blacklist and the boycott, the sympathetic strike, and all methods of direct or indirect intimidation are undemocratic and un-American." An equally small minority of Democratic congressmen supported specific exemption for labor. After all, one among them said, capital had enjoyed fifty years of congressional favors, "and it is just to have class legislation against them as much as to have class legislation for their benefit."[75] The greater number of Democrats, however, shared the sentiments of a representative from Maine who said of efforts to reform the Sherman Act, "It is simply an application of the old and sacred Democratic principle of equal rights to all."[76]

President Wilson also fervently believed in the principle of equal rights and asserted that providing labor exemption from judicial scrutiny (i.e., relief from equity procedures) was class legislation alien to the American way. From that conviction he would not budge.[77]

Nevertheless Congress worked to reform the Sherman Act and in doing so to assuage labor's grievances. As the Progressive Republican senator from Iowa, Albert Cummins, announced in May 1913, it had become obvious that a majority in Congress sought to protect labor unions and farmers' organizations from oppressive prosecution under the antitrust law, and now it was "the psychological moment to do so."[78] What Congress finally wrought, the Clayton Act of 1914, offered labor symbolic relief without real substance. It was clear why that was so. The congressional majority for reform simply would not countenance anything characterized as "class legislation," nor anything that compromised the principle of equal rights. Thus the bill, as enacted, could proclaim in lofty language that human labor was not "an article of commerce" and add that neither unions nor strikes were illegal under the law. It could even forbid federal injunctions against unions and strikes when labor's actions were otherwise legal. Such clauses and language enabled Gompers to laud the Clayton Act as labor's "Magna Carta." What the majority in Congress really intended was less than self-evident. One of the bill's floor leaders, a representative from North Carolina, said bluntly, "I will say frankly . . . that we never intended to make any organizations . . . exempt in every respect from the law." And the Democratic senator from New Jersey said of the Clayton Act's labor clauses, "It simply makes legal that which we all have been taught to believe was legal."[79] Anything else Wilson would have vetoed.

Even in 1914 a Progressive representative from Kansas understood the shell game Congress had played on labor. "After labor went to the courts and after the courts had sent it back to Congress," he suggested, "Congress sends labor back to the courts again. Eight to twelve years hence [actually it would be less] the courts will decide what the amendment which we are about to adopt means."[80] That was precisely what the congressional majority wanted, shifting political responsibility to unelected federal judges, who were better insulated from popular pressures and passions. The majority, moreover, could not have been ignorant of how Taft's judges on the Supreme Court were likely to interpret the Clayton Act's labor clauses. They knew just what they had accomplished.[81] Despite a subsequent historian's claim that the Supreme Court majority that ultimately gutted the Clayton Act's labor clauses disregarded Congress's manifest intention, it seems more likely that antilabor judges simply grasped the instruments handed them by more-cowardly politicians.[82]

Yet if the Clayton Act disappointed labor and if trade unions after 1914, as before, remained victims of legal injunctions, political exigencies kept the AFL and President Wilson in a firm embrace. In 1915 and 1916 the two partners would embrace each other more tightly and give growing evidence of their mutual affection.

Economic and political realities drove the Wilson administration in opposite directions on the labor question. Midway through his first term, whatever the substantive reality of his program, Wilson had become publicly identified as a friend and ally of the AFL. Republicans and most elements in the business community united to criticize the president for selling out the country to organized labor. Whether such attacks were based on the appointment of a partisan of unionism as secretary of labor, the alleged exemption of labor from antitrust legislation under the Clayton Act, or the president's decision to send federal troops to Colorado in 1914 in the aftermath of the Ludlow massacre with clear orders not to assist coal mine owners to resume production with strikebreakers, the critics had no doubt that Wilson acted as a servant for Samuel Gompers.[83] It was criticism made all the more telling by the economic contraction of 1913–15. As industry and agriculture contracted, prices fell, and unemployment rose, the president late in 1914 and 1915 sought a truce with business. Wilson declared his "New Freedom" accomplished, the time for reform past, the moment for an accommodation between the administration and capital ripe. Political realities, however, made such an accommodation chimerical. Wilson wanted a second term, and he knew that in 1916 he would face a reunited Republican party, one that ever since the mid-1890s had had a larger popular electoral base than the Democrats. This, then, was no time for Wilson to attenuate his party's base among trade unionists and other workers. In fact, the election of 1916 demanded that the Democrats build an even firmer coalition with labor than they had in 1912.

As a result, Wilson in 1915 and 1916 added substance to the symbolism of his labor politics. The erstwhile critic of class legislation now endorsed special legislation for merchant seamen (the LaFollette Seamen's Act of 1915), federal legislation to outlaw child labor (the Keating-Owens Act of 1916), and several other pieces of social welfare legislation providing special benefits for farmers, women, and children. He also appointed the social and legal reformer Louis Brandeis to the Supreme Court. How much of this second wave of Wilsonian reform was generated by political opportunism and how much by intellectual growth on the president's part through his association with labor leaders and social reformers is disputable. Evaluating individual human motivations is scarcely a scientific endeavor. Suffice it to say, that Wilson's new reforms achieved his political purposes.[84]

If any one action cemented Wilson's alliance with organized labor, it was his intervention in a railroad labor dispute in the summer of 1916. By then federal intervention in such labor controversies had a long history. That history had made two things clear. First, the federal government would not tolerate a strike that threatened to disrupt the national railroad system. Second, any labor dispute on the railroads that could not be resolved by the parties in conflict would be decided by federal intervention. Since the Pullman Boycott of 1894 no labor dispute had threatened to paralyze the nation's railroads. Disputes between operating railroad workers and management persisted, but few were resolved through the federal mediation machinery established by the Erdman Act of 1898. The Erdman Act proved so unsatisfactory to the unions and the companies that in 1913 Congress replaced it with the Newlands Act. Although the new legislation created a permanent Board of Arbitration and Conciliation, one that could offer its services to the disputants on its own initiative, it proved in practice as ineffective as its predecessor.[85] Thus when a dispute between the railroad brotherhoods and the railroads boiled over in the summer of 1916, no institutionalized federal machinery existed to resolve it.

It was also a time of inordinate crisis and tension. The nation was rent by a dual war scare, conflict with Mexico to the south and impending involvement in the Great War overseas. Americans were also swept up in Wilson's military preparedness campaign. All in all, it was a moment when no one in power would tolerate a threat to the nation's transportation system. And that is precisely why the unions chose to threaten a national strike unless the railroads acceded to labor's demand for a basic eight-hour day for operating employees. Actually the unions' demand was for higher wages, not shorter hours. The effect of a mandatory eight-hour day would be to recalculate overtime wages on a new basis, disregarding the current ten-hour standard, and hence raising wages some 25 percent across the board. That demand management refused to countenance; it posed too great a threat to the railroads' bottom line. With neither side willing to compromise the central issue in dispute, both parties realized that the federal government would intervene. The question, then, became who would benefit from state intervention?

On August 29 President Wilson acted. Previous conferences at the White House between the disputants had failed to resolve the conflict. Now, in a special message to Congress proposing a solution to the railroad labor dispute, Wilson played the consummate politician, appealing to his labor constituency and allaying the concerns of his business critics. He forthrightly extolled the justice of the eight-hour day (ignoring the unions' use of it as a device to raise wages) and demanded that Congress enact legislation to mandate the basic eight-hour day on interstate railroads. Wilson also asked for the establishment of a special presidential committee to investigate the economic impact of the reduced workday, and he promised the railroads rate relief if their actual costs rose substantially. The president requested two other measures, one long-term and the other immediate in its impact. He asked Congress first to require by law that before any strike could occur on an interstate railroad it had to be the subject of a full public investigation and, second, that in the case of military necessity, the president be authorized to seize all vital parts of the railroads and to conscript train crews and administrators as needed.[86]

In Congress the president's request precipitated heated partisan debate. Democrats rushed to enact the eight-hour and presidential commission provisions, neglecting Wilson's proposals for authorization to seize railroads and to establish public fact-finding commissions before strikes. Republicans condemned Wilson and the Democrats for surrendering the prerogatives of government to private special interests, leading one of the more moderate GOP critics to ask "whether modern combinations are stronger than the Government." The most common refrain in the Republican critique was the theme that the railroad brotherhoods had held a gun to Congress's head and that the Democrats had conceded to vulgar blackmail. "By this act to-day [the Adamson Act as the eight-hour bill was named]," declaimed a Republican representative from New York, "we take the first step away from the old democracy of Thomas Jefferson and the Federal policy of Alexander Hamilton to the socialism of Karl Marx."[87]

As that language implied, the Republicans felt comfortable in contesting the 1916 campaign partly on Woodrow Wilson's links to organized labor. And their presidential candidate, Charles Evans Hughes, stressed the Adamson Act as proof that the Democrats had sold the nation's birthright to the unions. For Wilson, by contrast, the Adamson Act was the final ingredient of his political strategy for 1916 and for the consummation of the Democrats' coalition with organized labor.

Organized labor fully reciprocated Wilson's attentions. Gompers called out all his troops to campaign for the president in 1916, and the old labor leader himself worked hard for the Democrats, publicly as well as privately. Such unions as the United Mine Workers and the International Association of Machinists, which were under strong socialist influence before 1916, enthusiastically fell in line behind Wilson. The railroad brotherhoods, as one might expect, grew perfervid in their support for the president. In the western states, which, in the event, proved decisive to Wilson's reelection, organized labor united behind the president as never before. Labor votes in the Pacific Coast states, most especially California, proved indispensable to Wilson's victory. By November 1916, then, organized labor had become a core constituency of the Democratic party, one that demanded increasing attention.[88]

As the United States careened toward war in the winter of 1916–17, things had never looked better for organized labor. With the economy booming as a result of European war orders, the labor market tightened and unions again grew. Another wave of labor militancy and strikes impended, this time with labor's political friends returned to power in the nation's capital. Only one dark, but then small, cloud moved across the otherwise bright horizon of trade unionism. In July 1916 a federal circuit court of appeals, citing the precedent of Loewe v. Lawler (the Danbury Hatters' case), ruled that the Clayton Act had not exempted trade unions from antitrust legislation and that in the case before it, a dispute between the UMW and an Arkansas coal company, the union must be enjoined from supporting a strike that unlawfully restrained interstate commerce.[89] The federal bench, thus, prepared itself to thwart any design by the Wilson administration to strengthen "unlawfully" the power of its trade union friends.

World War and

the Positive State,

1917–1920

Shortly after the passage of the Adamson Act in the late summer of 1916, Samuel Gompers observed that "a revolution was in progress — a real revolution . . . the agencies of power and control will no longer belong exclusively to the property-holding classes but will be shared by wage-earners . . . who shall have a representative voice in determining conditions under which they contribute their share in production as well as in the distribution of the proceeds of production."[1] The Adamson Act was only one sign of the revolution in relations between labor and management, unions and the state, that Gompers perceived in that summer. Another equally revealing sign for the AFL president was his appointment that same year by President Wilson to serve as a member of the Advisory Council on Labor of the newly created Council on National Defense (CND), the administration's attempt to organize the national economy in the event of war. Gompers took pride in the fact that he now sat among top corporation officials and cabinet members in planning for a war economy. Organized labor, it seemed, finally had its proper place in the councils of state and a share of national power.

Labor and the National Crisis

Labor's apparent rise to power derived from three closely related sources. First, it was a fitting climax to the political coalition that the Democratic party had built with the AFL in peacetime. Second, the European war and America's increasing involvement in it created its own imperatives. As the United States drifted slowly but steadily toward direct participation in the conflict, Washington policymakers realized that modern, total warfare required the cooperation of workers and their organizations. Third, the war overseas had changed power relations among domestic economic actors. Between 1904 and 1915 an employer counterattack had forced trade unionism on the defensive. Caught between judicial interdictions and a loose labor market, unions found it more difficult to recruit members, win strikes, and, in some cases, even survive. War, however, tightened the labor market by ending mass immigration from Europe and stimulating overseas demand for American products. By late 1915 American unions became more aggressive as workers grew restive and militant.

As unemployment declined and prices soared, workers reacted. Some changed jobs repeatedly, searching for ever higher wages and better conditions. Others joined unions to achieve the same goals. And many walked out on strike. The number of reported strikes doubled between 1915 and 1916, and in the latter year reached 3,789, the most ever recorded in U.S. history. The strike fever raged with singular intensity in the armaments industry, where machinists and metalworkers struggled for higher wages and the eight-hour day. Hardly a sector of the economy remained untouched in 1915–16. Oil-refinery hands in New Jersey struck; steelworkers in Youngstown, Ohio, stopped work; iron miners on Minnesota's Mesabi Range walked picket lines; clothing workers in New York City put down their tools; migratory grain harvesters in the Great Plains threatened job action against farmers; and a transit workers' dispute in New York City in September 1916 threatened a citywide general strike.[2]

Labor militancy intensified after America declared war on April 6, 1917. Between that date and October 6, 1917, more than 3,000 strikes occurred. For the whole year, 1917, over 4,400 strikes were reported, and more than one million workers struck, a situation repeated the following year. Between September 1917 and April 1918, citywide strikes erupted in Springfield, Illinois, Kansas City, Missouri, Waco, Texas, and Billings, Montana. Telephone operators, longshoremen, loggers, packinghouse workers, copper miners, and grain harvesters all struck industries defined as vital to the war effort. Even so conservative a union official as William Hutcheson of the United Brotherhood of Carpenters threatened to call his members out on strike unless the federal government granted the union closed-shop privileges on wartime contract work. With unemployment down to 1.4 percent by 1918 (mostly the frictional sort resulting from workers voluntarily changing jobs), it proved difficult to restrain working-class militancy.[3]

Such labor turbulence in wartime proved especially troubling to a prolabor administration in which Samuel Gompers exercised the kind of influence never before granted a labor leader. To be sure, Gompers cooperated enthusiastically in the Wilson administration's wartime program. He agreed that domestic questions should be subordinate to the overriding aim of winning the war. And he gladly signed no-strike pledges for the duration of the war, as did most of his associates in the labor movement. Yet despite Gompers's cooperation and union no-strike pledges, labor turbulence and strikes persisted. The labor leaders who signed the no-strike pledges could not keep their members on the job when employers refused to bargain with unions, increase wages, or reduce hours. Moreover, the cooperation of the so-called responsible labor leaders was posited upon certain minimal concessions by employers, which Washington would enforce: (1) Management would not discriminate against union members; (2) employers would bargain with union representatives; (3) wherever possible, wages would be calculated according to prevailing union rates; and (4) all workers would gain the basic eight-hour day.[4]

At least the administration had a basis for cooperation with Gompers and other AFL union leaders in achieving wartime labor-capital accommodations. But what was to be done in the case of the radical Industrial Workers of the World? Here was a labor organization whose leaders refused to sign no-strike pledges and who called on their followers to pursue the class war at home even in wartime. If the IWW and its leaders had limited themselves to rhetorical calls for class war, Washington officials might have been less troubled. The realities of a wartime economy, however, benefited the radical IWW fully as much as the moderate AFL. IWW locals in the western states recruited ever larger numbers of migratory farm workers, copper miners, and loggers. Their labor in greater demand than ever, such workers engaged freely in job actions for higher wages and shorter hours. By summer 1917, strikes among copper miners, loggers, and grain harvesters posed an immediate peril to the war effort. How could a war be waged without food to feed troops, copper to maintain communications (and produce munitions), and wood to build ships, planes, and cantonments?[5]

The Wilson administration had to answer that question and devise a wartime labor policy that simultaneously satisfied Gompers and his trade union allies, the militant workers who walked off the job whether as members of AFL unions or of the radical IWW, and employers on whose cooperation a successful war production effort depended. This task proved to be no simple accomplishment for Washington's wartime policymakers. Indeed, it took almost a full year to devise a consistent national labor policy, and even then, employers, labor leaders, and public officials quarreled over the terms and conditions of wartime labor planning.

The Wilson Administration Seeks a Labor Policy

In practice, the Wilson administration's wartime labor policy lacked uniformity and consistency. What was true for the War Industries Board (WIB), namely the ubiquity of bureaucratic conflict and the absence of an agreed-upon central plan for war production, was even more true for wartime labor policy.[6] By and large, President Wilson ceded the making of labor policy to subordinate officials, departments, and boards. He rarely coordinated actions on the labor front. The Labor, War, and Navy departments under Secretaries William B. Wilson, Newton Baker, and Josephus Daniels, respectively, generally favored trade unionism, as did several special wartime labor agencies. The Commerce, Agriculture, and Post Office departments (led by Franklin K. Lane, David Houston, and Albert S. Burleson, respectively) together with the separate military branches, the WIB, and the corporate dollar-a-year men equated unionism with radicalism and favored open-shop principles. The Justice Department, under the leadership of Attorney General Thomas W. Gregory, sometimes joined the advocates of trade unions and other times participated in the repression of unions. And the federal judiciary handed down rulings that on the one hand sanctioned a prolabor policy and on the other hand, as in the Supreme Court's decision in the *Hitchman* case, repudiated administration labor policy.[7]

By February 1918 wartime labor policy seemed so chaotic that reformer and journalist Robert Bruere described its contradictions in these words:

> Here were three branches of the Federal Government pursuing three radically divergent and hopelessly conflicting policies towards the wageworkers at the very moment when the nation was making a patriotic appeal to the workers to get out a maximum production. . . . The United States Department of Justice was arresting them, the President's Mediation Commission was telling them that they must organize into unions, and the United States Supreme Court was announcing that if they attempted to organize under certain conditions they would be guilty of contempt of court.[8]

Despite the evident confusions and contradictions about labor policy in wartime Washington, there were certain consistent patterns. One group of policymakers concentrated in the WIB and with friends in the Commerce Department and the military services was determined that federal labor policy must not alter the existing lines of power in society but instead scrupulously follow them and set them more rigidly in place. This group found authority for their position in an unpublished statement of the CND, signed by Samuel Gompers, that stipulated "that employers and employees in private industries should not attempt to take advantage of the existing abnormal conditions to change the standards which they were unable to change under normal conditions."[9] Precisely that position was enunciated by the chairman of the WIB, Bernard Baruch, who informed Secretary of Labor Wilson, "While I am in favor of making every possible concession, at the same time we certainly should preserve the *status quo* and not permit anything to be used as a leverage to change conditions from the standpoint either of the employers or the employees."[10]

What advocates of the status quo ante preferred was clear. Where unions had contractual rights to bargain for workers, employers would not repudiate such arrangements. Nor would they seek to disestablish existing union- or closed-shop situations. Yet they would retain an absolute right to decline to hire union members (even to the point of compelling employees to sign yellow-dog contracts), to refuse to bargain with nonemployees, i.e. union representatives, and to maintain their prewar wage rates and working conditions. In an economic environment that now favored workers, one in which labor was scarce and profits high, employers expected the government to protect them against labor militancy. They looked to their friends in Washington, of whom they had many, to enforce the CND's pledge to maintain the status quo in labor relations.

Labor also had its friends in wartime Washington, not only Gompers and other AFL officials who served on war production and labor policy committees but also influential members of the administration. These people read the CND labor policy statement rather differently than employers did. Labor Secretary Wilson interpreted the CND statement as applying only to working conditions (which he defined loosely) and not to the question of unionization. He defined the right to organize as the day's "burning issue" and declared that "capital has no right to interfere with working men organizing labor." And he influenced President Wilson to write the following to an intransigent antiunion Alabama coal operators' association: "It is generally acknowledged that our laws and the long established policy of our Government recognize the right of workingmen to organize unions if they so desire."[11]

Many federal officials, moreover, found labor more cooperative than capital. In his address to the 1917 AFL convention, President Wilson told delegates, "You are reasonable in a larger number of cases than the capitalists." More revealingly and privately, Secretary of War Baker confided to the president: "I confess I am more concerned to have industry and capital know what you think they ought to do in regard to labor than to have labor understand its duty. In my own dealings with the industrial problem here, I have found labor more willing to keep step than capital."[12] And at a cabinet meeting when Baker brought up a speech by Gompers to the CND in which the labor leader urged that union labor be recognized and union wage rates made universal, President Wilson agreed that union labor and the eight-hour day be endorsed.[13] Thus the spring and summer of 1917 saw a real battle over labor policy being waged in the nation's capital between the defenders of the status quo and the advocates of a new order for labor-capital relations.

The Conservative Approach to Labor Relations

Initially, the proponents of more-conservative labor policies seemed to gain the upper hand. There were many reasons for their early advantage. Uppermost was the reality that the bulk of war production planning fell within the sphere of corporate executives and attorneys who in private practice had served corporations and who now donated their services to the war effort. They far outnumbered such labor leaders as Samuel Gompers and Hugh Frayne, a prominent, longtime AFL official and organizer, on federal agencies, and their influence was greater. As a group, they preferred not to battle trade unions directly and, whenever possible, made tactical concessions on labor relations. But they drew the line at the issue of the closed, or union, shop and resisted government attempts to promote trade union growth. For them, preservation of the open shop and the nonunion employment contract remained the desideratum of public policy. Put simply, the open shop, by enabling employers to hire workers regardless of union affiliation, diluted union power and also imperiled union security. In a society in which the vast majority of workers remained nonunion, whatever the reason for their choice, open-shop hiring practices threatened to divest unions of influence. Only insofar as trade unions could require employers contractually to hire workers from a union roster (the closed shop) or compel new workers to join a union (the union shop) might they gain security.

Louis B. Wehle, a prominent attorney and Democratic party influential who helped set labor policies for the construction of cantonments and shipbuilding, best represented the conservative forces. Respectful of Gompers and not reflexively hostile to unions, Wehle fought the closed shop and resisted every effort to alter the prewar situation in labor relations. Together with Secretary of War Baker, Wehle devised an accommodation with Gompers that provided for the peaceful resolution of labor problems on federal contract construction. Baker and Gompers signed an agreement that created tripartite commissions — representing employers, unions, and the public — to resolve labor conflicts in construction and shipbuilding. The agreement also provided for union wages and the basic eight-hour day. But it left the union-shop issue ambiguous. Wehle, who administered the agreement, interpreted it to sanction the open shop and believed that Gompers had consented to such an interpretation. Gompers, in fact, was in accord with Wehle's approach only in comparison with William Hutcheson, president of the carpenters' union, who refused to cooperate and demanded the closed shop on all federal contract work. What Gompers actually expected to gain from the agreement is less than clear. Obviously, he disliked tripartite boards. On the basis of experience, Gompers suspected that public representatives would almost always side with employers, leaving the unions in a minority. Yet he also expected that the combination of union wage rates, an eight-hour day, and a tight labor market would promote the growth of unionism even in the absence of a mandated closed shop. And, basically, Gompers was right. Union membership soared in the shipyards and in general government construction because in the wartime situation a neutral federal labor policy did not help employers maintain an open shop. This, then, was a case where the policies preferred by the conservatives in practice operated to their disadvantage. The reality of union growth satisfied Gompers; employers' refusal to concede the union shop pleased Wehle and those who thought like him.[14]

On other fronts in the domestic class struggle, however, the conservatives had more success. As worker discontent and strikes in the western copper and lumber industries intensified in the summer of 1917, demands grew for prompt federal action. Rather than attack Gompers, the AFL, and trade unionism frontally, the antilabor forces concentrated their venom on the IWW, an allegedly subversive ally of Imperial Germany. On August 17, 1917, Senator Henry Ashurst of Arizona informed his colleagues that "IWW" meant simply and solely "Imperial Wilhelm's Warriors." The *Wall Street Journal* added: "The nation is at war, and treason must be met with preventive as well as punitive measures. When you hear the copperhead [IWW] hissing in the grass why wait until it strikes before stamping on it? Instead of waiting to see if their bite is poisonous, the heel of the Government should stamp them at once."[15]

As the halls of Congress rang to denunciations of the IWW, western businessmen and public officials besieged Washington with demands for assistance in coping with labor discontent. Local federal district attorneys faithfully transmitted these demands to their superiors in Washington. Like the local businessmen with whom they associated socially, the federal attorneys viewed strikes not as the behavior of discontented workers but as the outcome of subversive and even German influences.[16] Five western governors took their case for the repression of the IWW directly to the CND and the cabinet. Their agent carried to Washington a message suggesting that constitutional guarantees be suspended in the case of labor radicals who interfered with the war effort.[17]

Even before such pressure from the West overwhelmed Washington, the federal government had sent troops to patrol sites of war production in isolated regions of the country. Initially, the War Department assigned troops to protect railroads and public utilities from German espionage in Montana and Washington State, coincidentally the scene of much IWW activity. Before long, the definition of "public utilities" grew to encompass copper mines, forests, and grain farms. By July 1917 federal troops patrolled the mining districts of Montana and Arizona, the forests of western Washington and Oregon, and the farms of eastern Washington. Troops thus served as a guarantee that labor disputes would neither interrupt production nor undermine the war effort.

Military officers behaved in 1917 and 1918 much as they had in past labor disputes. Accustomed to strict discipline, they expected unionists and strikers to behave with military propriety. When workers instead proved unruly and disobedient, soldiers disciplined them. In Arizona, for example, an army officer forbade picketing, encouraged strikebreaking, and offered troop protection to all scabs. The army, moreover, failed to distinguish between AFL (legitimate) and IWW (illegitimate) strikes. The officers were most at home among western employers and county sheriffs, with whom they preferred to work closely despite orders from Washington to be absolutely impartial. Wherever they served in the American West, federal troops broke strikes, persecuted suspected labor radicals, and assisted local authorities in making unlawful searches and seizures.[18]

Even the AFL and some of its sympathizers supported military intervention in western labor disputes. They mistakenly believed that by rooting out the IWW, the troops would open industry to penetration by AFL unions. Or they believed, as did the U.S. attorney for western Montana, Burton K. Wheeler, that troops served as "the best deterrent upon lawlessness and prevent outbreaks of any kind." And for Wheeler and many others, a stable situation offered the best guarantee for the growth of legitimate trade unionism.[19]

How far such people as Gompers and Wheeler miscalculated the results of military intervention was clearly revealed in the lumber industry of Washington State. There IWW strikes and job actions had reduced the production of spruce deemed vital to the building of airplanes. There Washington governor Henry Suzzalo, labor economist Carleton Parker, and leaders of the AFL woodworkers' union schemed to restore spruce production by substituting patriotic AFL loggers for subversive Wobblies. The agent of their scheme was one Brice P. Disque, an army colonel and prewar progressive reformer. They planned to use the army and federal power to inveigle antiunion lumbermen into recognizing AFL unions and granting the eight-hour day. At first, Disque seemed amenable to the plan. Before leaving for the Northwest to restore spruce production, Disque met in Washington with such reformers as Newton Baker, Felix Frankfurter, and Walter Lippmann. The colonel seemed eager to serve the reformers' aims. Once on duty in the West, however, Disque behaved more like the typical army officer. He found the employers more gentlemanly and patriotic than the reformers or the AFL labor leaders. By early 1918 he devised a program that would simultaneously increase production, mollify workers, and satisfy employers. First he recruited a Spruce Production Division, composed of skilled loggers on active duty who were subject to military discipline; second, he convinced employers to grant the eight-hour day and improved working conditions; and third, he required all civilian workers to join the Loyal Legion of Loggers and Lumbermen (4Ls), which was, in effect, a company union. The 4Ls not only disposed of the IWW; it eliminated the AFL from the lumber industry, much to the consternation of the reformers and Gompers.[20]

Other influences also ran against labor in Washington during the summer of 1917. Although the Labor and War departments remained convinced that most labor conflict flowed from legitimate worker grievances and that recognition of

AFL unions would restore harmony, they found it difficult to hold firm against those who preferred to use federal power more repressively. Their moderation was compromised by Gompers himself, who joined in the outcry against the Wobblies and other labor radicals. With the AFL president leading the pack in condemning the IWW and demanding their suppression, Secretaries Baker and Wilson could scarcely stay the emerging federal campaign to crush the IWW. In August 1917, President Wilson assigned a federal judge to undertake a special investigation of the IWW aimed at acquiring sufficient evidence to prosecute the organization. At the same time, Assistant Attorney General William C. Fitts assured New Mexico senator Albert Fall that "something quite effective is under way with respect to the I.W.W. situation. . . . I do not think that you or any of your western friends will be disappointed if the results which we hope to obtain are achieved."[21] Less than a week after Fitts's letter to Fall, the federal government acted against the IWW. On September 5 Justice Department agents raided every IWW headquarters in the nation, the purpose being, as one department agent informed the attorney general, "very largely to put the I.W.W. out of business." By month's end a federal grand jury had indicted nearly two hundred IWW leaders on charges of sedition and espionage. Almost overnight a militant labor organization was turned into a legal defense society.[22]

With the IWW eliminated, Gompers had achieved a part of his aims, as had his reformer allies in the administration. Paradoxically, they had also endangered parts of their own more positive program for labor reform. The conservatives, who so gleefully crushed the IWW, did not distinguish AFL unions from subversive ones, responsible labor from irresponsible agitators. Thus the campaign against the IWW threatened to spill over into a general antilabor offensive, as had happened in the woods of the Pacific Northwest.

The Triumph of the Labor Reformers

Even as various branches of the federal government either repressed militant labor or shielded state and local authorities who engaged in extralegal antiunion activities, other influential officials in Washington planned a more positive response to working-class discontent. From the first, policymakers in the Labor Department had defined labor unrest as primarily an expression "of revolt at low wages and hard conditions in industry and impatience with the slow evolution of economic democracy through the organized labor movement." They seconded Gompers's advice to President Wilson that if employers recognized and bargained with bona fide AFL unions, unrest would diminish. Capital, however, not labor, the reformers reiterated, had refused to implement federal labor policies.[23]

Thus in August 1917 Gompers and Secretaries Wilson and Baker urged a new direction for policy. In an address to the CND and through direct appeals to the president, Gompers demanded the appointment of a special commission to investigate the wartime labor upheaval and to make recommendations for its resolution. The AFL leader got his wish. In September, President Wilson appointed the Special Mediation Commission, chaired by William B. Wilson and composed of two AFL representatives and two employers (both moderates who were amenable to bargaining with trade unions), to investigate labor disturbances that threatened the war effort.[24]

One of the strangest aspects of the president's Mediation Commission was that the man who agreed to serve as its secretary and who actually made its policies and dominated its activities — Felix Frankfurter — initially opposed its appointment. Then an assistant secretary in the War Department and an acolyte of Louis Brandeis who shared the justice's commitment to industrial democracy, Frankfurter told his wife, "I was opposed to the whole idea." His opposition derived from sound suspicions concerning Gompers's convictions and aims. "It will be fatal to the handling of the labor situation," Frankfurter informed Newton Baker, "to assume that Mr. Gompers controls all labor or even all organized labor with which the Government should deal, or to assume that all those who are not for Mr. Gompers are for the I.W.W." Instead the young reformer wanted to establish ties to "constructive and responsible radicals" such as Sidney Hillman, president of the Amalgamated Clothing Workers of America (ACWA), a union deemed dual and illegitimate by Gompers. But once the president appointed the Mediation Commission and staffed it according to Gompers's wishes, Frankfurter thought he could achieve his own goals best by going along.[25]

Frankfurter wasted no time in setting a direction for the commission. Even before it departed Washington, he prepared a detailed memorandum enunciating its guiding principles. Frankfurter asserted that most wartime labor unrest resulted from a combination of real material grievances and employer antiunion practices. He proposed that the mediators conduct in-depth investigations of working conditions in the troubled industries, that they recommend the creation of formal conciliation machinery to ameliorate workers' grievances, that they urge employers to deal reasonably with their employees, and that they convince workers that the war was not only to defeat autocracy abroad but also to establish industrial justice at home. In the end Frankfurter reached precisely the position that Gompers had begun with when, back in August, he had demanded a federal commission. Frankfurter now argued that industrial peace and justice could best be accomplished by requiring employers to bargain with AFL unions and rooting out the subversive IWW.[26]

Guided by Frankfurter's principles, the Mediation Commission investigated disputes in the southwestern copper industry, the Pacific Northwest woods, the West Coast telephone business, and the Chicago packinghouses. In January 1918 the commission reported its findings and recommendations to the president. Its report stressed four priority principles: (1) "Some form of collective relationship between management and men is indispensable. The recognition of this principle by the Government should form an accepted part of the labor policy of the Nation." (2) Employers should immediately establish grievance machinery to resolve problems equitably before they precipitate strikes; (3) The eight-hour day should be mandated as national policy; (4) Unified direction of wartime labor policy should be implemented.[27]

The commission had far less success in implementing its policies. In Arizona copper mine owners and state officials declined to cooperate in the commission's program for labor peace. Mine owners welcomed condemnation of the IWW, but they rejected recognition of AFL unions or any real voice for their employees in company affairs. Hence labor relations in the copper industry (in Montana as well as Arizona) remained tumultuous, and production failed to reach peak levels. In the Pacific Northwest, Colonel Brice P. Disque preempted the commission's recommendations. He created his own company union (the 4Ls), instituted the eight-hour day, and relieved lumbermen of dealing with both IWW and AFL unions. In the telephone industry and the packinghouses, where IWW influence was absent and strong AFL unions made their presence felt, the commission had more success. There its recommendations brought rapid trade union growth and a measure of industrial justice.[28]

Frankfurter and his fellow commissioners had their greatest success with President Wilson. Soon after receiving the Mediation Commission's final report and recommendations, the president asked Secretary of Labor W. B. Wilson to institute a more coherent and consistent federal labor policy. The labor secretary promptly invited representatives of capital, labor, and the public to meet together as a War Labor Conference Board (WLCB). He charged the board with devising a program to govern labor-management relations for the duration of the war. In March 1918 the tripartite board adopted principles much like those recommended by the Mediation Commission. It, too, defended the right of workers to form trade unions unimpeded by employers. But because it included business and public representatives, the board equivocated on the issue of union recognition. In keeping with policy proclamations that went back to McKinley's 1899 Industrial Commission, the War Labor Conference Board suggested that management be required to bargain with shop committees, not union representatives, and that unions neither coerce workers to join nor negotiate for the union shop.[29]

The NWLB

In the late winter of 1918 Washington still lacked a coherent, centralized labor policy. Despite the recommendations of the Mediation Commission and the War Labor Conference Board, bureaucrats and dollar-a-year men continued to fight for control of their self-defined turf. Wehle and his friends persisted in seeking autonomy for their tripartite production boards in shipbuilding and cantonment construction. William Gibbs McAdoo, President Wilson's son-in-law, who became railroad administrator in late 1917 when the federal government took control of the industry, refused to surrender the making of railroad labor policy to any other agency. William B. Wilson laid his claim as labor secretary to act as czar for labor policy, as did Felix Frankfurter when he became chair of the War Labor Policies Board (WLPB). To try to bring some order out of this chaos, President Wilson in April 1918 announced the appointment of a National War Labor Board (NWLB) to devise and implement labor policies for all war-related industries.[30]

Patterned somewhat after the Mediation Commission, the War Labor Board included an equal number of representatives from labor and capital (five each, chosen by the AFL and the National Industrial Conference Board, respectively) and cochairs representing the public. Gompers had initially opposed such a board because he believed that public representatives would ordinarily side with capital, leaving labor an impotent minority. The president's choice of chairs mollified the labor leader. Frank P. Walsh, one chair, was obviously a friend to unions. William Howard Taft, the other chair, equally obviously sympathized with employers. Thus Gompers seemed assured that the worst the board could ever do would be deadlock; employers could safely reach the same conclusion. The board also could not act unless it achieved consensus (never clearly defined), and even then it lacked coercive power. Moreover, President Wilson had already stripped the NWLB of much of its authority by exempting from its jurisdiction all economic sectors in which tripartite labor boards already functioned.[31]

In practice, the board dumbfounded both its friends and its critics. It acted decisively and usually in behalf of workers and unions. Altogether in its less than one-year life, the board docketed more than 1,100 cases of labor grievances or conflicts. They included everything from individual claims against small firms to disputes affecting Western Union; General Electric in Lynn, Pittsfield, and Schenectady; Bethlehem Steel; the Bridgeport, Connecticut, armaments industry; and transit companies in almost all the country's major cities. It dealt with wage claims, maximum-hours standards, and alleged company antiunion policies, among other issues. Most of the docketed cases were thoroughly investigated by field agents appointed largely by Walsh, apparently on the basis of their sympathy toward unions and reform. Walsh never hid his sympathy for unionism, although he never disclosed to his associates on the board that behind the scenes he assisted labor leaders in organizing the meatpacking and steel industries and defended radicals (mostly Wobblies) from repression. Publicly, at board executive sessions, he fought for the concept of the "living wage," a mandatory eight-hour day, and the right of workers to form unions with which employers must bargain. Walsh's outspoken radicalism made the five labor representatives almost moderate by comparison. More remarkable still, Walsh more often than not won the support of Taft, the erstwhile antilabor injunction judge. As one reporter observed of the former president, "He is for the Frank Walsh program and there never was a team of vaudevillians who did their act more in harmony than Taft and Walsh in conducting the affairs of the War Labor Board."[32] Taft's cooperation with Walsh enabled the board, over the opposition of its employer members, to institute the eight-hour day in many industries, to raise wages for transit workers, to demand equal pay for women doing equal work, to mandate representation election for workers off the company premises, and to require back pay as well as reemployment for workers discriminated against for union activities.[33]

In several instances, President Wilson saw to it that the board's rulings had teeth. Although the NWLB was conceived and authorized as a voluntaristic agency dependent on cooperation from the parties under investigation, Wilson's actions, in effect, made cooperation mandatory. When the Western Union Company refused to heed the board's ruling to employ and bargain with union members, the president ordered the firm seized and operated by federal administrators. One conservative newspaper whined that Wilson had destroyed "the only bar which employers could set up against the unionization of their shops." Wilson acted equally firmly against unions that refused to obey board rulings, as he did in ordering Bridgeport machinists back to work under threat of federal prosecution. Yet Wilson's actions were *not* antilabor in intent or result. First, in the Bridgeport case, as in the Western Union one, the president was carrying out the wishes of Walsh and the labor members of the board. Second, at the same time that Wilson ordered the machinists back to work, he threatened to seize the Smith and Wesson Gun Company for its violation of NWLB rulings.[34]

The NWLB had indeed instituted a mini-legal revolution by making the right to unionize real and by requiring employers to bargain collectively. As one business journal griped about one of the board's rulings: "We know of no legislation authorizing the [NWLB] . . . to require private business concerns to revolutionize their business methods. We cannot see that the War Labor Board . . . has any more right to prescribe collective bargaining than it has to prescribe red ink instead of black ink for the firm's letterheads."[35]

Felix Frankfurter tried to add force to the NWLB's policies in his position as chair of the War Labor Policies Board. Frankfurter, in fact, tried to make his position that of czar for all federal labor policy. The cochairs of the NWLB, leaders of the AFL, business associations, and several cabinet officials joined to fight Frankfurter's designs. With what little real influence he had, however, Frankfurter sought to establish as uniform federal labor policy "a condition of collective bargaining between employer and employee. It contemplates, and is based upon the existence of unions of employees and unions of employers."[36]

In less than a year federal wartime policies had transformed labor-management relations from a basically private arena to a semipublic one and, in the process, had upset the historical balance of power between workers and bosses in many industries. As William Z. Foster, the leader of the meatpacking and steel organizing campaigns, observed about developments in the spring and summer of 1918: "the Federal administration was friendly; the right to organize was freely conceded by the government and even insisted upon. . . . The gods were indeed fighting on the side of Labor. It was an opportunity to organize the industry [steel] such as might never again occur."[37]

The Upsurge of Unionism

Labor took full advantage of the new opportunities. Between 1917 and 1920, union membership grew by more than 2 million (from 2,976,000 to 5,034,000) for a total gain of almost 70 percent. For the first time in United States history, union membership approached 20 percent of the civilian nonagricultural labor force, a level more than twice as high as any previous peak. Along with the growth in union membership went steady advances in wages and widespread achievement of the basic eight-hour day.[38]

Union gains could be seen wherever the federal government intervened directly and persistently, and also wherever effective labor organizations and aggressive organizers functioned. In the men's clothing trade, which prospered on wartime military contracts, Sidney Hillman, president of the ACWA, established excellent relations with federal contract administrators. As a result, his union, barely two years old when the United States entered the war, more than doubled its membership.[39] In two industries that the federal government controlled during the war — one directly (the railroads) and the other indirectly (coal) — unions flourished. The United Mine Workers won equal participation with employers on the wartime Fuel Administration and used its influence there to advance the union into the hitherto nonunion Southern Appalachian coalfields. By war's end the UMW claimed more than 500,000 members, making it far and away the nation's largest union.[40] The story was much the same on the railroads. William G. McAdoo, the federal railroad czar, put out the welcome mat for labor leaders by eliminating all existing nonunion individual employment contracts. Federal Railroad Administration orders increased wages, standardized work rules, and improved working conditions.[41] Unions grew rapidly, especially the previously smaller nonoperating workers' unions. Between 1914 and 1920, for example, the Brotherhood of Railway Carmen expanded from 28,700 to 182,000 members. "A worker with a union card in his pocket," reported one carman, "will be looked after and has been assured by the government of this great country of ours that he will get a square deal."[42]

The most surprising gains in union membership occurred in industries with strong histories of antiunionism: meatpacking and steel. In both cases, the labor organizers looked to the federal government for support and received it. In fact, the union leaders in both campaigns, John Fitzpatrick and William Z. Foster, developed close and excellent working relationships with Frank P. Walsh. Between September 1917, when the Stockyards Labor Council was created in Chicago, and January 1918, the union succeeded in increasing dues-paying membership from about 8,000 to 28,229, and claimed between 25 and 50 percent of the industry's workers in the city. Unable to stop their employees from joining the union, the packers drew the line at recognition and collective bargaining. Federal pressure nevertheless compelled the packers to negotiate with union representatives, if not to recognize the union. At the end of January 1918, the employers conceded union demands on employment and shop conditions, leaving other disputed issues to be resolved by federal arbitration. In the arbitration hearings, Frank Walsh represented the unions. On March 30, 1918, the arbitrator, Judge Samuel Alschuler, handed down his award. He granted workers a basic eight-hour day with ten hours' pay, substantial wage increases, and overtime premiums. The union took credit for the award and used it as a basis for recruiting more members. Beginning in April, the NWLB made further specific rulings and awards, which added impetus to the union drive. By November 1918, the Amalgamated Meat Cutters reported 62,857 dues-paying members, more than twice as many as nine months earlier, and more than ten times as many as three years previously. "I think the foundations of unionism have been laid in the packing industry for a long time to come," Foster informed Walsh. Although the companies still refused formally to recognize the unions, in David Brody's words, "under the Alschuler administration, the unions assumed an important role both for the employees and management."[43]

A comparable development occurred in steel. There, too, as the journal of the Amalgamated Association of Iron, Steel, and Tin Workers reported: "The Government stands firmly behind the organized labor movement in its right to organize, and that is why it [the union] is going to push its work of organization into the steel industries." William Z. Foster transferred his attention from meatpacking to steel, as he took command of an AFL-sponsored joint organizing campaign modeled after the multiunion Stockyards Labor Council. In the summer and fall of 1918, steelworkers joined the unions by the thousands. Foster claimed between 250,000 and 350,000 members. The balance of power in steel had surely shifted. Judge Elbert Gary, chairman of the executive board of United States Steel, recognized as much when he observed that the best that employers could hope for was that labor questions could be evaded until the war was over.[44]

Federal wartime labor policies had an extraordinary impact on workers and unions. Wherever unions had real strength or solid footholds before the war crisis, they made enormous membership gains and often won de facto recognition, bargaining rights, and even the union shop. Where able and dedicated organizers worked to spread the union gospel, as in meatpacking, steel, and the railroad shops, labor's gains were also substantial. Only where unions had been absent in the prewar period, still fought among themselves, or lacked able organizers did the policies of the advocates of the status quo prevail. In those cases, the war and federal intervention caused no fundamental alteration in relations between labor and capital. Yet even there the war produced change. Nonunion workers also won the eight-hour day, improved working conditions, and formal grievance procedures. The *New Republic* did not seem too far wrong when it observed at the war's end: "We have already passed to a new era, the transition to a state in which labor will be the predominating element. . . . The character of the future democracy is largely at the mercy of the recognized leaders of organized labor."[45]

Federal wartime labor policies and Wilsonian rhetoric had fired the imagination of labor leaders. "What labor is demanding all over the world today," asserted Sidney Hillman, "is not a few material things like more dollars and fewer hours of work, but a right to a voice in the conduct of industry." Even the allegedly conservative Gompers sounded the same note. "We shall never again go back to prewar conditions and concepts," he told President Wilson's First Industrial Conference in 1919. "We demand a voice in the determination of the conditions under which we will give service. . . . We demand that the workers have the voice not only as supplicants but by right."[46]

In the fall of 1918, as the war ground to an end, Hillman wrote to his young daughter: "Messiah is arriving. He may be with us any minute — one can hear the footsteps of the Deliverer — if only he listens intently. Labor will rule and the world will be free." In more prosaic language, Harold Ickes, a prominent Progressive and reformer in Chicago, prophesied the immediate future. "The chief issue is likely to be the relationship between capital and labor. . . . We sense disturbances way down underneath our social structure."[47]

1919: Annum Mirabilis

Ickes was right, and so was Hillman. In 1919 both labor and capital awaited the "Deliverer." For radical trade unionists, Messiah appeared in the guise of the Bolshevik Revolution, or the British Labour party's plan for a New Order, or more simply as the triumph in America of trade unionism and industrial democracy. For employers, Messiah came as the armistice with its promise of the restoration of the status quo antebellum. Of such conflicting visions industrial warfare was made.

The year 1919 was like none other in American history. Industrial conflict reached unprecedented levels as more than 3,000 strikes involved over 4 million workers. Even police walked out. Race riots and bombings proliferated. Two American Communist parties appeared. The world had been turned upside down. So thought Warren G. Harding, who wrote to a friend in the fall of 1919: "I really think we are facing a desperate situation. It looks to me as if we are coming to a crisis in the conflict between the radical labor leaders and the capitalistic system under which we have developed the republic. . . . I think the situation has to be met with exceptionable [*sic*] courage." So, too, thought Joe Tumulty, President Wilson's confidential adviser, who observed of the February 1919 general strike in Seattle: "It is clear to me that it is the first appearance of the Soviet in this country."[48]

In this highly charged and tense situation, American labor faced a new set of economic and political realities. As the war drew to its end in the autumn of 1918, American employers resisted every effort by the federal government to plan for peacetime reconversion and reconstruction. Every attempt by the NWLB and the WLPB to do so collapsed as a consequence of the inability of union and employer representatives to agree on a postwar program of industrial relations. Almost without exception, management wanted the reestablishment of the prewar situation and the withdrawal of federal intrusion in private business affairs. Seeing what was happening, Frank Walsh resigned as chair of the NWLB, better to serve the unions in his capacity as an attorney. Frustrated by the inability of his WLPB to plan for the future, Felix Frankfurter wrote to friends, "now the starch is out of the administration. Cold feet prevail on a wide area . . . [Wilson's] subordinates are meek and timid. They have practically announced bankruptcy and have invited the Republicans as receivers. God Help us!" America, he told Walter Lippmann, was now "the most reactionary country in the world."[49]

Wilsonianism indeed seemed discredited politically. The Republicans had swept into control of Congress in the 1918 election, and their triumph flowed as much from disenchantment with Wilson's domestic policies, especially his alleged truckling to labor, as to his diplomacy. The 1920 presidential election seemed destined to confirm Republican national political dominance, a dominance now more threatening than ever to organized labor.[50]

President Wilson himself apparently remained of two minds on the labor question. In a special message sent to Congress from France in May 1919, the president singled out the question of labor's awakening as the great domestic issue for every nation. Moreover, he suggested that the question could be resolved only through a radical program of economic and political reform. "The object of all reform in this essential matter," he told Congress, "must be the genuine democratization of industry, based upon a full recognition of the right of those who work, to participate in some organic way in every decision which directly affects their welfare or the part they are to play in industry." Congress, he added, could do its share to promote industrial democracy by establishing a mandatory eight-hour day and abolishing child labor.[51]

When Wilson returned to Washington later in the summer of 1919, his advisers made him acutely aware of the new economic and political realities. With wartime inflation unabated, antilabor politicians fueled consumer resistance to union wage demands. Tumulty advised the president that high wages were bad for consumers and hence for Democrats. The new attorney general, A. Mitchell Palmer, sounded the same note. During the fall 1919 coal strike, he recommended against any concessions to the miners because they "will insure unreasonably high prices in all commodities for at least three years to come." Tumulty spelled out the implications of consumer politics lucidly for the president. Wilson already had assured his party of labor's support through the Clayton Act, the Adamson Act, and his wartime labor policies. If the administration continued to befriend labor, Tumulty warned, "The country at large would think that we are making a special appeal to labor at this time. If there is any class in this country to which we have been overgenerous it has been labor. I think that this class owes us more than they have been willing to give." Wilson learned his lessons well. In August he warned unionists about the perils of inflation. Strikes, he observed, "undertaken at this critical time are certain to make matters worse, not better — worse for them and for everybody else."[52] As the demand in Congress grew to outlaw strikes through mandatory arbitration, the president joined the outcry. In a speech delivered in Helena, Montana, on September 11, 1919, he called the strike by Boston's policemen "a crime against civilization" and added that public servants had no right to threaten the community through walkouts.[53]

Yet the Wilson administration did not completely desert its trade union friends. Many Wilsonians still believed in the right of workers to organize, unhindered by employer coercion. And they still encouraged employers to recognize unions and bargain with them. Now, however, they also feared labor radicalism, took the AFL's support for granted, and declined to compel employers to deal with unions.[54]

With the war over and Republicans in control of Congress, Judge Gary and his corporate friends finally had their preferred means for dealing with labor. In the packinghouses and railroad shops, employers refused to extend union recognition or bargain collectively. In both industries the unions in 1919 were unable to complete the unionization and perfect the organization they had begun during the war. And there was no longer an NWLB, a Judge Alschuler, or a sympathetic Railroad Administration to turn to.[55]

Even more revealing was what happened in steel and coal. In the former case, the union suffered a stillbirth; in the latter, the largest and most powerful union in the nation beat a strategic retreat. In steel, union leaders had believed in the words of John Fitzpatrick, that "the Government would intervene and see to it that the steel barons be brought to time, even as the packers were. . . . President Wilson would never allow a great struggle to develop between steelworkers and their employers." Wilson indeed sympathized with the unions' plight and desired to avert a strike in steel. But with the war ended, the president lacked the law or precedent to compel steel management to meet with labor. And so when the national strike in steel came on September 22, 1919, federal troops and marshals helped break it. In most steel districts, either local law officers or units of the National Guard sufficed to maintain order. In the Gary, Indiana, district, however, federal troops under the command of General Leonard Wood, acting under a declaration of martial law, protected company property, guarded nonunion workers, and weakened the resistance of strikers.[56]

The situation in coal was both more complicated and less decisive in its outcome. Unlike steel, the coal-mining industry was still governed by unexpired wartime legislation, and the UMW had a warm friend in the secretary of labor. Unlike the steel union, moreover, the UMW had a large and loyal dues-paying membership with a long and militant union tradition. Yet when the miners walked out on November 1, all the concerned administration officials except William B. Wilson defined the strike "as not only unjustifiable but unlawful." They maintained that the walkout was directed against the government, not the mine owners. "I am sure," wrote Tumulty, "that many of the miners would rather accept the peaceful process of settlement . . . than go to war against the Government of the United States." The miners instead chose to go to war. In response, the administration sought and obtained a stringent antistrike injunction. It also readied troops for duty in the coalfields, tapped the phones of union leaders, sent federal agents to spy on the UMW, and threatened alien strikers with summary deportation. In the end, union leaders called off the strike. Because the UMW was a large, stable union, it won a compromise wage award arranged through the intercession of William B. Wilson. The overall terms of the award, however, stripped the UMW of most of its footholds in Southern Appalachia and made it more vulnerable to employer counterattack.[57]

The events of the immediate postwar years proved that without allies in government, American workers lacked the power to defeat open-shop industry. In two years (1920–21) the labor movement had lost 1.5 million members and had been forced to retreat to its prewar bastions. After 1919 the great mass-production industries continued to operate on an open-shop basis.[58]

Wilson's Industrial Conferences: Harbinger of the New Era

How great the distance remained in 1919 between the aspirations of organized labor and the desires of corporate capital was revealed by the First Industrial

Conference, which President Wilson convened in October 1919. Conceived primarily to resolve the postwar labor-capital upheaval and specifically to avert the steel strike, the conference did neither. It deadlocked over irreconcilable union-management differences. The AFL unionists sought an equal role with management and government in the control of industry, a real form of corporate liberalism, or, as the labor leaders preferred to call it, industrial democracy. The business delegates, to the contrary, preferred the extirpation of unionism root and branch. They defined industrial democracy as the presence of shop committees or councils unaffiliated with outside unions and lacking the right to call strikes. It was the union movement and not the specter of violent revolution that unsettled most businessmen. Hence they looked to the state to curb the union drive for industrial power. The essence of the open-shop principle, which remained their goal throughout the conference, was, in Haggai Hurvitz's words, "the 'utmost freedom' of management to act without outside interference and not labor's freedom to be employed without discrimination."[59]

President Wilson tried to salvage a measure of hope from the ruins of the first conference. Appealing to Congress in December 1919, he again stressed the need to recognize labor's rights. "Government must recognize," he emphasized, "the right of men collectively to bargain for humane objectives that have at their base the mutual protection and welfare of those engaged in all industries. Labor must no longer be treated as a commodity." Wilson also took note of Congress's conservative sensibilities, issuing a warning to those unionists who sought to coerce the majority through direct action: "Let those beware who would take the shorter road of disorder and revolution."[60]

The president's message preceded the calling of his Second Industrial Conference. Herbert Hoover dominated the second conference. A world-famous mining engineer and wealthy entrepreneur, director of the wartime Food Administration, and organizer of relief programs for destitute Europeans, Hoover by 1919 had built a reputation as a leading progressive and Wilsonian liberal (in some circles he was even considered a potential Democratic presidential nominee in 1920). He was a policymaker known to favor scientific management, company-union cooperation, and harmonious collective bargaining. Influenced by Hoover, this second conference called for the recognition of trade unions and the institution of routinized collective bargaining. Early in 1920 there was no audience for such a message. The Second Industrial Conference ended as a footnote to the history of wartime labor reforms and the practice of industrial democracy.[61]

The message many preferred to hear in 1920 was the one encapsulated in an antistrike bill introduced into the Senate by Miles Poindexter and passed by a substantial majority. Senator Poindexter's bill made it a crime to interfere with or restrain the movement of commodities in commerce with foreign nations or among the several states. It even forbade speech and print advocating such action. Introduced ostensibly to outlaw railroad strikes, had it become law, it would have made illegal all but local industrial conflicts.[62]

A bill that did pass Congress in 1920 — the Transportation Act of 1920 — served as a harbinger of federal labor policies in the approaching new era. All the railroad unions had united along with the AFL to propose legislation (the Plumb Plan) to keep interstate railroads under federal management and ownership. Not only did Congress reject the union's proposal; the Senate included in its draft of the new railroad legislation that restored the industry to private ownership a clause forbidding strikes. Although the joint conference committee agreed to a final bill that eliminated the antistrike clause, it still failed to satisfy the railroad unions. For the unions knew that their theoretical right to strike had been nullified by the elaborate conciliation and arbitration machinery created in the Transportation Act's tripartite labor boards. They also knew from their own history that, after 1894, the right to strike existed only as a threat, not a reality. The threat, however, worked better against public managers than private owners. Hence the unions used all their political influence to defeat the bill. The passage of the Transportation Act of 1920 revealed graphically how far union political influence had fallen in the four years since the passage of the Adamson Act.[63] It boded ill for labor's immediate future. In the absence of a countervailing government presence on its behalf, trade unionism would see management's principles and programs prevail in the coming decade.

Interregnum:

The State as "Neutral,"

1921–1932

The mutual courtship between the Wilson administration and organized labor had ended with both partners unrequited. First in the off-year congressional elections of 1918 and then more resoundingly in the presidential election of 1920, the Wilson Democrats had suffered defeat. Despite the continued endorsement of the AFL and most labor leaders (the primary exceptions being John L. Lewis of the mine workers, William Hutcheson of the carpenters, and the officials of the railroad brotherhoods), the Democrats lost the support of too many working-class voters. The unions, too, suffered their share of setbacks in Wilson's last two years. The great steel strike had collapsed; the fate of Boston's police presaged the fate of most unionized public employees; unionism's most advanced wartime salients receded; and the president's First Industrial Conference proved that most employers still demanded the open shop and refused to bargain collectively.

Now with the Republicans returned decisively to national power, organized labor faced a more troublesome future. The Republicans owed few favors to the nation's labor leaders. Moreover, as a party, the Republicans were far more subject to the influence of "big business" and conservative lawyers than were the Democrats. During the preceding twenty years, it had been Republican members of Congress who had most steadfastly resisted labor law reform, and national and state bar associations that had condemned efforts to limit the equity jurisdiction of federal courts. Pessimists expected the more advanced labor policies of the Wilson administration to be swept away in a tide of reaction. Optimists hoped at best for the preservation of the status quo in federal labor policy and for some sort of minimal accommodation between organized labor and the administration of Warren G. Harding. Both had grounds for their respective hopes and fears.

Early Republican Labor Policy

Organized labor entered the 1920s with considerable resources. Between them, the AFL and the railroad brotherhoods claimed almost five million members in 1920–21. The brotherhoods seemed especially strong and secure on the nation's railroads and remained partly protected by federal railroad labor law (that despite the hostility of almost all unions to the Transportation Act of 1920). The United Mine Workers, too, commanded a mass membership (between 400,000 and 500,000) and great strength in the nation's coal mines. And the bulk of the AFL's core craft unions, especially those in the building and printing trades, held their members, as well as real job control in many cities. Labor, moreover, was not without influence in Congress. Influential members of the minority party still defended trade unionism, and they were usually joined by a small band of so-called progressive Republicans, the most liberal of whom were Fiorello LaGuardia in the House and George Norris and Robert LaFollette in the Senate.

Because of organized labor's real strength in 1921 (most labor leaders and unions remained as militant as they had been during and just after the war) and its influential friends in Congress, the Harding administration was in no mood to declare war on trade unionism. In the 1920 election Harding had appealed for the votes of working people, stressing his party's traditional commitment to prosperity through economic growth, high wages protected by wise tariff policies, and immigration laws that would protect American workers against foreign pauper labor.[1] Harding repeated those themes in his first message to Congress. The president emphasized what might be construed as the founding faith of the Republican party, the indistinguishability of capital and labor. In a variation of the old Lincolnian adage that the laborer of today was the capitalist of tomorrow, Harding asserted that the laborer was a capitalist and the capitalist a laborer. He defended the right of both to organize in their own interest but pledged to defend the public welfare against the depredations of either or both.[2]

More than soft words underlay the Republican approach to organized labor. The 1920s saw no sudden shrinkage in federal power to intervene in the domestic economy that had been established in the Roosevelt presidency, expanded in Wilson's first term, and magnified during the war. True, the most expansive of the wartime federal powers, agencies, and policies had been eroded in the reaction of 1919–20. But the Department of Labor remained an extremely active administrative agency, its mediation and conciliation service still frequently entering labor disputes. The new Railroad Labor Board (RLB), established under Title III of the Transportation Act of 1920, intervened more often and aggressively in railroad labor disputes than had any of its federal predecessors. And the Republicans did increase the power of federal administrative agencies to set tariffs and restrict immigration (new laws also raised tariffs and ended unrestricted immigration).[3]

Most encouraging to trade unionists were the principles and policies of the Harding administration's most active and influential cabinet member, the Secretary of Commerce Herbert Hoover. Chairman of President Wilson's Second Industrial Conference, Hoover carried to the Harding administration the labor policies he had first enunciated as the conference's chair. In simplest terms, he suggested that employers should freely recognize trade unions that their employees voluntarily chose to join and, more important, that employers should bargain collectively with such unions (precisely the demands of the labor representatives at Wilson's first conference.)[4] Hoover believed that if labor and capital, employees and employers cooperated to eliminate waste in industry, to use science in the service of higher productivity, and to stabilize employment, they could construct a high-wage economy, which was needed to consume the output of American mass production. Such cooperation in pursuit of "scientific management" could only be built, Hoover believed, on the basis of offering workers' organizations greater responsibility for the conduct of industry. He thus strove to convince employers to recognize and bargain with unions in order to maximize production and to achieve economic and employment stability.[5] For Gompers, who had opposed Harding in the 1920 election and now had few points of contact with the president, and also for John L. Lewis, who had endorsed Harding, Hoover served as their "man" in the new administration, the transmission belt for the ideas and policies of organized labor.

Even on the legal front, not all seemed bleak for organized labor in 1921. District and circuit court of appeals rulings handed down in April 1917 and May 1918, respectively, suggested that the Clayton Act could be read broadly to restrain the use of injunctions in all peaceful disputes between employees and employers over the conditions of work. In the case under consideration (Duplex Printing Press Co. v. Deering et al.), the International Association of Machinists, unable to win either a union contract or the eight-hour day through a strike against the Duplex Company, had called upon all its members to refuse to handle and install the company's printing presses. The IAM also asked Teamsters not to handle the "unfair" firm's products. The case originated in the New York metropolitan market, where the entirely peaceful boycott had operated successfully, causing the Duplex Company to seek an injunction against the IAM under the Sherman Act's clause covering restraint of interstate commerce. First, the district court judge and subsequently, on appeal, a two-to-one circuit court majority ruled that Section 20 of the Clayton Act exempted the IAM's action from judicial interdiction. Unless the union could compel Duplex to grant its demands, the better conditions the IAM had won for its members at all other manufacturers of printing presses were at risk. Hence three federal judges decided that the dispute was, in effect, a conflict between employees and employers over the terms and conditions of work, and as such it was covered by the Clayton Act. In the words of

Judge Learned Hand, "I think that the dispute here under any definition included the conditions of employment," and in those of his associate Charles Hough, "The remedy is political not judicial."[6]

Not even President Harding's appointment of William Howard Taft as chief justice of the United States noticeably dismayed the advocates of trade unionism. Once reviled by organized labor as an injunction judge, Taft seemed to have been altered by his experiences as cochair of the National War Labor Board. Tutored by his colleague Frank P. Walsh, impressed by the contributions of the trade union members of the board, and educated in the realities of industrial conflict by the cases that came before the NWLB, Taft had come to defend the rights of workers to join unions of their own choosing and to demand that employers bargain collectively with such unions. The new chief justice had also come to learn why industrial disputes often produced disorder and why unions pursued particular strike actions. Labor leaders could now realistically hope that Taft would bring his new knowledge and sympathy for trade unionism to bear on the labor cases that would come before the Supreme Court.

Other early actions by the Harding administration also hinted at an accommodation with organized labor. Harding's accession to office coincided with a sharp depression, which deflated prices, paralyzed production, and caused mass unemployment. Business leaders demanded steep wage cuts as the only answer to the problem. Under the influence of Hoover, however, Harding in October 1921 called an unemployment conference, to which he invited representatives of industry, labor, and the public, to provide other answers to economic depression. In place of wage deflation, Hoover suggested that the conference endorse a combination of voluntary action by industrialists to increase private investment plus state and municipal spending for public works.[7] Hoover also took a leading role in compelling the steel industry to grant its workers an eight-hour day. If not the sole administration champion of the eight-hour day, as his memoirs suggest, Hoover nevertheless could take the bulk of the credit for its achievement in the steel industry by 1923.[8]

The Hardening of Labor Policy: The Judiciary Acts

Other aspects of Republican dominance in Washington, however, boded ill for labor. For one thing, the president was not especially fond of Gompers and other labor leaders. Gompers reciprocated Harding's antipathy and attacked the Republican president with exceptional bitterness. Labor secretary James J. Davis tried to smooth Harding's ruffled feathers by reminding the president that Gompers "is a Democrat and it is hard for him to hand a glass of milk to a Republican."

Such hard feelings between the president of the AFL and the president of the United States led one historian to conclude that "there was little real communication and no bond of understanding" between organized labor and the Republican administration.[9]

Although that evaluation was not entirely true, as we have seen in examining the role and policies of Herbert Hoover, Harding's choice of a labor secretary scarcely pleased trade unionists. Accustomed to the active promotion of trade unionism by their friend and first secretary of labor, William B. Wilson, labor leaders could not hide their disdain for his successor, James J. Davis. A typical American success story, Davis had long since moved beyond his origins as a Welsh immigrant and skilled iron puddler and union member. By 1921, he was a veritable Babbitt, a typical small-town booster and joiner, proud of his membership in male fraternal orders and clubs too numerous to count. "If all the members of all the organizations to which he belonged had voted for him," Hoover later remembered, "he could have been elected to anything, any time, anywhere."[10] In his role as labor secretary, Davis played to the full the part of fraternal social secretary. He glad-handed, smiled, flattered, and had a knack, in Hoover's words, for "keeping labor quiet." In practice, however, he did precious little to promote unionism, encourage collective bargaining, or advance policies and legislation favored by organized labor. For trade unionists Davis's Department of Labor represented a setback in the sort of influence William B. Wilson had brought to the president's cabinet.[11]

The postwar depression of 1920–21 also undermined labor's influence and clouded its future. Economic contraction further decimated the ranks of organized labor. Mass unemployment made unions unable to resist general wage cuts and less successful in winning strikes, most of which were now defensive in aim. Newspaper stories and speeches that stressed union power and high wages as the causes for depression and high consumer prices fueled administration and congressional resistance to the interests and entreaties of trade unionists.

Even more disturbing to labor was a body of rulings in labor cases during 1921 and 1922 by the Taft Supreme Court. Wearing the judicial robes apparently caused the chief justice to revert to his earlier and strongly held views concerning the impropriety of most union strike action and the need for the judiciary to restrain such "criminal" behavior through injunctions. In a 1921 decision reversing a circuit court of appeals ruling (Duplex v. Deering), a majority of the Taft Court stripped the Clayton Act of most of the protection it provided strikers against injunctions. The court majority read the Clayton Act as narrowly as possible, declaring that disputes between employees and employers referred only to disagreements between a named company and its own workers, not to conflicts that indirectly concerned the material conditions of all workers in a trade or industry.

To give protection to the latter form of conflict, as the lower court rulings had done, the Taft Court suggested, would sanction general class warfare, a purpose the congressional majority could not have had in mind when it passed the Clayton Act. The Court also found that the Clayton Act failed to outlaw injunctions against the sort of secondary boycott instituted in the case under consideration.[12]

Not satisfied to interpret the Clayton Act narrowly, the Taft Court liberally used its power to declare state laws unconstitutional. In the same session of the Court, it struck down an Arizona law restricting the use of injunctions in labor disputes (a law specifically allowed by the state's constitution) because it deprived employers both of "property" without due process of law and equal protection of the laws."[13]

Other Supreme Court rulings also put trade unions at risk. In yet another 1921 decision in which Taft specifically read the Clayton Act to legitimize trade unionism and collective action by workers (American Steel Foundries v. Tri-Cities Central Trade Council), he practically outlawed most conventional forms of union strike picketing. The chief justice went almost so far as to find peaceful persuasion and picketing to be a contradiction in terms.[14] And the following year, in a ruling that ostensibly favored the United Mine Workers as plaintiff, Taft's decision imposed a potential threat to the security of all trade unions. In finding that the dispute under consideration had not really restrained interstate commerce (Taft ruled that the mining of coal was not by itself part of interstate commerce) and could not be enjoined under the Sherman Act and also that the UMW could not be held liable for the violent or criminal acts of individual members, the chief justice insisted that trade unions were in fact liable as institutions and responsible for the actions of their members during all authorized strikes.[15] Given the violence associated with so many American industrial disputes, Taft's decision posed a danger to union treasuries.

The nature of the judicial process in labor disputes rendered the Supreme Court's decisions in 1921 and 1922 all the more threatening to trade unionists. At that time the inferior courts showed a remarkable diversity of opinion in interpreting the Clayton Act and the validity of labor injunctions. Some judges issued sweeping injunctions reflexively and others found their power to enjoin limited either by the Clayton Act or the fact that manufacturing was not a part of the stream of interstate commerce.[16] The Taft Court rulings, in effect, unleashed the injunction judges and hobbled the ones more tolerant of strikes. Worse yet, the Supreme Court could not offer effective relief to trade unionists whose actions had been enjoined by lower court judges who exceeded their authority. By the time the Supreme Court found an injunction deficient, so much time had passed that the restraining order had already served its purpose.[17]

In such a legal environment many judges seldom hesitated to grant strike injunctions, more often than not on the basis of ex parte hearings without even formal affidavits. Injunctions forbade bricklayers from boycotting nonunion employers, machinists from refusing to install nonunion printing presses, and coal miners from unionizing the mines of West Virginia. As bad as the federal courts were in the 1920s, municipal judges and police likely exacted an even heavier price on trade unionists and strikers.[18]

The Coal Strike of 1922

Although the judiciary seemed to be committed to Chief Justice Taft's policy concerning labor — "that faction we have to hit every little while" — the Harding administration preferred to pursue a more neutral policy in labor-capital relations.[19] Events in the summer of 1922 quickly put the administration's neutrality to the test. Two massive national strikes, one by coal miners and the other by railroad shopcraft workers, clearly affected the national economy and demanded a federal response.[20] The forceful intervention of President Harding and Commerce Secretary Hoover illustrated how in practice neutrality worked to the disadvantage of workers and their unions.

The coal miners' strike, which began on April 1, 1922, was the most massive in American history. Both bituminous and anthracite miners struck. Miners at both union and nonunion properties put down their tools. More than 600,000 coal diggers in every state that produced coal walked a picket line at some time before the strike ended. On the surface a reflection of union strength and solidarity, the 1922 strike was in reality a reaction to the deteriorating position of the coal industry, its union, and the men who mined the mineral. Coal mining never fully recovered from the postwar depression. As the general economy revived in 1922, coal companies found themselves employing too many miners who dug too much coal. Simultaneously, in what was already a glutted market, the nonunion coal produced in Southern Appalachia undersold the product of the union mines. Unionized companies refused in 1922 to sign a contract with the UMW, which therefore left them at the mercy of their nonunion competitors. Rather than agree to a single uniform contract that covered the entire Central Competitive Field (CCF) and its outlying districts (which had been the arrangement since 1898), the operators sought separate district and local agreements that would enable them to respond better to market conditions and competitive realities. For the UMW, the operators' position threatened dire results. Already besieged by lower-wage nonunion miners, the union knew that if it acceded to the operators' demands, it would encourage the same sort of competition among union miners. A Gresham's wage law would operate, under which cheap labor would drive dear labor out of the marketplace. Thus the union had no choice except to call a national strike in which it hoped nonunion miners would join their union brothers in a struggle for uniform national standards.[21]

The scale and effectiveness of the strike brought demands for federal intervention to ensure that industry obtained enough coal to keep factories humming and that consumers had adequate fuel at a fair price to heat their homes. From the first, the Harding administration planned to satisfy such demands. Hoover, the cabinet member most responsible for dealing with the coal crisis, instituted a double-edged strategy. On the one hand, he encouraged the unionized operators to bargain collectively and come to terms with the UMW. On the other hand, he sought to ensure an adequate supply of nonunion coal for business and domestic consumers from suppliers whom he would not allow to profiteer from market circumstances. Hoover's strategy directly threatened the UMW, for markets once captured by nonunion producers were not likely to be rewon by their unionized competitors. Speaking for his union, John L. Lewis criticized the commerce secretary's policies. To which Hoover pleaded his innocence, assuring the UMW president that "the administration is not injecting itself into the strike; it is trying to protect the general public from the results of the strike."[22]

As the strike dragged on through April, May, and into late June, pressure built in Washington for a solution. A national railroad strike threatened for July 1 intensified the demand for a political resolution to industrial conflict. During the last week in June, Harding, Hoover, and even Labor Secretary Davis struggled to bring the miners' union and the coal operators closer together. All to no avail. Employers still demanded separate district contracts; the union, a standard national agreement. Even a private Saturday morning White House conference among the involved parties proved fruitless. Hoover then instituted the next element in his strategy to end the dispute. On July 9, Harding proposed that the miners resume work at the wages that had been in effect March 31, pending a full investigation of the coal industry by a special federal commission and an arbitration award covering wages and working conditions. The element of compulsory arbitration attracted the interest of the mine owners. The hint of a uniform national agreement elicited the interest of Lewis and his union. Yet the more Lewis studied the president's proposal, the more leery he became. First, it excluded all operating nonunion mines. Second, it also excluded several union properties. And, third, it proposed a solution that was anathema to all trade unionists, compulsory arbitration. Thus the union rejected Harding's recommendations, which only served to make the president more hostile to the miners than to the operators.[23]

Harding had already been advised by Hoover, in the event that his July 9 proposal failed, to "order the men back to work." The president almost did so. At a private conference with mine operators on July 17, Harding advised them to resume production, and he promised federal troops to protect their property. The next day he wired the governors of all coal-producing states, ordering them to protect coal mines and also informing them that federal troops had been alerted for strike duty. In his own way, the president was trying to bluff the strikers with the threat of military intervention.[24] The miners, however, realized that bayonets could not dig coal; the governors in the most heavily unionized states preferred not to risk real violence; and Harding and Hoover never had any intention of using troops to break a strike.

The president's suggestion that union operators resume production despite the strike and his talk of military intervention disclosed how shallow was the administration's neutrality in labor-capital relations. Well after the coal crisis had abated, Harding, in a special message to Congress on August 18 primarily concerned with the railroad strike, alluded to how the UMW would have put the nation at its mercy if it eliminated nonunion mines and how a national coal strike was a form of blackmail. And he never diluted his belief (shared by Hoover) that it was the government's obligation to protect an individual's right to work, an obligation that covered strikebreakers.[25]

The coal strike ended in mid-August, no thanks to the administration's intervention. What happened was quite simple. As nonunion coal captured more of the market, unionized operators feared protracting the strike. The combined impact of a three-month coal strike and a national railroad strike brought coal supply into equilibrium with demand, a situation that led to price increases and enabled operators to settle on union terms. In reality, the UMW's victory was as shallow as the Harding administration's neutrality. It failed to win recognition from nonunion companies, surrendered the rights of nonunion miners who had joined the walkout, and watched impotently as nonunion production gained a larger share of the market.[26]

The administration, or at least Hoover, came away with one gain from the 1922 conflict in coal: the appointment of a United States Coal Commission to investigate thoroughly the condition of the industry and recommend policies to restore its economic vitality. The commission's report, finally published in 1925, turned out to be, in the words of one scholar, "vague, platitudinous, and occasionally even meaningless." It also proved once again how neutrality in labor-capital relations offered nothing to workers and their unions. For the commission recommended that although national agreements contributed to labor stability, district, state, and even local contracts were equally acceptable. While applauding the UMW's contribution to the miners' welfare and the industry's health, it endorsed nonunion mines as a necessary restraint against a potential union monopoly and a guarantee for free competition in coal.[27]

The Railroad Shopmen's Strike

The 1922 railroad strike exposed the Harding administration's harsher side to trade unionism. In a situation even more complicated than that of the coal strike and one fraught with more perilous precedents for the strikers, the unions involved fought first the railroads and then the federal government. In a real sense, this strike marked an end to the wave of labor militancy that had originated in 1916, crested in 1919, and subsided after 1922.[28] Its defeat enabled the Republicans in national power to be less concerned thereafter with labor-capital relations and also to pursue policies more accommodative to the interests of trade unionists. The administration could act more moderately because the labor movement had been stripped of its aggressiveness and strength.

All the railroad unions had opposed the passage of the Transportation Act of 1920, which under Title III had established the Railroad Labor Board to address the industry's labor problems. Nothing that occurred after the RLB began to operate altered the unions' original objections to it. Instead, the RLB's policies intensified union antipathy. Based on the concept of a tripartite structure — capital, labor, and public members in equal number — the RLB was stacked against the unions. Not only did the industry and public members usually ally to reject union demands but Harding appointed labor members who were unacceptable to the railroad unions.

At first, however, the RLB caused few problems. Later, when the postwar depression hit, labor difficulties multiplied on the railroads and the RLB found itself trapped in an industrial relations quagmire. The railroads, plagued by shrinking freight traffic and ICC-ordered rate reductions, demanded wage cuts and changed work rules. In 1921 and 1922 the RLB ordered two rounds of wage cuts, which struck most heavily at the nonoperating workers and which the railroads implemented. It also issued rulings that ordered individual railroads not to sub-contract shop work out to nonunion shops and not to establish company unions for nonoperating employees. These rulings the railroads refused to implement. Finally, in 1923 in a case brought before the Supreme Court, the majority, speaking through Taft, ruled that Congress had not granted the RLB the power it needed to enforce its decisions. It must, Taft decided, rely solely on the power of public opinion.[29] That reality led one union leader to allege that the RLB "is clearly not a two-edged sword which cuts impartially in either direction. It has a blunt edge when used against the employers. Its blows have no force, but when this sword is turned against the employees it is sharp and cuts deep."[30]

Actually the labor situation on the railroads was even more complex than the fact that the RLB's decisions weighed unfairly on the unions. The brotherhoods, for example, generally survived the postwar onslaught against unionism on the railroads. Long accustomed to stable collective bargaining with the railroads and representing workers with irreplaceable skills, the brotherhoods were less susceptible to employers' attempts to weaken union influence. In fact, the railroads made no effort to uproot unions that they respected as conservative and responsible.

Instead, under the auspices of Hoover, the top railroad executives and the leaders of the brotherhoods met together in January, February, and March 1922 and agreed to bypass the RLB in reaching mutual understandings on all labor issues.[31]

The nonoperating railroad workers, especially those concentrated in the shops, proved more vulnerable to the employer counterattack. Only recently revitalized as a consequence of federal wartime labor policies, the shopcraft unions, of which the International Association of Machinists was the most important, felt themselves besieged on all fronts. Once before, in 1911–15 during a bitter, violent strike on the Illinois Central and Harriman railroad lines, the shopcraft unions had suffered a decisive defeat. Now, in 1921 and 1922, they again felt victimized. The railroads had implemented two wage reductions against them (but not against the brotherhoods), sent shop work out to nonunion firms, causing unemployment among shopmen, instituted piece-rate wage systems, and established company unions to replace independent ones. Unless they resisted, concluded the shopcraft union leaders joined together in the AFL's Railway Employee Department (RED), they would soon have no standards worth defending and no members to protect. For them a nationwide strike seemed the only alternative.[32]

Thus, throughout the month of June the leaders of the shopcraft unions took strike votes among their widely scattered memberships. The leaders, most notably Bert Jewell, head of the RED, were far more cautious than their followers and less eager to force the situation. Nevertheless, union members voted by overwhelming majorities to endorse a national strike for July 1 unless the RLB rescinded its wage cuts and the railroads restored previous work rules. The shop workers voted as they did with full knowledge that the brotherhoods would not support their cause and solid suspicion that several nonoperating workers' unions also would not sanction a strike, especially the Clerks and Maintenance of Way workers, whose members sometimes did walk out on their own volition.[33] On July 1, 1922, more than 400,000 shopmen and allied nonoperating railroad workers walked off the job in the first nationwide railroad strike since 1894.

The government responded almost immediately and forcefully. On July 3, the chairman of the RLB, Ben Hooper, a former governor of Tennessee, introduced a resolution that the board passed by a 5–2 majority (both dissenters were labor representatives). The resolution, in effect, declared that the strike was illegal, that the strikers had no claims to the jobs that they had voluntarily left (hence surrendering their seniority), and that their replacements were not strikebreakers but rather men acting with absolute moral and legal integrity. In so many words, the RLB branded the strikers as criminals, and its action soon became known as the "outlaw resolution." During the following week, Harding rose to the defense of the RLB and also condemned the strikers as lawbreakers violating the rulings of a legitimate federal agency (the Supreme Court decision declaring RLB orders unenforceable did not come until the following year).[34] The "outlaw resolution" and the president's endorsement of it led one union publication to observe: "This vividly illustrates the difference in treatment accorded by the Railroad Labor Board as between railroad officials and railroad employees. One is given 20 months' grace, the other three days. One is censured as 'disputants,' the other is 'outlawed' as criminals."[35]

Having first condemned the strikers and suggested that he would use federal power to break the strike, Harding hastened to assure the shopcraft workers of his goodwill and neutrality. By late July, both the president and the union leaders had good reasons to seek an accommodation. Although not totally effective, the strike caused enough damage to commerce and industry to raise a public outcry for its immediate resolution. Deserted first by the brotherhoods and then by several nonoperating unions, and now seeing replacement workers taking their jobs, the strikers sought a compromise. On July 31 Harding proposed a solution. He asked both sides to obey faithfully the decisions of the RLB and the railroads to withdraw all lawsuits against the RLB, promising that the decisions contested by the railroads would be reheard by the RLB and also that all strikers would be restored to their former positions with seniority and other job rights unimpaired. The strikers leaped at the compromise. The railroads declined, insisting that morally they had no choice but to protect the legitimate rights of loyal employees and new hires. In a last attempt to salvage his compromise, Harding proposed that the strikers return to work while the RLB determined the issue of seniority. Naturally the railroads accepted and the unions refused.[36]

For six weeks the Harding administration oscillated in its handling of the shopmen's strike. The lack of consistency apparently derived from the president's own vacillation. Members of his cabinet knew what they wanted. Davis, whose voice scarcely counted, and the more influential Hoover vigorously pushed a compromise. When the railroad executives rejected Harding's July 31 offer, Hoover, who personally delivered the proposal, dismissed its recipients as men whose "social instinct belonged to an early Egyptian period."[37] Hardliners in the cabinet, of whom the most outspoken was the attorney general and Harding's close friend, Harry Daugherty, wanted more-decisive action, steps reminiscent of those taken by Grover Cleveland in the Pullman Strike of 1894.

Finally, on August 18 in a special message to Congress concerning the industrial relations crisis, Harding revealed his deepest sentiments and prejudices. After a perfunctory condemnation of railroad management's failure to obey RLB rulings, the president tore into the strikers. He asserted that the shopmen's strike "revealed the cruelty and contempt for the law on the part of some railway employees, who have conspired to paralyze transportation, and lawlessness and violence in a hundred places have revealed the failure of the striking unions to hold their forces to law observance." Not satisfied with having condemned the strikers as cruel and criminal, Harding reiterated the point: "There is a state of lawlessness shocking to every conception of American law and order and violating the cherished guarantees of American freedom." Since the seniority issue was the primary point still in dispute, the president specifically defended the rights of the strikebreakers. "If free men can not toil according to their own lawful choosing," he proclaimed, "all our constitutional guarantees born of democracy are surrendered to mobocracy and the freedom of hundreds of millions is surrendered to the small minority which would have no law." And, finally, in words perhaps written by Daugherty and certainly uttered to the attorney general's delight, the president assured Congress, "I am resolved to use all the power of the Government to maintain transportation, and sustain the right of men to work."[38]

Harding's harsh language meant that the shopmen had lost their last chance for an acceptable compromise. It also implied that the federal government would soon move more decisively against the strikers. To be sure, even before the government acted repressively against the shopmen, their union leaders had begun a salvage operation. Realizing that the strike was all but broken, Jewell and his associates in the RED had opened discussions with some of the more moderate railroad executives, most notably Daniel Willard of the Baltimore and Ohio. Over the objections of Hoover and Davis, who were aware of the new negotiations, the cabinet hardliners, led by Daugherty, convinced the president, who by then did not need much convincing, that he should approve decisive action. So on September 1, the attorney general appeared in a federal district court in Chicago before Judge James Wilkerson to seek a restraining order against the strikers.[39]

Three weeks later, on September 23, at a time when the strike was practically over, Wilkerson handed down one of the most notorious injunctions in American legal history, one that in its scope and arbitrary restraints outdid even the infamous Debs-Pullman injunction. In fact, Wilkerson even cited the *Debs* case as a binding precedent (as well as every other Supreme Court antilabor ruling since 1894) in his declaration that the issue was not a labor dispute about working conditions but rather a war against the state. Such being the reality, he ruled that the Sherman Act provided the United States with the power to forbid every written, oral, and physical act in furtherance of the criminal conspiracy that was the shopmen's strike. In short, his order enjoined the officers of the RED, the separate shopcraft unions, and their members from engaging in any action concerning the strike.[40] In the words of Edward Berman, the Wilkerson injunction for the first time in modern American history declared illegal a strike against wage cuts and "appears to have completed the array of direct precedents upon the basis of which the courts may invoke the Sherman Act to prevent any kind of railway strike which involves interstate transportation."[41]

At the time, several federal judges were no less sparing in their condemnation of Wilkerson's ruling. In his own district court in North Dakota, Judge Charles F. Amidon cited the Clayton Act in refusing to grant an injunction against the shopmen. Then he turned to Wilkerson's ruling and commented that it "[is] not only in direct violation of the Clayton Act . . . but carrie[s] government by injunction into new fields. They virtually hold that the power of courts to issue injunctions in strike cases, not only has no limits in equity jurisprudence, but that Congress cannot frame a law to limit this power which courts may not nullify by skillful construction." Even earlier, before Wilkerson's ruling, Judge George M. Bourquin of Montana also cited the Clayton Act in refusing to grant an injunction. And Bourquin pointedly observed that the consequence of readily granting injunctions "is a disposition to view the courts as partners of the employers, and the judicial writs of injunction as weapons against employees however lawfully they be proceeding."[42] Amidon and Bourquin spoke for a minority on the federal bench and Wilkerson for the large majority — which is why even after the strike officially ended, he refused to lift his original injunction.[43]

Out of the shambles of the strike the union leaders saved what they could. From their negotiations with Willard and other more moderate railroad managers, they drew a compromise agreement. It provided that the signatory railroads would rehire the strikers in their former positions, would recognize and bargain collectively with the standard shopcraft unions, and could run as open shops (the unions also conceded most work rule disputes).[44]

The more-obdurate railroad executives ignored the unions. They refused to rehire strikers except on individual application as new employees, and they usually established docile company unions. By 1926 the railway carmen and also the clerks had lost the bulk of their 1920 peak membership, in both cases most of the loss coming after 1922. By 1924 a majority of the nonoperating employees on the eastern railroads and over one-third on the western roads were represented by company unions (in the South, for which data are less available, the proportion was probably comparable to that of the eastern lines).[45] The nonoperating railway unions and their members had paid dearly for what passed as neutrality in labor-capital relations in Republican Washington.

What William M. Leiserson wrote about labor law in the 1920s seems a fair description of the neutrality that the Harding administration practiced toward trade unionists during the industrial crisis of 1922:

The law recognized the equal freedom of employers to destroy labor organizations and to deny the right of employees to join trade unions. An employer could coerce or threaten his employees to keep them from organizing. He could discharge them if they joined a union, and he could refuse to hire any anyone who was a member. . . . Under such circumstances, to speak of labor's right to organize was clearly a misuse of terms. All that employees had was a right to try to organize if they could get away with it; and whether they could or not depended on the relative economic strength of the employers' and employees' organizations.[46]

The only way to alter this sort of neutrality was through political power. Thus in December 1923 the attorney for the railway unions, Donald Richberg, advised Bert Jewell of the RED that the unions should not turn to the courts for relief. "As the courts are at present constituted and influenced," advised Richberg, "they are the branch of Government most partisan in opposition to the claims of organized labor." The wisest course for labor would be "political action in getting new laws made by the legislatures and obtaining executive support of such laws."[47] Which is precisely what the labor movement chose to do between 1922 and 1924.

Labor and Politics

In the wake of its defeats in the summer of 1922, organized labor behaved more passively. Strikes became less common. By the end of the 1920s, the number of strikes annually had fallen to levels not seen since the initial wave of labor militancy in the 1870s. During his last two years as president of the AFL, Gompers acted the beggar, beseeching employers to give unions a break. It was his behavior and rhetoric in 1923 and 1924, not his previous policies and practices, that truly earned Gompers the appellation "labor conservative." His successor as president of the AFL, William Green, proved even less militant and more deferential to employers to whose Christian conscience he appealed. Those unions that had been in the forefront of labor militancy from 1916 through 1922 suffered the severest losses. The once mighty United Mine Workers were a battered husk by 1928; the Machinists never recovered from their defeat on the railroads; the socialist Brewery Workers were practically put out of business by Prohibition; and the socialist men's and especially women's garment workers suffered from factionalism and unfavorable economic trends. By contrast, the less militant and more conservative sectors of the labor movement — the building trades unions, the typographical crafts, and the railroad brotherhoods — either maintained their strength or grew slightly.[48]

Whipped on the industrial front, labor for a time turned to political action, as Donald Richberg had advised the railroad unions to do. With the railroad unions in the van, the entire organized labor movement participated actively in the 1922 congressional elections, seeking to defeat those legislators who had manifested hostility toward unions during the summer's industrial crisis.

In the short run, political action produced results. The new Congress included a far larger representation of so-called prolabor progressive Republicans and sympathetic Democrats. Buoyed by the 1922 results, the railroad unions brought all the nation's putative progressives — trade unionists, socialists, and independent reformers — together into the Conference for Progressive Political Action (CPPA). And in 1924, when the Democrats nominated a conservative Wall Street attorney, John Davis, to oppose the Republican nominee, Calvin Coolidge, the CPPA entered its own independent slate with Robert LaFollette of Wisconsin as presidential candidate and Burton Wheeler of Montana as vice presidential candidate. Coolidge's election by a landslide ended labor's foray into independent politics.[49]

Having used the "big stick" to beat trade unionists during the strikes of 1922, the Republicans offered several carrots to a now domesticated labor movement. The economic expansion of 1923–28 with its stable prices, steady wages, and easy consumer credit made the Republican carrots quite tasty to many workers. In tones and words redolent of William McKinley's "full dinner-pail" campaign, Coolidge in 1924 assured workers that Republican tariffs and immigration restrictions had kept their wages up and their cost of living down. And he assured the union minority within the American working class that his administration would encourage responsible collective bargaining and voluntary arbitration. "Republican rule," the president boasted, "has raised the wage-earner to a higher standard than he ever occupied before anywhere in the world."[50] Such labor leaders as John L. Lewis and Bill Hutcheson seemed to agree; both of them endorsed the Republican party in 1924 and again in 1928. The election returns, moreover, suggested similar sentiments among most working-class voters in 1924 and after.

One reason that Lewis supported Coolidge and the Republicans in 1924 was because Hoover had assisted the UMW president in obtaining a new contract from the CCF coal operators in 1924 without risking a strike. The soft-coal industry remained as economically troubled in 1924 as it had been two years earlier. Too many miners still dug too much coal. Nonunion Southern Appalachian mines still undersold their union competitors and grabbed a larger share of the market. In such a perilous situation, everyone — Lewis, Hoover, and the union operators — sought stability. The mine owners hoped to achieve it by compelling the union to make concessions in the contract, which would enable union mines to compete with their southern competitors. Each in his own way, Lewis and Hoover preferred to maintain high union wages by promoting scientific management in the more efficient mines, closing the less efficient ones, and eliminating strikes as a source of economic instability. The UMW and the CCF operators agreed to precisely such an arrangement at their bargaining sessions in Jacksonville, Florida, in February 1924. The so-called Jacksonville Agreement, to which Hoover acted as godfather, provided for a three-year contract that preserved existing terms, provisions, and conditions in the union mines and eliminated the threat of strikes. With due deference to Hoover, Lewis said of the agreement: "We must give economic laws free play. . . . It is survival of the fittest. Many are going to be hurt, but the rule must be the greatest good for the greatest number." To which the commerce secretary responded: "Mr. Lewis is more than a successful battle leader. He has a sound conception of statesmanship of long-view interest to the people and the industry he serves."[51]

In practice, however, the Jacksonville Agreement brought the UMW few lasting gains. It failed to stop nonunion mines from gaining a larger share of the market or to improve the balance sheets of union mines. Consequently, union operators, especially in western Pennsylvania, began to shut down or to violate the Jacksonville Agreement. Unwilling to risk a strike, Lewis turned to Washington for aid. He asked the man who had midwifed the settlement to compel the mine owners to respect it. A Republican administration once again demonstrated the real meaning of its neutrality in labor affairs. As counseled by Hoover, the administration in November 1925 deplored any breach of contract by mine operators but denied that it had been a party to the Jacksonville Agreement. "The government not being a party to contracts," Coolidge informed Lewis, "has no status in enforcement." Yet the same document warned Lewis that if the UMW struck to enforce contract terms, it would violate a binding agreement and "be a fatal blow at most collective bargaining." Don't strike, Hoover advised Lewis; go to court to resolve your union's grievances. No advice could have been more vexing to a labor leader in the 1920s.[52]

By the time the Jacksonville Agreement terminated in 1927, few of the larger operators respected it and the union was in parlous condition. Lewis again looked to Washington for help. Now the leader of what appeared to be a dying union, Lewis was rejected by Coolidge and neglected by Hoover. Instead Labor Secretary Davis offered his impotent influence in an effort to bring operators and union together. Nothing came of Davis's intervention because, as the leading mine owners informed him, "What would be our idea in meeting now and giving up the ground we fought for? We have definitely and permanently severed all relations with that organization. It is my sincere belief that freedom from union domination is the best assurance of future stability and peace for the industry and for the public." The owners' prescription for a cure to the soft-coal industry's ailments was the same as Hoover's: "the working of economic laws. . . . Governmental interference at any time . . . *would be hurtful.*"[53]

The situation in railroad labor relations and politics showed a similar pattern in Republican policy and state intervention. The unions remained deeply unhappy with the operations of the RLB and avoided its offices, as did most of the railroads. Aware of the railroad unions' political activities and influence in Congress,

Coolidge and Hoover repeatedly suggested revisions in federal railroad labor law, including elimination of the RLB. They based their suggestions on obtaining mutual consent from the railroads and the unions to any revisions. Largely satisfied with the outcome of the 1922 strike and the current status of labor relations, the railroads at first evinced no interest in amending the railroad labor law. The unions, however, persisted in turning to their friends in Congress to introduce bills that would eliminate the RLB, mandate representation for the standard national railroad unions (most railroads preferred system-bargaining, in which the company unions had a protected place), and sanction the right of railroad workers to form unions of their own choosing.[54] Such a bill sponsored by Democratic representative Alben Barkley of Kentucky and progressive Republican senator Robert Howell of Nebraska was introduced in the Sixty-eighth Congress but never came to a vote. Opposition from Republican floor leaders and the administration killed it.[55]

Having now thwarted railroad labor's legislative proposal, the administration sought to mollify the unions, especially the responsible, conservative brotherhoods. Coolidge once more publicly suggested amendments to federal railroad labor law, and Hoover again acted as middleman in bringing together labor leaders and railroad executives. This time the two sides could agree on a bill that was introduced in the first session of the Sixty-ninth Congress by Republican senator James E. Watson of Indiana and Republican representative James Parker of New York.[56] Backed by the administration, the Railway Labor Act of 1926 sailed through Congress on May 11 with only token opposition.

The act was one more example of the reality of neutral state intervention in labor-capital relations. It eliminated the despised RLB, provided a variety of new mediating agencies to resolve labor disputes, and called for specially appointed presidential mediation commissions that would investigate deadlocks, during which times strikes would be illegal. In return for surrendering the right to strike, the railroad unions gained specific legislative sanction for the right to bargain collectively and workers won theoretical freedom from employer coercion. For the brotherhoods the new law meant federal sanction for the representation they had won and the bargaining they had conducted since the late nineteenth century. For the nonoperating unions, the law legitimated what little they had salvaged through the Baltimore and Ohio agreement of 1922. The railroads also benefited. For them, the bill sanctioned system-based rather than nationwide bargaining, and it legitimated as valid the many company unions, which had been instituted on the railroads in the aftermath of 1922. It was a bargain in which no one lost. Not a single change in railroad labor relations occurred as a result of the new law. The unions surrendered a right they had never really had. After 1894 and 1922, everyone realized that the federal government would not tolerate a national railroad strike. Republicans could point to the Railway Labor Act as evidence of their friendship to workers and their respect for responsible trade unionists.[57] During floor debate on the bill, one representative, Meyer Jacobstein of Rochester, New York (a former mediator in the men's clothing industry), could even proclaim: "The American Government is recognizing collective bargaining in a legal way as it has never done before."[58] And in 1930 the Supreme Court under a new chief justice, Charles Evans Hughes, declared the act constitutional.

By 1926 leading Republicans had no difficulty defending their accommodation with organized labor. Its terms were strictly limited. As labor's best "friend" in the administration, Hoover had proved by his part in coal negotiations and in amending railway labor legislation that union rights were tightly circumscribed. Contractual obligations seemed to bind unions but not employers. If unions demanded the right to bargain collectively, they had to concede employers the right to run open shops and hire nonunion employees. In a speech that he delivered in 1926 extolling the Republican party's contribution to high wages, low prices, mass production, and labor peace, Hoover spelled out the terms of the accommodation. Unions had a right to exist and share equitably in the fruits of productivity, provided they eliminated featherbedding, used none of their money for political purposes, won no blanket exemption from antitrust laws, and tolerated the existence of nonunion competition to protect the community from union monopolies.[59]

If, by chance, the unions refused to behave, the federal courts remained on duty as effective custodians of the public interest. They proved especially decisive in making Hoover's version of union rights consistent with that of the Constitution. In case after case, judges declared attempts by trade unions to organize an entire industry or to uproot nonunion competition criminal conspiracies to monopolize interstate commerce in violation of the Sherman Act. If an inferior federal court happened to rule that the Clayton Act and elementary justice allowed trade unionists to combat nonunion employees or employers, the Supreme Court usually promptly overruled.[60] More often, the district courts enjoined union efforts to organize nonunion firms as prima facie criminal conspiracies, as happened several times to the UMW.[61] And, finally, when in 1927 a Supreme Court majority overruled district and appeals court decisions in favor of union stonecutters who refused to work on nonunion materials, Brandeis delivered a scathing dissent. "If, on the undisputed facts of the case," he lectured his colleagues, "refusal to work can be enjoined, Congress erected by the Sherman Act and the Clayton Act an instrument for imposing restraints upon labor which reminds of involuntary servitude."[62] Such, indeed, was the case as the 1920s drew to an end.

Yet Republican policies and practices seemed to work. Americans, millions of workers included, celebrated GOP prosperity, the "Golden Glow," and Hoover's new era. By 1927 and 1928 the number of strikes had declined to the level of the

1880s. As Republican candidate for president in 1928, Hoover promised to continue his party's labor policies, which promoted prosperity and harmonious relations between workers and employers. And a labor leader whose union had suffered more than most from Republican prosperity, John L. Lewis, delivered trade unionism's most fulsome campaign speech for Hoover. Speaking over a national radio network on October 17, Lewis credited the Republican candidate with having created "a new economic order" based on high wages, mass consumption, and a rising standard of living. To continue Hoover's "economic revolution" and guarantee the elimination of poverty, Lewis demanded that his listeners vote for Hoover. Republicans were so pleased with Lewis's speech that they published it as a pamphlet under the title "Hoover's Tonic Safest for Industry" and distributed it widely among workers.[63]

Hoover, the Depression, and Labor

The Republican accommodation with organized labor failed to survive Hoover's first year in power, for it had been built on that old Republican amalgam of tariffs, prosperity, high wages, and the full dinner pail. When the financial panic of October 1929 and the ensuing depression emptied workers' lunch buckets, there was little else the Hoover administration had to offer them. If Hoover proved more ambitious and adventurous in using federal power to combat economic depression than any of his predecessors as president, his policies and programs benefited business and agriculture more than labor. True, he encouraged and cajoled businessmen not to lay off workers or to cut wages. And for a time, at least, employers heeded the president's advice.

As the depression persisted and inventories mounted, businessmen had no choice but to reduce both employment and wages. The deeper the economy slid, the more daring Hoover became. He made federal funds available to agriculture through open-market purchases of farm products; he used the Reconstruction Finance Corporation to provide federal funds and credit to large banks, railroads, and industries. For workers and unions, however, there were not even crumbs to be had from the federal groaning board. Hoover resisted all pleas for direct federal relief for the unemployed, insisting that traditional private charities and local and state agencies could manage the problem in the customary American manner.[64]

As unemployment mounted in 1930 and 1931, unions suffered as much as individual workers. In the words of one UMW organizer, his area lacked enough union members to form a baseball team. Most unions lost members, few could sustain strikes, and such once flourishing unions as the UMW and the International Ladies Garment Workers' Union (ILGWU) verged on bankruptcy.[65]

Even when industrialists suggested to Hoover that the time may have come to promote trade unionism, the president remained unmoved. By 1931 the bituminous coal industry was in such bad shape that one large operator remarked, "Personally, I would much prefer to deal with the United Mine Workers than with these ruthless, price-cutting, wage-cutting operators who are a detriment to the industry." He urged the president to consider a plan to unionize the coal industry totally in order to eliminate cutthroat competition and establish a uniform livable wage everywhere. "Please think this over carefully," he asked Hoover, "and let me know what comments you have to make of a constructive nature that will benefit the industry." Hoover had no constructive comments. Instead, he sent the mine owners and John L. Lewis to see the secretaries of commerce and labor (Robert P. Lamont and William Doak, respectively), who were equally unreceptive to suggestions for a federal role in the coal industry. When the UMW influenced its friends in Congress to introduce legislation providing for the abrogation of antitrust laws in return for the recognition of trade unionism, the administration used its power to thwart such legislation.[66]

The congressional elections of 1930 altered the balance of power in Washington. Democrats in alliance with Progressive Republicans took control of the House while the large GOP majority in the Senate practically vanished. Suddenly legislation that organized labor had been demanding for twenty-five years — substantive reform of the much-abused labor injunction — seemed a real possibility. Ever since the Wilkerson injunction of 1922, sentiment had been building in all sectors of the political community for reform. The Taft Court's labor decisions stimulated such sentiment. Trade unionists and their congressional allies sought to restore the protections for labor that they thought had been won in the Clayton Act. Liberal scholars and attorneys such as Felix Frankfurter, E. E. Witte, and Donald Richberg urged revisions in equity procedures. And even good conservative Republicans like Senator George Wharton Pepper joined the reform advocates. Pepper and his ilk favored reforms suggested more than twenty years earlier by Theodore Roosevelt — not abolition of the labor injunction but procedural safeguards that would eliminate most ex parte hearings, require formal affidavits, and provide jury trials for all indirect contempts of court. From 1924 to 1932, however, every effort to offer unions relief from the labor injunction failed. Bar associations and employers' associations flooded Congress with letters and petitions in defense of the injunction. Republican leaders in Congress resisted change. The administrations of Coolidge and Hoover never supported such legislation. And even the labor movement split internally and with its congressional friends over how to obtain relief from the labor injunction.[67]

In 1928, however, Frankfurter, Richberg, and Witte drafted an injunction relief bill that they assured the chief advocate of reform in the Senate, George Norris, would pass constitutional scrutiny. In fact, their bill offered trade unionists everything they wanted and more. It declared the yellow-dog contract unenforceable in federal law, specified all the procedural reforms that such conservatives as Pepper favored, and stated that it was the public policy of the United States to endorse workers' rights to form unions of their own choosing free from employer coercion with the right to bargain collectively. And it specified a whole array of trade union practices, which federal courts would not be permitted to enjoin. Yet for almost four years, Norris could not get his bill to the floor. The AFL refused to endorse it and the administration opposed it.[68]

By 1932 everything had changed. The AFL fell into line behind the Norris Bill. The new Congress had large majorities in both houses favorable to action. On February 23, Norris formally introduced his anti-injunction bill into the Senate. Less than a week later, on March 1, the bill passed by a margin of 75–5, after only perfunctory debate and opposition. (The opposition never commanded more than 16 votes for amendments to cripple the bill.) Representative Fiorello LaGuardia introduced an almost identical bill in the House on March 8, and it, too, passed by a vote of 362–14. Because there were minor discrepancies between the two bills, a joint congressional conference committee had to resolve them. By March 18 the loose ends were tied and the Norris-LaGuardia Act was sent to the president for his signature.[69]

Although the administration had earlier tried to dilute the anti-injunction bill and to involve the most intransigent antiunion business leaders in negotiations about it, Hoover decided he had no choice but to sign the bill. A veto would only arouse further hostility among trade unionists and be overridden in Congress.[70]

In March 1932, then, organized labor had achieved special status in federal labor law. An overwhelming congressional majority had rendered the yellow-dog contract unenforceable in federal courts, stringently restricted the grounds on which labor injunctions might be granted, and declared trade unionism and collective bargaining to be public policy. Congress had extended to all workers the protections hitherto reserved for railroad workers under the Erdman Act and the Railway Labor Act of 1926. In the winter of 1932, however, this new union bill of rights was more a promise than a redemption.

Beneath the surface, though, forces were at work that would make federal labor policies serve the interests of trade unionism. W. Jett Lauck, John L. Lewis's economic adviser, sensed the changes in the popular and political barometers and advised his boss: "I am sure that *now* affords an opportunity which will never occur again for generations. You could take the leadership of . . . all classes of organized labor . . . farmers, bankers, business men and industrial leaders . . . a movement of real industrial statesmanship and accomplishment which you would start and lead to success." When Lewis balked at such grandiose notions, Lauck reminded him, "You are a Shakespearean scholar and you know that 'There is a tide in the affairs of men which taken at ebb leads on to victory,' or words to that effect." Lewis was tempted but in the summer of 1931 not yet ready to act.[71] Finally, in February 1933, a month before Franklin D. Roosevelt became president, Lewis told the Senate Finance Committee that the time had come to free industry from the grip of the investment bankers, to control prices and production in the national interest, to stimulate purchasing power among the masses of working people, and to offer wage and salary earners direct participation in the management of industry. It was time that labor had a new deal in the American economy, politics, and society.[72]

The New Deal

Labor Revolution,

Part 1, 1933–1936

In the late winter of 1933 few Americans knew precisely what to expect of their new president, Franklin Delano Roosevelt. Labor leaders shared the common perplexity. And they also shared the common fears concerning an economy in which between 13 million and 15 million men and women were jobless and in which by March 3, one day before the inauguration, most banks had closed their doors. Both the nineteenth-century model of entrepreneurial capitalism and Herbert Hoover's "cooperative" version had failed; the future of the people's republic itself appeared to be in doubt. "Even the iron hand of a national dictator," lamented the Republican governor of Kansas, Alfred M. Landon, "is in preference to a paralytic stroke."[1]

More than most Americans, the labor leaders knew what they wanted from the new administration. Most of all, they desired to rebuild the relationship that had existed between the AFL and the federal government during the previous Democratic administration of Woodrow Wilson. They expected the Department of Labor to serve as a conduit to the White House for trade unionism's policies and goals. Again they looked to a Democratic Congress to enact laws protective of working people and their labor movement. And again they relied on a friendly president to promote the growth of trade unionism under the aegis of the AFL.

Roosevelt seemed precisely the chief executive that labor wanted. His previous federal experience had occurred as an assistant secretary of the navy in the Wilson administration, a position in which he had been a central actor in the implementation of wartime labor policy. As governor of New York from 1928 through 1932, Roosevelt had maintained excellent relations with the state's labor movement, proved his strong commitment to protective factory and welfare legislation, and used his executive power and influence to succor the unemployed during the Great Depression. As candidate for president in 1932, he rallied those labor leaders customarily sympathetic to the Democratic party around his banner, and he dispatched a special emissary to inveigle the support (if not the open endorsement) of John L. Lewis.[2] What more could labor desire in a chief executive?

Much more, in fact — which proved a great disappointment to union leaders. The AFL expected Roosevelt to turn to the labor movement for his secretary of labor, to choose someone like the first occupant of the office, William B. Wilson. Instead the president selected Frances Perkins, who, from the AFL's perspective, brought two grave deficiencies to the office. First, she was a woman among trade unionists who prized their manliness. Few labor leaders (perhaps none) could conceive of a woman dealing effectively with grasping businessmen and tough union negotiators. Second, and not necessarily more important, Perkins lacked both personal and institutional links to the labor movement. Moreover, she was not known as an advocate of independent trade unionism. Rather, she perceived her function to be that of an advocate for all working people, among whom trade unionists were a small minority. This especially worried labor leaders because they knew that Roosevelt shared "Madame Secretary's" instinctive feelings on the labor question. The president and his secretary of labor were patrician reformers eager to assist the less fortunate from a sense of noblesse oblige. Labor much preferred a William B. Wilson type who could act as a real voice for trade unionism in the presence of a president unfamiliar with the history, practices, and aims of trade unionism. This was especially important because Roosevelt would exercise powers unprecedented in the peacetime history of the American presidency.[3] Indeed, from the moment he mounted the inaugural platform, Roosevelt would reach for the sort of power Woodrow Wilson commanded during war.

The similarities between the early labor policies of the New Deal (1933–35) and those of the wartime Wilson administration are almost uncanny. In his inaugural address, Roosevelt compared the current economic crisis directly to the national experience during World War I, called upon citizens to unite patriotically in combating economic depression, and promised to use his presidential power precisely as he would against a foreign enemy. Such analogies were not unique to the new president. They were part of a common discourse in the winter of 1933. In testimony before the Senate Finance Committee on February 17, 1933, John L. Lewis asked his auditors to act as if the nation were threatened by a foreign enemy, as if we faced an emergency comparable to 1917–18. He demanded the creation of a board of emergency control composed of representatives from industry, labor, agriculture, and finance, which would have plenary power to reduce the hours of labor, guarantee the right of collective bargaining, stabilize prices, and implement national economic planning. Some may criticize such a proposal as the beginning of a dictatorship, conceded Lewis, but "it is the form of procedure resorted to . . . during the crisis of World War, when the enemy was three thousand miles from our shore. Today the enemy is within the boundaries of the nation, and is stalking through every community and home, and, obviously, this proposal is the most democratic form of internal regulation that can be devised to deal with our economic and industrial collapse." Just so, agreed Roosevelt, a little more than ten days later.[4]

Not only ideas but also people linked the Wilson and Roosevelt years. Roosevelt had served in the Wilson administration, and Lewis had risen to power as a labor leader during and just after World War I. Bernard Baruch who headed the War Industries Board in Wilson's Washington; Louis Wehle, who had formulated World War I labor policies for the Army and Navy Departments; and Felix Frankfurter, who had played a central role in devising Wilsonian wartime labor policies, all influenced Roosevelt and the early New Deal. They were not alone. Hugh Johnson, who had been Baruch's loyal subaltern on the WIB during World War I, became the administrator of the early New Deal's primary economic planning agency, the National Recovery Administration (NRA). Men and women who had served apprenticeships on Wilson's Commission on Industrial Relations and his National War Labor Board returned to Washington to make and implement New Deal labor policy. The personal connections between Wilson's and Roosevelt's Washington multiplied beyond estimation.

The former wartime Wilsonians re-created in New Deal Washington the same contradictory policies, conflicting interests, and petty bureaucratic squabbling that had plagued World War I federal labor policies. Just as fifteen years earlier, federal officials beseeched all Americans to sublimate their more selfish interests to a common struggle against an alien enemy, the New Dealers demanded a similar spirit in their war against economic crisis. Those officials who had served their apprenticeships in the WIB or similar agencies valued a national unity in which prevailing private social and economic power relationships were set more firmly in place. They expected capital and labor to cooperate without altering the relative distribution of power between the two. The New Dealers, who had apprenticed in the Labor Department and the NWLB, and had come under the influence of Frankfurter, Frank P. Walsh of the CIR, and John R. Commons, again planned to use a national crisis to redistribute social, economic, and political power. They looked to the labor movement as the most effective single institution through which to create a more equitable social and economic order. And Roosevelt, like Wilson before him, fluctuated erratically between implementing the policies of the conservative reformers and their more radical adversaries.

Yet there were also essential, inescapable differences between the crises of

World War I and the Great Depression. The former demanded national unity in a situation in which all Americans could identify a common enemy and in which production and labor supply were rapidly reaching their respective limits. In 1917 and 1918 economic realities magnified the power of workers and their trade unions, required the government to allocate scarce labor and resources among alternative uses, and necessitated measures to restrain runaway price inflation. By contrast, in 1933 and 1934, federal officials pleaded for unity among citizens who identified each other as the enemy (labor versus capital; Main Street versus Wall Street; people versus plutocrats) and in an economy in which goods and labor were in excess supply. Now economic realities deflated labor power; demanded that the government put surplus labor and resources to use; and required price and wage inflation. It was a situation for which the New Dealers were unprepared by history, personal experiences, and, in many cases, inclination.[5]

One other factor clearly distinguished early New Deal Washington from Wilson's more rustic national capital. The leading congressional sponsors of labor legislation in the Wilson years came from the southern wing of the Democratic party. Labor's "magna carta," the Clayton Act, and the eight-hour bill for railroad workers, the Adamson Act, bore the names of Southerners. During the Roosevelt years, labor's friends in Congress came from the North and the West, both among Democrats and a small minority of so-called progressive Republicans. In the Senate especially, Democrat Robert F. Wagner of New York, Democrat David I. Walsh of Massachusetts, Democrat Edward Costigan of Colorado, Republican Robert LaFollette, Jr., of Wisconsin, Republican George Norris of Nebraska, and Republican Bronson Cutting of New Mexico advocated the cause of trade union-ism and were usually far in advance of the president on labor matters. The Southern Democrats now increasingly moved to the sidelines on labor matters, often influenced the president to modify the proposals introduced by labor's congressional advocates, and sometimes even resisted legislation to assist labor.

Certain causes, moreover, were never on the agenda, even for the most extreme New Deal reformers. First, all influential New Dealers, in whatever branch of government, favored a form of capitalism in which private institutions remained as free from intrusive state control as was compatible with social and economic stability. Socialism or full-scale state planning remained dreams shared by "uto-pians," not the central concern of policymakers. Nor did any New Dealers seek consciously to turn the world they inherited upside down. Instead they sought to make that world more equitable, workable, and livable. In seeking such goals, the New Dealers precipitated social, economic, and political struggles of unprece-dented proportions.

New Deal policies compelled Americans who shared abstract basic principles of democracy, equality, private property, and free enterprise to wage intense struggles over the translation of such principles into practice. They forced businesspeople, who never ceased screaming and struggling against the New Deal, to accommodate themselves to a new order of capital-labor relations. They required labor leaders to relinquish a portion of their treasured tradition of voluntarism and the private ordering of employment relations in order to establish unionism in all the basic sectors of the economy. And the New Deal demanded that all citizens respect the coercive state even in peacetime, whereas custom favored more voluntary principles. Finally, further New Deal reforms would unfold as much by accident as plan, and then largely as a result of the relentless push and shove of competing interest groups set into motion by Roosevelt's reforms.

NIRA and Section 7a: Success or Failure?

Labor policy and the role of trade unions did not bulk large in the minds of the president and his advisers as they plotted their initial response to the economic crisis. They were far more concerned with restoring vitality to the industrial and agricultural sectors of the economy than with enabling workers to organize. New Dealers were also eager to feed the hungry, succor the helpless, and employ the idle. They preferred to accomplish their aims by enlisting the cooperation of industrial and agricultural leaders rather than by igniting conflicts among competing economic interests and classes. Many presidential advisers, and Roosevelt himself, were uncertain whether the labor movement would participate cooperatively with their program. The AFL's favored antidepression prescription, the compulsory thirty-hours bill (with no reduction in wages), introduced in Congress by Senator Hugo Black of Alabama, did not fit into the New Deal scheme. For the Black Bill elicited bitter opposition from industrialists whose support Roosevelt desired and acid criticism from economists who believed that its passage would drive up labor costs and further retard economic recovery.

Yet Roosevelt preferred to enlist the AFL in the New Deal rather than force it into opposition. As his advisers drafted legislation to stimulate industrial recovery, they welcomed suggestions from such labor leaders as William Green, John L. Lewis, and Sidney Hillman. The result of this collaboration and of administration brainstorming was the National Industrial Recovery Act (NIRA), which provided minimal guarantees to organized and unorganized workers. Drafted primarily to exempt industrial concerns from the antitrust laws and to place the coercive power of the state behind efforts by industrialists to unite competitive firms in trade associations that would allocate markets and rationalize production, the NIRA also required participating firms to guarantee their workers minimum wages, maximum hours, the elimination of child labor, and the right to form unions of their own choosing. The proposed bill's Section 7a, the administration's major concession to the AFL, reaffirmed established federal policy. It reiterated language found in the Railway Labor Act of 1926 and the Norris-LaGuardia Act of 1932, which declared that it was the policy of the federal government to endorse the right of workers to form unions free from employer interference and to bargain collectively with their employers.[6]

Without exception, labor leaders endorsed the NIRA as introduced in Congress. By contrast, the leading industrialists vociferously opposed Section 7a, and they found friends in the Senate who criticized the section as a form of class legislation. Senator Pat Harrison of Mississippi, for example, proposed an amendment to the section which sanctioned company unions and the yellow-dog contract. Opposed on the floor by Senators Wagner, Norris, and Democrat Burton K. Wheeler of Montana, the Harrison amendment went down to defeat, 46–31, its supporters consisting of Republicans and Southern Democrats. The NIRA emerged from Congress on June 16 with its labor clauses intact.[7]

Labor leaders such as John L. Lewis proclaimed Section 7a the greatest single advance for human rights since Abraham Lincoln's Emancipation Proclamation. Secretary of the Interior Harold I. Ickes suggested that passage of the NIRA represented more than a New Deal. "It's a new world. People feel free again. . . . It's like quitting the morgue for the open woods."[8] The employers' hostility to Section 7a and the provisions of the rejected Harrison amendment, however, hinted at troubles to come in implementing labor's rights under the NIRA.

From its birth in June 1933 to its unmourned death in May 1935, the National Recovery Administration (NRA), the agency created to implement the provisions of the NIRA, found itself mired in controversy on the labor question. Part of the NRA's difficulties arose from the personalities and policies of its chief administrator, Hugh Johnson, and his assistant, Donald Richberg. The mercurial Johnson forever intruded into disputatious labor conflicts, worsening already bad situations. He promised trade unionists and employers mutually irreconcilable labor policies, and he persistently engendered conflicts with friends as well as enemies. Richberg began as a labor lawyer and an advocate of trade unions, but by 1933 he was midway through a political journey that took him from the left to the right. As an NRA administrator, he now saw himself more as a public defender than a union advocate. In this spirit, Richberg issued several antilabor edicts that prompted labor leaders to condemn him as a turncoat.

Johnson and Richberg, however, were only a part of the problem. More fundamental was the bitter-end resistance to trade unionism from the largest employers and some of their smaller brethren. Roosevelt compounded this employer resistance by repeatedly diluting his administration's commitment to the AFL and independent trade unionism whenever it seemed politic. In fact, in his original statement upon signing the NIRA, the president assured industrialists: "This is not a law to foment discord and it will not be executed as such. This is a time for mutual confidence and help."[9]

Labor both gained and lost from Roosevelt's approach to the implementation of the NIRA's labor provisions. To the president, power sometimes appeared to be the sole reality. Where trade unions already had power or were in the process of amassing it, Roosevelt helped labor leaders accumulate more of it. Where employers maintained the upper hand and unionists failed to build strength, Roosevelt's policies buttressed the power of industry. As the president, the NRA administrators, and special labor committees struggled to create a consistent New Deal labor policy in 1933 and 1934, they simultaneously generated a massive movement for trade unionism and thwarted its realization.

Developments in the coal-mining industry showed how Roosevelt and the New Deal generated an upsurge in unionism among workers. Already a decrepit institution in 1929 on the eve of the Depression, the UMW was even weaker in early 1933. By June 23, however, merely one week after the passage of the NIRA, Van Bittner, the union leader and organizer reported from West Virginia that the UMW's organizing campaign was like a dream, too good to be true. "We expect to be through with every mine in the state and have every miner under the jurisdiction of our union by the first of next week." Even heretofore antiunion southern West Virginia fell under the sway of the UMW. Similar patterns of unionization unfolded in every major bituminous coalfield. Employers seemed helpless in the face of union claims that the president (whether it was Roosevelt or Lewis was never specified) expected miners to enroll in the UMW.[10]

Miners clearly thought that they acted on the mandate of the New Deal. Operators did not know what to think. In the words of one impartial observer of the UMW organizing campaign, the operators "stood by with one eye on Washington, wondering what it was all about and not sure of themselves when the organizers kept reassuring the men that the federal government was behind them and their right to organize." Before the mine owners realized what had happened, he added, the UMW had completed its organization.[11]

For the union, the next step was to achieve recognition and a place on the NRA soft-coal code authority. Here, again, Roosevelt assisted labor out of his respect for power. By organizing the miners, the UMW had the potential to disrupt economic recovery through strikes. When employers refused to recognize the union and resisted full UMW participation on the code authority, strikes paralyzed coal production, especially in Pennsylvania. Consequently, both at private conferences in the White House and through informal communications, Roosevelt urged the mine operators to come to terms with the union. Unlike Hoover, Roosevelt lost no sleep over the union's ability to monopolize labor by organizing every mine in the country. As long as John L. Lewis agreed to cooperate in the president's recovery program, Roosevelt saw no reason to thwart the UMW's demands. Threatened by the union on the one hand, and besieged by the president on the other, the mine owners on September 21 conceded to every union demand except the union shop. The Bituminous Coal Code provided for full and equal participation by the UMW; operators promised to bargain with the union; Southern Appalachian firms also recognized the union; and operators agreed to check off union dues. As one northern mine owner wrote to Lewis, "I want to congratulate you on getting a code . . . which puts the United Mine Workers in every bituminous mine in the country."[12]

The mine owner's letter disclosed one reason for the union's revival in the soft-coal industry. A sick industry, beset by excess productive capacity, cutthroat competition, and enormous wage disparities, bituminous coal saw in the NRA code and the UMW a cure for its economic ailments. The code would temper competition, and the triumph of unionism would stabilize the industry's principal production cost, wage rates. This, then, was a case in which the interests of mine owners, miners, and the president coincided.[13]

For another, more significant, group of mine owners, the UMW appeared to be more peril than promise. The large basic steel companies all owned their own coal mines. Known collectively as the "captive mines," they produced solely for their corporate parents and did not sell their product on the open market. Among them there was no competition for customers and no substantial differentials in production costs. Thus, for the "captive mines," unionization offered no apparent benefits. For them, recognition of the UMW threatened the open-shop policy, which all the major steel companies practiced. The owners of the "captive mines" steadfastly resisted union recognition.

Unable to stop their miners from joining the UMW, the steel companies sought to defeat unionization by other means. They readily agreed to provide their workers precisely the same wages, hours, and conditions that the bituminous code guaranteed in the commercial mines. Several of the "captive mines," most notably the Frick properties owned by United States Steel, began to establish employee representation plans and company unions. All the steel companies, however, refused to bargain with the UMW.

Such employer recalcitrance tested Roosevelt's labor policies. In this instance, the president again showed himself to be respectful of power and the ally of a union that wielded it. The UMW used its power to strike the commercial as well as "captive" mines to compel presidential intervention in its dispute with the steel companies. Mindful of how coal strikes threatened economic recovery, Roosevelt on October 4 wrote to Myron Taylor, chief operating officer of United States Steel, that the term "working conditions" in the bituminous code encompassed the dues checkoff and collective bargaining. "I beg you to remember," the president implored the corporate executive, "that the old doctrine of 'pigs is pigs' applies. Coal is coal mining . . . as a matter of public policy, I must hold that the conditions of work in the captive coal mines must conform to the conditions of work in the average run of commercial coal mines." At a subsequent White House conference and in correspondence, Roosevelt refused to be swayed by the steel companies' claims that their labor policies protected the liberty of individual employees and guarded the right to work against union tyrannies. The president reiterated his principle of "pigs is pigs" and demanded that the captive mines bargain collectively with their employees' representatives. Roosevelt's firmness compelled the steel companies to agree to a compromise under which the National Labor Board (NLB) would conduct representation elections at all the captive mines in which employees would select representatives with whom the companies would bargain collectively.[14]

At the actual elections in late November, the miners in twenty out of thirty cases voted overwhelmingly for representative slates consisting of John L. Lewis, Philip Murray, Tom Kennedy (the three top UMW officials), and the respective district union directors. Still, the steel companies refused to bargain with the union, insisting through their attorneys, that legitimate bargaining could occur only between employers and their individual employees, not an outside institution. Finally, in January 1934, when the companies came to terms, they signed an agreement with Lewis, Murray, and Kennedy as individuals, not with the UMW as an organization. The NLB declined to rule whether such a contract constituted union recognition.[15]

The resolution of this dispute exposed flaws in early New Deal labor policy. Compelled by the president and the NLB to hold representation elections, to check off union dues, and even to bargain with union representatives, the steel companies refused to concede the principle of union recognition. They intended not to allow unions to dilute company authority. They rarely bargained in good faith, they schemed to replace independent unions with company unions, and they discharged militant union employees.[16] The steel companies' antiunion policies and tactics were not isolated incidents but essential elements in the basic corporate response to New Deal labor policies.

Struggles between workers, newly aroused to demand their rights, and employers, equally firm in resisting the upsurge in unionism, affected other sectors of the economy. In the summer of 1933 worker militancy resulted in a wave of strikes reminiscent of the prewar and World War I eras. The total number of strikes in the last half of 1933 exceeded that for any full year since 1921.

The pattern of union activism was determined in large measure by the number of firms and the average size of the firms in each industry. Where firms were highly competitive and wages formed their principal production cost, such as in the garment trades, collective bargaining became the standard practice. Thus the ILGWU rose from financial bankruptcy to a mass membership in the women's garment industry, and the ACWA tripled its membership in the men's trade.[17] In competitive industries, the AFL's more stable unions had always bargained with employers; now the economic recovery precipitated by the NRA's promise of higher prices brought an increase in union membership. But where large firms had rarely dealt with unions and had no desire to do so, they repulsed every effort by their workers to organize in 1933. Thus the strike wave that erupted in the summer of 1933, and especially those strikes that proved most difficult to settle, concerned the right to organize and union recognition in the steel, automobile, and electrical manufacturing industries. These disputes, moreover, imperiled Roosevelt's plans for economic recovery.

Hugh Johnson desperately sought to quell the industrial unrest. Convinced that workers acted on the mistaken belief that the president and the NRA expected them to join independent unions, Johnson issued a formal statement on July 7 proclaiming that "manifestly the purpose of the Act [NIRA] is to create and preserve harmonious relations and to prevent industrial strife and class conflicts." To make his meaning even clearer, he stressed that "it is not the duty of the Administration to act as an agent to unionize labor in any industry and . . . it will not so act."[18] Johnson's public statement notwithstanding, workers continued to unionize and demand recognition as their basic right under New Deal labor policy.

Finally, on August 5, Roosevelt attempted to restrain industrial unrest through the creation of a National Labor Board (NLB) authorized to investigate, mediate, and settle labor disputes under the terms of the NIRA and the president's Re-employment Agreement, which bound all employers to respect Section 7a. The NLB was clearly patterned on Woodrow Wilson's NWLB. It had a tripartite membership, with three representatives each from labor and industry, and a chair who represented the public, Senator Wagner. Like the NWLB's Frank Walsh, Wagner advocated industrial democracy and trade unionism. Like the NWLB, the NLB had amorphous authority and no legal mandate to enforce its decisions. It depended on the voluntary cooperation of employers and unions. Absent that, it could only ask Johnson or the president to penalize uncooperative parties.[19]

Despite its vague mandate and lack of power, the NLB, as directed by Wagner, acted forcefully. Not only did the board intervene in numerous labor disputes; more important, it enunciated policies conducive to the growth and triumph of independent trade unionism. It elaborated its basic principles through a decision made in a dispute affecting the full-fashioned hosiery industry in the Reading, Pennsylvania, district. The so-called Reading Formula encompassed several basic features. First, it compelled the affected parties to declare a truce while the board investigated. Second, it required employers to rehire all strikers without discrimination or prejudice. Third, it provided for a secret ballot representation election conducted by the board in which all eligible workers could participate and choose their own representatives as bargaining agents. Those elected agents might be outsiders — that is, independent union officials — and they would be authorized to bargain for all employees, a form of exclusive majority representation. And fourth, the NLB ordered employers to bargain collectively with their employees' elected representatives.[20]

In subsequent cases, the board refined its doctrine and began to elaborate a "common law" of labor relations. Its "common law" focused on three elements essential to equitable and democratic industrial relations. The law must protect workers from any form of employer coercion, however benign it might appear. Thus the board ordinarily found any company union to be a form of coercion. It defended the secret representation election as the only fair means to establish employee preferences. And it maintained that employers must recognize and bargain with unions freely chosen by their workers. Also, more often than not, the NLB ruled in favor of exclusive majority representation.[21]

The NLB's new "common labor law" aroused vociferous opposition from employers and also vigorous opposition within the administration reminiscent of such disputes during World War I. Employers who had established employee representation plans (ERPs) and company unions many years earlier, and the far larger number who had created them after the passage of NIRA, joined to criticize the NLB's condemnation of company unions as coercive devices. They found willing allies in the NRA administrators — Johnson and Richberg, who acted much like their World War I predecessors on the WIB, Bernard Baruch and John Ryan. On August 23, Johnson and Richberg publicly issued an interpretation of Section 7a that eliminated exclusive majority union representation, endorsed the open shop, and sanctioned noncoercive company unions. In defending the right of employers and employees to bargain individually and also to form company unions, they declared: "The law is not intended to enthrone any national labor organization or to dissolve any local organization."[22]

Within the administration, the advocates and opponents of independent trade unionism went their separate ways, each in turn seeking the ultimate sanction of the president. The NLB had great success in implementing its labor "common law" in the vast majority of cases it handled that concerned firms with between one and 250 employees (only two NLB elections covered units of more than 1,000 workers). Its most effective work resolved disputes affecting competitive firms that could not survive strikes.[23] Elsewhere the Johnson-Richberg approach prevailed. In cotton textiles, the administrators of the NRA code effectively eliminated the influence of trade unionists and usually ruled in favor of employers.[24] And early in October, Johnson and Richberg seemed to win the president's backing. Speaking on October 7 at the formal dedication of the Samuel Gompers Memorial in Washington, Roosevelt recalled Gompers's public service during World War I, especially the labor leader's pledge to maintain the status quo in industrial relations. The president specifically compared the current Depression to the Great War and asked all citizens to wage the new battle with comparable harmony. "Just as in 1917 we are seeking to pull in harness; just as in 1917, horses that kick over the traces will have to be put in a corral."[25]

The public statements of Johnson and Richberg as well as Roosevelt's harsh words for unruly citizens heartened those employers who resisted the NLB. Large firms continued to combat unions and to form their own company worker organizations. In two cases, major corporations directly challenged the authority of the NLB, and won. The Wierton Steel Company, after first agreeing to a NLB representation election, proceeded to conduct its own election among employees on company premises with company-defined choices. Naturally, the company union won by an almost unanimous vote. A second firm, the Budd Company of Philadelphia, a leading manufacturer of automotive equipment, simply refused to cooperate with the board and hold any election. Urged by Wagner to endorse the NLB rulings in the *Wierton* and *Budd* cases, Roosevelt equivocated. On December 16 the president issued an executive order (6511), which endorsed the board but failed to enlarge its authority or provide it with coercive power. About all the executive order occasioned was a public blast against the NLB by the NAM, which called on all employers to reject NLB-ordered elections.[26]

Still, the struggle for the president's support persisted. On February 1, 1934, Wagner and the NLB thought they had won. Roosevelt issued another executive order, No. 6580. This one, however, endorsed the Reading Formula and empowered the board to hold representation elections after which it might certify the choice of the majority as the exclusive bargaining agent for all workers. Only three days later, on February 4, Johnson and Richberg issued yet another public statement, which repudiated the NLB and its Reading Formula. NRA Release No. 3125 interpreted Executive Order No. 6580 to permit proportional representation, that is multiple bargaining units in a single firm, and also company unions. Wierton, Budd, and the NAM took this interpretation as a legitimation of their policies.[27]

After almost one year of the New Deal, labor seemed at a loss. It had a good friend in the NLB, but the board lacked power. It retained its old enemies among the great corporations and found new ones in Johnson and Richberg. And the president seemed of two minds, occasionally endorsing the policies of the NLB but rarely putting presidential power behind them. Small wonder that many labor leaders dismissed the NRA as the national runaround and that the mass worker militancy of July through October 1933 had abated by February 1934. Once the unions had reconquered the smaller firms and the competitive sectors of the economy in which they had traditionally built a strong presence, the American labor movement appeared to reach the limits of its power. Once again — as in 1892, 1894, 1901, 1909, and 1919 — the concentrated corporations in the basic industries had defeated trade unionism and maintained the open shop.[28]

The Labor Upheaval and Federal Policy, January–June 1934

Labor's friends in Washington were frustrated by the failure of Section 7a and the NLB to protect the right of workers to organize. They were even more puzzled by Roosevelt's deference to powerful employers. Among labor's allies none was more unhappy than the chair of the NLB, Senator Robert Wagner. His experiences in that position had convinced Wagner that few employers would voluntarily concede to employees the right to organize and also that the NLB lacked effective power. The senator's commitment to independent trade unionism was especially firm among those prominent in shaping New Deal labor policy.

Wagner saw trade unionism as a vital factor in a comprehensive scheme to refashion social and economic power in the United States. Trade unions would not only protect workers against autocratic employers (in Wagner's own words during Senate debate, "what does it profit a man to have so-called 'political freedom' if he is made an economic slave?");[29] they would also ensure that the economy distributed its rewards more equitably. By redistributing income away from profits to wages, unions would eliminate the lack of mass purchasing power that had caused the Depression.

Wagner's beliefs paralleled those proclaimed twenty years earlier in the staff report of Frank P. Walsh's Commission on Industrial Relations. As the CIR had stressed and Wagner now reiterated in 1934, the United States suffered from the maldistribution of wealth and income and the absence of industrial democracy. For Wagner, the only way to eliminate industrial anarchy, gross disparities in income, and worker insecurity was through the growth of trade unionism. And to achieve the industrial democracy and "law and order in industry" in which he so firmly believed, Wagner realized that the national state must use its power to foster trade unionism.[30]

Early in 1934 Wagner assigned his congressional staff and lawyers working for the NLB to draft legislation that would accomplish his purposes. The senator's draftsmen proved to be astute legal artisans and historians. They designed a bill that simultaneously addressed constitutional objections, outlawed the employer practices that most decisively weakened unions, and enunciated the language of democracy and individualism. As introduced in the Senate on March 1, 1934, the

Wagner Labor Relations Bill proposed to eliminate strikes as a restraint on interstate commerce by declaring illegal those employer practices that thwarted workers' freedom and caused strikes. In offering his new bill, Wagner declared that workers needed independent organization and equal bargaining power with employers to ensure the wider distribution of income, the full flow of purchasing power, and the prevention of cyclical depressions. Only collective bargaining could accomplish those goals.

To effectuate collective bargaining, the bill outlawed company-dominated unions; required employers to recognize independent unions; mandated exclusive majority representation; and established a seven-person board (two from business and two from labor with advisory roles plus three representing the public with effective power) appointed by the president as an independent quasi-judicial agency modeled on the ICC and the Federal Trade Commission (FTC). In drafting and defending his bill, Wagner explicitly left space for established unions to continue their customary practices (the closed shop remained legal where state law sanctioned it), guaranteed the right of workers to strike, and endorsed the Labor Department's conciliation service.[31]

On March 14, formal hearings opened before the Senate Committee on Education and Labor, chaired by David Walsh of Massachusetts. Wagner appeared as the first witness for the bill and reiterated his now standard reasons in support of its passage. He reminded the audience that the bill was a necessary response to the realities of industrial life. It neither denied employers their legitimate rights nor granted employees rights unavailable to their employers. The NIRA had granted firms the authority to join together in trade associations, and the NRA had enabled companies to do so without obstacle. The Wagner Bill simply offered workers the same alternative, the right to form collective organizations without undue interference. It was, Wagner stressed, "a direct attempt to meet modern evils with modern remedies. . . . [It] is based upon the studies and disclosures of hundreds of people who have observed the processes by which some employers dominate unions."[32]

For the next week, NLB staff members, academics, and trade unionists testified in favor of Wagner's bill. They all touched on the same basic points as the senator did and offered only marginal suggestions for change. Speaking for the labor movement, Bill Green and John L. Lewis demanded one change in the bill. They insisted that the proposed labor relations board consist of an equal number of industry and labor representatives with an impartial chair to represent the public. Green and Lewis feared a board in which public appointees would have the decisive votes. It reminded them of the Railway Labor Board and other similar government agencies on which the public members ordinarily ruled against unions. They preferred instead the sort of arrangement that from labor's perspective had worked so well in the case of the NWLB. In Lewis's strong words, "Labor wants a chance to participate on equal terms with industry, and it wants to assume the responsibilities of such participation." Somewhat paradoxically, they also wanted the board to be placed in the Department of Labor, whose secretary they disliked. Notwithstanding labor's antipathy to Frances Perkins, Green and Lewis considered her department to be trade unionism's special bailiwick in Washington.[33]

Even before the Senate committee heard from the bill's opponents, President Roosevelt delivered an almost fatal blow to Wagner and labor. The automobile companies had been among the most recalcitrant antiunion employers since the passage of the NIRA. They resisted every effort by their workers to form unions. Their initial NRA industry code specifically authorized them to hire and fire on the basis of merit, which the automobile companies used to discharge union militants. By early 1934, however, the union members in the industry seemed numerous and militant enough to threaten a strike over the issue of recognition. Roosevelt feared that a strike in such a vital industry would retard economic recovery. The AFL and its affiliates in the industry hesitated to challenge concentrated corporate power. The result was a presidential compromise. The unions called off the threatened strike in return for presidential intervention. On March 25, Roosevelt announced his decision. He removed the automobile firms from the jurisdiction of the NLB and placed them instead under a special Automobile Board chaired by Leo Wolman and without direct union participation. The settlement ruled out exclusive majority representation and legitimated both proportional representation and company unions. It established a diluted form of job seniority, which scarcely protected union militants, and no basis for effective collective bargaining.[34]

Considering how little the March 25 settlement offered workers for relinquishing the right to strike, it was puzzling, to say the least, that Roosevelt, in announcing the agreement, warned trade unionists that they had responsibilities as well as rights and must obey them ethically and morally.[35] The terms of the automobile agreement and Roosevelt's public statement seemed to repudiate the most essential aspects of Wagner's bill. The president had apparently condemned majority representation, endorsed company unionism, neglected collective bargaining, and demanded that unions as well as firms be regulated by law.

The next day, March 26, Walsh's Senate committee began to hear testimony from the adversaries of Wagner's labor disputes bill. Now the radio networks broadcast the hearings nationally, providing a forum for the bill's critics unavailable to its advocates. Corporate America formed a solid phalanx in opposing Wagner's measure. Whether in the words of corporate executive officers, business association leaders, attorneys, or company union members, the script remained the same. The bill was unconstitutional because it failed to distinguish between manufacturing and commerce (the former of which was not subject to federal regulation) and because it denied employers due process of the law by making the proposed labor board prosecutor, judge, and jury, all in the absence of conventional legal rules of evidence. Wagner's rationale, claimed all his critics, was based on an alien theory of class conflict that sought to upset the normal American harmony between employers and employees by restraining the employers' right to communicate with workers in order to instill a cooperative spirit and company loyalty. Moreover, the bill was clearly one-sided as shown by its refusal to restrain union coercion and its grant to unions of rights without responsibilities. Worst of all, if passed, it would foment discord, instigate strikes, and retard economic recovery. Time and again, the critics referred to the automobile settlement and Roosevelt's public statement of March 25 in making their case.[36]

The impact of Roosevelt's action could be seen most clearly in Wagner's own equivocation. When James A. Emery, representing the NAM, demanded that the proposed bill be amended to encompass intimidation or coercion from any source, Wagner responded: "Now, I think the act ought to be amended just as you suggested, that is, intimidation when it comes from any source, either a trade organization, or a company union, or an employer, ought to be made an unfair labor practice." Wagner also conceded that company unions might indeed be the free choice of workers and that he would not want to outlaw such organizations. "The free choice of the worker is the only thing I am interested in. . . . I am not wedded to language. . . . If better language can be proposed, I am not adamant."[37]

As Wagner compromised, Roosevelt moved a mite closer to the senator's position. The president did so for his own exigent reasons. As winter passed into spring, labor militancy reawakened. A particularly nasty and violent citywide conflict erupted in Toledo in May and similar strikes broke out elsewhere. At a press conference on May 25 devoted largely to the new wave of strikes, Roosevelt referred off-the-record to the Wagner Bill, "I would like to have it very much."[38]

The next day Roosevelt received a part of his wish. On May 26, Senator Walsh presented to the Senate for action his committee's amended version of the original Wagner Bill. As amended, the bill excluded domestic servants, agricultural workers, family employees, and any establishment with ten or fewer workers from coverage. It prohibited neither the company union nor the closed shop. It promised to protect workers from coercion by their employers yet guaranteed employers the right to communicate with their employees and even to pay them regular wages for their services to company unions during working hours. "The policy of the Government," proclaimed Walsh's report, "is founded upon the theory of collective bargaining, not upon the theory of class war, a conception foreign to industrial conditions in this country." Hence the bill, as amended, clarified rather than extended existing law governing relations between employers and employees. In other words, it left the situation just where it had been before Wagner introduced his original legislation.[39]

Even Walsh's amended version of the Wagner act seemed too ambitious for Roosevelt. At a press conference on June 15, the president again endorsed proportional and minority representation under Section 7a and declined to favor the rights demanded by AFL unions.[40] The next day, June 16, Senate Majority Leader Joseph Robinson of Arkansas introduced in the Senate the administration's own substitute for the amended Wagner Bill. Called the National Industrial Adjustment Act, it proposed the creation of a National Labor Relations Board with the power to investigate industrial disputes and to hold representation elections. Out of deference to Roosevelt, Wagner endorsed it and entreated Senate progressives such as Robert LaFollette and Bronson Cutting not to amend it to death. Give us a year to educate the country, pleaded Wagner, and we will reintroduce our own effective labor relations bill at the next session. Reluctantly, LaFollette went along with the senator from New York after moving an amendment that stated that nothing in the bill shall impede or prevent workers from striking, which passed easily. As the bill sailed through the Senate on June 18 by an overwhelming majority, Cutting declared, "The new deal is being strangled in the house of its friends."[41]

Even before Public Resolution 44, as the bill was known, became law, Roosevelt did a little more strangling. On June 28 he created a separate Steel Labor Relations Board, which replicated the one established in the automobile industry and also averted a threatened strike by offering more to the companies than to the union.[42] And the next day, in issuing Executive Order No. 6763, which established the first NLRB composed of three public representatives not tied to industry or labor, Roosevelt explained that its purpose was to achieve industrial peace not to promote trade unionism and collective bargaining.[43]

How far P.R. 44 diverged from Wagner's original intentions was best indicated in a letter written by A. H. Young, a vice president of United States Steel, concerning the resolution's introduction in Congress. "My guess," he wrote, "is that Congress will today pass the joint resolution . . . and that will end for the time being at least many of our troubles in that respect. Personally, I view the passage of the joint resolution with equanimity . . . my personal opinion is that it is not going to bother us very much."[44]

Instead, the passage of P.R. 44 coincided with the most violent and massive strike wave of the early New Deal. At exactly the moment Congress debated Wagner's proposal for a new national labor policy, workers and employers waged bloody battle on the streets of Toledo, Ohio. After the president signed the new legislation, the violent street-fighting spread to Minneapolis–St. Paul, San Francisco, and Kohler, Wisconsin. That spring and summer farm laborers and ranchers battled in the agricultural valleys of California. And as summer passed into fall, textile workers walked off the job in a massive national uprising involving more than 350,000 men and women in mills spread from Maine to Alabama.[45]

This new strike wave again graphically exposed the contradictions at the core of early New Deal labor policy. To some extent, Roosevelt's rhetoric and the New Deal's promise of substantial reform precipitated unrest and militancy among workers. The heady ferment of the New Deal not only liberated more-conventional AFL labor leaders from old inhibitions, it also revitalized radical leftists of every variety. The struggle in Toledo united the local AFL leaders with independent leftists from the American Workers' party. The battle in the Twin Cities saw former Wobblies and ex-Communists lead the striking local Teamsters. In San Francisco, an Australian immigrant sailor and close associate of Communists, Harry Bridges, commanded the militant longshoremen and seamen, whose demands resulted in a citywide general strike. And in California's fertile valleys Communists led the agricultural strikes.[46]

Unlike the Republican presidents of the 1920s, Roosevelt maintained a real neutrality in the face of labor militancy. In Toledo, the Twin Cities, and San Francisco, where strikers demonstrated singular solidarity, paralyzed local business, and fought the public authorities to a draw, Roosevelt declined to use federal power to smash strikes. Instead he preferred to mediate the disputes from behind the scenes, where he urged the governors of the affected areas to encourage collective bargaining between the disputants. In these cases, Roosevelt's neutrality brought clear gains for the strikers.[47] In textiles and California agriculture, however, federal neutrality brought grief to the strikers. In those cases, employers were more united and powerful than their employees and could rely on local and state officials to repress labor militancy. Harassed by sheriffs and deputies, intimidated by state troops, and replaced by strikebreakers, the textile and agricultural workers lost their struggles.[48]

The Hiatus, July 1934–July 1935

The first NLRB appointed by Roosevelt under P.R. 44 thus stepped into a boiling cauldron of labor discontent. Its three members, Lloyd K. Garrison, former dean of the University of Wisconsin law school, Harry A. Millis, an economist from the University of Chicago, and Edwin S. Smith, a former state labor official from Massachusetts, sought to implement Section 7a's promises to workers. Their opinions and principles represented the acme of the John R. Commons–Progressive era solution to labor relations.

Like Commons and his Progressive epigones, Garrison and his colleagues on the NLRB believed firmly in the concept of law and order in industry. They were eager to build a common law of labor relations that would grant a worker a "property" right in his job comparable to the employer's established rights to use of capital, that would enable workers to form independent unions as the best instruments for defending job rights; and that would require employers to bargain with the representatives of such unions. By implementing these three principles of labor relations, the new common law concept of labor relations would domesticate and perhaps eliminate industrial warfare. Most important, labor's rights would be established and guaranteed by a quasi-judicial, quasi-administrative board composed of full-time professional experts in the field, whose knowledge, wisdom, and impartiality would protect the public interest. In other words, the first NLRB sought to practice the Progressive notion of "scientific expertise" in service to society.[49]

On August 30, 1934, in a decision concerning a dispute between a Buffalo auto parts firm (Houde Co.) and its workers, the NLRB enunciated the full scope of its common law of labor relations. In *Houde* the board ruled that Section 7a's fundamental purpose was the promotion of collective bargaining. Hence all employees had the right to organize and bargain collectively free from employer interference. The NLRB further declared that the representatives elected by the majority of Houde workers in a secret board ballot should be the exclusive bargaining agents for all the firm's employees with whom the firm had a duty to bargain. What Garrison's NLRB had done was really quite simple. It reiterated the principles first declared by the NLB in the case of the Reading full-fashioned hosiery dispute and subsequently reformulated more precisely in the original Wagner industrial disputes bill of February 1934. Supposedly, Roosevelt personally endorsed such a law of labor relations. When Philadelphia socialite and attorney Francis Biddle replaced Garrison as chair of the NLRB late in 1934, he reported that the Labor Department's solicitor, Charles Wyzanski, informed him that the president had said: "It certainly took great courage to make that Houde decision. That's the sort of thing we want."[50]

In fact, nothing had really changed concerning the implementation or enforcement of New Deal labor policy. The NLRB made its rulings; employers ignored them; Johnson and Richberg continued to thwart the board; and Roosevelt, as usual, equivocated. No sooner had the NLRB made its *Houde* ruling than industry spokespeople and the NAM called on employers to defy the board. Employers maintained that Roosevelt's automobile settlement of March 25 and the public statements of Johnson and Richberg had established proportional representation, individual bargaining, and company unions as legitimate aspects of national labor policy. The Justice Department apparently shared employers' sentiments because it declined to bring suit against Houde at the NLRB's request. Justice's disdain for the NLRB encouraged employers to boycott board hearings. Wyzanski informed the president that the NLRB "is about to break down." Having as yet no alternative labor policy, Roosevelt, rather than risking the collapse of the NLRB, suggested that Attorney General Homer Cummings bring suit against the Houde company. So advised, the Justice Department on November 30 brought suit to require enforcement of the NLRB ruling. But, as Cummings warned, the case was weak and the federal courts failed to affirm the NLRB ruling.[51]

Roosevelt remained of two minds concerning labor policy. Having committed himself to defending the NLRB in the *Houde* case, he proceeded in January 1935 to repudiate the board's policies in the newspaper and automobile industries. Responding to newspaper publishers' reaction to an NLRB ruling concerning the American Newspaper Guild, Roosevelt substantially curtailed the board's authority. In a letter made public on January 22 (allegedly written by Richberg with the aid of Louis Howe), the president declared that the NLRB lacked jurisdiction in areas where code authorities already handled labor matters. That policy not only denied the board jurisdiction over newspapers where an NRA code board existed, but also in automobiles, steel, textiles, petroleum, shipping, and elsewhere where many such boards functioned and often without a hint of labor influence.[52] Then on March 31, despite the formal protests of the AFL, Roosevelt extended the life of the automobile code with its provisions endorsing minority representation and company unions.[53]

Worse was soon to come for the NLRB. At the end of February 1935, a case that had originated under the old NLB, the one concerning Weirton Steel's refusal to permit a representation election, resulted in an official federal district court decision. A year earlier, Charles Wyzanski had observed that "it will be hard to find a judge sympathetic with the policy of Section 7(a)." He was not mistaken. On February 27, Judge John P. Nields ruled that manufacturing was not interstate commerce and that the federal government lacked the constitutional mandate to regulate relations between employers and employees. *U.S. Law Week* immediately observed that "labor has suffered its most crushing defeat since the enactment" of the NIRA.[54] Nield's ruling and those of other federal judges practically paralyzed the NLRB. In March, Thomas Emerson, a board attorney, reported that "in every case where the employer has not consented to the holding of an election and the board has been compelled to use its power to order an election, the employer has succeeded in tying up the enforcement of the order almost indefinitely in the courts." By then, NLRB chair Francis Biddle had also concluded that Section 7a and its enforcement by the NLRB was "merely the expression of a paper right, a sort of innocuous moral shibboleth. Such paper rights raise hopes, but when they are shattered the reaction is far worse than if they had never been written in the statute books."[55]

Now Robert Wagner was again ready to reenter the fray. A year earlier he had promised to reintroduce his industrial disputes legislation when the nation would be better prepared to welcome it. During that interim, the nation had indeed received a practical education in industrial warfare. Americans had witnessed a succession of violent strikes in which clashes among armed police, troops, and workers had caused scores of deaths and hundreds of injuries. And in November 1934 voters had elected a radical Congress, one totally dominated by Democrats and progressives. Now the stage was better set for Wagner.

On February 21, 1935, the senator from New York introduced labor relations legislation designed to clarify Section 7a and create a permanent NLRB with enforcement powers. Wagner stressed that his proposal was not new; instead it perfected the bill introduced the previous year. Again he defended his proposal in language redolent with old democratic republican themes. It was an effort, Wagner stressed, to guarantee workers their basic rights as American freemen: the right to choose how they wanted to be represented at work free from coercion by their bosses and at liberty to choose that most basic of all American forms, majority rule. If they preferred company unions as a matter of free choice, workers could have them. Only employer-dominated unions would be made illegal. If workers and employers voluntarily desired closed-shop arrangements where they were legal, they could negotiate them. His bill, Wagner asserted, simply enforced existing substantive rights, those already established by the Clayton Act, the Norris-LaGuardia Act, the Railway Labor Act of 1926 and its amendments of 1934. It required no one to join a union, nor did it mandate the closed shop. It intended to extend citizenship rights for the individual worker from the public arena to the private workplace. Finally, to mollify those who were fearful of industrial conflict, Wagner pledged that the purpose of his proposal was to eliminate the causes of strikes not to induce workers to strike.[56]

In all its essential respects, Wagner's 1935 bill imitated the one introduced a year earlier.[57] It was even drafted the same way, through the joint collaboration of NLRB staff attorneys and Wagner's own staff led by Leon Keyserling. The attorneys did redraft the preamble to demonstrate more forcefully the law's constitutionality. They spelled out precisely how strikes affected the flow of interstate commerce, cited a long string of Supreme Court precedents, especially in labor cases, which linked unions and interstate commerce, illustrated how the proposal codified existing federal labor law, and, of course, how it promoted the general welfare.[58]

The reaction to Wagner's new proposal also repeated the previous year's experience. The administration again acted reluctantly. Not a favorable word came from the White House, and Labor Secretary Perkins again urged that any NLRB be lodged in the Department of Labor. Labor leaders once more demanded the bill's enactment while insisting that the Labor Department remain responsible for enforcing federal labor policies. Green and Lewis shared Perkins's view about where the NLRB should be placed. And during the formal Senate and House committee hearings, which ran from March 11 through April 4, employers remained an unbroken phalanx in opposition. In the course of a year nothing had changed in the language of resistance. Employers still challenged the proposal's constitutionality, only now they cited Judge Nield's *Weirton* decision to prove their point. They castigated Wagner's law as class legislation alien to the American way and as so absolutely one-sided that it would generate a tidal wave of industrial conflict.[59]

Senate debate on the Wagner Bill, which this time was reported favorably by the Education and Labor Committee with only minor amendments to strengthen it, opened on May 15 and lasted for only two days. The supporters clearly enjoyed a substantial majority. Only one serious challenge to the bill arose, an amendment by Democrat Millard Tydings of Maryland in favor of company unions, which sought to legitimate them through the subterfuge of forbidding intimidation or coercion from any sources, including unions and workers. Tydings's amendment lost by a vote of 50–21. A number of border state and deep South Democrats joined the Republican recalcitrants in the affirmative, but the key Southern Democratic leaders joined the majority. On May 16, the Senate voted 63 to 12 to pass the Wagner Act, with only two conservative Democrats in opposition (a number of Southern Democrats did abstain).[60]

Not till a month later did the companion legislation (the Connery Bill) come before the House. There, too, on June 19, the proponents had an overwhelming majority. Despite token opposition from Republicans who bewailed class legislation and Southern Democrats who defended state rights against an intrusive federal state, the Connery Bill, after debate stringently limited by a procedural rule, passed by overwhelming majorities. The one truly substantive difference between Wagner's bill and the House version, Connery's proposal that the NLRB be placed in the Labor Department, lost 130–48 on a roll call vote.[61] Actually by the time the House debated the proposal, it had Roosevelt's support. The president had no choice. A Supreme Court decision of May 27, the so-called sick chicken, or Schechter, case in which the court unanimously declared Title I of the NIRA to be unconstitutional, left the administration without a labor policy. Wagner's proposal was now the only available alternative. Thus with Roosevelt wanting it, the Congressional Joint Conference Committee experienced no difficulty or delay in reaching a resolution mutually satisfactory to a majority in both Houses. And on July 5, 1935, the president signed the new legislation.[62]

The New Labor Policy and the
New Labor Movement, July 1935–July 1936

Since its passage in the summer of 1935 the Wagner Act has generated heated political and historical controversy. At that time and since, opponents deemed it a revolutionary break with American constitutional traditions, which excessively enlarged the power of the national state and intruded on purely private economic transactions. Some members of the far left, mostly members of the American Communist party and a small minority within the ACLU, also perceived it as an improper expansion of state power that would police workers and debilitate their unions. In their more emotional moments, such leftists castigated the Wagner Act as the first savage thrust of American fascism.[63] And advocates for the cause of African Americans, especially the leaders of the NAACP, feared that the law would entrench trade unions in their exclusionary racial practices. In fact, the AFL, many of whose craft union affiliates did exclude nonwhite members, fought efforts to deny the benefit of the Wagner Act to unions that discriminated. The combination of AFL resistance and Southern influence in Congress defeated the NAACP's lobbying to amend the Wagner Act.[64]

Elements of both the 1930s rightist and leftist critiques entered into the work of so-called new left historians, sociologists, and political scientists during the 1960s. They described the Wagner Act as a central ingredient in a "corporate liberal" scheme to salvage American capitalism from crisis by enlisting trade union leaders in a crusade to wean workers from radicalism and discipline them on the job. For such analysts, Wagner's bill was the product of the class consciousness of farsighted monopoly capitalists who recruited accommodationist labor leaders to serve conservative purposes.[65] A larger number of contemporaries and subsequent scholars have considered the Wagner Act perhaps the most radical piece of New Deal legislation. One historian, surprised that a bill so radical sailed through Congress with only perfunctory opposition, suggested it was passed in a fit of absent-mindedness.[66] That verdict is not entirely fair. The sponsors of the legislation knew precisely what they were doing. For Wagner, his staff (especially Keyserling), the NLRB attorneys involved, and such senators as LaFollette, Costigan, Norris, Wheeler, Walsh, and many others, the NLRA represented a conscious effort to strengthen trade unionism. It also signified recognition that a national economy required national regulation and that a stable one needed a more equitable distribution of income and wealth. Although all of the bill's sponsors endorsed capitalism and none desired any form of socialism or collectivism, in 1935 their goals and policies were radical indeed. Compared with all previous federal labor legislation, the Wagner Act was so advanced, and the protections it guaranteed workers and unions so fulsome, that it carried the potential to transform radically the American social and economic order.[67]

What specifically did the Wagner Act do? Why did it frighten conservatives and exhilarate liberals and radicals? Why has it caused such controversy among scholars? The first two questions are easier to answer and should be addressed first. Simply put, the act codified all existing federal legislation which guaranteed workers the right to form unions of their own choosing. It also specifically outlawed yellow-dog contracts and spelled out precisely which employer practices interfered with the right of workers to choose their own collective bargaining representatives. More broadly speaking, it transformed the advisory rulings of the NLB and the first NLRB concerning representation elections, exclusive majority representation, union recognition, and the employer's obligation to bargain into statutory law. And in its preamble, which elaborated the federal government's constitutional right to regulate the relations between employers and employees in manufacturing in order to unclog the channels of interstate commerce, the act also declared trade unionism to be the single best instrument for establishing industrial democracy, spreading wealth and income more widely, and averting future depressions. Finally, it established a three-person NLRB with the authority to implement the law and the power to enforce its decisions by going directly to the circuit court of appeals.

Businesspeople and conservatives took umbrage at the law because it introduced federal power directly, deeply, and coercively into realms heretofore regarded as private and voluntary. They were equally frightened by its apparent assumption that the interests of employers and employees were not identical and that conflict rather than cooperation was the normal relationship between boss and worker. The law also implied a more collective view of social relations, one in which state regulation of conflict between corporations and unions replaced an assumed identity of interests between an individual employer and an individual employee. And most threatening of all was the implication that the federal government was now totally behind the effort of the labor movement to unionize workers; what else could be inferred from the Wagner Act's interdiction of all sorts of employer labor practices, including conventional communication with workers, without a comparable ban on union or employee behavior? Such anxieties led employers without exception to fight the Wagner Act before and after its passage. If there was a single "corporate liberal" anywhere in the American business universe willing to embrace either the new law or accommodative labor leaders, that person never testified before the Senate and House committees that held extensive hearings in 1934 and 1935. Between March 1934, when Wagner first introduced his legislation, and July 1935, when it became law, corporate America united against it. When Roosevelt signed the Wagner Act, the employers did not withdraw from the field of battle.

For the same reasons that employers and conservatives groaned, liberals and radicals gloated. As Senator Costigan pointed out during floor debate on the bill, it enacted the labor proposals of the most radical presidential commission in U.S. history, Wilson's Commission on Industrial Relations. In fact, Wagner took the recommendations of the CIR staff (the Walsh report) and combined them with the principles of John R. Commons (author of a CIR minority report) to create a consensus for reform, which the Walsh and Commons approaches to industrial relations could not build on their own. The NLRA wrote into the statute books many of the specific recommendations concerning worker rights, industrial democracy, and the distribution of income proposed by Walsh and his associates in 1915. It then created an NLRB to implement those rights, which was modeled after the Commons's notion of an independent, expert, professional administrative body designed to elaborate a law of labor relations and serve the public interest. Clearly, never before had the sanction and weight of federal power been arrayed so fully behind the claims of trade unionism and industrial democracy.

The Wagner Act was never intended to infringe on the customary private ordering of labor relations and job rights by the AFL and its craft union affiliates. It never intended to curtail the right of employers and unions voluntarily to make whatever arrangement they preferred, including the closed shop, as Wagner persistently reiterated. That is precisely why the NAACP and its allies had demanded the amendment of the law to forbid discriminatory actions by unions. The new law aimed not at altering collective bargaining where it already functioned but at establishing it where employers refused to recognize unions. To put it as bluntly as possible: For the labor movement of July 1935, the Wagner Act cost nothing and promised vast gains. It also left workers and their unions with an undiminished right to strike over wages, hours, conditions, and almost anything else, except representation rights, which would be decided by secret NLRB elections. Since the unions, not employers, sought such elections in preference to the strike, labor again surrendered nothing in the bargain. Even more basic, in requiring employers to bargain collectively with representatives of their employees, the Wagner Act defined no issue as outside the negotiating process. Private power, not public law, would determine the scope of collective bargaining.[68]

In July 1935, then, federal legislation gave the labor movement a charter for action. Whether the Wagner Act's promises to trade unionism could be realized in practice depended on the ingenuity of the labor movement, the character of the NLRB, the commitment of President Roosevelt, and the rulings of the federal courts.

The New Politics, June–November 1936

At first, the passage of the Wagner Act and the creation of the new NLRB brought few changes in the realm of industrial relations. The same employers who had resisted the NLB and the first NLRB proved equally resistant to new NLRB rulings. Automobile, steel, rubber, and electrical companies continued to discharge union militants, favor company unions, and refuse to hold board-ordered representation elections. Their attorneys assured them that the Wagner Act was unconstitutional and that federal courts would so find. Such legal counsel was also endorsed by a special lawyers' committee put together by the Liberty League, which consisted of fifty-eight of the nation's leading corporate and constitutional attorneys. The fifty-eight legal solons drafted a long brief in which they declared the Wagner Act constitutionally deficient in nearly every respect. For corporate America in 1935 and 1936, the Wagner Act NLRB merited the epithet accorded it by *Fortune*: "The G—— D—— Labor Board."[69]

The board nevertheless went about its business. The three people that Roosevelt appointed to administer it recruited a staff of aggressive young attorneys, established an economic research division under the direction of David Saposs, and rebuilt the regional offices and staffs established under the previous NLRB. The new board members also built on the "common labor law" precedents of their predecessors. They remained committed to ordering secret representation elections, the reinstatement with back pay of workers discharged for union activities, the elimination of company-dominated unions, and the necessity for exclusive majority representation. Because of employer resistance, however, the board devoted more time and energy to devising a legal strategy to withstand judicial challenges than actually to promoting industrial democracy and the growth of trade unionism.

Throughout the latter half of 1935 and the first half of 1936, conservative federal district court judges issued restraining orders and injunctions that made it practically impossible for the NLRB to implement the Wagner Act. Then, in the summer of 1936, the Supreme Court seemed to deliver a fatal blow to the board. Ruling in a case brought by the Carter Coal Company of Virginia against the Guffey Bituminous Coal Act of 1935, which regulated competition among soft-coal operators and promulgated a code of labor relations identical to the Wagner Act, the justices declared the law unconstitutional. A narrow 5–4 majority ruled that because the mining of coal did not directly affect interstate commerce (the old constitutional distinction between manufacturing and commerce was cited with all the usual precedents noted), the federal government lacked the authority to regulate matters that the Constitution left to the separate states. The constitutional mandate for the Wagner Act was now itself in doubt. As one board attorney concluded in the summer of 1936, "pending final determination of the constitutional questions, the board's activities in all fields except transportation and communications seem virtually at an end."[70]

If business resistance to labor and judicial interpretations concerning labor relations law remained unchanged after the passage of the Wagner Act, the character of the labor movement and the bases of national politics altered drastically. Two factors now converged and strengthened each other. As conservative, business-financed opposition to the New Deal intensified, Roosevelt increasingly looked to workers and their labor movement for mass support. Simultaneously, a small group of labor leaders, among whom John L. Lewis and Sidney Hillman were the most notable, realized that the president's political needs opened vast possibilities for a dynamic trade union movement.

Having watched the AFL fail to capitalize on the labor upheaval of 1934, especially in the steel and auto industries, Lewis knew that President Roosevelt reacted to demonstrations of power. Lewis, together with Hillman and a few other allies, insisted that if the AFL aggressively organized mass-production workers and threatened to use their power to paralyze production, the labor movement could wrest real gains from the New Deal. At the November 1934 San Francisco AFL convention, the Lewis faction seemed to prevail in its demands for a militant organizing campaign in the mass-production industries. As the convention adjourned, Lewis's friend and economic adviser, W. Jett Lauck, exulted: "You certainly brought about an epoch-making change in the A. F. of L. and have given everybody new hope about unionization and a strong, aggressive labor movement."[71]

Most AFL leaders, however, proved too indecisive to act militantly. Throughout the winter and spring of 1935 Lewis reminded his colleagues on the AFL executive council that their enemies believed labor was weak because of a lack of organization in the mass-production industries. Our enemies, as well as our potential allies in Washington, measure labor's strength, analyze its possibility as an adversary, he advised. "Our weakness to get anything is the absence of effective competent organization. . . . It is axiomatic . . . that you can get just about what you are ready to take." The more AFL leaders equivocated the more insistent Lewis became. Either the AFL will organize the mass-production industries, he intoned, "or the world is going to believe we are not going to try, or perhaps we do not want to." On the resolve of the AFL, warned Lewis, hinges "the destiny of the labor movement."[72]

When other labor leaders declined to join Lewis in the labor movement's rendezvous with destiny, even after the passage of the Wagner Act, the UMW president decided to act on his own. Defeated along with the other advocates of militant organizing at the 1935 AFL convention, Lewis brought all the union dissidents together in November in a new Committee for Industrial Organization (CIO). Lewis's CIO planned to use its influence with New Deal Democrats to unionize the mass production workers. It intended to deploy its mass membership as a power base from which to extract favors from Roosevelt. From November 1935 through November 1936, Lewis carefully made the CIO a vital part of the New Deal Democratic political coalition.[73]

By the summer of 1936 politics brought the CIO, the New Deal majority in

Congress, and the president into a tight alliance. Labor's allies moved in several directions simultaneously. In June, Senator James Byrnes of South Carolina introduced a bill making it a felony to transport people in interstate commerce with the intent to interfere with peaceful picketing. This so-called antiprofessional strikebreaker bill (aimed primarily at the notorious Pearl Berghoff agency) passed both houses on June 19 with no significant opposition and was signed the next day by the president.[74] The same session saw an even more notable victory for the CIO. The friends of labor and the NLRB united to authorize a special Senate subcommittee chaired by Robert LaFollette, Jr., to investigate the violation of civil liberties in the sphere of labor relations. LaFollette and his supporters made no secret of what they intended to do: investigate the use of private police, labor spies, professional strikebreakers, and violence by employers against unions. And they were not bashful about linking their investigations directly to the CIO organizing campaigns in steel and autos. Nor was the committee averse to using both NLRB and CIO staff in its field work. For LaFollette hoped to strengthen mass-production unionism and empower the NLRB. As the committee's historian has noted: "Its mandate from Congress invited it to become the cutting edge of the C.I.O.'s effort to muster public support for its campaigns and tactics." Or as Heber Blankenhorn, one of the principal supporters of the investigation, an NLRB staff member, and an ally of Lewis, recommended: "The principal job of this Board [NLRB] and of the LaFollette committee investigation is to clarify the country's mind in regard to the constitutional crisis. The bottom of that crisis is Capital-Labor relations."[75]

At the same time, Lewis and Roosevelt were solidifying their own political alliance. Together with Hillman and George Berry of the Printing Pressmen's union, Lewis had formed Labor's Nonpartisan League to amass labor support for Roosevelt in the approaching election. And it was to this new body, not the AFL, that the president now looked for assistance in the campaign. Roosevelt showed his concern for Lewis and labor in other ways. When obstruction by the Senate Majority Leader Joseph Robinson of Arkansas defeated an administration-endorsed bill (the Guffey-Snyder Bituminous Coal Act) to stabilize soft coal on June 20, two days later Roosevelt invited Lewis to the White House for a long private conference. The president pledged to protect the UMW in every way possible until Congress passed new coal legislation and also to support the CIO's unionization of steel. Then Roosevelt read the labor leader sections of the planned 1936 Democratic party platform, which contained strong labor clauses and a proposed amendment to strip the Supreme Court of the power to declare vital legislation unconstitutional. Lewis emerged from the White House to state publicly that he and his associates in the labor movement totally supported Roosevelt's reelection and all the president's policies.[76]

In July, Lewis launched the CIO organizing campaign in steel by linking it directly to the New Deal and the approaching election. In a national radio address of July 6, Lewis tied unionization in steel and the presidential election together as part of a process that would decide "whether the working population of this country shall have a voice in determining their destiny or whether they shall serve as indentured servants for a financial and economic dictatorship which would shamelessly . . . debase the soul . . . and . . . pride of a free people." Freedom could be won, Lewis told workers, only by breaking the shackles that bound them to industrial servitude, joining an industrial union, and voting for Roosevelt.[77] Throughout the remainder of the summer and fall the labor leader and the president coordinated their political activities. Lewis spoke for the Democratic party in all the principal coal-mining states and many major industrial states. He spent nearly $600,000 of UMW money, an unheard-of sum at that time, on the Democratic campaign. During the campaign's last week, Lewis and Roosevelt appeared together at a mass open-air meeting in Wilkes-Barre, Pennsylvania, timed to coincide with the anthracite miners' celebration of John Mitchell Day. Roosevelt delivered a ringing endorsement of the UMW, CIO, and collective bargaining.[78]

The election returns delighted Roosevelt and Lewis. It produced the largest presidential landslide in American history to that time and gave the Democrats total control of Congress. As Lewis proclaimed at a CIO executive board meeting held just after the election: "We . . . must capitalize on the election. The CIO was out fighting for Roosevelt. . . . We wanted a president who would hold the light for us while we went out and organized." The political lesson drawn by Lewis from the election results was self-evident: The CIO must maintain its aggressive organizing drive in steel and automobiles and look to the White House for support.[79] Events would soon test the strength of the Lewis-Roosevelt alliance and the depth of the New Deal's commitment to trade unionism.

The New Deal

Labor Revolution,

Part 2, 1937–1941

Roosevelt's reelection in November 1936 ushered the New Deal into the most tumultuous phase of its transformation of labor relations in the United States. Between January and April 1937, trade unionism accomplished what it had failed to achieve during the previous half century. Organized labor conquered the two most significant outposts of the open shop in mass-production industry, wresting a collective bargaining contract from General Motors on February 11 and one from United States Steel three weeks later. Both triumphs owed much to the support of New Deal Democrats at the national and state levels and to the awareness in some corporate boardrooms that big business had lost a good part of its customary political influence. Not only had organized labor won significant triumphs in mass-production industry. The beneficiaries had been the militant new unions in the CIO, the new national labor center, which for a time in 1937 displaced the AFL as the heart of the American labor movement.

Unions recruited more than three million members in 1937, an increase of nearly 100 percent, and they claimed almost 23 percent of the nation's non-agricultural workers, the greatest proportion as yet unionized in American history. And the largest share of those new members belonged to CIO affiliates. Finally in April and May the Supreme Court stamped its approval on the New Deal revolution in labor law and relations.

Yet the transformation ended almost before it began. By the spring of 1937 the militant unions in the CIO were battling more to protect what they had just won than to conquer additional outposts. And by autumn many of their newly enrolled members had stopped paying dues, leaving the CIO with a total membership that surpassed the AFL's membership only on paper. In reality, by the end of 1937, the AFL had many more dues-paying members than CIO. At the same time, New Deal Democrats suffered a series of political defeats. Despite his party's overwhelming majority in Congress, Roosevelt had lost control of the legislature. Congress rejected the president's proposal to "reform" the Supreme Court, procrastinated on administration proposals to enact a national minimum wage and maximum hours law, and refused to cooperate in Roosevelt's plans to reorganize the executive branch of government. Simultaneously, Roosevelt's budgetary decisions early in 1937 throttled an expanding economy, precipitating an economic contraction deeper than that of 1929–30, a situation that the president's political foes derided as the "Roosevelt depression."[1]

Thereafter labor militants and their advocates in the Roosevelt administration beat a strategic retreat. Not until the outbreak of war in Europe and the emergence of a national defense crisis in the United States would militant labor be able again to act aggressively and its friends in Washington partly contain the rising political power of the enemies of trade unionism.

"The New Unionism"

No sooner had the 1936 election returns been tallied than many commentators began to ask publicly what John L. Lewis expected from Franklin D. Roosevelt as recompense for the CIO's campaign expenditures. "With a man [Lewis] of his temper, his record, and his ambition," the *New York Times* noted, "it will be difficult to deal amicably."[2] The public did not have long to wait to learn what Lewis wanted.

On December 30, 1936, workers at two General Motors Fisher Body plants in Flint, Michigan, occupied the factories, stopped the assembly lines, and sparked the great General Motors sit-down strike of 1937. This conflict pitted the United Automobile Workers–CIO against the largest industrial corporation in the world. It also tested the strength of the CIO's alliance with the Democratic party, for its resolution required forceful intervention by Frank P. Murphy, the New Deal Democratic governor of Michigan, and manipulation behind the scenes by President Roosevelt.[3]

A day after the workers sat down and occupied the factories Lewis told the nation what labor wanted from "its" president. On New Year's Eve, 1937, Lewis, asserting his role as tribune for the nation's toiling masses, spoke on the NBC radio network. "The people of our nation," he reflected, "have just participated in a national referendum. By an overwhelming majority they voted for industrial democracy, and reelected its champion, Franklin Delano Roosevelt." Now, Lewis suggested, it was time for the agents of the federal government to enter the plants of General Motors, strip them of their deadly arsenals (exposed by investigators from the LaFollette Committee), and enable workers to exercise their rights as free men. "Labor," its putative leader proclaimed, "demands a new deal in America's great industries." Speaking directly to Roosevelt, Lewis challenged the president: "The time has passed in America when the workers can be either clubbed, gassed or shot down with impunity. . . . *Labor will . . . expect the protection of the Federal Government in the pursuit of its lawful objectives*" (emphasis added).[4]

From the first, two primary factors influenced Lewis's handling of the General Motors strike and the prospects for union success: power and politics. The strikers' seizure of the plants in Flint and their possession of millions of dollars worth of productive capital represented raw labor power. The impending accession to office of Democratic governors in Michigan, Ohio, Illinois, and Pennsylvania as well as Roosevelt's preelection promises to Lewis reflected labor's new political influence. So, too, did Lewis and the CIO's connections with the NLRB and the LaFollette Committee. Heber Blankenhorn, an experienced social reformer and advocate of progressive unionism, coordinated the activities of the NLRB and the Senate Civil Liberties Subcommittee in assisting the strikers against General Motors.[5]

The legal implications of the sit-down strike technique placed state and national Democratic officeholders in a perilous situation. By all established legal standards and judicial precedents (to be reiterated by federal circuit court and Supreme Court rulings over the next two years), the sit-downers had illegally trespassed on and confiscated the private property of General Motors. The firm had every right to expect judicial rulings ordering the strikers to relinquish possession of company property and for public officials to enforce court orders and evict the sit-downers. Which was why, at first, General Motors refused to bargain seriously with the union. Moreover, at the local level (the city of Flint and Genesee County), General Motors had the law on its side. Two attempts by local authorities to enforce the law, however, caused violent conflicts and no evacuation from the occupied plants.

In the past, perhaps, General Motors would have looked to the governor or the president to uphold the law and break the strike. But 1937 was not 1922, or 1919, or 1914, or 1894, or 1877. Now, instead, Democratic governors and a Democratic president preferred to promote unionization and collective bargaining rather than break strikes. Not that either Governor Murphy or President Roosevelt denied the illegality of the sit-down strike. Rather they perceived the situation in Flint as one in which two equally valid rights were in conflict — General Motors' right to possession of its property and the strikers' right to a union of their own choice and good-faith collective bargaining. Neither Murphy nor Roosevelt favored one right over the other. Let General Motors recognize the United Automobile Workers and bargain with it in good faith, thereby accepting its employees legal rights under the Wagner Act, and the strikers would evacuate the factories.

Throughout the strike, from its eruption on December 30 to its resolution on

February 11, Murphy and Roosevelt never deviated from their commitment to the principle of collective bargaining. Because the strike's fate would be determined in Flint, the governor played a more direct and decisive role than the president. When labor violence erupted in Flint, Murphy acted as many governors had done in comparable circumstances in the past: He sent the National Guard to Flint. Under Murphy's explicit orders, however, the state troops restricted themselves to maintaining the peace and the stalemate in the strike. In this case, the military actually protected the sit-downers against local police and vigilantes. Meantime, Murphy directly and Roosevelt indirectly, through his secretary of labor and the telephone, strove to bring management and labor together.[6]

Thinking the law on their side and buoyed by their history of successful antiunion activities, General Motors executives first refused direct negotiations with union officials and then bargained only on the most parsimonious terms. In fact, initially the company refused to bargain at all until strikers evacuated the plants. Next its negotiators maintained that they had to uphold the rights of both nonunion workers and potential AFL craft union members against the claims of the United Automobile Workers. For their part, union negotiators — especially. Lewis, representing the new industrial unionism as the leader of the CIO — held out for their maximum demands and refused to surrender their claim to exclusive representation. Lewis declared that the strikers would not evacuate company property until General Motors promised to bargain with no union other than the UAW.

While General Motors demanded that the governor enforce the law, Murphy and Roosevelt preferred to avert the bloodshed that would likely follow any attempt to evict the sit-downers through legal process. Lewis shrewdly played on the preferences and predilections of the governor and the president. At a widely attended press conference at UMW headquarters on January 21, Lewis reiterated the message he had delivered in his New Year's Eve radio address. "The administration asked labor for help to repel this attack [the campaign by the Liberty League in the election of 1936], and labor gave its help. The same economic royalists now have their fangs in labor. The workers of this country expect this administration to help the workers in *every legal way*, and to support the auto workers in the General Motors plants" (emphasis added). The next day Roosevelt mildly rebuked the labor leader, who responded to the president's criticism with aplomb. "I do not think," Lewis observed, "the President intended to rebuke the working people of America who are his friends and who are only attempting to obtain rights guaranteed them by Congress." Lewis was right. Over the next several days Roosevelt and his secretary of labor, Frances Perkins, forcefully denounced the executives of General Motors for refusing to bargain with the UAW.[7]

Lewis was even more blunt in his approaches to Murphy. He played on the governor's political ambitions, reminding him of labor's voting power in Michigan. "If you break this strike that washes us up and washes you up. General Motors fought you in the election and when we are gone you are gone. If you stand firm you will aggrandize your political position enormously and there will be talk of Governor Murphy in 1940." Then Lewis, Heber Blankenhorn later recalled, "picked up a cartoon contrasting a large and growing Governor Murphy, pro-C.I.O., with a dark and diminishing Governor Hoffman of New Jersey, anti-C.I.O."[8]

Lewis's tactics produced large dividends. As long as the strikers remained in possession of the occupied plants and Murphy and Roosevelt declined to use force to evict them, the General Motors negotiators had few options. The more the firm began to concede, the more Lewis demanded. As the concessions to the union from General Motors grew in number, one UAW leader turned to Lewis and quipped, "We've got 'em by the 'balls,' squeeze a little harder." Which he did, not only to the company men but also to the governor and the president. By the time the company and the union signed an agreement on February 11, General Motors pledged not to discriminate against union members or interfere in any way with workers' rights to join a union; it promised to bargain with the UAW concerning all its demands; it agreed not to influence its employees against the UAW; and it undertook an obligation for six months after production resumed not to deal with any other union or representative of its employees without Governor Murphy's permission.[9]

The UAW victory at Flint legitimated the CIO as a national trade union center. Within a month of its triumph over General Motors, the UAW claimed 166,000 members. By mid-October, it reported a total dues-paying membership of 400,000. The example set by the Flint workers proved contagious. The year 1937 witnessed 477 sit-down strikes affecting 400,000 workers. Twenty-five of the strikes occurred in January, 47 in February, and 170 in March. Lewis's evaluation of the strike's significance was even more to the point. "GM strike," he exulted, "CIO faced a united financial front — GM settlement broke it."[10]

Lewis's remarks had been occasioned by an even more remarkable happening than the signing of a contract between General Motors and the UAW. For on March 2, 1937, United States Steel and the Steel Workers Organizing Committee (SWOC)–CIO agreed to a collective bargaining agreement without enduring the pain or ritual of a strike.

Why had big steel surrendered without a battle? Again the answer must be found in the altered balance of political power exemplified by the New Deal. The election of 1936 not only returned Roosevelt to power by a landslide. In local communities and states long dominated by the steel industry, labor's candidates swept into office.[11] In this more hospitable milieu for unionism, thousands of workers joined SWOC and scores of company unions declared their independence. Once more a national steel strike impended, this time at a moment of rising prices, increasing productivity, and company profits. In 1937, unlike 1919 and 1934, however, the steel industry could not rely on the state to help it avert or smash a strike. Executives in steel watched events in Flint with trepidation. They noticed that neither Murphy nor Roosevelt had enforced the law against the sit-downers. Myron C. Taylor of United States Steel drew the clearest lessons from Flint. Rather than risk a violent strike in steel, which would disrupt his company's erratic recovery from economic depression and in which he could not be sure of victory, Taylor compromised. In secret negotiations with Lewis, which occurred intermittently during the General Motors strike, Taylor finally agreed to recognize SWOC and bargain collectively with its representatives. As Lewis told his fellow CIO officials, "GM strike — sweeping effect on steel."[12]

The fortress of the open shop, the company that for decades had used every weapon at its command to combat trade unionism, had conceded to CIO without a struggle. The United States Steel–SWOC agreement, coming just three weeks after the General Motors–UAW settlement, proved the potency of the CIO and how its alliance with the New Deal had transformed American political and economic realities. As Lewis also told the CIO executive board: "As years go by, this period will be marked as epoch in life of labor organizations — and economic, social, political history of America. Gigantic implications."[13]

A Switch in Time:
The Supreme Court Revolution

Trade unionism's sudden and startling triumphs in the automobile and steel industries owed far more to a militant rank-and-file movement and to a sympathetic response in the executive branch than it did to the Wagner Act and the NLRB. At the time the CIO challenged General Motors and United States Steel, the NLRB lacked the power to enforce its rulings and the Wagner Act remained in a constitutional limbo. Most corporate attorneys and constitutional law experts continued to insist that the NLRA was unconstitutional and advised company executives not to implement NLRB orders. Their advice was legitimated by several federal circuit courts of appeal decisions that ruled the NLRA unconstitutional. Federal judges applied the precedent of the Supreme Court in the Carter Coal case of 1936, which declared manufacturing outside the stream of interstate commerce. As the attorney for Jones and Laughlin Steel, Earl F. Reed, told the justices of the Supreme Court in February 1937, as they listened to arguments concerning the constitutionality of the Wagner Act, "What the petitioner [NLRB] is asking is that the traditions and precedents of a century be cast aside and that we change the meaning of the Constitution by a judicial decree and say that things that for a century have not been the business of the Federal Government are now to be subject to regulation." [14]

Political realities, not statute law, controlled the actions of business, labor, and New Deal Democrats in the late winter of 1937. General Motors conceded to a union contract not because the law was on the side of its workers. Quite the contrary. It did so only because New Deal Democrats at the state and national levels refused to enforce the law in the company's favor. For the same reason, United States Steel recognized independent trade unionism rather than risk a costly strike. Such labor leaders as John L. Lewis meantime preferred to combine the raw power of militant workers with the political exigencies of New Deal officeholders, rather than resort to the NLRB and representation elections, to win new salients for unionism in mass-production industry.

On the other side, Roosevelt and his New Deal allies needed mass political support from labor as never before. The more assertive the president grew in his demands for domestic reform legislation, the more resistance he encountered in his own party, in Congress, among the opposition, and from the business community. Only labor, most especially the unions and workers associated with Lewis and the CIO, wholeheartedly endorsed Roosevelt's plan to restructure the Supreme Court, to enact minimum-wage, maximum-hour legislation, to provide more-generous financing for public housing, and to reform the administrative branch of government. From January through April 1937 and indeed on into the elections of 1938, the more opposition to his program intensified, the more Roosevelt turned to Lewis, Hillman, and the CIO for support. This explains why in the winter of 1937 the dynamics of New Deal politics worked to the advantage of mass-production unionism, as events in the automobile and steel industries had shown. [15]

As workers fought in the streets of Flint and CIO leaders bargained with corporate executives, attorneys for the NLRB plotted a legal strategy to win constitutional sanction for the Wagner Act. They used great care in selecting which NLRB cease-and-desist orders to pursue in the federal circuit courts of appeal, which circuits to bring suit in, which decisions to appeal to the Supreme Court, and also in amassing the economic and legal evidence to establish their claims. The board attorneys chose as test cases some that decisively affected interstate commerce (interstate bus lines and national communications agencies); others that involved large corporations whose operations had an obvious interstate component (Jones & Laughlin Steel and Fruehauf Trailer); and a small men's clothing firm (Friedman-Harry Marks). They expected no judicial demurrer to federal and NLRB regulatory power in the first set of cases. They were less certain of how judges would rule in the cases concerning large manufacturing concerns, and it was in those instances that the NLRB was most eager to establish the constitutionality of its mandate. The final case was chosen to determine precisely how far judges would allow federal power to reach in regulating labor relations.[16]

Just as General Motors and the UAW were negotiating the final terms of their agreement, the Supreme Court on February 10 and 11, 1937, heard oral arguments in the five cases that had come before it testing the constitutionality of the Wagner Act. Throughout the remainder of that month, March, and the first part of April, as labor militancy intensified and the wave of sit-down strikes spread fear among more-conservative citizens, the nine justices, who during their previous two Court terms had declared large parts of the New Deal program unconstitutional, pondered their decision. If the past were to be a guide, the prospects looked bad for the NLRB. The same nine justices who had found the NIRA and the Guffey Coal Act unconstitutional (by different majorities) and a majority of whom had always distinguished sharply between interstate commerce and actual manufacturing remained on the bench.

Finally, on April 12, 1937, Chief Justice Charles Evans Hughes delivered an opinion for the narrowest of majorities, five to four. In a simultaneously strong yet ambiguous ruling (he failed to repudiate directly precedents that distinguished manufacturing from interstate commerce), the chief justice upheld the constitutionality of the Wagner Act and the operations of the NLRB. Hughes's opinion pertained to all three appeals concerning manufacturers (Jones & Laughlin, Fruehauf Trailer, and Friedman-Harry Marks), and he declared decisively in each case that their production entered the stream of commerce and hence was subject to reasonable federal regulations.

Having placed manufacturing within the purview of federal power, Hughes next endorsed the labor relations philosophy of Robert Wagner, which prized the rights of workers to organize unions and bargain collectively and for which he found precedent in Chief Justice William Howard Taft's ruling in the case of American Steel Foundries v. Tri-States Labor Council (1922). The chief justice also affirmed that the NLRB's procedures and decisions evidenced respect for all the rules of legal due process and were justified by the evidence. About the only solace Hughes offered businesspeople and conservatives, who had expected the Court to rescue them once again, was his passing observations that the Wagner Act allowed employers to hire and fire as they chose (cases of union discrimination excepted) and that it did not compel employer and union to agree on a contract.[17]

The chief justice selected the key swing voter in this ruling, Owen Roberts, to deliver the majority opinion in the less disputatious cases concerning federal power over interstate commerce, those involving the Associated Press and a Washington-area bus company (the latter case did not even engender a dissent).[18]

That Hughes, with assistance from Roberts, had produced a constitutional revolution, one that rewrote the definition of interstate commerce and the federal power to regulate it to the advantage of organized labor, was revealed by the dissents in two of the cases. In the Jones & Laughlin case, one of the Court's "four horsemen" (those reactionaries whom Roosevelt had dismissed publicly as belonging to the era of the horse and buggy), James McReynolds, castigated the majority for overturning more than a century of legal precedent. Through the alchemy of the "stream of commerce" doctrine, the majority had not only repudiated the accepted distinction between commerce and manufacturing; it had also rewritten the rules of federalism and violated state rights. Worse yet, McReynolds declared, the decision had sullied American principles of individual liberty. "The employer and employee," he asserted in phrases redolent of the Court's past, "have equality of right, and any legislation that disturbs that equality is an arbitrary interference with the liberty of contract which no government can legally justify in a free land."[19] In the Associated Press case, Justice George Sutherland saw an even more frightful example of abuse of liberty. "For the saddest epitaph which can be carved in memory of a vanished liberty," he lamented, "is that it was lost because its possessors failed to stretch forth a saving hand while yet there was time."[20]

The sources of this constitutional revolution were clear. One was the voters' mandate in the election of 1936. Another was Roosevelt's plan to "reform" the Court. And most important was the rise of the CIO, the growing assertiveness of militant workers, and the spread of industrial warfare. As Heber Blankenhorn reflected, credit for the constitutional revolution should go to environmental factors, "that is, to the 'facts of industrial relations.' "[21] Or as the justice department solicitor, Charles Wyzanski, later remembered: "Right along I have said that the cases were won not by Mr. Wyzanski but either by Mr. Roosevelt or, if you prefer it, by Mr. Zeitgeist."[22]

The following month, in another five-to-four decision, the Court further extended the rights of labor. An opinion delivered by Brandeis declared a law enacted by the state of Wisconsin to free peaceful picketing from judicial restraint to be constitutional. Brandeis also ruled the closed shop and union work rules as permissible objectives of action. To the small contractor who brought the case on the basis that the union's rules and actions interfered with his right to earn a living and to protect his personal property, Brandeis replied, "One has no constitutional right to a 'remedy' against the lawful conduct of another." As usual, the four conservatives dissented, seeing in the majority opinion one more attack on the inviolability of individual free contract and one more setback to the right of American citizens to liberty, property, and the free choice of occupation.[23]

Within a span of six weeks, the Supreme Court had declared that workers had a right to join unions of their own choosing and to bargain collectively with their employers; that the federal government had the power to enforce those rights in almost all sectors of the economy; that the NLRB was a constitutionally permissible administrative agency charged with implementing labor's legal rights; and that states were free to permit all forms of peaceful union picketing. In a real sense, then, the Supreme Court had finally extended to all workers rights theretofore reserved only to those directly involved in interstate commerce. It had also made federal regulation of general labor relations an ongoing administrative concern rather than an episodic happening as it had been in the past. In the complex bargain that ensued for labor from this revolution in law, workers won precious new rights, while their unions were clearly transformed from private, voluntary organizations into quasi-public institutions charged with implementing aspects of public policy.[24]

The Conservative Revanchistes

Even as the coalition between militant labor and New Deal Democrats was producing its greatest victories in the automobile and steel industries, the forces of conservatism organized their counterattack. Newspapers and magazines regularly reported the sit-down strikes and other manifestations of worker discontent as cases of riot, instances of worker unruliness and public disorder that subverted law and order. Republicans in Congress and outside cited the same events to prove that Roosevelt and other New Deal Democrats had mortgaged the public interest and traditional American liberties to John L. Lewis and the CIO. The Republicans also appealed directly to the self-interest of Southern Democrats, who feared federal intrusion into state control of both racial and labor relations. Business interests naturally attacked New Deal labor policies as an affront to the rights of private property and a derogation of the principles of free enterprise. And the AFL increasingly criticized the NLRB for favoring the CIO, which, claimed the AFL, subverted the law by undermining the existence of unions as voluntary institutions. Transformations in racial relations also formed a subtext to the AFL's critique of the NLRB and won it sympathy among Southern Democrats. The new CIO unions had far more success in organizing African American workers than the AFL affiliates ever did, and the civil rights policies and practices of several CIO unions stood as a warning to those traditional craft unions that still excluded nonwhite workers.[25] The AFL also accused the CIO of harboring communists. By mid-summer 1937, Republicans, Southern Democrats, corporate interests, and AFL leaders had formed an informal alliance to reform the labor policies of the New Deal.

While automobile workers fought General Motors in the streets and factories of

Flint, the halls of Congress rang with denunciations of the sit-down tactic. Re-publicans naturally accused Roosevelt, Frank Murphy, and their Democratic allies of serving as the lackeys of John L. Lewis. "The most ominous thing in American life today," said Republican senator Hiram Johnson of California, "is the sit-down strike. . . . If the sit-down strike is carried on with the connivance or the sympathy of the public authorities, then the warning signals are out, and down that road lurks a dictatorship." Such Republican denunciations were to be expected. More sur-prising were the ripostes of such New Deal Democrats as William Connery, chair of the House Labor Committee and coauthor of the Wagner Act. "I think I speak for every member of the Committee," Connery said on February 4. "Not one of the members of the Committee on Labor endorses sit-down strikes. We do not believe that any man has a right to go on the property of another and then cease work." Equally significant was the shift in attitude among influential Southern Democrats who had heretofore endorsed New Deal labor policies. Admitting that he lacked knowledge of who actually was responsible for the illegal and un-American sit-downs, Senator Allen Ellender of Louisiana asserted: "I am told that John L. Lewis is the leader of the movement. If Mr. Lewis is, I brand him as a traitor to American ideals and a menace to the peace and prosperity of our nation."[26]

By early April the coalition of Republicans and Southern Democrats had reached the point of introducing antistrike laws and resolutions in Congress. The New Deal Democrats and their progressive Republican allies, such as Robert LaFollette, were placed on the defensive. Rather than defend the right of workers to sit-down or other militant tactics used by the CIO, labor's congressional advocates used the findings of the LaFollette Committee as a basis for counter-attack. They condemned employers for their practices of illegal and violent methods of labor relations. Both in Congress and in the arena of public opinion, however, labor's allies were on weaker ground than their opponents.

Republican critics of Roosevelt had now found an ideal weapon with which to club the New Deal. They lumped together the sit-down strikes, Roosevelt's proposal to reform the Supreme Court, and anti-lynching legislation (this last theme was the work of Southern Democrats) as part and parcel of the president's un-American, unconstitutional program. In fact, the minority Republicans played a subordinate role to Southern Democrats in the antilabor offensive.

During debate on the Guffey-Vinson Coal Act, Senator James Byrnes of South Carolina (formerly a supporter of New Deal labor policies) added an amendment that, in effect, outlawed not only sit-down strikes but also strikes by former employees on company property (this latter clause would have made strikes in all Southern textile company towns illegal). And the most impassioned advocate of the Byrnes amendment was his fellow Southern Democrat, Walter George of

Georgia. In the end, the best the defenders of labor could accomplish was to pass on April 7 by a margin of 75 to 3 a Senate Concurrent Resolution that condemned sit-down strikes as illegal and contrary to sound public policy. As a sop to the New Dealers, the resolution also condemned as contrary to sound public policy employer espionage and violations of the Wagner Act.[27]

The shifting mood in Congress and the nation-at-large swiftly made itself felt in the Roosevelt administration and among New Deal Democrats in general. When SWOC engaged in battle against the so-called Little Steel companies beginning on May 26, 1937, the strike leaders suddenly found themselves bereft of allies in state capitals and the White House. Wherever steelworkers waged war against the Little Steel firms in the company towns of Pennsylvania, Ohio, Indiana, and Illinois, local authorities cooperated with the firms in coordinated strikebreaking operations. Street-fighting, violence, and death punctuated the conflict, none so infamous and publicized as the "Memorial Day Massacre" in South Chicago near the gates of a Republic Steel mill, during which police killed ten demonstrators, wounded thirty others by gunshot, and beat scores of others with billies and ax handles. "Wounded prisoners of war," observed the LaFollette Committee subsequently, "might have expected and received greater solicitude."[28]

This, then, was an occasion when the CIO should have used its vaunted influence among Democrats to combat company and police violence. After all, the governors of Pennsylvania, Ohio, Indiana, and Illinois had been elected with CIO support. And Roosevelt, now frequently castigated as labor's lackey, had also personally promised Lewis to assist SWOC's organizing campaign. Lewis did urge the president and the four New Deal governors to use state power to thwart corporate terror. Instead, the governors of Indiana and Ohio dispatched militia units to strike-torn cities in order to disperse pickets, protect property, and guard strikebreakers. In Pennsylvania, where the lieutenant governor, Tom Kennedy, was secretary-treasurer of the UMW, the state followed a neutral policy that in practice benefited the companies. And as for Roosevelt, when Lewis on June 21, referring to labor's casualties in the Memorial Day Massacre, demanded, "Labor will await the position of the authorities on whether our people will be protected or butchered" — the president responded a week later with the comment "the majority of the people are saying just one thing, 'A plague on both your houses.' " When reporters read Roosevelt's statement to Lewis, the CIO leader, according to one journalist present, "said nothing, but his heels drummed against the desk's lower panels with a violence that just missed reducing them to splinters."[29]

The president acted as he did because of political realities. He was aware of the shifting sentiments in Congress (his Court reform proposal had already been defeated, along with other New Deal reforms) and his declining support among Southern Democrats. Some of his most influential advisers, including Harry Hopkins, warned him against getting involved in a dangerous situation from which he had little to gain politically. The CIO movement in mass-production industry, reported one presidential confidante, "is a complicated situation, and full of all kinds of dynamite, political as well as social." He then advised Roosevelt to allow the Little Steel strike to come to its natural end, a defeat for SWOC. "Nothing the President could now say [July 2] would make any difference. If he chided the employers, he would once again be charged with playing Lewis's game. Time is needed for things to cool off. . . . I think Lewis will be willing to compromise. There is a strong reaction against the C.I.O., and Lewis will need time to reorganize his forces."[30]

Roosevelt found such advice persuasive. In the summer of 1937, then, the president retreated from his firm support of CIO and mass-production unionism and maneuvered to free himself from the quagmire of labor-capital conflict.

Other factors also motivated the president to pursue a more cautious labor policy. In response to the brisk economic recovery of late 1936–early 1937, Roosevelt had cut federal expenditures in order to achieve one of his fondest ambitions: to balance the federal budget. The result of parsimonious fiscal policy was disastrous. The economy collapsed. Consumption, production, and employment levels fell between August and October 1937 to those of the early Depression years. Two million workers lost their jobs between Labor Day and year's end. By early winter 1938, unemployment, poverty, and even starvation reapproached the levels of 1933.[31]

The president's badly timed budget cuts undermined the New Deal's coalition with militant labor as represented by CIO. They also undercut the Keynesian "politics of productivity." Unemployment hit hardest those durable goods industries in which CIO membership was concentrated. All across the board, the CIO found itself losing members, income, and influence. Like the president, Lewis had one response to the situation: retrenchment. The most dedicated enemy of CIO within the AFL, John Frey, gloated in April 1938, "The C.I.O. is slipping definitely as an industrial movement." Not only had it lost thousands of members, falling well behind the AFL in that respect, but the CIO had, according to Frey, lost most of its political influence.[32]

Crusaders on the NLRB

Just as the tide began to turn against labor, the NLRB entered the fray full blast. Its existence and procedures having been validated by the Supreme Court on April 12, the board subsequently increased the number of hearings it held by 341 percent and its decisions rendered by 362 percent. In almost every case the board ruled against employers and for workers. It ruled against the unfair labor practices defined in the Wagner Act with firmness and promoted collective bargaining with dedication. The mostly young people and recent law school graduates who served the NLRB as hearing examiners and trial attorneys acted almost as missionaries for worker rights and trade unionism. They were indeed true believers in their cause.

The board began to set a variety of precedents favorable to union organizing campaigns. Where a sufficient number of employees signed union pledge cards, the NLRB bypassed formal representation elections and certified the union in question as exclusive bargaining agent. In elections, the board counted only actual ballots cast, eliminating the influence of the always large number of nonvoters. This, too, worked to the advantage of unions. As a rule, the NLRB permitted workers discharged for union membership and those on strike legally to vote in representation elections. Moreover, by and large, the circuit courts of appeal and the Supreme Court upheld the board's rulings. In the words of *Business Week*, "NLRB calls the tune and business dances to a new set of labor relations rules."[33]

In many ways, the early NLRB encountered more problems as a result of the split in labor's ranks (CIO versus AFL) than as a consequence of its enforcement of worker rights against employer coercion. The overwhelmingly liberal and even radical board employees sympathized strongly with the more militant and socially conscious CIO. Even the more conservative board members perceived the CIO as more active, democratic, and progressive than the "backward" AFL. In the spring and summer of 1937 field workers reported that employers were favoring the AFL in order to thwart CIO organizing efforts. Rather than allow their employees free choice through representation elections, many employers signed closed-shop contracts with AFL affiliates, which were "attempting to take advantage of an antipathy among employers directed toward the CIO as being communist and radical." When the AFL obtained a contract as a result of employer influence or coercion, the NLRB was not hesitant to invalidate such agreements. Worker preferences seemed to validate the board's sympathy for the CIO. CIO affiliates defeated AFL affiliates in three-quarters of all elections in which both were on the ballot, and by average majorities of 83 percent. Overall, the CIO won 82 percent of all elections in which it was on the ballot, compared with the AFL's 56 percent.[34]

Upset as the AFL leaders were by their poorer showing in representation elections than their competitors from the CIO, they were even more vexed by the NLRB's apparent preference for the CIO, its disdain for traditional craft lines of jurisdiction, and its proclivity for voiding AFL contracts with employers. That the board sympathized more with the CIO and ruled against the legality of several AFL collective bargaining agreements is beyond dispute. That the NLRB disregarded the rights of craft workers is a more disputable charge.

For the board, the preferences of workers and the requirements of harmonious collective bargaining transcended the traditional jurisdictional claims of AFL affiliates. If a majority of workers voted overwhelmingly to be represented by a single industrial union, the NLRB refused to separate small minorities of craft workers into separate bargaining units. If a firm had no history of bargaining with its skilled workers and if establishing separate craft and industrial bargaining units would disadvantage employees in negotiations, the board refused to do so. Where employers had a history of bargaining with craft units and a majority of skilled workers preferred to have their own union, the NLRB sanctioned such arrangements. This approach the board codified in what became known as the Globe doctrine, a means of eliminating disputes between craft and industrial unions on the basis of history, custom, and free elections. Nothing in the principles of the Globe doctrine favored the CIO, yet a small group of AFL leaders saw the NLRB's principles and practices as a direct attack on a half century of trade union tradition and practice.[35]

The rising discontent among AFL leaders with the operations of the NLRB added additional fuel to the intensifying opposition in Congress to New Deal labor policies. As early as April 7, 1937, Senator David I. Walsh introduced an amendment to the NLRA in the Senate, sponsored by the AFL and requiring the NLRB to designate a craft union as the appropriate bargaining unit whenever a majority of employees of a particular craft should so decide. This amendment directly challenged the board's right to determine which group of workers represented a legitimate bargaining unit as well as to weigh bargaining history and custom in making its decision. Taken by itself, the AFL amendment offered little threat to the NLRB. Weighed in conjunction with rising employer and Republican hostility to the NLRB, the AFL's attitude portended real trouble for the New Deal. By the summer of 1937 Republican senator Arthur Vandenberg of Michigan called for amendments to the NLRA that would grant employers rights equal to those of their employees and place restraints on unions as well as companies. In December, Senator Edward R. Burke, Republican of Nebraska, charged the NLRB with violating the will of Congress and engaging in a variety of unconstitutional practices. He demanded that the Senate Judiciary Committee undertake a full-scale investigation of the administration of the Wagner Act by the NLRB. In his criticism of the board, Burke amalgamated the indictments levied against it by the Chamber of Commerce and the AFL. For the time being, however, the Democratic majorities on the Labor and Judiciary committees had sufficient strength to beat back the antilabor attack.[36] The emerging alliance among Republicans, Southern Democrats, big business, and the AFL, however, spelled real trouble for the NLRB and other New Deal friends of labor.

The NLRB under Siege

Throughout the year 1938 the NLRB continued to win victories for its rulings in courts of law, but it steadily lost approval in the court of public opinion. Part of the problem was the bad press that the agency received — which was to be expected because the large newspapers, press agencies, and radio networks themselves represented big business and had been the "victims" of board rulings. Another part of the problem arose from the increased feistiness of Southern Democratic opponents of the New Deal.

Not content to castigate the NLRB for its antipathy to business, such Southern congressmen as Representatives Martin Dies of Texas and Howard Smith of Virginia publicly charged the NLRB with serving a CIO-Communist plot to subvert the nation. Dies turned the hearings of his House Committee on Un-American Activities into a forum for witnesses hostile to the CIO and the NLRB. Among the first of such witnesses was John Frey, who submitted a list of more than fifty CIO officials alleged to be Communists and also tied them to friends on the NLRB. And, of course, business interests used the National Association of Manufacturers and the Chamber of Commerce to unleash a steady barrage of publicity and press releases hostile to the NLRB.[37]

By far the largest share of the NLRB's political problems flowed from the conflict between the AFL and the CIO. A fact of life in the labor movement ever since John L. Lewis had founded the CIO in November 1935, the split between the two labor centers had become one of unrelenting warfare by 1938. All pretense of cooperation in organizing the unorganized had collapsed. In fact, the executive council of the AFL had declared open war against the CIO. Lewis, in response, accepted the AFL's challenge, and in November 1938 transformed the CIO from a provisional committee into a constitutionally autonomous national labor center. As AFL and CIO affiliates battled for the loyalty of workers, they drew the NLRB deeply into labor's civil war.[38]

Because the CIO generally had more success in NLRB representation elections and also because the board had invalidated several contracts between employers and AFL affiliates, AFL leaders condemned the board publicly and privately. On several occasions, Green personally, and the executive council officially, approached Roosevelt to demand changes in the policies of the NLRB. In a speech to the Massachusetts State Federation of Labor in August 1938, Green swore never to compromise with the CIO and pledged, "We will mobilize our political and economic strength in an uncompromising fight until this Board [NLRB] is driven from power. . . . The Board is a travesty on justice." At the October 1938 convention of the AFL in Houston, Texas, Green, Frey, and Matthew Woll indicted the New Deal, blasted Roosevelt's reform program, and demanded revisions in the policies and composition of the NLRB. A report from the executive council condemning the alliance between the NLRB and the CIO and proposing nine amendments to the NLRA to strip the board of much of its power to determine legitimate bargaining units, sailed through the convention without opposition.[39]

In this case, the small group of leaders who controlled the AFL worked as efficiently as ever. As the AFL's attorney, Joseph Padway, later recalled about the resolution's adoption, "there was one peeping 'no' heard from the back of the room, and the president put the question again very loudly. He said, 'I will call for the question again;' and it was unanimously adopted." Both before and after the convention, Padway and his principals on the executive council cooperated with attorneys formerly associated with the Liberty League and still serving the NAM and large corporations to build a common front against the NLRB and for revisions in the NLRA.[40]

President Roosevelt, as well as the NLRB, found himself caught between the competing labor centers. On the one hand, the president needed labor support more desperately than ever as congressional opposition to his program intensified. Beset by enemies in his own party as well as among Republicans, Roosevelt could scarcely afford foes within the labor movement. Yet labor unity held as much peril as promise for the president. Undiluted support from trade unionists might assist Roosevelt in enacting his stymied domestic reform agenda. It might also pressure the president to seek more-radical reforms, which would worsen internal conflicts in an already divided Democratic party. And worse yet was the prospect that in a united labor movement power would flow not to the New Deal's friends but to its most resolute and even reactionary union enemies, such people as Frey, Woll, and William Hutcheson, the president of the carpenters' union and the most prominent union Republican.

Thus Roosevelt simultaneously urged the leaders of the AFL and the CIO to negotiate a peace agreement and seemed not especially displeased when every such effort collapsed. For most of 1938 and the early part of 1939, the White House acted as a private and mostly silent broker in AFL-CIO peace negotiations. Because the president refused to support either AFL or CIO proposals (politically he could not afford to alienate either group of labor leaders), the two labor centers preferred war to peace. And their conflict continued to dilute the strength of the New Deal as a domestic reform movement.[41]

The congressional, state, and local elections of 1938 proved to be a referendum on the New Deal, and they showed just how precarious Roosevelt's position had become. In the Democratic primaries, Roosevelt, with complete support from the CIO, sought to defeat candidates who had opposed the president's program. The AFL endorsed the putative Democratic reactionaries. In every case but one, Roosevelt's enemies won. The November general election brought even more bitter news to the president. The Republicans gained 81 seats in the House and 8 in the Senate, the greatest midyear turnover in seats since 1894. Although Democratic majorities remained firmly in control of both houses, within the Democratic party the balance of power had shifted in favor of the more conservative Southerners. At the state and local levels, the returns proved even more dismaying for

New Dealers. In Michigan, the governor most closely associated with labor and its CIO wing, Frank Murphy, lost his bid for reelection, and badly at that. And in numerous industrial cities, the CIO failed to translate its mass union membership into an equally solid electoral phalanx.[42]

The results of the 1938 election presaged an even more coordinated political attack on the NLRB as the symbol of New Deal labor policies. By 1939 an informal coalition among Republicans, conservative (mostly Southern) Democrats, corporate interests, and the AFL was firmly in place.

Congress Attacks the NLRB

The new political balance of power on questions of labor policy manifested itself almost immediately in the first session of the Seventy-sixth Congress. From January through April 1939, a group consisting mostly of Southern Democrats and northern Republicans introduced bills to amend the Wagner Act and to strip the NLRB of much of its authority. The more extreme measures demanded the repeal of the NLRA or cut off appropriations for the operation of the NLRB. The less extreme proposed to exempt all agricultural labor (including workers involved in food processing and distribution) from the act or to amend it in order to grant employers rights equal to those of their employees. Other conservative congressmen called for a special committee to investigate the work of the NLRB.

The measure that commanded the greatest support and appeared most likely to succeed was the one first introduced, on January 25, by a prolabor, New Deal Democrat from Massachusetts, Senator David I. Walsh. Walsh's proposed bill bore the imprimatur of the AFL and proposed numerous amendments to the NLRA. Some served particular demands of the AFL — requiring the labor board to respect all majority votes by units of craft workers and curtailing the board's power to invalidate legal contracts between employers and unions. Others satisfied the concerns of employers — permitting employers to request a representation election, preventing the NLRB from establishing a bargaining unit of more than one employer, ceding the courts broader review power over NLRB decisions, and granting employers the right of noncoercive free speech.[43]

The Walsh amendments represented the solidification of the alliance built between the AFL executive council and attorneys for the NAM and several large corporations. On January 26, Gilbert Montague, an attorney for the NAM, congratulated Joseph Padway, staff counsel for the AFL: "Under all circumstances I think that you did a wonderful job on the NLRA amendments as reported in the newspapers of last evening, and I extend to you and the Federation my sincere and hearty congratulations."[44] The following month William Green blasted the NLRB in an article printed in *Fortune*. Green leveled the usual charges against the board for favoring the CIO and subverting employers' constitutional rights. He also levied a savage ad hominem indictment against Donald Wakefield Smith and Edwin Smith, the two board members he considered most hostile to the AFL and employers, who, Green suggested, were dupes of communism. He reiterated the AFL's intention to amend and clarify the Wagner Act. Green also promised a campaign to clean house among NLRB employees. Through the AFL's efforts, he pledged, "we are confident that the interests of labor, industry, and the public will be better protected in the future."[45]

Green, the NAM, and congressional conservatives found support for their position in a series of decisions handed down by the Supreme Court on February 27, 1939.[46] For the first time, the nation's highest tribunal ruled the NLRB deficient in its proceedings and unfair in its decisions. Although the critics of the NLRB delighted in the Court's findings, their pleasure was premature. The Supreme Court's decisions of February 27 remained rare exceptions to its more general affirmations of NLRB procedures and decisions.

As political pressure intensified to amend the Wagner Act and reform the NLRB, the administration and its labor advocates again beat a strategic retreat. The prolabor Democrats in control of the Senate Education and Labor Committee (Elbert Thomas of Utah) and the House Labor Committee (Mary Norton of New Jersey) declined to hold hearings on the proposed legislation. Their opponents charged that Thomas, Norton, and their committee allies acted at the behest of the White House. What will we do about the NLRA, asked one border state antilabor Democrat. "Are we going to permit this fiery dragon to continue to suck the blood of American business and destroy American institutions and ideals?" And one of the most reactionary Southern Democrats, a representative from Georgia, swore that unless the House Labor Committee held hearings on the proposed amendments, he would move that a special congressional committee be appointed to investigate the NLRB.[47]

In the Senate, Robert Wagner eloquently tried to defend his creation from its critics. He appeared before the Education and Labor Committee to testify against the proposed amendments to the NLRA. Wagner defended the board against all the charges levied against its procedures. It had been authorized to promote the right of workers to organize and to bargain collectively while simultaneously moderating industrial conflict. Wagner provided detailed statistics to prove his case, facts and numbers that demonstrated that the number of union members had increased enormously while the incidence of strikes had declined substantially after the Wagner Act had been ruled constitutional. His statement also stressed that, despite the Supreme Court's rulings of February 27, the federal judiciary had invariably decided in favor of the board.[48]

Neither Wagner's data nor his eloquence could protect the board from its critics.

Instead, President Roosevelt tried a different ploy. On April 25, 1939, Roosevelt chose William Leiserson to replace Donald Wakefield Smith as a member of the NLRB. The president hoped that Leiserson's appointment would mollify the AFL and business without unnecessarily irking the CIO. Roosevelt was partly right. By 1939 Leiserson had built a long and successful career as a private, state, and federal labor mediator-arbitrator. Both union officials and management had always found his approach to industrial disputes to be sound and sensible. A disciple of John R. Commons, Selig Perlman, and the Wisconsin approach to labor relations, Leiserson brought to the board an attitude and an approach far different from that of its original members.

In many respects Leiserson's relationship to his new colleagues replicated the experience of the John R. Commons group on Frank P. Walsh's Commission on Industrial Relations. In 1914 and 1915 Commons had rebelled against Walsh's one-sided emphasis on corporate misbehavior and on establishing workers' legal rights, because he argued that this failed to promote a framework for harmonious labor-management relations. Likewise, in 1939 and 1940, Leiserson declared war against the lawyers who dominated the NLRB. He found them too fond of abstract legal principles and insufficiently attuned to the subtleties of sound industrial relations. Instead of promoting more-stable bargaining relationships between employers and employees, Leiserson believed that the board's attorneys encouraged unionists and workers to fight the authority of their bosses. Leiserson also suspected that some board employees acted as they did because of their connections to the Communist party. He particularly distrusted the board's secretary, Nathan Witt, whom Leiserson identified as the hub around which Communist activities revolved. Leiserson accepted his appointment by the president as a mandate to extirpate subversive influences from the board, to reform its "irregular" procedures, and to promote more harmonious relations between companies and unions.[49]

If Roosevelt thought that his appointment of Leiserson to the NLRB would silence the critics, he was mistaken. The president's concession only strengthened the resolve of the board's enemies to further their cause. The AFL continued to work closely with corporate attorneys and congressional conservatives in the campaign to amend the Wagner Act. Green and his fellow executive council members increasingly acted like a herd of rogue elephants off on a destructive rampage. They disregarded the pro–Wagner Act, pro-NLRB sentiments of the bulk of their affiliates and members. Worse, they refused to recognize that the AFL had in fact gained more than the CIO from the Wagner Act and its administration by the board. Despite the several NLRB decisions that had gone against the AFL, from 1938 through 1940 the AFL grew much more rapidly than the CIO did. The existence of the Wagner Act and the threat of adverse NLRB rulings induced many employers to recognize AFL unions and to bargain collectively with them rather than risk penetration by an affiliate of the CIO. New Deal labor policy had created an environment in which conventional AFL unions could recruit more successfully and function more effectively than ever. This, Green and his associates refused to recognize. Instead, they built a working political coalition with some of trade unionism's most resolute enemies.[50]

Leiserson, who had been appointed to the board partly to mollify the AFL, proved more supportive of the Wagner Act than Green and his associates. Yet Leiserson inadvertently furthered the anti–Wagner Act, NLRB campaign as much as the AFL did. In his eagerness to root out subversive members, curtail Witt's authority, and implement policies more accommodative to the AFL and business, Leiserson built a public and private record that labor's political enemies used to excellent advantage. His disdain for board attorneys, especially his antipathy to Witt, prompted Leiserson to amass a file of numerous cases in which the board had allegedly violated rules of judicial procedure and equitable industrial relations.[51]

Only firm control of their respective committees by Senator Thomas and Representative Norton stymied the antilabor forces in the spring and summer of 1939. The congressional conservatives, however, were not to be denied. Certain of their power in the House, the conservatives decided to use their strategic leadership positions to outflank labor's defenders. On June 22, Representative Howard Smith of Virginia, chair of the Rules Committee and one of the Democrats whom Roosevelt had tried to purge in the 1938 election, introduced a resolution requesting the appointment of a special committee to investigate the NLRB. Despite claims by Representative Norton and her prolabor allies that jurisdiction over all labor legislation properly belonged to the Labor Committee, Smith took his proposal before his own Rules Committee, which reported it out on July 6. Two weeks later a slightly amended Rules Committee proposal (HR 258) calling for the creation of a special five-person House committee to investigate the NLRB passed by a majority of 254 to 134. On August 5 Smith announced the appointment of the committee, consisting of himself as chair, two antilabor Republicans, Charles Halleck of Indiana and Harry Routzohn of Ohio, and two prolabor Democrats, Abe Murdock of Utah and Arthur Healy of Massachusetts.[52]

The creation of the Smith Committee placed the NLRB and its defenders completely on the defensive. Moreover, in the summer of 1939, they had less reason than ever to expect firm support from Roosevelt. By then, his New Deal was in shambles as a domestic reform movement, his influence in Congress a shadow of its former self, and his own interests consumed by foreign affairs. The new political realities led NLRB chair Warren Madden to cooperate with Leiserson in purging Witt and his allies from the board and to introduce new procedures more favorable to craft unionists and employers.[53] Nothing could now slake the thirst of Howard Smith and his conservative congressional allies. They were committed to restoring to employers the power that had been theirs before New Deal Democrats had rewritten national labor law and the NLRB had implemented the new law to the benefit of militant labor.

The NLRB under Investigation

The Smith Committee opened its initial public hearings into the NLRB on December 11, 1939. Prior to the open hearings, investigators from the committee went through all the NLRB's records and papers meticulously. They had a field day. Board members and employees, Witt especially, had mixed private, off-the-record materials with official papers. Leiserson, apparently consciously, had filed memoranda that could later be used to damage the reputation of Witt and the policies of the latter's followers on the board. From the board's papers alone, Smith had ample circumstantial evidence to construct an incriminating case against the NLRB.

Then over more than two months, in thirty-seven days of public hearings, Smith gave his committee's counsel and hostile witnesses freedom to pillory the board. He conducted the hearings with acute awareness of public relations and used every available opportunity to generate publicity adverse to the NLRB in the newspapers. While the Senate and House labor committees provided a forum for witnesses sympathetic to the board, the Smith investigation dominated the news. Together with the investigations into "un-American" activities by Martin Dies, the Smith Committee hearings indelibly etched into the public mind the alleged links among communism, the CIO, and the NLRB. Even Leiserson, who testified during this period in defense of both the Wagner Act and the board, subverted his own goal. Because of his antipathy to Witt in particular, lawyers in general, and Communists in toto, Leiserson generated a mass of evidence that Smith was able to use against the board.[54]

Even before the committee completed its public hearings and before the board's defenders had the opportunity to make their case, Smith and his Republican colleagues issued an intermediate report, on March 29. This report pulled no punches. It was an unadulterated brief for the prosecution case against the NLRB. Smith, Halleck, and Routzohn asserted that the Wagner Act intended neither to promote unionization nor to sanction compulsory collective bargaining. Because the NLRB had chosen to promote unions and required employers not only to bargain with them but to sign contracts, it had, according to the committee majority, violated its own charter of existence. The report then charged the NLRB with fifteen separate instances in which it violated the Wagner Act, disregarded the requirements of legal due process, and acted unconstitutionally.

Most of the evidence to establish the charges came from a handful of court decisions unfavorable to the NLRB, the AFL's own bill of particulars, internal records of the board, and Leiserson's testimony. One would never have known that the circuit courts and the Supreme Court had nearly always found for the NLRB; or that the board had adjudicated most of the disputes that came before it to the satisfaction of both parties. The majority then proposed twenty-one amendments to the Wagner Act, all of which diluted its benefits to labor. Among the amendments were proposals to rewrite the preamble to the Wagner Act in order to strip it of its prolabor, pro–collective bargaining bias; to diminish the board's authority to reinstate discharged employees; to redefine agricultural labor so as to eliminate millions of workers from protection under the Wagner Act; to turn collective bargaining into a process without purpose; to guarantee employers free speech and the right to petition for elections; to change representation rules to favor the AFL and small craft units; to require the board to adhere to legal rules of evidence; and to grant federal courts greater authority to review NLRB election procedures.[55]

On April 11, Representatives Healey and Murdock issued a minority report, which refuted, point by point, the majority's indictment of the NLRB and its proposed amendments. The minority minced no words in arguing that the Wagner Act was intended to strengthen unions and collective bargaining. Healey and Murdock demonstrated how the NLRB had done just that, while also having a moderating impact on industrial conflict. "Industrial democracy must not again be disfranchised," they warned the NLRB's critics. "The attack upon the National Labor Relations Act has failed in the courts. We submit that on the evidence this attack in the National Legislature must also fail."[56]

The minority effectively rebutted the Smith majority's preliminary report. It failed, however, to stall the congressional attack on industrial democracy. Even before Murdock and Healey made their dissent public, the House moved against the NLRB. First, the coalition of Republicans and Southern Democrats cut the board's appropriations.[57] Then on April 4 the House Labor Committee, whose chair, Mary Norton, perceived herself as the NLRB's defender, recommended four changes in the board: (1) to expand it to five members (enabling Roosevelt to appoint more people like Leiserson); (2) to make the Globe doctrine concerning the rights of craft workers part of the law; (3) to allow employers to request elections when faced by rival unions; and (4) to make exclusive representation contracts inviolate for one year.[58]

Just how far the balance of power on labor questions had shifted in Congress was shown in mid-May 1940, when Robert LaFollette introduced his bill (S. 1970) to outlaw oppressive corporate labor practices. The result of the LaFollette Committee's three-year-long investigation into employer violations of civil liberties, S. 1970 ripened into a bitter fruit. Senate debate focused not on LaFollette's purposes but on charges by Southern Democrats that alien workers and subversives in league with the CIO were endangering the national defense. The Southerners proposed amendments that would limit the employment of aliens, Communists, and Nazis. As amended, the LaFollette Bill passed 47 to 20, but it never even came to a vote in the House.[59]

By May 1940 the House was totally involved in Howard Smith's campaign to amend the Wagner Act. Smith used his own power as chair of the Rules Committee and the support of Republicans to strip Norton's Labor Committee of its primary jurisdiction in the sphere of labor relations. By a vote of 292 to 106, the House on June 4 passed Smith's special rule to debate his proposed amendments to the NLRA (HR 9195). Before the debate ended, Smith engineered a great coup. He won William Green's consent to most of his proposed amendments. Green negotiated with Smith because the Virginia congressman defended his amendments in the name of worker rights and the prerogatives of voluntary, private organizations. Smith stressed the right of workers to free choice without union coercion, that workers should not be compelled to join a union as a requirement of employment. He also insisted that employers had as much right to communicate with their employees as union organizers did. And several of his amendments offered protection to AFL craft unions and managerial prerogatives against arbitrary NLRB decisions that allegedly favored radical, Communist-influenced and coercive CIO affiliates. To solidify Green's endorsement of such goals, Smith accepted four amendments proposed by the AFL. Two restored the Wagner Act's original preamble with its commitment to unionism and collective bargaining. The other two made minor revisions in NLRB procedures to render them marginally more protective to workers in general and the AFL in particular. Having gained the AFL's cooperation, Smith had no trouble in inducing the House to pass his revised amendments by a vote of 258–129.[60]

Although the Senate never acted on the Smith amendments (as Roosevelt and labor's friends expected, Elbert Thomas's Labor Committee buried them), by the end of 1940 the antilabor coalition had achieved many of its primary aims. The NLRB felt the heat and reacted to it. It became far less aggressive in pursuing labor's rights. In August, Madden's term as chair ended, and in the absence of an immediate replacement, the board usually deadlocked between the approaches of Edwin Smith and Leiserson. That stalemate was broken by the president on November 25, when Roosevelt, less than a month after his reelection, appointed Harry Millis, an economist from the University of Chicago and a practitioner of the Commons-Leiserson style of industrial relations, as the new chair of the NLRB. On Millis's appointment, *Business Week* observed, "subtly, perhaps, but surely, the Board may be counted upon to change its line . . . [and] from now on business can expect to find the Board's agents more tolerant to its problems and points of view."[61]

The magazine was right. The new Millis-Leiserson majority restaffed the board and refashioned its doctrines. Millis discharged Nathan Witt and all the radical attorneys associated with him. They encouraged employers to petition for representation elections. They refused to certify unions on the basis of signed cards and similar evidence of preference in the absence of elections. And they evinced a clear preference for the AFL's style of business unionism and its mode of collective bargaining. When the Smith Committee presented its final report on December 30, although the majority still condemned the NLRB and endorsed amendments to the Wagner Act, it took cognizance of the changes in board policy wrought by Millis and Leiserson.[62] In Millis's own words, the board had begun an "orderly retreat" in which it moved to a far less prolabor orientation. Now the board grew more concerned with employer rights and more tolerant of company labor practices. In the words of one observer, "it is difficult to justify the Board's present position except on the ground that labor unions must be left to achieve their objectives without aid from the Board." When Edwin Smith's term ended in August 1941, more bad news came for militant labor advocates. Roosevelt replaced Smith with Gerard Reilly, who was more conservative than Leiserson and Millis and also more probusiness. Green and the AFL rejoiced, for Smith had been their special bête noir. Smith's departure and Reilly's appointment concluded the radical prolabor, pro-CIO phase of the NLRB's history.[63]

For a time, it also marked the end of Roosevelt and Congress's battle over domestic issues. As the president drew the nation deeper into the cauldron of world war, he preferred not to battle with conservatives inside and outside Congress over his labor policies. He still sought to assist his union friends, but not at the expense of losing support among Southern Democrats and business interests whose backing he needed for foreign policy.

The conservatives in Congress, however, did not suddenly forget labor in 1941. Southern Democrats and Republicans continued to attack the CIO and criticize the NLRB. Now a new note crept into congressional debate. Not only were union militants charged with fostering antibusiness attitudes; they were accused of sabotaging the defense effort and serving the Soviet Union. Pointing to strikes against strategic defense industries, especially airplane plants in California, many members of Congress accused CIO unions of sheltering "reds" and the NLRB of protecting the left. This, they suggested, exposed the nation to the same situation — Communist unions hindering defense production in the interest of the Nazi-Soviet Non-aggression Pact — that had led to the fall of France in June 1940. Even labor's friends in Congress joined in lambasting Communist influence in the unions of aircraft workers. They drew the line in refusing to join their more conservative colleagues in an effort to enact a law outlawing the right to strike in all defense-related industries.[64]

The Federal Judiciary and Labor

Bereft of strong support in Congress and partly deserted by a president preoccupied with foreign affairs, the labor movement between 1938 and 1941 paradoxically discovered new and firm friends in what historically had been the least sympathetic branch of the federal government, the judiciary. Roosevelt's appointees to the judiciary were numerous enough by the end of his second term to tip the balance of power in favor of the NLRB and labor's rights. Where circuit court judges still reflected the pre–New Deal legal order, the new Roosevelt Supreme Court usually reversed lower court decisions in labor cases. The federal judiciary's support of the NLRB and labor was all the more remarkable considering how far the political balance of power in Congress, in the states, and among the electorate had swung against trade unionism. Pressure from Congress, business, and the AFL had prompted Roosevelt to reshape the NLRB, and the board in turn to moderate its commitment to trade unionism. Yet at the same time, many federal judges, especially a majority on the highest court, took a much more expansive view of the NLRB's power and labor's rights.

It is true that the federal courts as early as 1937 began to restrain militant unionism and to interpret the Wagner Act in a less radical manner.[65] Moreover, several decisions handed down by the Supreme Court in 1937 and 1939 seemed to echo older judicial doctrines concerning the rights of workers and employers rather than to reverberate to the sounds of industrial citizenship and democracy.[66] Yet a majority of federal judges (at least among those on the Supreme Court) delivered opinions that resonated to the tones of the present (judges are seldom tribunes of the future), whereas only the minority opinions of Justices Hughes, Roberts, and sometimes Stone echoed the past.

While a few decisions of the high court went against labor, their impact must not be exaggerated. Such decisions usually provided the judges relatively little room to maneuver. In the case of NLRB v. Mackay Radio and Telegraph Company, for example, a majority of judges ruled that, under the Wagner Act, an employer has the right to hire replacement workers during an economic strike (that is, a non-unfair labor practices dispute).[67] Still, the Supreme Court's actual opinion reiterated the basic provisions of the Wagner Act concerning the protection of the job rights of strikers, while simply defining more precisely the employers' prior legal right to hire replacement workers, which the Wagner Act had never abrogated. The ruling, in fact, endorsed the opinion of the dissenter in the lower court and reversed the circuit court's decision. The majority ruled that legal strikers remained employees even during an economic dispute, that it was an unfair labor practice to refuse to rehire strike leaders, that the NLRB had the power to order an employer to reinstate workers discharged for their activities during a labor dispute, and that, in doing so, the board had not acted arbitrarily or capriciously.[68]

The courts did twice limit the NLRB's power to define as unfair certain employer labor practices. These, however, were extremely complex decisions in highly sensitive cases concerning the conflict between the AFL and the CIO. In two instances the NLRB had voided contracts between an employer and an affiliate of the AFL. In each instance, the federal courts repudiated the board's findings that the employers had engaged in an unfair labor practice. Instead, the judges ruled that the contracts between employers and AFL unions evidenced a commitment to fair collective bargaining, provided a means to avert strikes, eliminated restraints on interstate commerce, and hence promoted the purposes of the Wagner Act. As long as employers did not use their power primarily to eliminate trade unions, the judges agreed, firms were free to hire whomever they pleased and to bargain with whomever they preferred.[69]

The decision that stands out as the clearest symbol of the judiciary's antipathy toward militant labor occurred in the case of NLRB v. Fansteel Metallurgical Company and concerned the rights of sit-down strikers. The case had originated during the wave of sit-down strikes in 1937 and affected a firm that had refused to recognize unions. Fansteel had also violated almost every aspect of the Wagner Act. The sit-down itself turned violent because of the company's resolve to evict the strikers through the use of force. In the aftermath of the strike, local authorities prosecuted union leaders and other workers charged with criminal behavior. Many of them were found guilty and punished. Fansteel refused to rehire not only any of its convicted employees but also many others who had been neither convicted nor indicted. The NLRB ordered the firm to desist from its unfair labor practices, to recognize the union, and to reinstate with back pay the discharged employees, including some found guilty in court. The board argued that conviction was a sufficient penalty for criminal behavior and that discharge from work was a pretext for the company to break the union. The company appealed the NLRB's order to the circuit court of appeals, which found for Fansteel, and the board then appealed to the Supreme Court.

On February 27, 1939, Chief Justice Hughes, speaking for the majority, endorsed the NLRB's finding of unfair labor practices against the company but reversed the board's order of reinstatement for workers discharged for violent behavior. As might be expected, Hughes castigated the sit-down as an illegal seizure of private property. In such a case, he added, to require the reemployment of the guilty parties in order to remedy an unfair labor practice "would be to put a premium on resort to force instead of legal remedies and to subvert the principles of law and order which lie at the foundation of society."[70]

For Hughes and the majority to have ruled otherwise, in fact, would have been truly astounding in 1939. It would probably have generated a popular outcry against the "Roosevelt Court" as great as that against its predecessor in 1935 and 1936. Two years earlier a joint resolution of Congress had declared sit-down strikes to be a violation of public policy. Robert Wagner himself had publicly repudiated the sit-down tactic, as also had the president, the AFL, and by 1938, most of the CIO's leaders. There was simply no way in February 1939 that the Supreme Court would have allowed the NLRB to protect sit-down strikers, especially at a time when Congress was considering legislation to strip the board of much of its authority.

We should not make too much of the Fansteel decision. The vast majority of Supreme Court rulings between 1938 and 1941 sustained both the letter and the spirit of the Wagner Act, and the authority of the NLRB and the rights of labor. In numerous cases the judges affirmed the power of the board to decertify company unions and to deny employers the fruits of unfair labor practices.[71] In such decisions, the majority ruled that a history of company unionism was sufficient to establish a pattern of employer coercion. The Court still allowed the NLRB to invalidate contracts between employers and AFL craft unions, where evidence suggested that they were the result of unfair labor practices. It also validated the board's power to determine the scope of bargaining units, including multiemployer ones, and declared that such certifications based on representation elections were not subject to circuit court review. The majority approved the NLRB's policy of holding runoff elections and removing company unions from representation election ballots.[72]

Two decisions handed down in April 1941 further extended the NLRB's authority. In one, the majority ruled that the NLRB had the power to order an employer with several plants to recognize the same union as the exclusive bargaining agent for all employees, despite the fact that a clear majority of workers in one plant preferred their own independent company union. In the other, the Court decided that it was as much an unfair labor practice to refuse to hire a union member as to discharge one (here the Court implicitly repudiated its own earlier defense of the employer's undiluted right to hire).[73] In an even more significant previous opinion (January 1941), the majority offered one of its broadest assertions of NLRB power. In a case involving the H. J. Heinz Company, Stone, speaking for the Court, ruled that it was an unfair labor practice for a firm to refuse to sign a contract with a union after the two had reached agreement in the process of collective bargaining. The employer who refuses to sign a contract, Stone declared, "impairs the bargaining process and tends to frustrate the aim of the statute [Wagner Act] to secure industrial peace through collective bargaining."[74]

On these issues and many others, the Supreme Court majority perceived the reality of labor-management relations far differently than did the majority in Congress and even than the Millis-Leiserson majority on the NLRB. The congressional majority, Millis-Leiserson, and lower federal courts thought it was time to treat employers and workers more equally. So too argued the sixth circuit court of appeals, declaring in December 1940 in a case concerning the Ford Motor Company that Henry Ford had an equal right of free speech, since with the passage of the Wagner Act "the servant no longer has occasion to fear the master's frown of authority or threats of discrimination for union activities, express or implied."[75] The Supreme Court, however, demurred. On December 22, 1941, speaking for the majority in another employer free-speech case, Frank Murphy observed, "Slight suggestions as to the employer's choice between unions may have telling effect among men who know the consequences of incurring that employer's strong displeasure."[76]

The Roosevelt Court did more than reaffirm the power of the NLRB. It also firmly established picketing as a protected aspect of free speech and emancipated unions from the clutches of the antitrust laws. In an April 1940 decision invalidating an Alabama statute that restrained workers' right to picket, Murphy ruled, "In the circumstances of our times the dissemination of information concerning the facts of a labor dispute must be regarded as within that area of free discussion that is guaranteed by the Constitution."[77] In the same term of the Court, the majority substantially curtailed the Sherman Act's applicability to strikes. Although the majority declined to find unions exempt from the Sherman Act and refused to overturn old decisions, which it disingenuously claimed to concern only secondary boycotts, it declared that strikes to limit hours, raise wages, or even establish the closed shop were beyond the reach of antitrust legislation.[78]

Less than a year later, Felix Frankfurter extended this ruling. Frankfurter declared that Section 20 of the Clayton Act had originally intended to exempt all normal union activities from the Sherman Act. The Supreme Court had diluted that exemption through its decisions in the 1920s. Congress then reacted by passing the Norris-LaGuardia Act (Frankfurter was one of its authors). Reading his own version of legislative history in which he had been an active participant, Frankfurter declared that socioeconomic realities, the Clayton Act, and the Norris-LaGuardia Act taken together placed all normal, legal union activities, including boycotts as well as strikes, beyond the purview of the Sherman Act, criminal conspiracy, and judicial restraint. In response to Frankfurter's opinion in U.S. v. Hutcheson, the Court's minority, Hughes and Roberts, dredged up old legal doctrines lamenting the majority's surrender to alien notions of class. To turn union labor into a special exempt legal category, they implied, was to unleash the forces of class war.[79] Frankfurter thus completed what he had set out to accomplish more than twenty years before on Wilson's NWLB. He solidified the victory of the New Deal labor relations regime through a judicial transformation in the conception of property rights and free speech.

What the federal judiciary had accomplished by the end of 1941 in the sphere of labor law was truly amazing. Alone among the branches of the federal government, it had not retreated far, if at all, in the face of an aggressive and growing antilabor movement. Despite a few rulings partly adverse to the NLRB and trade unions, the federal judiciary — the Supreme Court especially — had substantially extended the rights of workers, unions, and the NLRB. If the New Deal had failed by 1941 to achieve a total transformation in industrial relations, the federal judiciary had indeed experienced a legal revolution with enormous implications for the American labor movement. Just how far that revolution had proceeded was captured in the words of a circuit court of appeals decision upholding the authority of the NLRB: "Perhaps the cackle of the farmer's hen as she announces the completion of her daily chore, or the squeal of his pig in its struggle to become a porker, are beyond this boundary line [federal power under the commerce clause], but of this we give no assurance."[80]

The federal government's labor policies and their impact on the American labor movement during the New Deal years bore a striking resemblance to events during the Wilson years. In fact, early New Dealers consistently compared their political response to the crisis of depression to their predecessors' reaction to world war. Once again also, the Democratic party built a close working alliance with organized labor (in this instance more the CIO than the AFL) and became the preferred choice of most working-class voters. New Dealers transformed the recommendations of Frank P. Walsh's Commission on Industrial Relations (1911–15) into law (the Wagner, Social Security, and Fair Labor Standards acts, among others) and reincarnated Wilson's National War Labor Board in the body of the National Labor Relations Board. Unlike its World War I precursor, however, the NLRB had real coercive power, which it used to promote fair representation elections and collective bargaining.[81]

The New Deal reforms, like those of the Wilson years, stimulated the growth of trade unionism, especially in sectors of the economy theretofore resistant to the labor movement. However precariously, by 1939–40 industrial unions were a real presence in the towering heights of the economy, and automobile, steel, rubber, and electrical goods employers had lost much of their previously undiluted power over workers. The AFL benefited as much or more than the CIO from this revolution, and in 1940 it was by far the larger of the two labor centers. Together AFL and CIO members composed almost 20 percent of the nonagricultural labor force, and unions were poised to become an economic, social, and political power in the land.

By 1938, the New Deal experiment in labor policy also seemed to be in danger of ending as an abortive reform in a manner similar to the reforms of the Wilson years. In 1919 and 1920, popular attitudes, as expressed in voting preferences, had shifted drastically against trade unionism; business interests and their allies in the Republican party had initiated a vigorous antilabor crusade; big business challenged and defeated labor in a series of postwar strikes; Wilsonian Democrats retreated hastily from their most advanced and exposed prolabor positions; and organized labor fell into a decline from which it would not recover until the coming of the New Deal. In 1938 and 1939, the labor movement seemed to relive a large part of the Wilsonian experience. Business recovered from its defeats of 1936 and 1937 and fought trade unionism with a renewed vigor, especially in the mass-production industries. The coalition of Southern Democrats and Republicans in Congress stymied the New Deal and imperiled its most progressive labor laws. Roosevelt, like Wilson before him, withdrew from his most exposed political positions on the labor question and listened more carefully to business and antilabor opinion. And the CIO, like the AFL between 1919 and 1922, appeared to be on the verge of collapse. Even more eerily, Martin Dies, Howard Smith, and several AFL leaders began to fan the flames of a new red scare.

One dominant reality, however, distinguished the Roosevelt years from the Wilson years. Wilson's greatest labor reforms had occurred during the war years and disintegrated during the postwar conservative restoration. The New Deal, by contrast, had set its labor policies in place in peacetime, had established a government agency (the NLRB) with the coercive power to enforce them, and had appointed a federal judiciary that would legitimate them. Instead of providing temporary concessions to unions in order to establish labor peace during war, the New Deal fostered collective bargaining between unions and management as a permanent feature of the economic landscape. When war came, trade unions could use the political and legal victories won during the 1930s to undertake a giant membership drive, which became a bonanza for union-building. The war also completed the transformation of trade unions from voluntary, private, craft-based associations into mass industrial institutions that would be subjected to persistent and intensive state regulation.

War and the Creation

of a New Industrial State,

1940–1946

Just as the congressional conservative reaction against New Deal labor policies peaked in 1940, United States foreign policy drew the nation deeper into the morass of European war. With the fall of France in June 1940 and Britain's isolation as Hitler's solitary enemy, Roosevelt pursued policies designed to expedite American defense production and provide our British allies with all the aid possible short of an American declaration of war. His major domestic reform initiatives already killed by Congress, Roosevelt was probably relieved to focus on events overseas, an arena in which he could rely on the sympathy and support of most Southern Democrats.

From the summer of 1940 through the autumn of 1941, he inched the nation step by step closer to open war with Germany. Even before the Japanese attacked Pearl Harbor on December 7, 1941, the United States and Germany had been waging undeclared naval warfare in the North Atlantic. The Japanese attack simply hastened the moment of American belligerency and partly relieved Roosevelt of full responsibility for leading the American people into war.

The movement in 1941 from quasi neutrality to quasi belligerency to total warfare altered the balance of power between labor and capital. Labor remained on the defensive politically, unable to achieve its legislative agenda, but the war stalled antilabor initiatives in Congress while the courts continued to interpret labor law in the spirit of 1935. The decisive factor, however, became the economy. Trade unions operated in a milieu unlike anything they had experienced since the halcyon years of World War I. The labor market tightened, skilled workers grew scarce, and employers acted less hostilely toward unions. The CIO unions in the mass-production industries, led by automobiles, steel, electrical construction, rubber, and shipbuilding, recovered from their severe setbacks of late 1937 and 1938 and experienced a second burst of great growth. The more mature and stable affiliates of the AFL, which had grown even in the slack time of the "Roosevelt depression," increasingly demanded and won closed-shop contracts, an achievement that boosted membership substantially.

As the nation prepared for a difficult and global war, labor leaders and corporate executives alike realized that the federal government would mandate a wartime system of labor-management relations. Both trade unionists and employers remembered their experiences during World War I with the labor policies of the Wilson administration. Both, however, drew different lessons from those experiences. Employers had been upset by the policies of the NWLB and the great trade union advance of 1917–19. Trade unionists recalled their failure to consolidate wartime gains and the debacle that unions suffered in the steel and meatpacking industries after the war. Yet labor's and business's reactions to the crisis of 1940–41 echoed their behavior during the World War I years.

Corporate spokespeople insisted that a national emergency must not be the occasion to transform the status quo in labor-management relations. They demanded a federal policy that would lock into place the existing relationship between employers and workers, tolerating the closed shop where it functioned, legitimating the open shop elsewhere, and enabling nonunion firms to remain union-free. Business expected to coordinate a military-industrial policy under which the state disciplined labor through no-strike pledges and binding contracts.

Labor leaders envisioned a different kind of wartime quid pro quo. They expected to use the crisis to build union strength. If the government sought labor's cooperation, the state would have to grant unions security and their leaders an equal share with business leaders in policy-making. In exchange for pledging not to strike and promising to discipline their rank and files, labor leaders demanded that the state require corporations to recognize unions, bargain with them in good faith, and deduct union dues from the payroll, in effect creating a secure union shop. They now saw themselves, in C. Wright Mills's famous phrase, as "new men of power," and they insisted on being treated as such.

In 1940 and 1941 labor was in a much stronger position to advance its interests than in the World War I years. Although the labor movement remained divided institutionally and politically[1] (as it had not been during the Wilson years), competition between AFL and CIO affiliates fostered union growth. Total union membership by 1941 was three times as great as it had been in 1916 and included a mass membership in the basic industries, where it had been largely absent a quarter of a century earlier. Labor again had a friend in the White House, firm advocates in the Labor Department, and sympathizers scattered throughout the federal bureaucracy. And this time it also had the law (NLRA) clearly on its side, an administrative agency to enforce the law (NLRB), and a Supreme Court more tolerant of union tactics. Thus many labor leaders sought to obtain the full and equal participation in wartime policy-making that had been denied them during the Wilson years.

Instead labor found its larger design thwarted. Despite all their friends in Washington, labor leaders discovered themselves less in demand than business leaders and found their advice disregarded. As in the Wilson war years, so in the Roosevelt era the federal government acted in a contradictory manner in the realm of labor policy. The cabinet bureaus and agencies most closely associated with the military rarely evinced sympathy for trade unionism, instead awarding numerous lucrative contracts to antiunion firms. Almost all the chief administrators of wartime labor policy were drawn from corporate enterprise or the social science-legal mandarinate. Whether former businesspeople, academics, or attorneys, they treated labor leaders and workers as clients, not equals. Even labor's ally in the White House rarely had time to befriend his advocates in the unions. Roosevelt focused on war and diplomacy, considering domestic affairs a diversion from the nation's more vital interests. Still, despite its handicaps during the war years, the labor movement emerged in 1945–46 much more powerful and secure than it had been in 1940, let alone in 1919–20, appearing to many of its friends and enemies as a new power in the land.

The Trade Union Offensive

Ever since its initial triumphs in the winter and spring of 1937, the CIO's organizing campaign in the mass-production industries had stalled. In 1940 the Little Steel companies still refused to recognize SWOC, the Ford Motor Company spurned the UAW, Westinghouse fought the United Electrical Workers, and the big four meat packers rejected unionism. Even where CIO unions had won recognition and contracts — General Motors, Chrysler, Studebaker, General Electric, and United States Steel, for example — their gains were not yet secure. None of those companies tolerated the union shop, nor would they grant unions sole and exclusive bargaining rights for all workers employed by the firms. Indeed, in contract renegotiations during 1939 such firms drove hard bargains, declining to increase wages and demanding that the unions discipline their unruly members.[2]

As the nation increased defense production, however, the CIO unions found themselves in a more favorable position. The mass-production firms received the bulk of the new federal military contracts, which guaranteed them a substantial rate of profit. As the labor market tightened and firms with defense contracts hesitated to diminish profits by taking strikes, CIO leaders grew more aggressive.

Philip Murray, who replaced John L. Lewis as president of CIO in November 1940, immediately urged his executive board to endorse a vigorous and extensive organizing drive. "I tell you frankly and candidly," Murray advised his fellow trade unionists, "that I don't give a tinker's damn about national defense interfering with our work. I feel that we ought to go ahead just the same as if that kind of situation were not in our midst. Organize and fight and do the job as we originally intended to do the job five years ago."[3] Lewis intended to do the same in his own union empire, coal mining. In his case, the defense crisis would be used to eliminate the remaining wage differentials between southern and northern miners and to gain union security in the captive mines owned by the steel companies.[4]

The CIO sought to achieve its goals in two ways. Initially, first Lewis and then Murray tried to use the power of the state to unionize workers in the major defense industries. They demanded that the federal government *not* award contracts to firms that the NLRB had declared to be in violation of the Wagner Act. Among the primary defense contractors under NLRB censure were Bethlehem Steel and Ford Motors. Threatened with the loss of their federal contracts, such firms, reasoned Lewis and Murray, would implement NLRB orders, hold representation elections, recognize the victorious unions, and bargain collectively. Federal officials, however, refused to award defense contracts solely on the basis of a firm's compliance with national labor legislation. Thus the CIO resorted to raw power. It conducted massive strikes (or threatened them) against those employers who refused to bargain with unions. In the winter and spring of 1941, the CIO took on Ford, the Little Steel companies, the airplane industry, the major meat packers, and such traditional antiunion firms as International Harvester and Allis Chalmers. The number of strikes and the total number of workers involved in the year 1941 surpassed that for any year during the 1930s, including 1934 and 1937, and approached that for 1919. John L. Lewis waged two national coal strikes, one against the southern mine operators in the spring and another against the captive mines that dragged on through the summer to the end of the fall. Fully 70 percent of all the strikes involved affiliates of the CIO, and most of those concentrated in defense-related industries.

Labor came out of these battles with enormous gains. Ford not only recognized the UAW, it was the first automobile company to grant the union shop. Both the Little Steel companies and the meat packers dropped their resistance to unionism, and federal intervention compelled many firms in airplane production, shipbuilding, and other lines of defense work to grant forms of union security. Along with union recognition went wage increases, more-stringent provisions for seniority, and an enhanced role for the union on the shop floor.[5]

In their own quiet, less obtrusive manner, the affiliates of the AFL also benefited from the defense crisis. Less prone to strike or to call workers to the barricades, these unions claimed as members highly skilled workers in especially short supply in defense work. They also appealed to employers as less militant, less threatening, and more responsible than their competitors in the CIO. As a consequence, employers often voluntarily recognized an affiliate of the AFL rather than risk an organizing drive by the CIO or a representation election. Just as often, employers granted the skilled construction and metalworkers closed-shop agreements. Thus, as employment rose in closed-shop defense production, AFL membership soared.[6]

The union offensive increased total membership by more than 17 percent, bringing it to an all-time high of between 10.2 and 10.5 million members. Union successes, however, also caused further political losses and complicated the formulation and implementation of Roosevelt administration labor policy during the defense and war crisis.

Antilabor Politics

Labor's rising assertiveness in 1941 provided its congressional enemies with additional cause to attack trade unionism. Their campaign to amend the Wagner Act having been frustrated by the tactics of the administration and the Senate Education and Labor Committee, the conservatives tried a new tack. They no longer proposed amendments to the NLRA. Now they focused on strikes in sensitive defense industries and on the closed shop — which, they charged, levied a compulsory tax on workers eager to do their patriotic duty without seeking permission from irresponsible union bosses. Throughout the year 1941 the halls of Congress rang to charges that France had fallen to Germany the previous year because "subversive" unions had refused to allow their members to cooperate in the war effort. The behavior of Communist-influenced unions in the CIO before the Nazi invasion of the Soviet Union on June 22 lent credence to such allegations. The same fate awaited the United States, warned the congressional conservatives, unless radical union leaders were punished, subversives eliminated from the labor movement, and the right to strike in defense industries denied.

Southern Democrats led the assault against labor in both houses. Senator Harry Byrd of Virginia demanded that the administration have the power to prevent strikes in defense industries. "The majesty of the Government of the United States must be sternly and firmly exercised to destroy the peril which now exists to our national security," he warned. Other Southern senators applauded Byrd's sentiments, adding that unless labor leaders ended strikes in defense industries, unions should lose federal protection. Their favorite form of punishment was to suggest the enactment of a new law that would establish the "right-to-work" in all defense industries, that is, to outlaw all forms of union security.[7]

As the number of strikes multiplied in the spring and summer of 1941, congressional rhetoric heated up. "Is John L. Lewis bigger and more powerful than the United States Government?" asked a querulous Senator Byrd. "In my opinion," declared Senator Price Daniel of Texas, "the maintenance of 'Freedom to Work' . . . means more to the domestic affairs of this country and to the future of the Nation than the temporary decision on any matter concerned with the present World War." And with those words, Daniels on September 25 introduced a joint resolution that proposed an amendment to the Constitution guaranteeing "Freedom to Work" (the open shop).[8] Few Democrats from the North or the West rose to defend the rights of strikers in defense industries, and most Republicans kept quiet or softly seconded the sentiments so loudly proclaimed by their Southern Democratic allies.

The polls Elmo Roper conducted for *Fortune* on public opinion added weight to the charges levied against labor by congressional conservatives. In June two-thirds of Roper's sample favored a ban on all strikes in defense industries, and another third desired the same in all defense-related industries. More than two-thirds of his sample demanded that the federal government establish an agency with the power to compel settlements in labor-management disputes. Those in the sample not associated with unions or management (the so-called middle Americans) were almost unanimous in their condemnation of defense strikes.[9]

Thus, the closer the nation drew to direct participation in the war, the more strongly congressional conservatives demanded antistrike legislation. On December 1 the House debated three bills that sought to limit the right to strike, two fueled by antilabor animus and the third originated as a compromise by labor's political friends. The first bill was introduced by Representative Carl Vinson of Georgia, chairman of the Naval Affairs Committee. Vinson simply proposed to outlaw all strikes in defense industries. The second came from labor's old enemy, Howard Smith, and also outlawed strikes and added a ban on closed and union shops as well as the loss of other vital rights that unions had gained through the Wagner Act. The third, or compromise bill, which came from the Labor Committee, proposed a sixty-day cooling-off period during which strikes would be banned while federal mediation occurred. If mediation failed to settle the dispute, the president would have the power to seize the affected plant. Vinson and Smith allied to overwhelm the moderates represented by the Labor Committee. First Smith moved that his bill be made an amendment to Vinson's, which passed the House on a roll call vote of 229–158. Then, on December 3, the Vinson Bill, as amended, passed 252–136.[10]

The amended Vinson Bill suffered the same fate as Smith's previous efforts to modify the Wagner Act. Senator Elbert Thomas, chairman of the Education and Labor Committee, buried it, as he did similar proposals arising in the Senate. How long Thomas could have held back the antilabor tide seems debatable. The

Japanese attack on Pearl Harbor, however, ended temporarily the congressional assault against trade unionism. On December 16, nine days after the Japanese attack, the leading antilabor senators agreed to postpone consideration of anti-strike legislation pending the results of an emergency industry-labor conference convened by President Roosevelt.[11]

The Roosevelt administration, which had been struggling to implement an effective defense-related labor policy since late in 1939, was now under even more pressure to do so. On one side, congressional conservatives, especially the Southern Democrats whose support Roosevelt needed for his foreign policy, sought to limit the right to strike. On a second front, labor leaders demanded that the president invalidate defense contracts with all firms that refused to obey federal labor laws. And on a third front, corporate executives urged the administration to uphold the status quo in labor relations, to reject compulsory arbitration, and to preclude mandatory cooling-off periods. Both labor and management demanded that Roosevelt cede them a larger role in making national policy, in return for which they would police the industrial peace.

The Administration's Dilemma

From the outbreak of the war in the late summer of 1939 until the Japanese attack on Pearl Harbor, the Roosevelt administration found itself torn in two. In many ways its response to the defense crisis replicated the situation during the early New Deal and the first stages of the NRA. Again Roosevelt desperately needed the cooperation of big business, for the largest corporations dominated the sectors of the economy considered most vital to the defense effort. Yet once again the stimulus to the economy generated by the defense effort intensified labor militancy and caused strikes that disrupted military preparedness. For most of the years 1939, 1940, and 1941, neither business nor labor evinced an inclination to sacrifice its own vital interests to a common cause. Thus Roosevelt faced a dilemma in which he needed the support of big business to reorganize the economy for an all-out defense effort without causing desertions among his trade union allies, which were now more crucial than ever to the Democratic political coalition.

By the fall of 1939 it had become clear to the leaders of the CIO that Roosevelt had begun to consult businessmen concerning defense production without offering trade unionists an equal share in the planning. This led John L. Lewis, among others, to demand for labor an equal role with business on all federal war planning agencies.[12] More directly and simply, Lewis called on the president to deny contracts to firms found in violation of federal labor laws. The CIO president had in mind Ford Motor and Bethlehem Steel, both beneficiaries of substantial military contracts and both having been charged by the NLRB with violations of the

Wagner Act. When no presidential executive order ensued, Lewis asked, "Is the law just for the weak and lowly, or is the law to be enforced against the powerful and the strong?"[13]

In late 1939 and the first half of 1940, Roosevelt's problems were largely with the CIO, whose affiliates were engaged in organizing campaigns against major defense contractors. What complaints the AFL had at the time were directed more to CIO challenges to craft union jurisdictional claims than to employers or to an absence of labor influence on federal defense agencies. The president's first priority, then, was to mollify those in the CIO who were unhappy with labor's role in the defense program. Roosevelt appealed directly to those CIO officials most amenable to his influence, notably Sidney Hillman and Philip Murray. Thus as the defense buildup intensified in the spring of 1940 after the fall of France, Roosevelt recalled his experiences as a federal administrator during World War I. On May 28, 1940, he announced the establishment of a National Defense Advisory Commission (NDAC) patterned after Woodrow Wilson's World War I agency and on which he designated Sidney Hillman as labor's representative (a choice parallel to Wilson's designation of Gompers for a similar role in 1916). At a press conference that day, Roosevelt explained in this way his choice of Hillman: "For heaven's sake do not attribute it to me because somebody will call me names — he [Hillman] is just half way between John Lewis and Green."[14]

Actually the president had dissembled for the press. He knew that the choice of Hillman was totally unacceptable both to the AFL (Green) and to Lewis (it was partly the reason for the latter's opposing Roosevelt in the election of 1940). Moreover, Roosevelt made his choice without consulting any labor leaders, a direct affront to the presidents of both national union federations. Roosevelt knew precisely what he was doing. The CIO, not the AFL, was creating problems for the defense effort. The appointment of Hillman would draw the CIO into cooperating with Roosevelt's design and render it unable to oppose defense labor policies with a single voice — that of Lewis. What the president had achieved was best expressed in the words of Lee Pressman, chief counsel for the CIO: The method of Hillman's appointment had "made Hillman a Government representative in the ranks of labor, rather than a representative of the ranks of labor in the field of Government."[15]

The acuity of Pressman's comment quickly became apparent as Hillman acted in his new advisory capacity to the president. In June, Hillman set up a labor division within the NDAC; in July he appointed John Keenan from the AFL and John Owens from the CIO as members of a labor-management advisory staff; and in early August he established a separate labor policy advisory committee. Yet as far as labor was concerned, the operative word was always "advisory." Hillman might consult trade unionists and seek their advice, but most policy decisions in the area of labor relations continued to be made either by dollar-a-year industrialists serving on the NDAC or by federal officials. As Lewis informed the CIO executive board in June, Hillman's policies were totally unacceptable. "Labor wants a seat at the council table. . . . It wants to cooperate and not be driven to the work bench or the factory. . . . Labor as represented in the CIO wants a partnership in this enterprise."[16]

What Lewis and the CIO wanted even more was a presidential executive order denying defense contracts to firms found to be in violation of the Wagner Act by the NLRB. Here, too, Hillman disappointed his associates in the CIO. Echoing the president's line, Hillman maintained that the exigencies of defense and the need to assist the British against the Nazi onslaught had to be accorded priority over the cause of the CIO.[17] In September, when the administration and Hillman inched closer to satisfying Lewis's demands through a ruling by the attorney general declaring that decisions by the NLRB were binding until federal courts ruled otherwise, business leaders, the military, and conservative politicians quickly compelled the president to retreat. On October 8, William Knudsen, the General Motors executive and Hillman's business counterpart on the NDAC, told an audience of businessmen in Milwaukee, "We don't want any part of the Russian system over here." Moreover, he assured them that the NDAC would not deny contracts to firms until federal courts definitely declared them in violation of the law. "The Defense Commission has no authority and does not want to undertake the job of enforcing the labor laws." Despite subsequent feeble efforts by Hillman and Roosevelt to link the award of federal contracts to implementation of the Wagner Act, Knudsen's policy prevailed. Federal defense planners refused to use their contract power as an indirect method to compel collective bargaining and to accomplish what Congress declined to mandate through direct legislation.[18]

As the pace of defense production accelerated, it became harder to resist the demands of organized labor. Trade unionists, especially the more highly skilled ones, who were in short supply, felt powerful enough to wrest their demands from reluctant employers. Affiliates of the AFL gained substantially, while those in the CIO mounted militant new organizing campaigns against such antiunion firms as Ford, Bethlehem Steel, Allis Chalmers, and the "big four" meat packers. As union membership mounted and labor's strength grew, Philip Murray, who had replaced Lewis as president of the CIO in November 1940, demanded for trade unionists an absolutely equal share in the organization of defense production. In December 1940 he proposed to Roosevelt that the federal government create a council in every major industry consisting of equal numbers of union and management people and chaired by a public official. Such councils would have complete responsibility for running the industry, and labor would become, in effect, codirector for corporate America.[19]

Naturally, business leaders resisted the Murray proposal and made clear to Roosevelt that their cooperation in the defense effort depended on government's respect for corporate prerogatives. Eager to satisfy business and also to mollify labor, Roosevelt on January 7, 1941, created the Office of Production Management (OPM). He appointed Knudsen and Hillman as codirectors, ostensibly awarding labor a full and equal share in defense planning. In practice, however, labor's role remained insignificant, and the committees that Hillman staffed with trade unionists were always labeled "advisory."[20] Why Knudsen made policy and Hillman only advised was explained by Bruce Catton: "A president of a corporation, taking a leave of absence . . . from his desk and being sworn in as a government official, ceased to be 'a representative of industry' and became, in fact and in substance, a government official, fit to be entrusted with the exercise of government authorities; a union man, similarly taking leave from his job and being sworn in as a government official, remained 'a representative of labor from start to finish.' "[21]

This reality left labor with no choice but to accomplish its aims through confrontation. Beginning in January 1941 and not terminating until December 6, 1941, a wave of strikes challenged the remaining major antiunion employers. Neither the OPM nor the NLRB had much success in eliminating industrial conflict, especially among primary defense contractors. In most of these disputes, both unions and firms refused to compromise their core demands (usually union security versus the open shop), and the customary forms of federal mediation through the Labor Department failed.

As strikes increasingly interfered with the defense effort, Roosevelt acted. On March 19, 1941, the president established a National Defense Mediation Board (NDMB), consisting of an equal number of representatives (four) from industry and labor (half AFL, half CIO), and three public members, one of whom, William H. Davis, served as chair. The executive order creating the NDMB authorized it to act only in a mediatory capacity; the board could neither arbitrate labor disputes nor compel obedience to its recommendations. Moreover, it could only consider disputes certified to it by the secretary of labor.[22]

The NDMB had enormous success in resolving the disputes that came before it, with the exception of the one insoluble dispute that caused its dissolution. Of the 114 cases it considered (111 of which were handled satisfactorily by subpanels), the board settled 96 to the satisfaction of both parties. The most contentious issue it faced was that of union security. On this question the public members held the balance of power, for the industry and union representatives refused to compromise the issue of the union versus the open shop. When forced to act, the public members formulated policy on a case-by-case basis. Eight times they recommended forms of union security; four times they rejected such an approach; and twice they recommended compromises. The most common form of union security granted was the "membership maintenance" clause, which provided that once a contract was negotiated, all current union members remained on the books for its duration. In one case, the board awarded the closed shop to skilled workers at Bethlehem Steel's Shipbuilding Division, arguing that since other firms in the industry had granted the closed shop Bethlehem must do the same in order to establish uniformity in a vital defense industry. In a comparable case, however, in which the public members recommended against the closed shop, that of the mine workers' union dispute with the captive coal mines, the ruling caused the board's collapse. Because the three public members arrogated to themselves the right to determine whether employers were antiunion and thus whether unions needed special protection, the labor members, even more than their industry counterparts, felt labor's vital interests to be at the mercy of people whose judgment they could not always trust.[23]

In truth, the success of the NDMB owed more to the realities of the economic situation than to its ad hoc policies or specific rulings. As excess industrial capacity diminished, unemployment declined, and profits soared, many firms grew more receptive to unions and collective bargaining. After a massive but short strike, Ford not only recognized the UAW in April but granted it a union shop. Later in the spring, the Little Steel companies finally agreed to bargain with SWOC, as did the big four meat packers and several major lumber firms with CIO affiliates in their sectors. Where companies refused to respect economic realities or to grant union security in return for no-strike contracts, however, the NDMB found itself stymied and simply left the dispute to the discretion of the president.

Roosevelt's personal intervention into labor warfare in the year 1941 strengthened the claims of trade unionism — but at a price. The president stressed that he would not tolerate strikes in sensitive defense industries, yet he assured trade unionists that he would protect their interests. True, he used federal troops to break a strike against the North American Aviation Company conducted by a local of the UAW. In this instance, however, Roosevelt had the support of UAW and CIO leaders, who evinced little sympathy for the strike leaders in California, whom they dismissed as irresponsible left wingers carrying out the wishes of the Communist party to support Soviet foreign policy. And after the troops broke the strike, the federal government compelled North American Aviation to grant the UAW local union security and to pay wages comparable to those previously won by the AFL machinists' union. Roosevelt also dispatched troops to seize a shipbuilding firm (Federal Drydock) that had refused to implement a "maintenance of membership" agreement, in this instance using federal power to discipline corporate enterprise and reward unionism.[24] In the coal industry, Roosevelt had also used federal power to ensure that Southern Appalachian mine operators matched northern wage rates, a victory for the UMW that increased its power in bituminous coal.[25]

A second labor dispute in coal initiated by Lewis and his union caused graver difficulties for the president and destroyed the NDMB. Having by the summer of 1941 achieved the union shop and uniform wage rates in all the nation's commercial soft-coal mines, the UMW thought the time propitious to conquer the last holdout against union security in the industry, the mines owned and operated by the basic steel companies (the captive mines). By then 95 percent of workers in the captive mines had joined the union. Clearly, absent a national emergency, Lewis could have called a strike, which would have compelled the steel companies to grant the union shop. It was equally evident that the companies were amenable to ceding union security as a surrender to either union or state power. Corporate executives refused to relinquish the open shop voluntarily, for to do so threatened the labor relations policies they practiced in the steel and shipbuilding industries and the principles enunciated by the industry members of the NDMB. As the chief operating officer of United States Steel, Myron Taylor, informed Roosevelt in a personal and confidential memorandum on October 25, the directors of his company "would abandon the defense of the freedom of the workers to join or not to join a union only if you issued an executive order . . . or if Congress enacted legislation which took from the shoulders of the Board the responsibility for that decision. In either of those instances, I am confident that the corporation would promptly comply."[26]

Throughout the dispute, however, Roosevelt refused to mandate a union shop. Neither politically nor ideologically antipathetic to the principle of union security, the president acted cautiously. At a time when congressional conservatives were condemning labor agitators and introducing "right to work" bills, Roosevelt scarcely desired to resist a rising political tide by ordering the union shop in the captive mines. Instead all parties to the dispute preferred that the NDMB resolve it. Thus on September 15, Lewis called a strike, which the secretary of labor certified to the NDMB as an emergency dispute. Two days later, Lewis proposed to reopen the mines for thirty days while the board studied the situation. It seems apparent that Lewis, the steel executives, and Roosevelt all expected the NDMB to rule in favor of the union shop; after all, the board had already ordered Bethlehem Steel to implement a closed shop for its shipyard division workers.

For more than a month the NDMB pondered a decision without resolving the issues in dispute. It simply returned the issues in dispute to Lewis and Taylor for private resolution. In Lewis's words, "The Board now emerges with a report devoid of conclusions as to merit, evasive as to the responsibilities of the Board, and dumps its own sorry mess into the already over-burdened lap of the Chief Executive." The UMW chief saw no alternative other than to order the miners back out on strike. The president had no choice but to condemn a walkout that allegedly disrupted essential defense production and to appeal to the miners' sense of patriotism. In any event, the miners walked out on October 28, precipitating a second round of presidential intervention.[27]

Had Roosevelt so desired, he undoubtedly could have taken a hard line against Lewis. The press, members of Congress of both parties and of liberal and conservative persuasion, and a host of others condemned the union leader. As Democratic politician Sherman Minton informed the president, "He [Lewis] is hated like no one else in America. Now is the time to clip his wings."[28] Roosevelt, however, preferred persuasion, compromise, and consensus. He prevailed upon Lewis and Taylor to return the dispute to the NDMB, whose chairman, William H. Davis, promised a firm decision if the miners returned to work. Again expecting a ruling in favor of the union shop, the disputants were stunned on November 10, when the NDMB rejected the union shop 9–2, with only the CIO's representatives in the affirmative. As a result, Philip Murray and Thomas Kennedy, the CIO men, resigned from the board, causing its collapse.[29]

As a strike once more seemed likely, Roosevelt urged the disputants to reach a resolution voluntarily. He threatened the union with antistrike legislation and the companies with federal seizure of the mines. Above all, he refused to mandate the union shop by executive order. "I tell you frankly that the Government of the United States will not order, nor will Congress pass legislation ordering a so-called closed shop." Yet the steel companies resisted the union shop, precipitating yet another strike in the captive mines.

Faced with the third strike in three months in a strategic industry, Roosevelt finally engineered a compromise solution. He appointed a special arbitration committee consisting of Lewis, Benjamin Fairless of United States Steel, and John Steelman, formerly chief of the Labor Department's Mediation and Conciliation Service, to resolve the dispute. It was an ingenious solution. Lewis would favor the union shop; Fairless would demand the open shop; and Steelman would cast the deciding vote. All the parties to the dispute knew precisely how Steelman would vote. He had been chosen by Roosevelt expressly because he favored the union shop. Yet to make the arbitration board's ruling appear to be the result of voluntary agreement between private parties and not state compulsion, Steelman resigned his federal office before joining the panel. The board's decision satisfied Lewis, mollified the steel industry, which would grant the union shop only under duress, and relieved Roosevelt of having to use force to break a national emergency strike.[30]

Nobody really noticed what Steelman had wrought. He announced the decision on December 7 — the same day that the Japanese bombed Pearl Harbor. The defense crisis had become a total war. And the entry of the United States into the war would create a system of labor-capital relations in which the private parties practiced voluntarism, but only at the risk of state coercion.

The Wartime Labor Relations System

Ever since the war had erupted in Europe and the Roosevelt administration focused on foreign affairs and defense (war) planning, the control of labor policy had slipped steadily away from the NLRB, where it had been placed by the Wagner Act. In 1940 and 1941, basic labor policy had been set either in the White House or by the NDMB. There the divisive issues of union security, wage stabilization, and the content of collective bargaining played themselves out. After Pearl Harbor and the declaration of war by the United States, the NLRB receded more deeply into the background.

Only ten days after the Japanese attack on Pearl Harbor, Roosevelt convened a meeting of the nation's leading labor leaders and corporate executives to discuss how best to maintain industrial production without interruption. The businesspeople and the union officials jointly condemned lockouts and strikes during the duration of the war, but they failed to reach agreement concerning fundamental relations between unions and management. As had happened during World War I, corporate representatives insisted upon the *status quo ante*, demanding that open shop, nonunion enterprises remain as such during the war emergency. Union leaders, however, in return for relinquishing the right to strike, demanded union security, which they typically defined as the union, or closed, shop. Unable to unite employers and unionists behind a common program, the president promised to resolve the impasse in wartime labor relations through the creation of a National War Labor Board, modeled partly on the World War I NWLB and partly on the more recent NDMB.[31]

Like its predecessors, the new NWLB consisted of an equal number of labor leaders (representing the AFL and the CIO) and corporate executives (nearly all from giant enterprises that dealt with unions) plus public representatives, who held the effective balance of power. The president charged the board with the power to resolve questions of both union security and wage equity. Its public members, drawn about equally from the legal and the academic communities, held the balance of power on the board, thus shaping its policies and determining its decisions.[32]

As the NWLB and its public members made wartime labor policy, the NLRB operated in the shadows. As the historian of the NLRB has written, "For the first time since the passage of the Wagner Act the governmental labor relations action was someplace else as the aura of excitement and trail blazing adventure passed from the NLRB to the NWLB."[33] Not only did the making of policy pass to another state agency, but Congress for the first time since the passage of the Wagner Act diluted the authority of the NLRB to remedy unfair labor practices. At the urging of John Frey of the AFL, congressional conservatives used the appropriation process to deny the board funds to investigate and repudiate contracts negotiated between AFL unions and employers behind the backs of workers. Thereafter, it became possible for a minority of workers to repudiate the preferences of a majority.[34] Overall, during the war years, the NLRB continued to conduct representation elections, holding more such votes than at any other time, and to investigate charges of unfair labor practices. When Congress passed antistrike legislation in 1943, the NLRB, its staff now decimated by appropriations cuts and conscription, wasted precious time administering strike votes among rank-and-file workers. The heroic age of the board had reached its end.[35]

Into the breach charged the NWLB, led by its public members. Union leaders were insistent that the war not be used to roll back dearly won labor standards, that unions be able to use tight labor market conditions to recruit members and build union shops, and that workers be protected against wartime price inflation. Employers were equally insistent that war production demands take precedence over such labor standards as maximum hours of work and overtime pay premiums, that nonunion firms remain open shops, and that wage inflation be restrained. Of the three issues most often before the board, the union security issue proved the most nettlesome. As industry representative Roger Lapham said: "As to union status, this should be a simpler issue than wages. . . . Yet, the truth is, of the two, it is the more troublesome because neither management nor labor seem able to discuss it without an emotional pounding of the table."[36] With labor and management far apart on the issue of union security, the public representatives spoke decisively.

Such public members as William Davis (chair of the board), Lloyd K. Garrison, and Frank Graham, and the bureaucrats who served them shared a common approach to labor relations. They believed strongly that unions and collective bargaining had a vital role to play in making capitalism more equitable and democracy more meaningful. Without a fairer distribution of national income, the economy faced disaster. Without some measure of industrial democracy at work, political democracy lost its substance for working people. Committed to the New Deal Keynesian "revolution" and the Wagnerian conception of industrial democracy, Davis, Garrison, Graham, and their younger acolytes tried to use the NWLB to build an American wartime version of corporatism, in which representatives of labor and capital would jointly plan the wartime industrial relations system. Their vision of how such a system might work was expressed best by Graham in his opinion in the case that put precisely such a method into practice. Graham observed that efficient wartime production depended on equally responsible unions and workers. Union security, he suggested, would induce union leaders to behave responsibly and to cooperate with management in observing faithfully the terms of the contract. Responsible union leaders would discipline unruly members who disrupted production; workers, secure in their union rights, would correct the abuses of irresponsible or demagogic leaders. By establishing a more stable basis for union-management relations, the NWLB, Graham asserted, could "contribute to a united concentration on the supreme task of winning the war."[37]

A dispute between the Little Steel companies and the United Steelworkers of America (USWA) provided the occasion for the NWLB to put the policy of its public members into practice. The steel industry in general, and Little Steel in particular, had traditionally fought all aspects of union security, enshrining the open shop as a hallowed principle of industrial relations. Industry executives and their supporters on the NWLB did not want to alter existing practices in the industry. The steelworkers union, however, could not relinquish its right to strike without a guarantee that secured its control of workers in the industry. Because the war's impact on labor recruitment transformed work forces in industry, everywhere putting to work employees new to the job and without previous union experiences and loyalties, it threatened union security.[38]

How could a union such as that of the steelworkers promise to discipline its members and ensure uninterrupted production if it could not compel workers to join and protect members against company discrimination? The answer to the union's dilemma, as supplied by the NWLB, was the principle of "maintenance of membership." Under that principle, once a contractual agreement had been reached between a company and a union, members of the union would not be allowed to withdraw for the duration of the contract. All such labor-management contracts were to be binding until the war ended. For the unions, such a policy guaranteed a modified union shop. For the public members of the NWLB, the principle compelled companies and unions to deal with each other cooperatively, management to respect union security, and labor to discipline its rank and file in the interest of maximum production. For employers, "maintenance of membership" implied dilution of the open shop, and the industry representatives resisted its implementation until Roger Lapham broke with his colleagues when the policy, as applied by the NWLB, provided workers with a fifteen-day escape period to leave the union, a practice that in theory diluted the principle of compulsory unionism but that in practice few workers used.[39]

From its enunciation in the Little Steel decision of July 12, 1942, until the end of the war, the principle of "maintenance of membership" secured the place of CIO unions in mass-production industry. In August 1942 the board established the principle in a set of formal rules and thereafter awarded "maintenance of membership" to all unions that it deemed to behave responsibly. In a manner of speaking, the NWLB put into practice the industrial relations system favored by the originators of the Wagner Act, compelling management to deal with the chosen representatives of their unionized employees, who in return for having a voice at work would guarantee uninterrupted production. In the words of an industrial relations professional who served on the board and later prepared the official report of its accomplishments, economist Milton Derber, "the Board turned out relatively little that was new, it did extend what it regarded as the best existing practices to industrial areas hitherto untouched by such concepts" (Little Steel, for example).[40] In 1943 the board extended further the practice of union security by awarding, over business opposition, the automatic dues checkoff in order to ensure the loyalty of labor leaders who were still nervous about the allegiances of new workers.[41]

Other aspects of wartime labor relations under the NWLB system brought to mind echoes of experiences under the Wagner Act and the NLRB. Just as the Wagner Act, as implemented by the NLRB, guaranteed unions the right to organize workers and compelled employers to bargain with their workers' chosen representatives, so, too, did the NWLB offer workers and their unions comparable guarantees. And just as the NLRB could not compel employers to reach a contractual agreement with unions, the NWLB's public representatives insisted that management and labor must cooperate and bargain voluntarily. But there was one essential difference in the wartime system of industrial relations. Before the war employers could bargain collectively without reaching an agreement and suffer no penalty. During the war, however, despite the NWLB's paeans of praise for voluntarism and "American democracy," management and labor bargained in the shadow of coercive state power. Union leaders knew full well that if they failed to keep the rank and file under control, they risked the loss of union security and military intervention. Corporate executives realized equally well that if they refused to reach agreements with labor, the NWLB could mandate settlements, as happened in the case of the Little Steel companies, backed by the full coercive power of the national state. To put the realities as bluntly as possible, the rhetoric of voluntarism cloaked a wartime industrial relations system that operated effectively only to the extent that the state monopoly of legal coercion held labor and management on a tight tether.[42]

The limits of voluntarism in labor-management relations were illustrated even more graphically in the NWLB's decisions concerning the heart of conventional collective bargaining, i.e., the determination of wage rates and working conditions. Here, too, the public members established the agenda and made the rules. On these issues public members and industry representatives allied against the union leaders. Charged by President Roosevelt to restrain inflation and ensure maximum production, the NLRB used the precedent-setting Little Steel ruling to limit the wage increases available to workers in all industries. Applying a complicated formula that sought to protect workers against the inflation that had already occurred between the outbreak of war and July 1942 but that guaranteed that wage increases would not surpass price rises, the board effectively reduced the ability of more powerful unions to benefit their members financially.[43] This led one labor member of the board to rage that the decision "wipes out collective bargaining and it makes every negotiation in this country break off . . . and really sets up this Board as the controller of wages in this country. . . . With one clear sweep you wipe out collective bargaining."[44] The board kept its labor members in line only because it applied its wage stabilization policy on a flexible, case-by-case basis (one that conferred special benefits on the lowest-paid employees) and, in the words of a public member, always added "enough sweetening in the wage situation to keep leaders of organized labor slightly satisfied."[45]

While the NWLB set the rules under which labor-management relations were governed during the war years, and the rules guaranteed a substantial increase in union membership, other aspects of federal wartime labor policy denied workers and their unions full participation in the war production effort. Having already seen its Murray Plan for tripartite committees (labor-industry-government) to administer war production and the Reuther Plan for a comparable arrangement in the automobile industry rejected by the president and the Office of Production Management (OPM), which Sidney Hillman chaired jointly with William Knudsen, the CIO hoped to resurrect tripartitism in a different fashion. On January 24, 1942, Roosevelt had abolished the OPM, replacing it with the War Production Board (WPB), to which he appointed Hillman as head of the Labor Division. Hillman promptly discovered that labor's role was to be distinctly secondary and that Donald Nelson, the chair of the WPB, and his closest advisers, corporate dollar-a-year men, would make policy. By April 1942 Hillman was gone and no comparable labor leader replaced him.[46] Consequently, corporate enterprise gained in influence, although Nelson made one small overture to organized labor. In March 1942 Nelson announced the establishment of joint labor-management committees to plan production. Although he made it clear that such committees would not bargain collectively, process worker grievances, or impinge upon managerial authority — they existed only to expedite war production — Nelson stirred a hornet's nest of opposition from the business community. "It's just raising hell among the businessmen," Nelson told his assistant Bruce Catton. "People are calling me up from all over. They don't like it, they're afraid of it, they're saying it won't work, they're calling it another of Roosevelt's revolutionary ideas."[47] Business railed against the new committees because labor, most especially the CIO, greeted their creation with enthusiasm. For labor leaders, the advisory committees, however limited their responsibilities, offered the prospect of moving in the direction of Phil Murray's plan for industry councils. Clint Golden, a former adviser to

Murray in the USWA and the CIO and now a vice-chair of the WPB, asserted that the committees "were shaping new relations between management and labor and are building patterns of democracy." *Business Week* was closer to the mark in suggesting that Nelson's aim was to "direct unions from their demand for a bigger voice in the management of industry to . . . their proper role — stimulation of the individual worker to greater effort."[48] However much Nelson's aim was to protect management from union intrusion on its prerogatives, the executives of the largest corporations saw clearly that even token recognition of unionism's role in production planning threatened managerial freedom. As Ford spokespeople told an associate of Nelson's, the labor-advisory committees were a "political vehicle designed . . . in an effort to push labor farther into the management of industry."[49] Much as trade unionists tried to use the committees as a device to enlarge worker participation in company planning, Nelson and his corporate allies made it clear that the promotion of labor-management committees "is not designed to increase the power or position of any union. . . . It does not put management in labor or labor in management."[50]

One other aspect of federal regulation of wartime labor relations distinguished the World War II experience from that of World War I. Between 1940 and 1944, as had also happened between 1916 and 1919, African American workers swelled the ranks of wartime defense employees. This time even larger numbers of African Americans left the Old South to find relatively high-wage jobs in the war industries of the North and the West. This time, however, civil rights organizations, especially the "March on Washington Movement" (MOWM) led by A. Philip Randolph, the president of the Brotherhood of Sleeping Car Porters, demanded that the federal government enforce nondiscriminatory hiring practices in private industry. Partly to ward off a threatened mass protest on Washington, President Roosevelt on June 19, 1941, signed Executive Order 8802 establishing the president's Fair Employment Practices Committee (FEPC). During the next four years, through a series of public hearings, published reports, and specific findings, the FEPC tried to eliminate discrimination in the labor market. It sought to open employment to African Americans everywhere, and to obtain for Hispanic Americans in the Southwest equal wages and promotions at work. Employers, Southerners and Southwesterners fought the attempt by a federal agency to alter their customary racial practices. While the CIO unions generally cooperated with the FEPC as part of their commitment to civil rights and in behalf of their many African American and Hispanic American members, the AFL and some of its most influential affiliates resisted federal attempts to eliminate racial discrimination in the labor market. The AFL even joined with business groups, Southern Democrats, and conservative Republicans in resisting the establishment of a permanent FEPC after the war. Although the FEPC had limited success in altering employment practices except where it was supported by CIO unions committed to racial equality, its existence suggested that no longer could federal regulation of labor relations neglect the subject of union as well as management discrimination. In one more realm of activity, the state threatened to transform a traditional aspect of the private ordering of employment practices.[51]

By 1943 the wartime labor relations system was firmly in place. The NWLB supervised relations between unions and managements, ensuring that responsible unions effective in controlling their members obtained security against employer antagonism and that employers and consumers were protected against wage-led inflation. The WPB operated to achieve maximum industrial production with union cooperation while circumscribing trade union power at both the managerial and the shop-floor levels. And the FEPC sought to eliminate racial discrimination in the job market. Such a system could not long satisfy workers nettled by sticky wages and labor leaders convinced that their contributions to the war effort and industrial production warranted greater influence for trade unions in corporate affairs.

The Wartime System under Attack

By 1943 the wartime labor relations system was in deep trouble. Workers realized that voluntarism did not govern the relations among unions, employers, and the state. Laboring for companies guaranteed profits under wartime cost-plus contracts, employed often under closed-shop, union-shop, and maintenance-of-membership arrangements, and offering their labor in a sellers' market, workers understood that within a conventional system of collective bargaining they could wrest substantial increases in wages and other benefits from employers. In fact, however, the rulings of the NWLB and the National Wage Stabilization Board (NWSB) denied workers the gains that might otherwise have been theirs as a consequence of their market power and organizational security. As the leader of the mine workers, John L. Lewis, put it, the government had adopted "a paradoxical policy that runs to the premise of rewarding and fattening industry and starving labor."[52] The truth at the core of Lewis's comment led workers to rebel simultaneously against their employers, the state, and even their own union leaders. By 1943 a wave of wildcat strikes threatened the war production effort and the NWLB program of labor relations.[53]

Nowhere was the discontent and rebelliousness greater than among mine workers, and no workers had a leader more eager to challenge the wartime system of labor relations. Coal miners felt themselves to be the special victims of the Little Steel decision and the government's unceasing demands for greater production. The NWLB's attempt to curb inflation caused miners' wages to lag behind those of other industrial workers, and more-intensive labor regimes in the mines produced work injuries that matched casualty rates among troops at the front. Voicing the sentiments of his members, Lewis taunted: "When the mine workers' children cry for bread, they cannot be satisfied with a 'Little Steel Formula.' . . . The facts of life in the mining homes of America cannot be pushed aside by the flamboyant theories of an idealistic economic philosophy."[54]

Dissatisfaction among coal miners first flared in the anthracite fields of northeastern Pennsylvania in January 1943, where angry workers walked out of the pits in wildcats to demand a wage increase of two dollars a day. Lewis simultaneously expressed the discontent of his followers and whipped them back into line. Aware, however, that coal miners were gravely dissatisfied with the government's wage policies and unlikely to remain passive in the future, Lewis decided to use the rank-and-file discontent for his own ends. Indeed, he was prepared to use the power of the miners to embarrass Roosevelt politically and to undermine the authority of the NWLB. To do so, Lewis was willing to violate labor's no-strike pledge and to confront the prospect of state coercion that lay at the heart of the wartime labor relations system. He could do so with relative impunity because of his autocratic control of the UMW and also because employers no longer threatened the security of the union and what amounted in practice to a completely closed shop in the industry.[55]

Negotiations between the UMW and soft-coal operators in the late winter of 1943 ended in stalemate, and Lewis threatened to call the miners out on strike. Meantime on April 22, the administration turned the handling of the dispute over to the NWLB. The mine operators gladly took their case before the board, in the expectation that the government would uphold the employers' battle against inflationary wage increases. Lewis and his union boycotted the board hearings and instead prepared to strike. Over the opposition of the NWLB and the president, who condemned the threatened strike as a war "against the United States government itself," miners walked out of the pits in the last week of April. Stymied in their efforts to keep the mines operating, federal officials were elated when Roosevelt delivered an ultimatum to Lewis and the miners. Unless the miners returned to work by the morning of May 1, said Roosevelt, "I shall use all the power vested in me as president and as Commander-in-Chief of the Army and Navy to protect the national interest and to prevent further interference with the successful prosecution of the war."[56]

May 1 came and the miners stayed out. Roosevelt had few options. He could not conscript hundreds of thousands of miners and make them dig coal productively, nor could he afford to use an equal number of troops to do so. Instead, the president seized the mines and placed them under the control of Secretary of Commerce Harold Ickes, whom he ordered to bargain with the UMW, but only within the parameters already set by the NWLB. Feeling that he could negotiate amicably with Ickes, Lewis ordered the miners back to work on May 4. Lewis was partly right. He and Ickes had little trouble cutting a deal between themselves. Their problem was that the NWLB would not sanction an agreement acceptable to Lewis and that Roosevelt endorsed the board's position. The result was continued stalemate and further strike actions by the miners. Roosevelt felt absolutely frustrated as the dispute and the intermittent strikes dragged on through the spring and summer, and into the fall. At one point soon after the government had taken over the mines, the president wrote in response to the question of whether Ickes could reach an agreement with the union, "No! U.S. cannot make an agreement with its employees."[57]

Congressional conservatives were quick to take advantage of the anger toward unionism precipitated by the coal miners' tactics. How, asked newspaper columnists, radio newscasters, and private citizens, could a union threaten the nation's security in the midst of world war by denying war industry a vital product? How, demanded antilabor members of Congress, could an autocratic union leader such as Lewis threaten the war effort? Stymied in peacetime in their efforts to amend the Wagner Act, weaken the NLRB, and curb labor's power, the congressional conservatives used the widespread anger against Lewis and the miners to accomplish their aims. Legislation originated in the Senate by Tom Connally of Texas and in the House by Howard Smith of Virginia (the same Smith who had conducted the hearings on the NLRB) passed both houses of Congress on June 15. The Smith-Connally Act (more formally, the War Labor Disputes Act), as it was known, authorized the NWLB to subpoena parties to appear before it, made NWLB decisions final and binding, conferred on the president the power to seize industries threatened by strikes and set criminal penalties for those who struck properties under government control, and required NLRB-supervised strike votes and a mandatory cooling-off period before a strike might begin. Ten days later, Congress passed the act over a presidential veto.[58] The act expressed conservative displeasure with union power and the arrogance of John L. Lewis. It failed to make coal miners work; neither could its approach to labor discontent assure uninterrupted production, and that is why Roosevelt vetoed it.[59]

In the end, Lewis and his miners got their way. Ickes, the union leader, and the coal operators cut a deal in which the miners obtained a substantial increase in daily wages while ostensibly holding the line against wage inflation. Rather than increasing the hourly rate paid underground miners, the new agreement provided portal-to-portal pay, for the first time reimbursing workers for the time they spent traveling to and from the mine face (underground miners were credited with three-quarters of an hour travel time daily). When the NWLB balked at approving a contract that raised wages above the stabilization level, Roosevelt had Ickes negotiate precisely such an agreement with Lewis, leaving the board no choice other than to approve a contract signed by a member of the cabinet.[60]

The miners' strikes (three in all), which roiled the nation from the spring of 1943 until settlement on November 3 and from which Lewis emerged triumphant, challenged the wartime labor relations system and the president's authority to stabilize wages. Lewis's decision to play the politics of confrontation rather than mediation also proved clearly that state coercion, not voluntarism, controlled wartime labor relations. The NWLB three times repudiated contracts that had been voluntarily negotiated between Lewis and the operators. Only when Ickes and Roosevelt became direct parties to the contract and one branch of the state, the more powerful office of the president, overruled another were the coal strikes ended.

Yet, in the end, labor probably lost more as a result of Lewis's challenge than it gained. The material rewards won by the miners proved to be far smaller than their symbolic victory. The UWM's new contract, in fact, scarcely breached the NWLB's wage stabilization policy. Moreover, in response to the many other unauthorized strikes precipitated by the miners' militancy, the NWLB modified its policies enough to mollify those labor leaders who preferred to cooperate with the government's wartime labor relations system. Although the board refused to approve contracts that raised minimum wages much above the Little Steel award level, it did sanction agreements that rewarded workers materially through fringe benefits related to employer-financed retirement, health, and vacation plans.[61] Those labor leaders who kept their members in line might still bring home the bacon. Increasingly, the NWLB awarded leaders of "responsible unions," those who proved their loyalty by condemning the tactics of Lewis and wildcat strikers, union security and compulsory dues checkoff.[62] In the final analysis, however, the miners' strikes bequeathed to the labor movement a bitter legacy. They fed rising public antagonism against trade unions and fueled the influential antilabor members of Congress and their many allies who came to honeycomb the federal administrative bureaucracies during the war years. After the war, these conservatives had their revenge.[63]

Peace and a Labor-Capital Crisis

The end of the war in August 1945 found organized labor and its remaining advocates in the national administration in an awkward dilemma. The death of Roosevelt in April 1945 brought the untested Harry S. Truman to power. Truman, moreover, promptly surrounded himself with the more conservative elements in the Democratic party. In Congress, the coalition of Southern Democrats and northern Republicans held the upper hand and was busily writing antilabor amendments into the NLRA. Some labor leaders could even imagine another 1919, a postwar restoration and ensuing depression during which the great corporations and their allies in the state would ally to roll back the union tide.[64]

Such realities explained why labor leaders, especially those in the CIO, strove, as the war came to its end, to maintain labor-capital peace at home. They continued to honor the no-strike pledge, to endorse wage-price stability, and to seek the sort of corporatism exemplified by the tripartite NWLB. That was why in March 1945 the leaders of the AFL and the CIO joined with Eric Johnston, the president of the United States Chamber of Commerce, to endorse a "Labor-Management Charter," which in somewhat contradictory fashion lauded trade unionism, collective bargaining, and unfettered free enterprise. Johnston appeared to represent those corporate executives who were more friendly to organized labor, such as Donald Nelson, who wrote that labor's behavior during the war years "proved its own maturity . . . the labor movement in America had come of age."[65]

To a large degree, however, the labor leaders misunderstood the attitude of such putative "corporate liberals" as Eric Johnston on the labor question. Despite their kind words for responsible unions and moderate collective bargaining, Johnston-style corporate leaders shared more with antiunion congressional conservatives than with AFL and CIO officials.[66] For example, in a book published in 1944, Johnston wrote: "Measured in numbers, economic weight, political influence, or by any other yardstick, labor is a power in our land. It can well afford to throw off its underdog psychology. It need no longer be sorry for itself." Having accorded labor power equal to that of management, Johnston proceeded to suggest that labor be judged by the same standards as business and that unions' unfair practices, which he defined in precisely the same manner as most antilabor conservatives did, be banned.[67] "Corporate liberals" such as Johnston sought to revive the Hooverian welfare capitalism of the 1920s, a "people's capitalism" based on high wages, mass production, and mass consumption, and in which nonmonopolistic unions could participate as long as they respected efficiency, higher productivity, and managerial prerogatives. Conservatives could, as Johnson did, take Robert Wagner's original defense of workers' rights against their employers and turn it into a critique of monopolistic unions that denied to individual workers their democratic rights to property and free contract.[68]

As the war came to its end, however, organized labor was in a far stronger position than it had been in 1919, and its leaders were not of a mind to settle for Hooverian-style corporate welfarism. By the summer of 1945, unions represented nearly 35 percent of the civilian labor force and had established themselves securely in all sectors of mass-production industry. Organized labor, especially as exemplified by the CIO's Political Action Committee (PAC), represented the largest single organized bloc in the Democratic party, and its leaders had enjoyed five years of exercising unprecedented power in the formulation of wartime labor policy jointly with corporate and state officials. In peacetime, labor expected to share and expand the sort of corporate tripartitism that had governed wartime labor relations. And that is what union officials expected to obtain at the labor-management conference that Truman convened in November 1945.

The differences between Johnston's conceptions of an ideal labor-management system and those favored by labor leaders spelled doom for Truman's conference. Union officials desired to gain an equal voice with management and public officials in making policy; they expected the state and capital to commit themselves to a reconversion program in which real standards of living would rise as government price controls regulated inflation; and they hoped that management representatives would legitimate the type of union security arrangements that had prevailed during the war years. Management's representatives at the conference, by contrast, sought to validate managerial rights against union incursions and to proscribe such unfair union practices as secondary boycotts and sympathy strikes. No longer reflexively antipathetic to collective bargaining or to state intervention in labor relations, management had discovered as a result of its wartime experiences that responsible unions could discipline unruly rank and files and that, in Howell Harris's words, "federal regulation of labor relations could be to its advantage, so long as the government entered on the side of 'order' and against the exercise of labor power."[69] Despite a rhetorical style that hinted at continued labor-management cooperation in peacetime, the conferees had too many fundamental differences concerning industrial relations to reach consensus. Even labor leaders could not agree among themselves, as evidenced by John L. Lewis's attack on CIO conferees, whom, the UMW leader charged, were seeking "a corporate state, wherein the activities of the people are regulated and constrained by a dictatorial government."[70]

In fact, even while the conferees were meeting in Washington, industrial warfare erupted across the nation. As the conferees discussed the future of industrial relations, 200,000 automobile workers organized in the UAW walked out of the plants of General Motors, beginning a strike that would last more than one hundred days. In January 1946, 300,000 meat packers, and 180,000 electrical workers followed suit, and soon afterward 750,000 steelworkers struck. In the twelve months following Japan's surrender in August 1945, 4,630 strikes involved five million workers, and cost more than 120 million workdays. Not only did workers strike the nation's largest mass-production enterprises but citywide general strikes paralyzed such medium-sized industrial cities as Rochester, New York, Stamford, Connecticut, and Lancaster, Pennsylvania.[71]

These disputes, which left scarcely an industry or a region of the country untouched, constituted the first peacetime test of the alignment of political, economic, and social forces that had formed during the Great Depression and World War II. Their resolution would determine the place and role of workers and their unions in the postwar era. As it turned out, the labor policies of the Truman administration, partly shaped by debates in Congress and partly determined by White House estimates of popular political sentiments, fit well with the corporate community's eagerness to set limits to trade union power.

As workers and employers fought their battles around factory gates and on city streets, the halls of Congress echoed with denunciations of union monopoly and labor radicalism. Southern Democrats and their northern Republican allies introduced a rash of labor laws that stirred memories of the 1938–40 sessions of Congress and attempts to amend the Wagner Act in the interests of employers. In the House, Republican Francis Case of South Dakota introduced a bill that curtailed workers' right to strike and amended the Wagner Act in order to curb the power of the NLRB. Indicative of the changed balance of political power, not only did the House pass the Case Bill by a substantial majority but, in May 1946, the Senate, theretofore a death chamber for antilabor legislation, did likewise. Only a veto by President Truman stalled the antiunion political express.[72]

Truman, however, did his own part to engender antilabor politics and sentiments. During the dispute between the UAW and General Motors, the president equivocated, in the end deserting his friends in the labor movement and rewarding his enemies in the corporate world, such as General Motors, which fought the strike largely to defend managerial prerogatives in the realm of capital investment, product pricing, and innovations in the labor process. A presidential commission that Truman appointed to mediate the steel strike proposed a settlement that endorsed managerial prerogatives, provided for wage increases to be matched by price increases, and, in general, spelled death for the wartime system of wage-price controls in the interest of the community. As a benchmark for all the other settlements in mass-production industry, the steel award set in motion a wage-price inflationary spiral that cost consumers dearly and also damaged union prestige.[73]

In addition, the president attacked labor more directly. Beset by conservative critics in Congress and in the public-at-large, Truman grew more defensive when coal miners and railroad workers walked off their jobs in May 1946. Speaking to Congress, the president condemned the railroad strikers, threatened to conscript them, and called for antistrike legislation. The miners' strike offered Truman an opportunity to prove that the government was not beholden to "labor bosses" and that the state could discipline unions. First, during the spring 1946 dispute, Truman placed the soft-coal mines under government control and had Interior Secretary Julius Krug arrange a settlement with Lewis. Then when the mines were returned to private ownership and the UMW again reached an impasse in its effort to implement the agreement with operators, Truman denied the miners the right to strike. Counseled by his closest political advisers, most notably Clark Clifford, that the best way to contain the congressional conservatives, maintain Democratic political control in Washington, and have a chance to be elected in his own right in 1948, was to challenge "big labor" as personified by John L. Lewis, Truman did just that. "It is not that the president is spoiling for a fight with Mr. Lewis," a White House insider disclosed to reporters. "It is as simple as ABCs, however, that the Administration must find out sometime whether the power of Mr. Lewis is superior to that of the Federal Government." The president established state supremacy through a federal court injunction against the miners' strike. Held in contempt by a federal judge and facing onerous financial penalties, Lewis in December 1946 called the miners back to work, then fled in defeat to his holiday retreat in Florida. Truman simply gloated, for as his right-hand man, Clifford, noted, the president "was his own man at last."[74]

Truman may have become his own man; he may have defeated Lewis and labor; he may even have bettered his chances of being elected president in 1948. But he had not braked the conservative political resurgence. At the same time that Truman was challenging Lewis in November 1946, Republicans took majority control of the Congress. Corporate capital had set limits to labor's claim to power in the strikes of 1945–46. If management in 1945–46, unlike 1919, chose to accept unions and tolerate collective bargaining, it did so only on terms and within limits that business defined. Truman had defeated Lewis and proved the state's primacy over labor. Yet he still needed the political support of the CIO and as many labor leaders as hè could woo in the AFL, which was why he had vetoed the Case Bill. And the Republican majority in Congress could await expectantly the new session in 1947, during which — in coalition with their sympathizers among Southern Democrats — they could enact (anti)labor legislation even in the event of a presidential veto.

An Almost Perfect Machine:

Industrial Relations Policy

in an Age of Affluence,

1947–1973

In the quarter century after the end of World War II, the United States appeared to learn the lessons of its previous experience in postwar reconstruction. World War I ended in a bitter and bloody battle between labor and capital in which workers and their unions lost all their footholds in mass-production industry and suffered grave defeats. Industrial conflict gave way to deep depression, which, in turn, precipitated an employer attack against high wages that succeeded by 1922 in lowering nominal wage rates substantially. The federal government, which had sheltered workers and unions in its warm embrace during the war years, lost its ardor for labor's cause during the 1920s. The flawed prosperity of the 1920s, in which workers did not receive a growing share of the fruits of rising productivity culminated in the Great Depression of the 1930s, followed in turn by the eruption of a second world war.

The aftermath of World War II produced a different reality. Industrial conflict left unionism in place wherever it had intruded and grown during the war years. The federal industrial relations policies set in place during the New Deal remained in operation, and unions still looked to the state through the NLRB to protect their interests. A Democratic administration dependent on the votes of working people and closely tied to the CIO and elements of the AFL held power, at least until 1953. And Congress even enacted the Full Employment Act of 1946, a bill that, however innocuous its actual provisions, declared it the responsibility of the state to regulate the economy in order to guarantee jobs for workers. Moreover, the New Deal "judicial revolution" had created a federal judiciary far more sympathetic to the claims of workers and their unions. No deep depression ensued, although conversion from a war to a peace economy caused temporarily heavy unemployment and price inflation. Once the adjustment from a total war to a partial peace economy took place, workers enjoyed the fruits of higher productivity in the form of steadily rising real wages and incomes. More workers than ever before could enjoy what Walt Whitman Rostow called the era of "high mass consumption." The United States had indeed learned to practice what historian Charles Maier has characterized as the "politics of productivity" and others have defined as Keynesian or neo-Keynesian economics.[1]

So successful did the practice of the "politics of productivity" appear that its primary practitioners and theoreticians in the realm of industrial relations, frequently one and the same people who staffed university industrial relations programs and served the American Arbitration Association, declared the American system near perfect, a thing of wonder in which bargaining and decision-making could be ceded to private parties. A form of neo-voluntarism came to characterize industrial relations, one that extolled "free" bargaining between unions and corporations unimpeded by an intrusive state or the demands of political parties. This American system of nonpoliticized, non-state-regulated collective bargaining was idealized as the model for all other labor movements and for public policy elsewhere, especially for the nations of Western Europe, which had suffered from politicized labor movements and intrusive states.[2]

In this chapter I intend to suggest why so many scholars, practitioners, and participants in the industrial relations system assumed its perfection, believed it to be based largely on voluntary, nonstate actions, and deemed "industrial pluralism" a fitting counterpart to the political pluralism that ensured all citizens equal, equitable, and democratic public rights.[3] Industrial pluralism combined with neo-Keynesian economics — that is, the practice of the "politics of productivity" — wrote an end to the struggle over the distribution of income and wealth that had characterized national politics and industrial relations policy since the emergence of a modern industrial nation. As the old disputes that had triggered conflict and struggle between workers and employers dissolved, new issues emerged to roil industrial relations and to disturb both unions and employers. As workers, through their unions, won elements of industrial citizenship, African Americans and women demanded equal treatment at work. Increasingly, questions of race and gender came to dominate industrial relations policy. And, finally, the quite real success of "industrial pluralism" created the conditions that subverted its dominance, for it was a system that carried within itself the seeds of its own destruction.

From a Laboristic State
to Countervailing Power

At war's end in 1945–46, labor in the United States had never seemed so strong. Fully a third of all civilian, nonagricultural employees belonged to a union, and the majority of them enjoyed contracts that guaranteed some form of union security. Many people inside and outside the trade unions expected the proportion of organized workers to grow in the future, and, in fact, unions experienced no perceptible shrinkage in membership comparable to what had happened after World War I.[4] The votes of working people seemed absolutely vital to the continued success and dominance of the Democratic party, and the CIO, in particular, through its Political Action Committee (PAC) participated actively in politics at all levels and usually through the Democratic party.[5] C. Wright Mills's "new men of power," the generation of labor leaders in office at war's end, together with their Democratic allies appeared eager to push ahead with New Deal reforms until they had built, in the words of economist Sumner Slichter, a "laboristic society."[6]

The image of labor as a power in the land as well as the looming inevitability of a "laboristic state" was just that, an image that cloaked a more ambiguous reality. For all the gains that the unions had made during the war years and preserved in the postwar strike wave, for all the power that labor leaders appeared to wield, the United States lacked a unified labor movement, one that acted with solidarity on both the industrial and the political fronts. Not only did the AFL and the CIO remain at odds, sometimes subverting each other's organizing and political campaigns, but John L. Lewis, still the most notorious, if no longer the most powerful, of labor leaders, led his mine workers along a curiously independent course, and the CIO waged its own internal wars.

A closer look at labor reveals the disarray in its ranks. Although the AFL had benefited enormously from the New Deal "revolution" in labor policy and law, some of its more powerful leaders remained active Republicans, and it endorsed the campaigns of several antilabor Republicans, including Fred Hartley of New Jersey. The leaders who were Republicans and whose influence inside the AFL accounted for some of the organization's singular political endorsements represented unions, mostly in the building trades, whose market power was so secure that they could function without the assistance of the NLRB and other federal agencies (indeed, they were precisely the leaders who perceived the NLRB as more sympathetic to the CIO and federal labor law as less likely to benefit traditional craft unions).[7] John L. Lewis also led an organization that, through closed-shop contracts, automatic dues checkoff, and the solidarity of miners, could function safely without state assistance. Hence Lewis increasingly criticized federal labor policy, used rhetoric redolent of Gompersian voluntarism, and implored fellow labor leaders to consider building a movement without NLRB legitimation.[8]

By contrast, the CIO still desperately needed allies in the national state, protection from the NLRB, and a sympathetic federal judiciary. Unfortunately, the CIO and several of its larger affiliates (as well as many smaller ones) fought among themselves in a battle between Communists and anti-Communists. Although the conflict would not culminate until 1949–50, when the CIO indicted, tried, and expelled eleven affiliates for allegedly following the Communist party line rather than CIO policy, it was already in 1946 starting to tear the mass-production union movement apart.[9]

The internal struggle within the CIO also affected the organization's most ambitious postwar organizing drive, "Operation Dixie," an effort to bring trade unionism to the vast majority of unorganized Southern workers, especially in the textile industry. Operation Dixie had a double purpose, to organize the largest nonunion region of the country and to restructure the Democratic party through the politicization of a biracial working-class electorate that would remove from office conservative, antilabor Southern Democrats. Operation Dixie collapsed as a result of concerted employer-state resistance, race and red-baiting, and splits among CIO organizers and unions. The failure of Operation Dixie exposed the weakness of the CIO, the persistence of racism, the depth of anticommunism, and the appeal of individualism among Southern workers; it also left the Southern Democratic party largely in the hands of antilabor "Bourbons."[10]

Organized labor's weaknesses exposed unions to a successful managerial counterattack. Initially, in the postwar strike wave of 1945–46, the largest enterprises in the mass-production sector preferred to endure protracted conflicts rather than cede unions influence in what they defined as managerial prerogatives. With few, if any, exceptions, management retained for itself the unchallenged power to make decisions concerning investment, pricing, and technological change. Rather than bear the incalculable costs of breaking unions, management offered its workers wage increases and attractive fringe benefits in return for contractual recognition of "managerial prerogatives."[11]

Many other large enterprises felt no need whatever to deal with unions. Even during the turbulent 1930s and the peak unionization of the war years, these firms operated as open shops unencumbered with collective bargaining. Some functioned with part-company, part-independent unions that passed muster with the NLRB as non-company-dominated organizations. Others dealt with completely independent, unaffiliated plant-specific unions. And still others treated their workers so well and made them feel so much a part of a common enterprise that such firms were never seriously threatened by unions. In this nonunion sector of the economy, no substantial number of employees longed for conventional trade unionism; they preferred to consider themselves part of a common corporate culture that guaranteed all its members equitable treatment, fair wages, promotions up internal job ladders, and job security through seniority.[12]

Given the internal divisions in the labor movement, the inability of unions to conquer new frontiers, and the quite successful postwar managerial counterattack against trade unionism, the new Republican majority in Congress and its Southern Democratic allies chose precisely that moment to "equalize" power between labor and management by amending the Wagner Act. In fact, the origins of the congressional campaign to curb labor had less to do with the overweening pride and power of labor's "new men of power" than with the history of the Wagner Act and subsequent efforts to revise it in the immediate prewar years. To make the Wagner Act palatable to a large congressional majority and to ensure that it passed constitutional muster with the courts, the legislation's original drafters and sponsors had stressed the rights of individual workers and the law's ability to reduce substantially the number of industrial conflicts. In fact, however, the passage of the Wagner Act had absolutely no impact on the incidence of strikes, one notable strike wave, that of 1936–37, occurring in the immediate aftermath of its passage, and another, more massive wave of strikes erupting in 1945–46.[13] Moreover, its critics alleged that the Wagner Act, in freeing workers from employer domination, had sometimes placed them at the mercy of unscrupulous and tyrannical labor leaders. Since 1938 Republicans inside and outside Congress, together with their Southern Democratic allies, had been harping on those issues. Harry Truman seemed to share a part of those beliefs in 1946 when he railed against the unpatriotic behavior of the leaders of the railroad brotherhoods, whose striking members he threatened to conscript into military service, and that notorious union tyrant John L. Lewis, whose coal miners refused to obey presidential edicts and legal rulings. Popular resentment against the demands of unionized workers and dictatorial labor bosses helped Republicans regain a majority in Congress in 1946 for the first time since 1928.

It thus seemed inevitable that the new Congress taking office in January 1947 would revise the Wagner Act. Truman sought to preempt Congress and allay the fears of his party's union constituents by offering his own suggestions for revisions in national labor policy. In his State of the Union message on January 6, 1947, Truman recommended four policy changes, only two of which, one to curb jurisdictional strikes and the other to restrain "illegitimate" secondary boycotts, affected labor's rights under the Wagner Act. Afterward, however, neither the president nor the Democrats in Congress introduced legislation to modify labor relations policy.[14] Instead, Republicans acted quickly to move labor legislation through Congress. At the end of January 1947, the Senate Committee on Labor and Public Welfare began hearings on the subject, and less than two weeks later, the House Committee on Education and Labor opened its own hearings. By April 10, Representative Fred Hartley of New Jersey had introduced his committee's bill in the House (known as the Hartley Bill), and a week later Robert A. Taft introduced a comparable bill bearing his name in the Senate.[15]

The specific provisions of the two pieces of legislation and the debate precipitated by their introduction in Congress echoed the controversy that had surrounded the Smith Committee's attempt to revise the Wagner Act between 1938 and 1940. Once again a House committee acted precipitately in its hearings, reports, and recommendations, scarcely offering the minority a fair and equal opportunity to participate. Once again the Senate, where organized labor had more influential supporters, including several Republicans, appeared to act more cautiously and sensibly. And once again northern Republicans and Southern Democrats castigated Communist-influenced unions, corrupt labor bosses, and union tyrants, fervently defending the rights of individual workers against the likes of John L. Lewis. In the words of a Republican congressman from New York, the Hartley Bill "restores to American workers and employers alike, the rights guaranteed them by the Constitution. . . . This bill is antiabuse, not antilabor. It . . . puts the interest of John Q. Public above the interest of John L. Lewis. It is a bill which is for the American workman and against the dictators who have so effectively enslaved him." Or, as a Democrat from Texas echoed, "it will protect the public interest against the actions of power-drunk labor bosses. . . . Let us come to grips with the real problem this Nation faces. Do we or do we not want to curb the power of John L. Lewis and his kind over the economic life of the Nation?"[16]

How, precisely, did Representative Hartley and Senator Taft propose to guarantee the constitutional rights of individual workers and employers, curb the actions of "power-drunk labor bosses," and protect the public against coercive strikes? Simply put, the separate pieces of legislation specified as unfair and illegal particular trade union practices (creating a category of unfair labor practices to match the Wagner Act's category of unfair management practices), established a category of management rights to balance union rights, enabled workers more easily and freely to choose nonunion employment options, limited union rights to strike and boycott, and offered both employers and workers the ability to challenge unions more effectively. Many of the specific provisions were drawn directly from the Smith Committee's prewar proposals, the amendments to the Wagner Act originally proposed by the AFL, and rulings made by the NLRB after 1941 that diluted parts of the Wagner Act (one of the people most responsible for drafting the Taft Bill was Gerard Reilly, a former NLRB member).

Although the Hartley Bill appeared manifestly more hostile to trade unionism than the Taft Bill, the two were actually quite similar. If Hartley and his House allies recommended the elimination of union security arrangements in order to guarantee all employees the "right to work," as well the outlawing of industry-wide collective bargaining, while Taft and his senatorial colleagues tolerated the union shop if a certified majority of workers chose it and industrywide bargaining if employers and unions voluntarily preferred it, those were distinctions without a difference. After all, Taft accepted the abolition of the closed shop and agreed that the separate states should have the option of making union security arrangements illegal. Industrywide collective bargaining, moreover, was the exception in American industrial relations, especially in the mass-production sector. The Hartley and Taft versions also concurred that jurisdictional strikes and secondary boycotts be outlawed; that employers be granted a broad definition of free speech rights in addressing their employees; that both employers and individual workers be allowed to ask the NLRB for decertification elections; that judges be allowed to issue antistrike injunctions in many circumstances; and that the president have the power to interdict strikes by declaring a national emergency. These were only some of the many restrictions that the Taft and the Hartley bills imposed on trade unionism. Other features of the proposed legislation limited unions' right and ability to create welfare funds, restricted their use of union resources for political purposes, and required all union officials to sign noncommunist affidavits or forego the benefits of the NLRB.[17]

Despite impassioned pleas from New Deal representatives and senators warning against precipitate change in a national industrial relations policy that had worked well for a decade, their voices and arguments had little impact on Congress. Not even the words of Senator Robert Wagner, then fighting a losing battle against death, and read to the Senate by a colleague from Montana, influenced members to vote against the Taft Bill. Not even suggestions by Wagner himself and the young representative from Massachusetts, John F. Kennedy, that the Hartley and Taft bills would "assist the Communist Party in the promotion of widespread class warfare, industrial chaos, and economic depression" swayed many minds.[18] On April 17 the House voted overwhelmingly in favor of the Hartley Bill, as Republicans and Southern Democrats, a few exceptions notwithstanding, allied to form a veto-proof majority. A month later, the Senate passed the Taft Bill with an equally large majority, once again composed in the main of Republicans and Southern Democrats. Almost immediately, the two houses resolved to submit the legislation to a joint conference committee for further consideration. In a masterful stroke of political strategy, the joint conference committee eliminated the severest antilabor provisions of the Hartley Bill, including its outlawing of the union shop, the dues checkoff, industrywide bargaining, and many forms of picketing. Hartley later claimed that he had included such provisions in his bill only as a device to render the Taft proposals more moderate and more acceptable to the largest congressional majority.

The "compromise" Taft-Hartley Bill, as reported by the conference committee, completed the work begun by Howard Smith, the National Association of Manufacturers, and several AFL leaders a decade earlier. It weakened the NLRB by splitting it administratively and subjecting its rulings to greater judicial review; it granted employers additional rights while rendering a number of union practices illegal; it diluted union security by banning the closed shop, placing restraints on the establishment of union shops, and allowing states to eliminate all forms of union security (Section 14b); it reestablished the right of federal courts to issue antistrike injunctions, in effect amending the Norris-LaGuardia Act; and it authorized the president to declare certain industrial disputes to be national emergencies and, on that basis, curtail the right to strike.[19] The bill sailed through Congress as easily as its predecessors had, and with majorities as large (320 for, 79 against, and 30 not voting in the House; 68 for, 24 against, and 3 not voting in the Senate).[20]

Immediately after the passage of Taft-Hartley, Truman conferred with his closest advisers concerning how to react in terms of statecraft and politics. It was clear that the House had the votes to override a veto, and that Truman would have to shift at least four votes in the Senate to uphold a veto, not a strong likelihood, given Republican solidarity and the political considerations that motivated most Southern Democrats. Labor leaders, whether from the AFL, CIO, or independent unions, beseeched Truman to veto what they were quick to condemn as a "slave labor act." The nation's most expert practitioners of "pluralist" industrial relations, people who had served on the NLRB and the NWLB, who taught in the leading schools of industrial relations and who wrote treatises on the subject, overwhelmingly favored a veto because, in their estimation, Taft-Hartley intruded the state and its courts too deeply into an arena best suited to voluntary private negotiations. And Truman's closest advisers also recommended that he veto the legislation in order to keep the labor vote in the Democratic column, hold the faith with old New Dealers, and prepare for the 1948 election.[21]

On June 20 Truman sent his veto message to Congress and that same evening addressed the nation on network radio to explain his decision. In his formal message to Congress and address to the American people, Truman struck the same basic chords. To a Congress and a public traditionally suspicious of an intrusive state, he suggested that Taft-Hartley substituted government mandates for voluntarily negotiated agreements between workers and employers. To an audience antipathetic to labor militancy and strikes, he warned that Taft-Hartley would increase the number of strikes by embittering union-management relations. To a nation that long preferred to see itself as free from the class barriers and struggles of the old world, he implied that Taft-Hartley was an example of class-motivated legislation — the product of wealthy businesspeople and reactionary Republicans — that would turn American politics into a steaming cauldron of class conflict. To loyal old New Dealers and trade union advocates, he condemned Taft-Hartley as a blatant form of union-breaking and worker oppression. To Americans increasingly sensitive to the threat of communism at home and the Soviet Union abroad, he insinuated that the law would, in effect, increase what it claimed to eliminate — communist influence in the unions. It would, moreover, weaken trade unions as "a strong bulwark against the growth of totalitarian movements." And, finally, in words redolent of Theodore Roosevelt's distinction between "good" and "bad" trusts, Truman told his radio audience that the vast majority of "good" unions and unionists must not be punished for the sins of a small minority of "bad" labor leaders. Further to assuage the fears that many Americans harbored about omnipotent and corrupt trade unions, he promised to support reforms in the labor law, as he had already done in his State of the Union message, that would eliminate unfair and corrupt union practices without putting in peril the future of trade unionism and the practice of collective bargaining.[22]

The veto message and the radio address were brilliant pieces of political propaganda, but they did little to sway congressional attitudes and votes. Both Houses of Congress quickly overrode the presidential veto, a result that Truman expected and perhaps even wanted. After all, Truman himself had suggested during the strike wave of 1945–46 that many unions had grown too powerful and their leaders too dismissive of the public interest. He had also demanded that the president be granted more authority to regulate and restrain unruly unions. Moreover, he had been a senator at the time that congressional efforts to amend the Wagner Act had peaked, and he had not then been an ardent defender of New Deal labor policy. And Truman certainly knew that between 1945 and 1947 many states, even some in the industrial heartland, had amended their own labor laws to eliminate the features most conducive to trade union growth and success.

Hence, as one NLRB member, James Reynolds, intimated years later in an oral history interview, Truman may have been practicing an extraordinarily adept version of Machiavellian statecraft. According to Reynolds, just before the president drafted his final veto message, Truman declared that he knew that Congress had the votes to override. All the better, for Truman realized that the Wagner Act needed amendment, that labor had sometimes gone too far in its behavior and demands, and that "we're going to have a pretty good law on the books in spite of my veto." More important, the veto would keep the labor vote Democratic, enable Truman to win the 1948 election, and thus guarantee the accomplishment of a far greater objective than labor law reform, the containment of Soviet Communism and the reconstruction of Western Europe through the Marshall Plan.[23]

Reynolds's version of Truman's motivation for vetoing Taft-Hartley implies that the president did not consider it a "slave labor act" or a drastic reversal of New Deal labor policy. It suggests further that Taft had indeed diluted the harshly antilabor provisions of the House bill and that, in the Ohio senator's words, the new law would only deter coercive and violent union organizing and "not be directed against the use of propaganda or the use of persuasion or any of the other peaceful methods of organizing employees." Rather than depriving workers of fundamental rights, Taft assured Americans in a response to Truman's veto, the new law only curbs the arbitrary power of "labor bosses" and protects union members, workers, and their wives against unjustified strikes and arbitrary closed-shop agreements. Taft also implied that the amendments reinforced the aim of Wagner's original law, to liberate the worker from industrial thralldom by guaranteeing his constitutional rights as an American citizen to do as he pleases.[24]

Supporting evidence buttresses the case for seeing the Taft-Hartley Act as a continuation of New Deal labor policy in a slightly diluted form. Ever since the NLRB had been reconstituted by Roosevelt in the wake of the Smith Committee investigations and hearings, its new members and their even more conservative successors had been issuing decisions that prefigured some of the reforms enunciated in Taft-Hartley. Other provisions of Taft-Hartley codified the rights of craft workers and units long demanded by the AFL. The postenactment experience of unions revealed no significant changes in the incidence of strikes, the rates of unionization, and the stability of unions. In fact, the unions that should have been most severely constrained by the law's limitations on jurisdictional and sympathy strikes, secondary boycotts, and arbitrary internal union practices flourished in the aftermath of its passage, none more so than the Teamsters and the construction trades unions, the primary practitioners of jurisdictional strikes, common situs picketing (a form of sympathy strike), and boycotts of unfair employers and their suppliers. Nor did the giant CIO unions in the mass-production industries suffer under Taft-Hartley. Whether in automobiles, steel, electrical goods, or rubber, unions and managements bargained collectively and reached agreements that provided union security (usually in the form of a union shop with automatic dues checkoff), employment stability, and steadily rising real wages. The CIO campaign to organize the South was imperiled well before the passage of Taft-Hartley and the subsequent enactment of state right-to-work laws. Indeed, unions achieved their peak absolute and relative membership (union density) in the era of the Korean War, four to six years after the passage of Taft-Hartley. A cynic responding to all the furor surrounding the law's enactment, Truman's veto, and labor leaders' condemnation of Taft-Hartley as a "slave labor act" might have been justified in concluding, "The more things change the more they stay the same."[25]

Truman's entire pattern of behavior during the struggle over Taft-Hartley — and that of many Democrats who supported him — suggested that trade unionists had no choice but to accept a substantial revision of their rights under the Wagner Act. After labor failed to refashion Southern politics and industrial relations and, so to speak, came to accept its role as one of many competing and countervailing interest groups in the Democratic party, it could scarcely defeat legislation that sought, in the words of its sponsors, to guarantee equal rights for employers and employees as well as to protect the public interest from unscrupulous private parties. The majority of trade unions that still needed the shielding embrace of federal law and agencies to insulate them against antiunion employers could not escape tighter regulation of their own activities.

That being the case, how do we explain the apoplectic reaction of the leaders of both national labor federations, dedicated New Dealers, the vast majority of the academic and legal practitioners of "industrial pluralism," and most historians who have studied the subject? The answer, I believe, is plain enough. We should consider more carefully the language used by the sponsors and advocates of amending the Wagner Act, whether in the ranks of the Republican party, the business community, or the media. Their language dripped with antiunion venom, even in the case of the moderate Taft, persistently associating unions with coercion, intimidation, violence, corruption, and crime, and their leaders with greed, tyranny, and communism. However much such critics of corrupt and dictatorial unions presented themselves as the defenders of oppressed and threatened individual workers, the true advocates of constitutional liberty, their real aim was to diminish union power at the workplace and the polling place. There is simply no doubt that the sponsors of the Taft-Hartley Act sought to diminish the influence and power of trade unions quite in contrast to the creators of the Wagner Act, who had aimed at protecting the collective power of workers in order to distribute income more equitably and establish industrial democracy alongside political democracy.

The sponsors of both the Wagner Act and the Taft-Hartley Act used the language of constitutional liberties, democracy, free expression, and individual rights — but for different ends. The former expected the guarantee of those rights to produce worker solidarity, collective action, a strong labor movement, and a more equal distribution of wealth and income. The latter assumed that the protection of such rights would diminish collective behavior, dilute union power, and motivate workers to act in a nonclass, individualistic manner. Both were partly right and partly wrong. The Wagner Act failed to create a solidaristic labor movement although it boosted the power of trade unions immeasurably, because far too many Americans refused to think and act in terms of class. Taft-Hartley failed to strip unions of their influence and power because far too many workers trusted their unions and their leaders to defend them against arbitrary and uncaring employers.[26]

Clearly, Taft-Hartley did not enslave American workers nor diminish the material gains most unions won for their members. Over the next twenty-five years, unionized workers enjoyed steadily rising real wages and incomes as beneficiaries of the successful practice of the "politics of productivity." A political economy of growth conquered one based on the redistribution of wealth and income. If the minority of the labor force that was unionized (at its peak no more than one-third of civilian, nonagricultural employees) benefited disproportionately from its collective strength, substantial evidence shows that union power pushed up the wages and earnings of the nonunion majority as well.[27]

The advocates of Taft-Hartley had perhaps built better than they knew, or, in Truman's alleged words, enacted "a pretty good law." A decade after the passage of Taft-Hartley, labor economist Richard Lester could write a book describing a mature labor movement that behaved responsibly, bargained peaceably with its putative adversaries, felt absolutely secure, and acted with all the characteristics of a "sleepy monopoly."[28] About the same time, sociologist and former labor reporter for *Fortune* Daniel Bell characterized trade unions as the "capitalism of the proletariat."[29] Economist John Kenneth Galbraith, in a book published in 1952, captured best the sort of world that Robert A. Taft, Harry S. Truman, and perhaps some New Dealers thought had been created by the end of the 1940s. In Galbraith's reformed American political economy, big business, big agriculture, big labor, and big government balanced each other through a system of countervailing power that served the general interest.[30]

The Twilight World of Countervailing Power

In the post–Taft-Hartley world of countervailing power, "big labor" remained the single most effective political voice and mobilizing institution for the masses of ordinary citizens. The New Deal–Fair Deal wing of the Democratic party depended on the material support of the labor movement in the form of political education, campaign funds, voter registration drives, and election-day voter services. In some cities and states, the Democratic party organization and the local labor movement, especially after the merger of the AFL and the CIO in 1955, grew almost indistinguishable. Labor lobbying and votes provided the margin to enable national administrations and Congress to expand social security and other key elements of an emerging limited welfare state. One scholar has not exaggerated much in crediting organized labor with the creation of modern American liberalism.[31]

Yet, however much organized labor influenced the reformist wing of the Democratic party, however much its political muscle enabled labor lobbyists and their allies to broaden the benefits and add to the beneficiaries of the welfare state, it could not influence Congress to eliminate the features in the Taft-Hartley Act that labor found most obnoxious. That was so for various reasons. When labor demanded improvements in social security, or endorsed raising the minimum wage, or favored public programs for improved health care and education, it addressed the needs of nonunion members and expressed the interests of masses of citizens and voters outside its immediate constituency. In those instances, it was able to build broad-based popular coalitions that influenced members of the Democratic party and Republicans in Congress who otherwise were unsympathetic to trade unionism. When organized labor sought to repeal Taft-Hartley, it appeared to be acting defensively as a narrow and greedy special interest, a group whose political philosophy many condemned as "the public be damned."

Thus, although Truman and the Democratic party won the election of 1948 partly with organized labor's votes and on the basis of the party's pledge to repeal Taft-Hartley, once returned to office, the Democrats did little more than pay lip service to repeal. Neither Truman nor his loyal followers in Congress were willing to risk precious political capital in a struggle in behalf of a group increasingly identified as a selfish special interest. Democrats preferred to offer organized labor symbols rather than substance. Labor and the Democrats had formed the strangest of political marriages. Truman Democrats could not win elections or control their own party without support from organized labor. Labor could not exert influence in the national state or hope to expand the welfare state except by working within and through the Democratic party. If Democrats gave labor leaders real positions of authority and power in the party or repealed Taft-Hartley, they would alienate masses of nonunion voters. If the labor movement, in the words of Walter Reuther, tried to capture the Democratic party, it would destroy the only political institution through which it might influence policymaking at the level of the national state. Such were the practical political arrangements of modern American liberalism and countervailing power.[32]

Despite such political realities, organized labor continued to pour its resources into a campaign to repeal the "slave labor law." It marked candidates for office who had supported Taft-Hartley, especially Senator Taft, for defeat. It insisted that the Democratic party remain true to the plank in its platform that favored repeal. Taft and most of his political allies remained immune to labor's opposition. The best that the unions could win from the Democrats was a joint presidential-congressional initiative in 1951 to amend the Taft-Hartley provision that all union-shop agreements required a two-thirds membership majority vote before they could be implemented. Because so many negotiated agreements provided for the union shop, the NLRB was swamped administratively and financially in conducting such elections. Because nearly all the elections ended in practically unanimous votes for the union shop, Truman and Taft both agreed that the provision requiring such elections should be deleted from Taft-Hartley, and Congress did so promptly.[33]

For a generation, New Deal and Fair Deal Democrats had made and controlled national industrial relations policy. However much public sentiment, congressional attitudes, labor law, and its administration by the NLRB had shifted away from the original New Deal commitment to promote trade unionism, most administration Democrats remained the friends of labor, and organized labor acted as the single largest power bloc within the Democratic party. All of that changed with the election of Dwight D. Eisenhower as president in November 1952 and the approaching installation of a Republican Congress in January 1953. (It is worth noting that in the election of 1952 the AFL broke with its hoary tradition of not endorsing presidential candidates to support the Democratic nominee, Adlai E. Stevenson, a candidate not especially warm or sympathetic to organized labor. AFL leaders, except for some who remained Republicans and kept close ties to the party, feared the worst from a Republican victory.)

The worst did not happen. To be sure, Eisenhower's appointees to the NLRB were more conservative than their predecessors and more attuned to the interests of business, but, in practice, they adhered to the board's established policies and precedents. The new president, moreover, made direct overtures to sectors of the labor movement with whom he and his advisers thought that the Republicans might build an effective coalition, one that might wean trade union voters away from the Democrats and transform the Republicans into a new national majority party.

Two developments illustrated Eisenhower's wooing of organized labor. First, he chose Martin P. Durkin, an old-line AFL craft unionist and leader in the plumbers' union, to serve as secretary of labor. Second, he encouraged Durkin to recommend amendments to Taft-Hartley that would eliminate those aspects of the law that impinged most unfairly and negatively on the practices of construction and trucking trades unions.[34]

As part of Eisenhower's attempt to use his personal popularity to benefit his party, he also strove to lead fellow Republicans into an accommodation with the New Deal, to urge them to accept the state's responsibility for promoting the general welfare, especially through expansion and improvement of social security and associated welfare programs. Eisenhower's brand of "modern Republicanism" necessitated that the state practice "the politics of productivity" with the mutual cooperation of big business and big labor. It was a policy fully consonant with Galbraith's concept of countervailing power and what many scholars since have described as the practice of corporatism. Whether defined as countervailing power or corporatism, such state policies provided labor a participatory role as an *organized* constituency.[35]

Eisenhower's overtures to organized labor were easier to make than to solidify in practice. Durkin had no difficulty in recommending nineteen amendments to Taft-Hartley, none of which drastically revised the law but nearly all of which benefited AFL craft unions. And Eisenhower seemed amenable to endorsing

Durkin's proposals, as did "Mr. Republican," Robert A. Taft. Nevertheless, many old-style Republicans in the administration and in Congress had not yet made their peace with organized labor. Secretary of Commerce Sinclair Weeks and Secretary of the Treasury George Humphrey, for example, resisted Durkin's effort to amend Taft-Hartley, and they had far more influence within Republican circles than did the ex-plumber. Although Eisenhower deemed Weeks an unbending conservative, the realities of Republican party politics made it impossible for the president to support Durkin.[36] After Taft's death in mid-summer 1953, Eisenhower lacked the ability to forge a consensus among Republicans concerning the need to amend Taft-Hartley in order to woo trade union voters. Frustrated in his attempt to alter labor law and feeling himself an alien among the corporate executives in the cabinet, Durkin resigned his position on August 30, 1953. Durkin's resignation, following Taft's death a month earlier, ended Republican attempts to court organized labor, but only temporarily.[37]

Eisenhower and several of his advisers, including the new secretary of labor, James P. Mitchell, continued to court trade unionists. In a message presented to the September 1953 convention of the AFL, Eisenhower simultaneously endorsed Taft-Hartley as "a substantial contribution to the quest for sounder labor-management relations" whose practice had "confirmed its essential soundness" and suggested that Republicans were open to remedying defects in the act, so long as such changes respected "the legitimate rights of individual workers, their employers, and the general public."[38] Although influential cabinet members, especially Treasury Secretary Humphrey, urged Eisenhower not to seek substantive changes in Taft-Hartley, the president, his labor secretary, and congressional Republicans more sympathetic to trade unionism resurrected Durkin's original nineteen amendments. In a special message to Congress on labor-management relations delivered on January 11, 1954, Eisenhower proposed amendments to Taft-Hartley. He suggested that the restriction on secondary boycotts be altered to enable construction trades unions, among others, to engage in traditional actions against union employers who subcontracted work to nonunion operators; that NLRB be denied the right to consider employer decertification election petitions or those from a competing union during an economic strike; that unions in the construction, amusement, and maritime industries be allowed to negotiate what amounted to closed-shop, or hiring hall, contracts and that, in those trades, union-shop agreements take effect within seven days of employment; that unions not be held responsible for the actions of individual members; and that Congress study whether to regulate union welfare and pension funds.[39] These proposals, all save the one concerning union votes during strikes, benefited solely AFL affiliates, and exemplified the administration's effort to win the more traditional and conservative sector of trade unionism for Republicanism.

Eisenhower failed to win enough congressional Republican support for his suggested amendments, and hard-core conservative Republicans together with their Southern Democratic allies rejected alterations to Taft-Hartley. Trade unionists too, particularly those in the CIO like Walter Reuther of the automobile workers, rejected Eisenhower's proposals as too timid.[40] The president's failure to reform Taft-Hartley and attract AFL unions to the Republican party presaged the merger between AFL and CIO that was consummated in December 1955.

In a special telephone message on December 5, 1955, to the AFL-CIO merger meeting, Eisenhower expressed succinctly "modern Republicanism's" vision of the labor movement's role in American affairs. After complimenting trade unionists for all they had done to promote the general welfare of the republic, the president warned them against the class struggle doctrines of Karl Marx, "a lonely refugee scribbling in a dark recess of the British Museum." Class sentiments, Eisenhower declared, had no place in a society in which labor, "respected and prosperous," formed a part of the middle class that cooperated harmoniously with employers in an "economy where the barriers of class do not exist." He assured his auditors that as long as unions practiced teamwork with managements that the state would not interfere in the voluntary and private realm of collective bargaining.[41]

Industrial Relations and Industrial Pluralism

During the 1950s and 1960s the industrial relations system, as described by Eisenhower, seemed to work. Collective bargaining between unions and managements created an affluent society in which rising real wages enabled workers and their families to consume with abandon. Such labor lawyers and industrial relations experts as Archibald Cox, John Dunlop, Clark Kerr, and David Feller, to name only a few, tutored union officials, corporate administrators, and federal judges in how to interpret basic labor law and implement collective bargaining with minimal direct state regulation.

The industrial relations system that these theorists and practitioners helped institutionalize was built on an amalgamation of "industrial pluralism" and a common law of contract implementation. It aimed, in Cox's words, at building the "kind of day-to-day cooperation between company and union which is normally the mark of sound industrial relations — a relationship in which grievances are treated as problems to be solved and contract clauses are only guideposts in a dynamic human relationship." These experts sought to define precisely which subjects unions and managements should bargain about and to eliminate from the arena of mandatory bargaining those issues least amenable to compromise. They defined wages, fringe benefits, working conditions, and work rules as mandatory bargaining subjects; investment decisions, pricing policies, technological innovation, plant location (and relocation), they deemed matters for voluntary bargaining. They also sought through the establishment of a common law of industrial relations to reduce the number and intensity of disputes that precipitated strikes and litigation.

Whereas during the 1930s and into the early 1940s, the primary goal for unions and workers had been to win a binding contract through collective bargaining, by the 1950s and 1960s, the salient issues concerned contract implementation. The industrial relations experts and labor lawyers typically suggested that unions and managements should resolve contractual disputes through formal grievance procedures culminating in binding arbitration. Indeed, they recommended that both unions and managements negotiate agreements that provided for binding arbitration as a substitute for the right to strike during the duration of a contract. And the impartial industry-union umpires and arbitrators, recruited largely from the universe of industrial relations experts and labor lawyers, would do justice to the disputants by basing their rulings on past practices and precedents, the core of a common law of contract implementation. Put as simply and plainly as possible, this form of industrial relations would guarantee economic stability, put corporatism into practice, protect the rights of individual workers through institutionalized, nondisruptive collective action, and reduce direct state regulation.[42]

The NLRB and the federal courts adopted "industrial pluralism" in their rulings. Both the labor board and the federal courts enforced Taft-Hartley limitations against jurisdictional strikes and secondary boycotts, issuing in the case of the latter antistrike injunctions. Despite the existence of the Norris-LaGuardia law, the Supreme Court and lower federal courts enjoined workers from striking or taking other forms of direct economic action against employers in cases in which the existing contract contained a no-strike clause or provided for binding arbitration. Federal judges also legitimated corporatism by subordinating the rights of individual workers to the larger interests of their unions. Several associate justices of the Supreme Court used the bench as a platform from which to enunciate the law of industrial pluralism. In the famous Steelworkers Trilogy ruling of 1960, William Douglas declared that "the collective bargaining agreement . . . calls into being a new common law — the common law of a particular industry or of a particular plant. . . . A collective bargaining agreement is an effort to erect a system of industrial self-government."[43] Two years earlier Justice William Brennan had emphasized that "the goal of federal labor policy . . . is the promotion of collective bargaining; to encourage the employer and the representative of the employees to establish, through collective negotiation, their own charter for the ordering of industrial relations [an industrial common law], and thereby to minimize industrial strife."[44]

In practice, "industrial pluralism" and its common law of contract implementation did not substantially reduce the incidence of strikes and other disputes. It did, however, lend to most strikes a ritualistic character in which the future of the union and the achievement of a collective agreement were never in doubt. Industrial conflict lost its association with militancy, unruliness, and violence. It became a tactic used by both sides to wrest from its adversary the best possible agreement. Conducted primarily when the contract terminated, the strike became a choreographed performance featuring company and union negotiators. The autonomy and rights of individual workers, and the oft-romanticized rank and file, seemed to vanish. Common law contractualism, as David Brody has so astutely observed, bound workers so tightly into a web of rules and procedures that they lost many rights and their ability to challenge either their employers or their union. Brody, to be sure, also realizes that the same web of contractual rules bound employers, who were no longer free to treat workers arbitrarily or abuse them with impunity. "Industrial pluralism" and its contractual principles simultaneously liberated and imprisoned the individual worker, enabling her to challenge the employer without fearing immediate punishment yet rendered her unable to make such a challenge without the full support of the union.[45]

Voluntarism versus Coercion

A similar paradox lay at the root of national industrial relations policy. Business interests, trade unionists, and public officials all extolled the virtues of voluntary collective bargaining, the concept that labor-management relations worked best in the absence of state regulation. Yet, as Wayne Morse, had observed during the Senate debates that preceded the passage of the Taft-Hartley Act, when "labor and employers, by conduct which jeopardizes the public interest, insist upon abusing their freedom, I do not know what else our Government can do but attempt to restrict such harmful actions." Yes, Morse admitted, government intervention and compulsion always cost the loss of private freedom, but the general interest must prevail.[46] Throughout the postwar era, frequent and decisive state intervention buttressed a voluntaristic industrial relations system.

Although Truman had vetoed the Taft-Hartley Act and then sought its revision, he seldom hesitated at using its provisions to enjoin national emergency strikes. In the spring of 1948 and again in the winter of 1950, Truman used the act to enjoin strikes in the coal industry. More frequently even than the president used Taft-Hartley's injunction provisions, he established presidential fact-finding boards of inquiry to investigate industrial disputes during mandated sixty-day cooling-off periods. Truman appointed fact-finding boards and resorted to antistrike injunctions in disputes involving aluminum, steel, maritime, and railroad workers, as well as coal miners.[47]

Truman did not limit himself to intervening in labor disputes solely under the provisions of Taft-Hartley. Between 1948 and 1952, he often acted in much the same manner as he had in 1945–46, when he engaged in open warfare with John L. Lewis and threatened to draft railroad workers. In the spring of 1948 Truman placed the railroads under federal control and directed the secretary of the army to operate them in order to avert a national strike.[48] And, in July 1950, he issued an executive order placing the Rock Island Railroad under federal control, once again to avert a strike that threatened to damage national defense and security. The impending strike on the Rock Island coincided with the outbreak of the Korean War.[49] Using World War II precedents as a guide, Truman established a National Wage Stabilization Board to regulate labor-management bargaining and to restrain price inflation. When unions, managements, or both balked at board rulings, Truman used presidential power to seek antistrike injunctions or to impose government seizure of the industries affected.[50]

The most egregious example of presidential intervention in a labor dispute occurred during the steel strike of 1951. Union and management negotiators in the steel industry had failed to compromise their differences on the issue of wage increases. On December 22, Truman requested the NWSB to investigate the dispute. Although the board recommended a wage-price increase for the steel industry, the companies rejected it, and the steelworkers union prepared to strike on April 9. The steelworkers had remained on the job without a contract since the old one had expired on December 31, and their patience had reached an end. Late on the evening of April 8, Truman addressed the nation on network radio, castigating the steel enterprises for scorning the national interest by refusing to honor the board recommendation and praising the union for its good sense in accepting the board's decision. Then he informed his audience that, as of midnight, the federal government would seize the industry. The following day he reported to Congress on his seizure of the steel industry, suggesting that Congress might wish to pass legislation legitimating and regulating federal control of the steel industry. Truman, however, met opposition on many fronts. Congress members, angry that the president had declined to use Taft-Hartley national emergency strike procedures, deemed seizure of the steel industry an arbitrary, dictatorial act more fitting a fascist or communist state than a democratic one. The steel companies took their case to federal court, winning a series of rulings that culminated in a Supreme Court decision declaring Truman's action an arbitrary, unconstitutional step that lacked congressional authorization and ordering the president to return the mills to the private companies.[51]

Truman's precipitate seizure of the steel mills may have been as much a political act as one determined by the president's perception of the national interest during a military conflict. Most of his previous interventions in labor disputes had occurred when unions had the upper hand in their confrontations with management and could use their power and the threat of strikes to best advantage. This time Truman intervened to uphold labor's claims and to discipline a non-cooperative management, in the process tightening labor's links to the Democratic party, particularly among its friends and allies in the CIO.

Although President Eisenhower was less inclined than Truman to use state power to regulate private economic arrangements and owed no direct political debts to labor, especially the CIO, he also did not shrink from using Taft-Hartley to avert national emergency strikes. Much as Eisenhower preferred to see management and labor reach agreement without state intervention, he felt that he had no choice but to intervene when industrial disputes undermined his definition of national security. He sought an injunction in August 1954 to end a strike at the Atomic Energy Commission facilities in Kentucky, and in October 1959 he asked for an injunction to stop longshoremen on the East and Gulf coasts from striking.[52] And like Truman, he also found himself involved in 1959 in yet another steel industry dispute. Eisenhower tried to distance himself from both the steelworkers union and the companies. He refused the union's request to appoint a presidential board to investigate the issues in dispute although the union president, David MacDonald, was the CIO leader for whom Eisenhower felt the greatest affinity.[53] When negotiations failed to produce an agreement and a long, bitter strike ensued, Eisenhower finally acted under Taft-Hartley to appoint a board of inquiry. Subsequently he sought an injunction to end the strike, arguing in precisely the same language of national security and public interest that Truman had used. Although Eisenhower privately found management more at fault than labor, he used state power more neutrally than Truman, never seeking to ensure a settlement especially favorable to the union position. Yet he urged management always to give due credence to union concerns about their institutional and their members' job security.[54]

Just as had been the reality during the World War II years, so, too, in the postwar years, the administrators of federal industrial relations policy extolled voluntarism in principle while they practiced public regulation of private bargaining between management and labor. Presidents and their appointees sought to ensure that privately negotiated collective bargaining agreements served the general interest. Unions and managements in sectors of the economy that impinged directly on the national economy and security — mass-production enterprises, basic communications and transport, and defense-related industries — especially bargained under the watchful eye of federal officials. During Truman's tenure in office, and later during the administrations of Kennedy and Johnson, labor leaders tried to please their Democratic allies by negotiating contracts that linked wage increases and other benefits to rises in productivity, hence restraining inflation. Those unions that refused to practice collective bargaining in the national interest experienced direct federal intervention into the bargaining process. In return, Truman and also Kennedy, on occasion, held employers to the same standard, as happened when they castigated steel management for refusing to bargain in good faith with the steelworkers union.

Indeed, by the end of the Truman years, American trade unions had built a relationship with Democratic administrations that prefigured the comparable relationship that would emerge in Western Europe between trade unions and Social Democratic or Labor parties. In both instances, trade unionists, eager not to see their political allies slip from power, tolerated a degree of regulation in the national interest by the state that they would not accept so readily from those that they identified as political enemies. It was precisely this sort of relationship that Eisenhower tried to build with labor leaders, however unsuccessfully.

By the 1950s, then, the labor movement found itself firmly subject to state regulation. The merger of the AFL and the CIO was intended to revitalize labor as an organizing and political lobbying force. It did neither. Instead, labor united behaved, in Richard Lester's phrase, as "a sleepy monopoly," unable to unionize the unorganized effectively and with minimal influence on a Republican national administration. Still damning Taft-Hartley as a "slave labor act," the AFL-CIO sought revisions to eliminate the law's restrictive provisions governing union practices.

Corrupt Unions and Labor Law Reform

For more than twenty years, ever since New Deal policies had placed the influence of the national state behind trade unionism and collective bargaining, conservative critics of union power in the business community, the Congress, the Republican party, and society at large had been condemning labor leaders as autocrats enmeshed in a web of corruption and crime. To these critics of the labor movement, individual union and nonunion workers needed their constitutional rights protected against corrupt "labor bosses." All Americans, moreover, required protection against abusive, coercive, "blackmailing" union practices that Taft-Hartley had failed to eliminate. These conservatives found their case for state regulation of trade unionism buttressed by the hearings and findings of a Select Senate Committee appointed in 1957 to investigate improper relations in labor-management relations. Better known as the McClellan Committee on "labor racketeering" and named after its chair, Senator John McClellan of Arkansas, the committee appeared to be a bipartisan effort to probe a real problem. Not only was the committee chaired by a Democrat, albeit a Southern conservative, but its chief counsel was Robert F. Kennedy, the younger brother of Senator John F. Kennedy, an ally of labor, an opponent of Taft-Hartley in 1947, and a member of the investigating committee.

The committee's investigations exposed a sordid pattern of crime and corruption in a number of unions, nearly all of which had been AFL affiliates before the merger, and in none as gross as in the Teamsters union. The committee's exposé caused the fall of one Teamsters president, David Beck, and transformed another, James R. Hoffa, into a symbol of all that was wrong with the American labor movement. By exposing the extent of corruption prevalent among unions and revealing Teamster links to criminal elements, the committee proved a part of the conservative critique of trade unionism and also made the pressure for changes in labor law irresistible.[55]

The committee investigation coincided with another effort by the Eisenhower administration to reform basic labor law in a manner that would mollify elements in the labor movement close to the Republican party and assuage the corporate constituency dominant in the party. In a special message to Congress on January 23, 1958, the president proposed recommendations to deal with "the disclosures of corruption, racketeering and abuse of trust and power in the labor-management field." In keeping with a traditional focus on rights, he called for legislation "to protect the basic rights of the individual worker" as the best means "to maintain the integrity of trade unionism." He recommended that the Department of Labor be responsible for regulating all union and employer financial dealings that concerned the administration of welfare and pension funds, that union treasuries be used only for the benefit of members, that unions be required to submit detailed annual reports on their financial condition to the department, and that the department be authorized to take legal action against unions that violate their fiduciary responsibility to members. Eisenhower also suggested again that Taft-Hartley be amended to tighten restrictions against secondary boycotts, except in the case of the building trades, which would be authorized to "boycott" nonunion subcontractors and sign representation contracts with an employer prior to an NLRB certification election, and to deny unions the right to picket as an organizing tactic except in precisely defined situations. As a sop to the AFL-CIO, still a potent if not dominant political force, the president proposed the elimination of the statutory prohibition denying economic strikers the right to vote in representation elections.[56]

Congress devoted much of the remainder of the year 1958 to drafting legislation that would remedy the situation exposed by the McClellan Committee. It proved a fruitless task. Most Republicans, their corporate allies, and a majority of Southern Democrats preferred legislation that would subject unions to closer public regulation and tighten restrictions against coercive union tactics. Northern and western Democrats and their allies in the AFL-CIO and among the community of industrial relations experts favored reforms that regulated corrupt practices without intrusive state regulation and amendments to Taft-Hartley that liberated unions from restrictions that curtailed their ability to organize and bargain effectively. The administration had no program to support other than the one that the president had recommended in January, proposals that failed to command the support of a congressional majority.[57]

Labor reform thus became a prominent issue in the 1958 election. The AFL-CIO vigorously opposed candidates favorable to stricter state regulation of union internal affairs and state right-to-work referenda. The economy, moreover, worked to the advantage of labor, a deepening recession and rising unemployment combining to reinvigorate the old New Deal electoral coalition. When the votes were tallied, labor appeared to have won a great victory. In six of seven states in which right-to-work laws were on the ballot, the voters rejected them. Seventy percent of the congressional candidates supported by the AFL-CIO won, some of the most prominent Republican antilabor candidates lost badly, and the advocate of reforms acceptable to labor, Senator John F. Kennedy, triumphed in a landslide. The new Congress would be overwhelmingly Democratic in both houses, a situation that the AFL-CIO dearly desired.[58]

When the new Congress convened in January 1959, the prospects for labor law reform seemed good. Not only were Democrats in control of both houses, but Senator Kennedy assumed command of the reform effort in the upper house and the committee in the lower house responsible for labor legislation now had a majority more sympathetic to trade unionism. Among the members Kennedy had appointed to an advisory panel on labor law revision were Archibald Cox and Clark Kerr, two of the most vigorous advocates of "industrial pluralism" and labor-management voluntarism, and Arthur Goldberg, council to the AFL-CIO. Cox especially would play an active role in drafting the labor law reforms proposed by Kennedy, revisions that subjected internal union affairs to regulation in the least intrusive manner and that amended the provisions in Taft-Hartley found most noxious by labor. Kennedy even gained the cooperation of several northern Republicans, including Senator Irving Ives of New York, a former associate of the "industrial pluralists" at the New York State School of Industrial and Labor Relations, who agreed to cosponsor Kennedy's bill.[59]

What Kennedy and his allies wrought never came to pass. The struggle in Congress to reform national labor law in 1959 exposed weaknesses in labor's political influence; the continued vitality of the Republican–Southern Democratic congressional coalition; and how trade unionists, lobbyists, members of Congress, both parties, and the president continued to practice the politics of the past. Labor's impotency stemmed from two causes, one internal, the other external. Never did labor address Congress and its committees as a single voice. If the AFL-

CIO accepted some regulation of internal union affairs in order to eliminate corruption, the Teamsters union and the United Mine Workers opposed state regulation. The building trades accepted reforms that relieved them of several Taft-Hartley restrictions yet accepted amendments that further restrained the economic activities of other unions. Walter Reuther of the automobile workers and David MacDonald of the steelworkers, the two largest former CIO unions, disagreed about how stringently corrupt union practices should be regulated. The members of Congress negotiating with labor's leaders and lobbyists promptly realized that they were dealing with a fragmented power bloc. Labor's internal divisions only worsened its external, public image. Representing at most 30 percent of the nonagricultural labor force, organized labor appeared to much of the nonunion public largely as portrayed by the McClellan Committee and the media, an institution immersed in violence, corruption, and crime, an institution that had to be regulated more rigorously in order to protect the rights of the individual worker.[60]

Labor's splits and the general public's low estimation of unions provided Republicans and Southern Democrats in the House with the opportunity to enact legislation far more restrictive of labor's rights than Kennedy's bill was. In a House that was narrowly balanced between friends and enemies of labor, the conservative coalition could amass enough votes to defeat a compromise measure sponsored by the Democratic leadership. The end result was a piece of legislation bearing the names of Robert Griffin, a Republican from Michigan, and Philip Landrum, a Democrat from Georgia. The Landrum-Griffin Bill, a proposal that subjected union internal affairs to tight public regulation, offered the building trades unions some relief, and denied all other unions the ability to use boycotts and picketing to organize. It was, in the eyes of its sponsors, bipartisan legislation.

The struggle over labor reform, arising only five years after the Supreme Court's school desegregation decision and three years after the rebirth of the "modern" civil rights movement in the Montgomery bus boycott, revealed how anachronistic the debate over union regulation had become. The antiunion conservatives had sought to make state regulation of unions more stringent by including a "bill of rights" protecting all union members from arbitrary, autocratic, and discriminatory actions. Ordinarily such a proposal would have raised a red flag for Southern Democrats still committed to the principle of legal segregation. How could Senator McClellan of Arkansas, who introduced such an amendment to the Kennedy Bill in the Senate, and the northern Republicans in the House propose a union members' "bill of rights" and expect to keep the support of Southern Democrats?

The only rational explanation for their behavior is that civil rights and nondiscriminatory procedures truly lay outside the consciousness of McClellan and many of the Republicans. When the link between a union "bill of rights" and the rights of nonwhite workers became public, northern Republicans assured their southern allies that the legislation's provision for jury trials in cases brought under the law would preserve the "Southern way of life." In their eagerness to diminish union power further, Republicans in the House sponsored a bill that they promised would not strengthen the claims of African Americans and would enable Southern states to preserve their low-wage, nonunion labor force.

How little anyone in Congress, the trade unions, the administration, and the "industrial pluralist" community thought about the relationship between civil rights and labor reform in 1959 is quite amazing. Perhaps more astonishing is the suspicion that Republicans in Congress traded their commitment to civil rights legislation in return for Southern Democratic support of their antilabor program. When Alan K. McAdams interviewed members of Congress for his study of the political and legislative history of Landrum-Griffin, he met numerous Republicans, none of whom spoke for the record, who admitted to discarding their party's commitments to civil rights legislation in return for Southern Democratic support of tighter restrictions on unions. McAdams was forced to conclude that conservative Republicans were so antipathetic to unions that they simultaneously sacrificed the rights of African Americans and enabled Southern states to woo northern employers with the promise of nonunion, low-wage workers.[61]

The congressional endgame that produced Landrum-Griffin resembled the politics of Taft-Hartley, but with one salient difference. As had happened in 1947, Congress in 1959 appointed a joint conference committee to resolve the differences between the House and the Senate. Once again the legislators in the House loaded their bill with punitive antiunion features that they could trade away to the Senate negotiators in order to ensure a final bill more to their liking. The bill, produced by the conference committee, soon to be known as the Labor-Management Reporting and Disclosure Act of 1959 (more popularly as Landrum-Griffin), did precisely that. It subjected the internal affairs of unions to detailed public scrutiny; it incorporated a mini-bill of rights for union members without suggesting any legislative intent to promote civil rights; it further tightened restrictions on secondary boycotts and strikes as well as proscribed forms of picketing; it offered building trades unions some of the relief they had long been demanding; and it exempted the clothing trades unions from the harshest limitations on secondary boycotts, ostensibly to enable such unions to eliminate sweatshops. The difference came in the form of a radio and television address that Eisenhower delivered on August 6, 1959, in which he demanded that Congress enact a labor law to eliminate the racketeering and corruption exposed by the McClellan Committee. It was past time, the president said, "to protect the individual rights of union members — within their unions" and to outlaw "the blackmail picket line and the secondary boycott."[62]

The passage of Landrum-Griffin closed a chapter in the history of state regulation of industrial relations that had begun with the Railway Labor Act of 1926, included the Norris-LaGuardia Act of 1932, the Wagner Act of 1935, and the Taft-Hartley Act of 1947. Since 1959, no additional legislation affecting the nation's industrial relations system has passed Congress. In some ways the passage of Landrum-Griffin, much as Taft-Hartley had done, ratified the American system of "industrial pluralism."

Only a year after the passage of Landrum-Griffin, the doyens of "industrial pluralism" published a set of essays in which they announced their satisfaction with the prevailing system of industrial relations in the advanced industrial world. In one of the essays, titled "Pluralistic Industrialism," the authors declared that ideology as a force that moved societies had vanished, as a time of realism replaced an age of utopias. We now live in an age, they exulted, "in which there is little expectation of either utter perfection or complete doom." In language redolent of Galbraith's countervailing power and Bell's "end of ideology," they described a society that was administered by managers increasingly benevolent and skilled, who would know when and how to respond and anticipate the inevitable. For them, the United States was ruled by a "benevolent political bureaucracy" allied to a "benevolent economic oligarchy" served by a "tolerant mass." Their "new realism" they described as "essentially conservative," with conditions changing only slowly and equilibrium the rule. In their conservative, balanced society the state would not wither away, for it had to "set the rules of the game within which . . . conflict will occur, enforce these rules, and act as mediator." It also had to set the rules for voluntary organizations, ensuring that the rights of membership and the rules of participation are uniform and equitable. In their estimation, that was precisely the sort of balanced system that the United States enjoyed in 1960, one in which corporations and trade unions bargained voluntarily, subject to state regulations that ensured fair treatment to all individuals affected directly by the actions of private organizations and that protected the general or public interest against the extortionate actions of private parties.[63]

A decade later, in 1970–71, the Department of Labor used the provisions of the Landrum-Griffin Act to ensure fair play and equitable treatment for members of the United Mine Workers of America, after a corrupt leadership rigged the 1969 election during which union insurgents sought to depose President Anthony "Tony" Boyle. Boyle not only stole votes; he had his opponent, Joseph Yablonski, murdered. Acting under the provisions of Landrum-Griffin (state and federal authorities also indicted, convicted, and imprisoned Boyle on civil and criminal charges), the Labor Department ordered a new union election in 1972, which it supervised and which elected Arnold Miller and a reform slate to govern the UMW.[64] Finally, between 1988 and 1991, the Teamsters union, whose imperious and often corrupt leaders had kept the McClellan Committee investigators so busy, felt the full weight of federal intervention into internal union affairs. Acting together, the Department of Labor and federal courts placed the union under a judicial trusteeship and supervised an election that in December 1991 returned a slate of reformers led by President Ron Carey to power in the Teamsters union.[65] In the cases of the UMW and the Teamsters, the Department of Labor and the federal courts had interceded into union internal affairs to set uniform and equitable rules that protected the rights of all members equally.

From Redistributional Politics to Race and Gender

The piping prosperity of the 1950s and 1960s and the apparent triumph of "industrial pluralism" plus a generous welfare state neatly eliminated questions concerning wealth and income distribution from the political arena and the agendas of state administrators. John Kenneth Galbraith captured the new economic realities in two books, one published in the 1950s and the other in the 1960s, that described the evolution of "countervailing power" into an "affluent society" governed by a class of professional managers and technocrats, including union leaders, who created a "new industrial state."[66] What Charles Maier labeled the "politics of productivity" had won its greatest triumphs, producing in the post–World War II world a stable and democratic political economy in the United States and Western Europe.[67]

Just when the "industrial pluralists" and the theorists of the "end of ideology" relished their greatest triumphs, however, a new set of divisive issues related to race and gender fractured politics, state agencies, and the labor movement. Civil rights, the "black liberation" movement, dominated the domestic scene and the politics of the 1960s with unintended results for labor and national industrial relations policy. Ever since the emergence of the CIO in the 1930s and especially after the alliance built between the NAACP and the United Automobile Workers in Detroit, the labor movement and the civil rights movement had been closely linked. The AFL, to be sure, and especially many of its oldest craft unions, had a less admirable tradition on civil rights, but after the merger of the AFL and the CIO in 1955, George Meany, the president of the merged union movement, endorsed civil rights legislation and encouraged federation lobbyists to work closely with their counterparts in the civil rights movement. Union members' electoral influence and labor lobbying in Congress and the White House played a decisive role in securing the enactment of the civil rights acts of 1964, 1965, and 1972, legislation that affected basic union practices and traditions.[68]

Title VII of the Civil Rights Act of 1964, which had been endorsed by the AFL-CIO lobbyists, aimed to eliminate discrimination from private labor markets and created a new federal agency, the Equal Employment Opportunity Commission (EEOC), to enforce its mandate. Title VII revised federal labor and industrial relations policies in two vital respects. First, it rendered illegal customary craft union practices, especially common in the building and associated trades, that regulated access to union apprenticeship programs and full membership in a discriminatory manner. Second, it rendered suspect labor-management agreements that included seniority guarantees and promotion opportunities that were discriminatory in impact. The NLRB customarily had done little to alter union or management practices that had a discriminatory impact. The EEOC, by contrast, sought to open the skilled crafts and their unions to minority membership and to ensure that collective bargaining agreements did not use seniority clauses and other devices to limit opportunities for minority workers.[69]

Soon the AFL-CIO found itself in conflict with EEOC rulings and judicial decisions under the terms of Title VII. Craft unions had traditionally limited access to apprenticeship programs and to membership in order to monopolize the labor market and their bargaining power. In practice, however, such policies discriminated against minority workers, and the EEOC and the federal courts ordered several craft unions to set aside places in their apprenticeship programs for minority workers. The craft unions perceived those requirements as a direct threat to their bargaining power and their members' income and job security.[70] The former CIO mass-production unions, despite the fact that many of them had long promoted the rights of minority workers, also fell afoul of Title VII rulings. Because they operated primarily in sectors of the economy in which employers retained the unilateral power to hire and to assign jobs to new employees, collective bargaining contracts that provided job security and promotions on the basis of seniority often discriminated against minority workers. Commission and judicial rulings also demanded that those collective bargaining agreements be amended to eliminate the discriminatory impact of seniority provisions affecting layoffs and promotions. By 1977, so many craft and mass-production unions had found their practices and traditions condemned under the new civil rights laws, that the AFL-CIO, according to one advocate of the new equal opportunity regime, had attacked "not only . . . women workers and blacks locked into segregated seniority structures" but had repudiated "the fundamental premises of Title VII."[71]

The split between the labor movement and the civil rights communities over new federal policies in employment and collective bargaining law consisted of several paradoxes. First, it is quite unlikely that most of the civil rights legislation of the 1960s and 1970s would have been enacted in its final form without the endorsement of the labor movement and its lobbyists. Second, the mass-production unions, which felt the sting of several of the EEOC and judicial rulings as badly as did the more exclusionary craft unions, had perhaps done more to advance the economic, social, and political rights of minority workers than any other basic institution in the United States.[72] Third, the unions that had done the most to advance the cause of minority workers, especially the UAW, suffered most grievously from internal conflicts generated by the civil rights movement and the burgeoning of black consciousness and nationalism.[73] Yet the fact remained that many contracts determined seniority rights on departmental and occupational (skill) lines rather than on a plantwide basis, a reality that condemned many nonwhite workers with long job tenure to less-secure employment than white workers who occupied more-skilled jobs. Decisions by the EEOC and also rulings by federal judges sought both to widen definitions of seniority and to open the skilled trades to nonwhite workers, a process that involved such unions as the steelworkers and automobile workers in conflict with aspects of state regulation.

A similar process played itself out in the arena of gender, unions, collective bargaining, and federal labor relations law. As the fires of the civil rights movement cooled in the late 1960s, the advocates of women's rights turned up the heat. Here, two factors combined to put women workers, trade unions, and state administrators at odds with each other. Just as had been the case with minority workers, craft union rules and basic collective bargaining agreements disadvantaged women workers. Like nonwhite employees, women tended to be recent hires and to be assigned by employers to job classifications with the poorest prospects for promotion (as a group, women workers tended to have discontinuous employment patterns, entering and leaving the labor force in response to family and personal considerations). Women thus clustered in the lower-skill and lower-wage classifications in both union and nonunion settings. Even where men and women performed the same jobs with the same classifications, men tended to earn more and to enjoy greater security, a situation that unions committed to "equal pay for equal work" did not always remedy.[74] The rapid growth in the number of women entering the labor market and seeking full-time employment magnified the impact of Title VII on unions and collective bargaining under federal law. Once again the EEOC and the federal courts issued rulings that violated the customary practices and contractual relationships of craft and mass-production unions.[75]

Throughout the 1960s and into the early 1970s prosperity and relatively full employment salved the wounds suffered by the labor movement as a result of the enforcement of Title VII and its own inability to amend industrial relations law. In fact, the union movement seemed to be conquering new frontiers, as President Kennedy extended to federal employees the same collective bargaining rights enjoyed by workers in the private sector, and many states did likewise. The ranks of unions with jurisdiction in the public sector — the American Federation of State, County, and Municipal Employees, the American Federation of Government Employees (federal), and the American Federation of Teachers, to name only three — swelled with new members. Industrial pluralism still seemed to be working, and political scientist Karen Orren, writing in 1986, could justly observe that instead of serving in national politics as the "Little Sir Echo" of Theodore Lowi's increasingly debilitated interest-group pluralism, "unions have been at the heart of postwar political and economic affairs, with an aggressive, broad, and successful political strategy." This was especially true during the presidency of Lyndon B. Johnson, when AFL-CIO lobbyists and their allies in Congress cooperated to enact the "Great Society" reforms, the broadest expansion of the American welfare state since its inception during the New Deal. Trade unions, "free collective bargaining," and organized labor's alliance with the Democratic party were, in Orren's words, a stable feature of American society that "should be understood not as the haphazard or second-best phenomena they are so often considered to be, but as emblematic expressions of postwar liberal society."[76]

Epilogue: The Death of Industrial
Pluralism and the New Deal System

The celebration of industrial pluralism by its exponents in the 1950s and 1960s and by Karen Orren in the 1980s honored a system that had reached full maturity and was about to experience senescence. For a quarter of a century after World War II, the world economy, driven first by the United States economy and then by those of Western Europe and Japan, had enjoyed an era of unprecedented expansion and prosperity. As had happened repeatedly in the history of the world economy, contraction and crisis followed expansion and stability.[77] That would be precisely the case in the United States and elsewhere in the world during the 1970s. A series of economic shocks, including the artificially induced oil scarcities of 1973–74 and 1978–79, the challenge of competition in the global marketplace from the rising economies of Germany, Japan, and smaller East Asian nations, and rapid price inflation, delivered a savage wallop to the American union movement.

Everywhere one looked at the end of the 1970s, the public sector excepted, one saw unions in disarray. Union density fell substantially for the first time since the Great Depression. The mass-production unions created in the aftermath of the Wagner Act and World War II fell on hard times, as corporations struggled to survive global competition by economizing, substituting cheaper capital for dearer labor, or downsizing altogether and laying off workers by the thousands. Even the craft unions, which had long enjoyed a protected position in the labor market and enviable institutional stability, found themselves under attack from large and small nonunion employers. Technological innovations decimated the printers union, the oldest and most stable of craft unions, in the newspaper business, long its stronghold. Worse yet, employers, who since World War II had accepted trade unionism, collective bargaining, and the federal industrial relations regime, now attacked unions and the entire structure of industrial pluralism.[78]

By the 1970s, what remained of the labor movement could no longer rely on the national state and its agents to promote and protect the union cause. The New Deal–Fair Deal–Great Society coalition, which exemplified Karen Orren's labor-based modern American liberalism, had collapsed beyond repair. The electoral triumph of Richard Nixon and the Republicans in 1968 heralded a new politics distinctly unfavorable to the prospects of labor. Hence it came as no surprise that the NLRB and the federal courts handed down rulings less supportive of organizing initiatives and employers' contractual obligations, or that unions lost an increasing proportion of NLRB representation elections and that employers learned how to use the NLRB and national labor law to thwart union organizing.[79]

The return of the Democrats to national power in 1976 with the election of Jimmy Carter and a Democrat-controlled Congress disclosed labor's political impotency. Having used all its resources and political skills to return the Democrats to power on a platform that endorsed labor law reform, the labor movement found itself unable to cash in its political chips. A congressional majority composed of Republicans, old-line Southern Democrats, and new-style managerial-class, suburban Democrats defeated labor's and the administration's effort to modify the NLRA in a manner that would accelerate NLRB representation elections and curtail employers' power under the law to thwart unionizing drives. A Democratic Congress would not even enact a bill that Eisenhower Republicans had once recommended, legislation to enable building trades unions to picket construction sites when any single union had a dispute with a contractor (common situs picketing). Listening to their nonunion constituents more concerned with high prices and high taxes than with the right of unions to organize and to a corporate world that was united in its opposition to labor law reform, the congressional majority dealt the AFL-CIO's cause a fatal blow. In frustration with the action of Congress and the behavior of the corporate executives, Douglas Fraser of the UAW damned his former associates in the Business-Labor Advisory Council as the proponents of a new class war in which the powerful aimed to crush the powerless. And other labor leaders, such as Lane Kirkland, who replaced Meany as president of the AFL-CIO in 1979, even suggested that the NLRA be repealed and that unions be liberated to slug it out with employers.[80]

The failure of the trade unions to reform national labor law during the presidency of Jimmy Carter presaged the graver difficulties that they would face when the Republicans returned to national power in 1981. All the factors that had operated during the 1970s to reduce union density, enhance employers' resistance to unionization, and strip labor of political influence returned with a vengeance during the 1980s.

The domestic and global economic changes that devastated the trade unions in the late 1970s and that the Carter administration managed poorly, ensured a Republican political triumph in the election of 1980. The election of Ronald Reagan accelerated the decline of trade unionism and also the transformation of federal industrial relations policy. As the new Republican administration began to put its administrators and policies in place, a labor reporter for the *New York Times* observed that organized labor, confronted with aggressive managements, an unsympathetic national government, and a clear desire by Republicans to rewrite fundamentally New Deal labor policies, "neither understands the workplace trends nor, when it does see trends, is it able to come up with imaginative strategies to counter them. It is . . . unable in the face of conservative strength to mount a united effort to save old programs or to come up with new ones."[81]

The president promptly demonstrated just how much policies and practices were changing when he used the full coercive power of the state in the summer of 1981 to break a strike led by the union of air traffic controllers (Professional Air Traffic Controllers Organization, PATCO), the people who managed the traffic patterns that enable commercial aircraft to fly safely in and out of airports and across the nation's skies. The strike itself was precipitated by the hard-nosed bargaining tactics of federal negotiators, who declined to reach a compromise with PATCO. Reagan and his appointees, in language redolent of Grover Cleveland during the Pullman Strike of 1894 and Warren G. Harding during the shopmen's strike of 1922, condemned the strikers as disloyal citizens who tried to use their power over a vital artery of commerce to extort unjust gains from the American people. And in practices reminiscent of 1894 and 1922, Reagan used federal marshals, troops, and judicial writs to break the strike. With newly hired controllers drawn from the ranks of the active military, retired air force controllers, and newly recruited civilians manning airport control towers (as well as a number of PATCO members who crossed picket lines), the president ordered all strike leaders arrested (many of them were brought to court chained and manacled) and all those who refused to return to work discharged permanently from federal service and rendered ineligible for reemployment in any federal position.

Reagan's response to the strike was truly draconian, a warning that although federal and other public employees had recently won the right to unionize and to bargain collectively, they never had the right to strike, a right that, Reagan told a convention of the carpenters union, such labor leaders as John L. Lewis and Philip Murray had relinquished when the Wagner Act was passed in 1935.[82]

The Reagan administration's response to the PATCO strike symbolized how the Republicans in power believed management should respond to labor. It suggested that employers should seek to break strikes through the use of replacement workers (strikebreakers), legal rules, and police power. It also prompted employers to take the offensive, often locking workers out and telling them that unless they returned to the job under revised and less favorable contract terms, they would be permanently replaced. In a loose labor market with substantial unemployment, persistent substitution of capital for labor, and company "downsizing" as a strategic response to shrinking market share, such threats and anti-union practices worked. Newspaper headlines, worker concessions to management called "givebacks," and a persistent decline in union membership told the story of what was happening. Through the decade of the 1980s, headlines blared: "Why Walkouts Don't Work as They Used To"; "Business Brings Back the Lockout"; "Tougher Tactics to Keep Out Unions"; "Union Membership Falls Sharply: Decline Expected to Be Permanent"; "There's No Recovery in Sight for Unions:" "Big Labor Tries to Ends Its Nightmare."[83]

New appointments to the NLRB and the federal judiciary liberated management from previous restraints on antiunion activities. In 1984, Donald Dotson, the new chair of the NLRB, explained his preference for deregulation of industrial relations, implying that the Wagner Act originally intended to promote good relations between employers and employees, not unionism and collective bargaining. Under his administration, the board responded dilatorily to complaints concerning management discrimination against union members or union organizing drives. The board tended to be more sympathetic to management actions, scarcely surprising since Dotson during his pre-board career had served as a management attorney and the board's new solicitor (chief legal adviser) had been recruited from the antiunion National Right to Work Committee. It scarcely surprised labor, for example, when the board ruled on January 24, 1986, that employers bound by a union collective bargaining contract had no duty to bargain about moving to a nonunion site unless the contract required bargaining on such management rights.[84]

At the same time, federal district, circuit, and Supreme court rulings upheld the NLRB. The federal courts also issued some of their own rulings, which further curtailed union rights under the law. The courts ruled that employers could close facilities to escape unions or move operations from unionized to nonunion sites, unless specific contract clauses denied them the right to do so prior to collective bargaining. The Supreme Court ruled that unions could not punish or otherwise discipline members for crossing picket lines and returning to work during economic strikes. In 1989 the Court decided that in certain cases management, when reemploying strikers, could ignore contractual seniority privileges. A year earlier the Court had restricted how unions could use the dues paid by nonmembers (that is, workers who benefited from union services under agency shop agreements), denying unions the right to use such funds for general educational, research, or political purposes. Previously, the Court had limited the ability of unions to use members' dues for political purposes, if the members objected to such use. And in

1992 the Supreme Court denied unions the right to organize on employers' property, even in the case of a shopping mall parking lot that was open to general, unrestricted public access.[85]

Throughout the decade of the 1980s labor found itself unable to reverse the economic and political trends working against it. However much the AFL-CIO strove to reinvigorate the labor-Democratic alliance, voters rejected it in 1984 and 1988, a majority of all working-class voters and probably even a majority of white union members voting Republican. The old coalition had been permanently frayed by the politics of race, low taxes, anti-inflation, and resentment.[86] Even with a Democratic majority in the Senate in 1992, labor's friends failed to secure enough votes to act on a bill that would ban management's use of permanent replacements for striking workers. And at that year's AFL-CIO convention, Secretary of Labor Lynn Martin asked the delegates why the administration should pay any attention at all to a labor movement that represented a shrinking proportion of the nation's labor force and that seemed incapable of adjusting to the reality of global economic competition and a labor force transformed by technology, immigration, race, and gender.[87]

Perhaps more indicative of the low estate to which trade unionism had fallen was the position increasingly taken at the end of the 1980s by the industrial and labor relations authorities. From the emergence of labor-capital relations as a major national issue in the late nineteenth century through the Progressive years, the interwar era, the New Deal, and the age of affluence, such experts had consistently advocated and favored public policies that promoted trade unionism, adversarial collective bargaining, and industrial democracy. In the late 1980s and early 1990s, the same authorities deemed traditional union practices, established public policies, and adversarial industrial relations as outmoded customs in a universe of high technology, well-educated workers, and global competition. Now they demanded that employers and workers practice new forms of alternative industrial relations in which cooperation replaced conflict, mutualism transcended class distinctions, and unions cooperated or became superfluous. In the new world of enlightened human relations–based company personnel practices, unions might grow redundant. Unions, it seemed, had to adapt to nonadversarial, alternative industrial relations regimes or disappear.[88]

In the course of little more than a century, a cycle has played itself out in the arena of public industrial relations policy. In the late nineteenth century, a small proportion of workers belonged to unions, few of which had real bargaining power with larger employers, most of whom resolutely refused to recognize collective action by their employees. Public policy privileged individualism over collective behavior and acted harshly against workers and worker organizations that demonstrated class-based solidarity and militancy. Over the course of the next seventy-five years, public policies and practices, while never abjuring the rights-based and individualistic traditions of politics and law, increasingly promoted collective responses to industrial relations through unions. As a consequence, a larger proportion of workers joined unions, until union density reached one-third or more of all civilian nonagricultural workers between 1946 and 1954, and far greater union densities marked the basic manufacturing, construction, mining, and transport sectors of the economy. Thereafter, union density fell slowly but steadily, although until the mid-1970s the absolute number of union members continued to rise. Today, however, union density has fallen to the lowest levels in more than fifty years, and all indications suggest that the decline in union membership has become irreversible. Public policy and practice, moreover, resemble more the world of the late nineteenth century than that of the New Deal order, as politics and law once more privilege individualism and define militant collective action as unacceptable, "un-American," and illegal.

Conclusion

Where does this history of the state and labor in modern America leave us? What are its meanings or implications? Let me return to the several theories of the state in capitalist society that I discussed explicitly in the introduction and implicitly throughout the book and offer one possible reading and interpretation of the historical record. Those who controlled the American state rarely served capital or labor directly; nor usually did they act as disinterested and impartial honest brokers. Several tacit premises governed the making of policy by public officials. The predominant goal of public policy-makers was political stability and social peace. That goal, moreover, made administrators antagonistic to all forms of unruliness and uncontrolled mass upheavals. Although those in political power tended to respond to shifts in the external balance of social, economic, and political forces, business interests commonly prevailed. Entrepreneurial investment decisions remained the keys to stability and social peace. Hence the state never deliberately enacted and implemented policies that might harm capital.[1] Still, as happened during the World War I and New Deal years, state policy had unintended consequences, which altered the balance of power between labor and capital. This was so because in contemporary democracies the voting rights possessed by all adults partly offset the preponderance of economic power held by capital. Elected public officials could not simply serve the interests of a small minority, however influential, over those of a *mobilized* majority.[2]

To seek to credit autonomous state institutions and actors for shaping and making history is a frustrating and fruitless search. Federal industrial relations policies were not designed at the behest of enlightened and far-seeing employers who knew how to pacify their employees and tame trade unions. Nor were they the handiwork of state managers who realized better than employers how to preserve the essence of capitalism and ensure its expanded reproduction. Nor were they the triumphs of a mobilized, militant, and insistent working class that demanded that the state serve its interests. No autonomous factors or actors walked the historical stage. Whether we consider the role of class relations in society-at-large or the state as historical actor (through any of its branches and institutions, including the judiciary), we must realize that each acted in terms of its own history and imperatives and also in response to the actions of the other(s). Class relations, the law, state administrators — each shared a logic and an institutional memory of its own. In real life and in actual history, institutions and actors were so inextricably intertwined and interdependent that actions taken by one always affected the others and produced a continuous feedback effect.

In a *relatively* autonomous state, the administrative capacities of different agencies and the skills of their professional bureaucrats in large measure determined their ability to pursue policies and goals as defined by the state rather than by pressure groups, lobbyists, or voters. Historically, the Labor Department and its associated agencies lacked the administrative capacity, as defined by budgets, bureaucratic scale and skill, and a history of triumphs, to turn their policies into unchallenged writ. Labor and welfare agencies, the Social Security Administration excepted, lacked the resources and the influence wielded by the legal, financial, agricultural, and military-defense branches of the state.[3]

If the varying administrative capacities of state agencies rendered consistency and common logic absent from the arena of national labor policy, federalism and separation of power further complicated the story. Federal and state labor policies often did not move in harmony, some states modeling their industrial relations approaches after the dominant national model of industrial pluralism, while others, both before and after the passage of the Taft-Hartley Act in 1947, rejected industrial pluralism in favor of policies that privileged individualism, nonunion settings, and alternative industrial relations systems. This was especially true of the southern states, the majority of which rejected industrial pluralism, and whose representatives in the federal state after 1937 persistently opposed pro-labor, pro–collective bargaining initiatives. Formal separation of powers enabled Southern Democratic members of Congress and their Republican allies to wage guerrilla political warfare against more prolabor elements in the executive and judicial branches of the national state. Using their power to investigate, to control the purse strings of government, and to endorse or reject presidential appointees (as well as the filibuster in the Senate), Southerners and their allies in Congress influenced the president and the NLRB to adopt practices more consonant with noncollective approaches to industrial relations.[4]

To be sure, the relation of class forces partly determined how the state acted in the realm of industrial relations. Between the 1870s and the end of World War II, class was an inescapable reality of American society, economics, and politics. Whether expressed in the form of industrial conflicts or political movements such as farmer-laborism and populism in the late nineteenth century, socialism and trade unionism in the early twentieth century, and the New Deal and mass-production unionism in the mid-twentieth century, class divisions influenced policy-making. For three quarters of a century fierce debates and struggles concerning the equitable division of national income and wealth generated intense political heat. From the Industrial Commission report of 1900 through the Commission on Industrial Relations report of 1915 and the Wagner Act of 1935, the proponents of reform asserted that popular democracy and republican government necessitated collective action by working people to wrest for themselves an equitable share of national income and industrial democracy.

Although reformers and working-class leaders stressed collective action, more individualistic forms of thought and practice dominated national culture, institutions, and legal doctrines. What the legal scholar Mary Ann Glendon calls "rights talk" bulked large in the debates over national industrial relations policies. Both the proponents and the opponents of trade unionism, collective bargaining, and industrial pluralism used "rights talk." Advocates of trade unions and collective action emphasized the *right* of workers as individuals to choose, free from the coercion of employers and anachronistic legal codes that offered workers only a "counterfeit liberty." The critics of trade unionism and collective action used similar "rights talk" to vindicate the choices of working people who elected to reject unions in the name of individual free choice.[5]

In paradoxical fashion, individualism and "rights talk" simultaneously strengthened and weakened collective movements, whether based on class (trade unions), race (civil rights), or gender (women's movements). Workers' ability to resist employers, to join unions, and to act collectively found justification in the theory and language of natural, constitutional, and democratic rights. Trade unionism and collective bargaining, argued its defenders, were corollaries of democracy, the signs of a true individualism. The same rights theory and language, however, validated employers' antipathy to closed or union shops as well as individual workers' "right to work" free from coercion in the guise of compulsory unionism. The contradiction between "rights talk" as the basis for both collective action and individualism plagued the civil rights and women's movements. If African Americans (other minorities as well) and women deserved their full civil, social, and economic rights as equal citizens of a democratic republic, they could not demand such rights collectively, asserted the critics of affirmative action, at the expense of other individuals entitled to an equal array of natural, civil, and constitutional rights. Trade unionists, African American protestors, and feminists all discovered that the "rights talk" that they used to vindicate their collective movements also strengthened the hand of their enemies who preferred to build society and polity on the basis of individual free choice.

The tension between individualism and associationalism, which lay at the heart of modern American thought and culture, doomed movements constructed solely in terms of class. In their imaginative reconceptualization of the orthodox Marxian model of class relations, Ira Katznelson and Aristide Zolberg suggest a four-level, or four-stage, process of class formation. The first level consists of the structure of capitalist economic development, which divides people into wage-givers and wage earners, the superordinate and the subordinate. Level two concerns how people actually organize their lives in real places and real ways. The third level involves how people living in real places form social groups based on shared dispositions. Finally, level four encompasses social groups, better defined as classes, that organize themselves and act through movements to modify society and their place within it as a class.[6]

Clearly, in the American case, economic structure divided society into wage-givers and wage earners. Equally obviously, in the years from the 1870s to the end of World War II, most working people resided in neighborhoods of their own kind that fostered shared dispositions based on common ethnicity, religion, and race, as well as class. And at times, masses of working people also organized themselves in economic and political movements to control the society and economy in their interest.[7] Yet, as a graduate student of mine observed in a seminar paper that used a metaphor drawn from baseball, you don't score a run unless all four bases are touched in proper sequence. All workers touched first base, the level of economic structure; nearly all workers touched second, living in common neighborhoods where social interaction was part of daily life; workers, however, failed to touch third simultaneously, causing many to pass others illegally on the base paths, producing outs instead of runs; and only a minority ever touched home plate, having previously touched first, second, and third bases in sequence. The persistence of individualistic patterns of behavior added to the ethnic, racial, and gender divisions that fragmented the working class ensured that American workers would hit no home runs socially, economically, or politically.

Are there any lessons for the labor movement or for public policy-makers in the realm of industrial relations in my reading of history? Frankly, I distrust those who turn to history for lessons, or guidance, or sanction. I find history more often abused than used. Let me for a moment, however, act as one of those abusers, and make the following observations: First, no sharp line ever separated state from society, public from private, coercion from voluntarism. Second, for working people and their movements, the state liberated as well as leashed; it offered a real as well as a counterfeit liberty.

The history told in this book records as many instances of state intervention fostering collective action by working people as of cases in which the state repressed working-class militancy. At no time, however, did the state serve the interests of either capital or labor directly. Nor did state managers originate, adopt, and implement policies in a universe free from external social, economic, and political pressures. The state may have had a memory and a history of its own, but it did *not* act autonomously. Public policies resulted from real conflicts among peoples, groups, and classes (what Marxists once called class relations) and not from a shared consensus that united all or most citizens.

Both in the state and civil society, moreover, structural and conjunctural factors generated greater conflict and less consensus. Federalism and the constitutional separation of powers set separate states in competition with each other and sometimes in conflict with the national state, while the executive, legislative, and judicial branches of government often went their own ways. In civil society, a united working class never challenged a monolithic capitalist class. Business interests splintered sectorally, regionally, and by size and scale of enterprise. Inside and outside the labor movement, working people fractured by occupation, ethnicity, religion, race, and gender. And enormous numbers of citizens identified neither with the capitalist nor with the working class, preferring to see themselves as a protean "middle class," who personified true "Americanism."

At those historical conjunctures when labor seemed least fragmented internally and most successful at identifying its interests as "American" — the Wilson and World War I years, the New Deal, World War II, and the era of affluence (1946–73) — it mobilized its own members for political action alongside numerous "progressive" allies in order to wrest from the state the policies that created industrial pluralism and modern liberalism (the welfare state). When labor failed to unite internally, coalesce with reformist allies, and identify itself with the national interest, as happened in the late nineteenth century, the 1920s, and the Reagan years, business interests dominated politically and workers suffered.

To emphasize the rights of individual workers at the expense of initiatives by the state and civil society that promote collective action breeds as many perils as possibilities. Both radicals and conservatives, for example, have condemned the industrial relations regime that arose in the aftermath of the Wagner and Taft-Hartley acts, the decisions of the NLRB, and the rulings of federal judges. Both have suggested that workers would benefit if liberated from the clutches of bureaucratic union leaders and the web of legal rules that bind them.[8]

More than ten years ago, in 1981 at the start of the Reagan administration, I asked the following questions: Given the current distribution of political and economic power in the United States, would unleashing managements as well as unions from legal restraints work to the advantage of labor or capital? In a society in which employers, at best, merely tolerate unions, in which many union members have only the shakiest allegiance to their organizations, and in which an increasing proportion of the labor force is unorganized, does one serve the interest of workers by railing against trade union bureaucracy and autocracy and demanding more rights for the individual worker against union leaders? In answering those questions, I observed that antilabor employers and conservative politicians as well as their academic cum intellectual sympathizers talk the language of individual rights (rights talk) and seek to extend workers' "democratic" rights. And I asserted then that American workers and their labor movement needed, as never before, solidarity and collective action to endure the onslaught of Reagan Republicanism and its corporate allies. How the labor movement can build solidarity and maintain its collective strength without diminishing rank-and-file initiative or union democracy remains problematic.[9]

To win a true — as distinguished from a counterfeit — liberty, labor must cultivate, secure, and expand its organizational strength simultaneously in the workplace, the community, and the public arena. The success and security of working people depend both on collective economic power and political action to mobilize great masses of voters in order to influence the state and increase the administrative capacities of the agencies that serve workers and their organizations. To gain real liberty in the future, as it has on occasion done in the past, labor must build coalitions with other social movements of racial minorities, women, and new immigrants as well as more advantaged sympathizers in order to create a political majority that pressures the state and its administrators to revitalize modern American liberalism. Such a coalition can look sanguinely to past popular political mobilizations that won their adherents new rights, a better standard of living, and greater security as citizens of state and society.

To those who believe that true liberty can be obtained only by turning the existing world upside down or inside out, by discarding root and branch the political principles and legal doctrines that have shaped the making of public policy since the 1870s, I cite the cautionary advice of E. P. Thompson. Dubious about the claims of radicals who prophesied a world of egalitarian relations built on working-class power once the restraints associated with bourgeois legal rules had been eliminated, Thompson, speaking as a historian, observed that he "can bring in support of [such utopian projections] . . . no historical evidence whatsoever." "Watch," this newly liberated and empowered working-class Thompson wrote, "for a century or two before you cut your hedges down."[10] Amen!

Notes

Abbreviations

ACWA	Amalgamated Clothing Workers of America
CUA	Catholic University of America, Washington, D.C.
AFL	American Federation of Labor
AFL-CIO	American Federation of Labor-Congress of Industrial Organizations
ALHUA	Archives of Labor History and Urban Affairs, Wayne State University, Detroit
CIO	Congress of Industrial Organizations
CIR	Commission on Industrial Relations
COHC	Columbia University Oral History Collection, New York City
CR	*Congressional Record*
FDRL	Franklin D. Roosevelt Library, Hyde Park, New York
HCHL	Herbert C. Hoover Library, West Branch, Iowa
HSTL	Harry S. Truman Library, Independence, Missouri
LC	Library of Congress, Washington, D.C.
LMDC	Labor-Management Documentation Center, Cornell University, Ithaca, New York
NA	National Archives, Washington, D.C.
NLRB	National Labor Relations Board
NRA	National Recovery Administration
NWLB	National War Labor Board
NYPL	New York Public Library, New York City
NYSSI&LR	New York State School of Industrial and Labor Relations, Ithaca, New York
OF	Office Files
PPF	President's Personal Files
PSF	President's Secretary's Files
PSULA	Pennsylvania State University Labor Archives, State College, Pennsylvania
RG	Record Group
SHSW	State Historical Society of Wisconsin, Madison, Wisconsin
WSU	Wayne State University, Detroit, Michigan

Introduction

1. Miliband, *The State in Capitalist Society* 1.

2. See most notably the collection of essays edited by Evans, Rueschmeyer, and Skocpol, *Bringing the State Back In*.

3. Wilentz, *Chants Democratic*, and Fink, *Workingmen's Democracy*.

4. Buhle, "Gender and Labor History," and Kessler-Harris, "A New Agenda for American Labor History"; Kessler-Harris, *A Woman's Wage*; Scott, *Gender and the Politics of History*; Scott, "On Language, Gender, and Working-Class History"; and Palmer, *Descent into Discourse.*

5. Fox-Genovese and Genovese, "The Political Crisis of Social History," 212.

6. For a withering critique of the tendency toward sentimentalization in labor history, yet one that fails to appreciate the real contributions to scholarship made by Gutman, Montgomery, and their epigones, see McDonnell, " 'You Are Too Sentimental.' "

7. For the theme of "republicanism" as an explanatory device for understanding American history and especially the alacrity with which it was seized by labor historians, see Rodgers, "Republicanism."

8. On the parlous state of the labor movement and trade unionism in the 1980s, consult the following works: Goldfield, *Decline of Organized Labor*; K. Moody, *Injury to All*; Kochan, Katz, and McKersie, *Transformation of American Industrial Relations*; Hecksher, *The New Unionism*; and Weiler, *Governing the Workplace.*

9. *New York Times*, February 2, 1984, sec. 2, p. 6; April 15, 1984, sec. 4, p. 5; June 8, 1985, sec. 1, p. 6.

10. Weiler, "Promises to Keep."

11. Lipset, "North American Labor Movements" and *Consensus and Conflict*, 1–8.

12. Leuchtenberg, "The Persistence of Political History."

13. The three most representative examples of this school are Weinstein, *The Corporate Ideal in the Liberal State*; Kolko, *Triumph of American Conservatism*, and also his textbook *Main Currents in American History*; and Radosh, *American Labor and United States Foreign Policy*, and his essay "Corporate Ideology of American Labor Leaders from Gompers to Hillman." For perhaps the most sophisticated and convincing version of this interpretation, see Sklar, *Corporate Reconstruction of American Capitalism*, revising his influential earlier essay "Woodrow Wilson and the Political Economy of Modern United States Liberalism," which first appeared in *Studies on the Left* and was later reprinted in Weinstein and Eakins, *For a New America*. For the most recent elaboration of the "corporate liberal" *cum* C. Wright Mills's "power elite" interpretation, see Domhoff, *The Power Elite and the State.*

14. Only recently have labor historians shown renewed interest in the state, as evidenced in Montgomery, *The Fall of the House of Labor*; Dawley, *Struggles for Justice*; and Sklar, *Corporate Reconstruction of American Capitalism*. Yet even in those cases, the relationship between the state and labor fails to occupy center stage. Montgomery remains more concerned with the shop floor than with public policy; Sklar focuses more on the corporation than the trade union; and Dawley is perhaps more concerned with the new holy trinity of class, race, and especially gender than with the actions of the state. For other works that examine the role of the state but stress its repressive functions in the sphere of industrial relations, see Palladino, *Another Civil War*, and Dawley, "Workers, Capital, and the State in the Twentieth Century." For approaches by historians who view the relationship between the state and labor in a far more dialectical manner, see Fraser, *Labor Will Rule*; Plotke, "The Wagner Act, Again"; J. Greene, " 'The Strike at the Ballot Box' " and "The American Federation of Labor"; and Stromquist, "Looking Both Ways" and "The Politics of Class."

An indication of the absence of historians from the debate over the role of the state in labor history can be seen in the decision of Ira Katznelson and Aristide Zolberg to choose two political scientists, Amy Bridges and Martin Shefter, to write the essays on American workers in the nineteenth century for their coedited volume on comparative labor history, *Working-Class Formation*. By contrast, the essays on France and Germany were written by historians.

15. Block, "The Ruling Class Does Not Rule: Notes on the Marxist Theory of the State"; cf. Gold, Lo, and Wright, "Recent Developments in Marxist Theories of the Capitalist State"; and Jessop, "Recent Theories of the Capitalist State."

16. Skocpol, "Bringing the State Back In," and Weir and Skocpol, "State Structures and the Possibilities for 'Keynesian' Responses to the Great Depression in Sweden, Britain, and the United States"; also Weir, Orloff, and Skocpol, "Introduction: Understanding American Social Politics" and "Epilogue: The Future of Social Policy in the United States"; and Skocpol, "Political Response to Capitalist Crisis"; cf. Ferguson, "From Normalcy to the New Deal," and Vittoz, "The Economic Foundations of Industrial Politics," 365–412, for somewhat differing versions of state policy in the New Deal era. See Skowronek, *Building a New American State*; three articles by Orren — "Union Politics and Postwar Liberalism," "Organized Labor and the Invention of Modern Liberalism," and "Liberalism, Money, and the Situation of Organized Labor"; and Plotke, "The Wagner Act, Again."

17. Tomlins, *The State and the Unions*, 328, for "counterfeit liberty." For other versions of Tomlins's argument as expounded by legal scholars, see, for example, Atleson, *Values and Assumptions*; Stone, "Post-war Paradigm"; Klare, "Traditional Labor Law Scholarship and the Crisis of Collective Bargaining," and the following responses stimulated by it: Finkin, "Does Karl Klare Protest Too Much?" and Klare, "Lost Opportunity"; Atleson, "Reflections on Labor, Power and Society," and Stone, "Re-Envisioning Labor Law." Also see Klare, "Labor Law as Ideology," and Lynd, "Government without Rights," and the comments by Duncan Kennedy and Melvyn Dubofsky in *Industrial Relations Law Journal* 4 (1981): 450–506.

18. "Towards Permanent Exceptionalism," 140–41.

19. Forbath, *Law and the Shaping of the American Labor Movement*. Hattam, "Economic Visions and Political Strategies" and *Labor Visions and State Power*. For the work of an economist who also stresses the repressive functions of the state, see Friedman, "Strike Success and Union Ideology" and "Worker Militancy and Its Consequences."

20. Here I share the sentiments of Karen Orren and David Plotke in their articles cited above in note 16. Orren, moreover, has recently published a book, *Belated Feudalism*, that argues that the sort of legal doctrines and judicial rulings cited by Forbath and Hattam to explain the apolitical and voluntaristic behavior of the American labor movement actually transformed the labor movement into the key political actor in twentieth-century American political liberalism.

21. Brody, *Workers in Industrial America*, viii, 127.

22. *Charleston News and Courier*, July 28, 1877, as cited in E. Foner, *Politics and Ideology*, 126–27.

23. National Civic Federation, *Industrial Conciliation*, 204.

Chapter 1

1. Chandler, *The Visible Hand*. Also see Chandler's more recent history of the same developments, *Scale and Scope*, esp. chaps. 1–4.

2. On these themes, see especially the two books by Chandler cited above.

3. Daniel Nelson, *Managers and Workers*; Brody, *Steelworkers in America*.

4. Montgomery, *Workers' Control in America*, chap. 1, and *The Fall of the House of Labor*, chaps. 1–3; Gutman, *Work, Culture, and Society*, chap. 1.

5. Ulman, *Rise of the National Trade Union.* Cf. Jackson, *Formation of Craft Labor Markets.*

6. Dubofsky, "Workers' Movements in North America"; Montgomery, "Strikes in Nineteenth-Century America." Edwards, *Strikes in the United States*; and Bennett and Earle, *Geography of American Labor and Industrialization.*

7. See the books and articles cited above, and especially Montgomery, "Strikes in Nineteenth-Century America," for the shifting character and goals of strikes.

8. For Lincoln's view on labor, see Randall, *Lincoln the Liberal Statesman*, 187–89, and Lincoln, *Collected Works*, 4:24.

9. Montgomery, *Beyond Equality.*

10. *CR*, 43d Cong., 1st sess., 1874, Appendix, 393.

11. Ibid.

12. Cited in Keller, *Affairs of State*, 189. On the theme of the private market as the regulator of relations in society, see Hovenkamp, *Enterprise and American Law*, chaps. 15–17, and "Labor Conspiracies."

13. The one major exception might have been Abraham Lincoln's dispatch of federal troops to the anthracite district of Pennsylvania during the Civil War, ostensibly to suppress resistance to conscription among Irish immigrant workers but also to cow striking coal miners. On this, see Palladino, *Another Civil War*, chap. 7.

14. For the tendency of state court judges to find most forms of labor action during strikes illegal, see Forbath, *Law and the Shaping of the American Labor Movement*, chaps. 2–4, passim. For a more generous reading of state and federal legal precedents concerning the right to strike, see Hovenkamp, *Enterprise and American Law*, chap. 18.

15. Gutman, *Work, Culture, and Society*, chaps. 6–7; Salvatore, *Eugene V. Debs*, chap. 2.

16. William Roscoe Thayer, *The Life and Letters of John Hay*, 2:5, cited in Wilentz, "Rise of the American Working Class," 117.

17. Bruce, *1877: Year of Violence*, chap. 5.

18. On this, see ibid., chaps. 6–12.

19. Cited in Dulles and Dubofsky, *Labor in America*, 113.

20. Cooper, *The Army and Civil Disorder*, 253. For the official army version of events, see U.S. Congress, Senate, *Federal Aid in Domestic Disturbances*, 189–205.

21. Cooper, *The Army and Civil Disorder,* 60–61.

22. Ibid., 76–81.

23. Bruce, *1877*, 279, 289.

24. U.S. Congress, Senate, *Federal Aid in Domestic Disturbances,* 322–23.

25. Bruce, *1877*, 298–99.

26. Cited in Eggert, *Railroad Labor Disputes*, 36–37; Bruce, *1877*, 258–59.

27. Bruce, *1877*, 255; Eggert, *Railroad Labor Disputes*, 37.

28. McMurry, "Legal Ancestry of the Pullman Strike Injunctions," 235–56.

29. Cited in Cooper, *The Army and Civil Disorder*, 7.

30. Ibid., 210.

31. Bruce, *1877*, 317.

32. *CR*, 45th Cong., 1st sess., 1877, 296–98, 301, 312, 326.

33. *CR*, 47th Cong., 1st sess., 1882, 4924, 5430, 6996.

34. For a fine sample of the testimony, see Garraty, *Labor and Capital in the Gilded Age.*

35. Leiby, *Carroll Wright and Labor Reform*, 69–70.

36. Fink, *Workingmen's Democracy*.

37. Dubofsky, *Industrialism and the American Worker*, 62.

38. *CR*, 48th Cong., 2d sess., 1885, 1620–36, 1778–97, 1832–40.

39. In re Wabash Railway Co., 24 Federal Reporter (1885), 217–21.

40. See Hovenkamp, "Labor Conspiracies," 924–25, for the quotation and also for the argument that judges interpreted the law identically for business and labor, although, in practice, uniformity in judicial interpretation weakened union rights. By contrast, Forbath, *Law and the Shaping of the American Labor Movement*, asserts that judges singled out workers and their unions as victims of a conservative and corporate form of ideological hegemony. Cf. Keller, *Affairs of State*, 404, for an interpretation more consonant with Hovenkamp's; and Twiss, *Lawyers and the Constitution*, and Paul, *Conservative Crisis and the Rule of Law*, for the older interpretation of the federal courts as conservative instruments of a corporate ruling class.

41. *CR*, 49th Cong., 1st sess., 1886, 3349.

42. Ibid., 3393.

43. Ibid., 3394.

44. Ibid., 3728–29, 3760; see also *Messages and Papers of the Presidents*, 7:5112.

45. *CR*, 49th Cong., 1st sess., 1886, 3760–65; Eggert, *Railroad Labor Disputes*, 74.

46. *CR*, 49th Cong., 1st sess., 1886, 8030.

47. U.S. Congress, House, *Investigation of Labor Troubles in Missouri, Arkansas, Kansas, Texas, and Illinois*, xiv, xxiii–xiv.

48. *CR*, 49th Cong., 2d sess., 1887, 2375–76.

49. *CR*, 50th Cong., 1st sess., 1888, 3105–6.

50. Ibid., 3096–109, 8608.

51. Ibid., 4507, 4744, 4768; Leiby, *Carroll Wright and Labor Reform*, 107.

52. Railroads in receivership because they were unable to pay their obligations to bondholders and other creditors and hence had declared bankruptcy came under the direct control of federal judges who acted as the receivers. Such judges ruled that railroads in receivership had temporarily become public property and, as such, were subject to direct judicial administration in all aspects of their business, including labor relations. On this issue, see Forbath, *Law and the Shaping of the American Labor Movement*, 66, 68, 72–74.

53. McMurry, *The Great Burlington Strike of 1888*, 117–23; Eggert, *Railroad Labor Disputes*, 90.

54. Chicago, Burlington, & Quincy Railway Co. et al. v. Burlington, C.R. & N. Railway Co. et al., 34 Federal Reporter (1888), 481–88. For the peculiar place of railroads in late-nineteenth-century legal history and the means used by judges to distinguish them from other types of business enterprise in order to subject their operation to state regulation, see Hovenkamp, *Enterprise and American Law*, chap. 12.

55. Casey v. Cincinnati Typographical Union, No. 3., et al., 45 Federal Reporter (1891), 135–47.

56. *Messages and Papers of the Presidents*, 7:5359–60.

57. *Report on Labor Troubles in the Anthracite Regions of Pennsylvania*, cxxii.

58. Wall, *Andrew Carnegie*, chap. 16; see Wolff, *Lockout*, for a full but journalistic history of the conflict. Both have now been surpassed by Krause, *Battle for Homestead*, 12–43, 329–50.

59. U.S. Congress, House, *Employment of Pinkerton Detectives*; U.S. Congress, Senate, *Investigation of Labor Troubles*.

60. Coeur d'Alene Consolidated Mining Co. v. Miners' Union of Wardner et al., 51

Federal Reporter (1892), 260–68; for the full legal history of the dispute, see Dubofsky, "James H. Hawley and the Haywood Case."

61. These machinations can best be followed in the relevant correspondence in the Norman H. Willey Papers, Idaho State Historical Society, Boise.

62. These maneuvers are fully detailed in Telegrams and Correspondence, Idaho Congressional Delegation, Pertaining to Coeur d'Alenes, Idaho State Historical Society.

63. Cooper, *The Army and Civil Disorder*, 170; Dubofsky, *We Shall Be All*, 30–33; U.S. Congress, Senate, *Federal Aid in Domestic Disturbances*, 222–24.

64. Dubofsky, "Hawley and the Haywood Case," 25–27; *We Shall Be All*, 33–34.

65. Wolff, *Lockout*, 221. On the political fragmentation of the working class, see Oestreicher, "Urban Working-Class Political Behavior," 1257–86.

66. Walter Q. Gresham to Morris Ross, August 1, 1892, Gresham Papers, LC, cited in Morgan, *From Hayes to McKinley*, 441.

67. For a perspective suggesting that judges did not always favor the interests of capitalists and that particularly on issues of health, safety, and the public interest, they showed some solicitude for the powerless, see Hurvitz, "American Labor Law and the Doctrine of Entrepreneurial Property Rights." Hovenkamp's findings that judges did not consciously favor capital over labor and indeed tried to treat both parties identically lends support to Hurvitz's interpretation. See *Enterprise and American Law*, chap. 18.

68. U.S. v. Workingmen's Amalgamated Council of New Orleans et al., 54 Federal Reporter (1893), 994–1000.

69. Berman, *Labor and the Sherman Act*, 37–40; Eggert, *Railroad Labor Disputes*, 115–17.

70. Mason, *Organized Labor and the Law*, 123–43. For a more recent and slightly more convincing version of the same interpretation, see Hovenkamp, *Enterprise and American Law*, 228–34.

71. Waterhouse et al. v. Comer, 55 Federal Reporter (1893), 149–59.

72. Toledo, A.A. & N.M. Railway Co. v. Penn. Co. et al., 54 Federal Reporter (1893), 730–45.

73. Ibid., 746–58, at 751. For evidence of Brewer's influence on other judges, see Burt, *Constitution in Conflict*, 237–39, 242–44.

74. Farmers' Loan & Trust Co. v. Northern Pac. R. Co. et al., 60 Federal Reporter (1894), 803–24. Burt, *Constitution in Conflict*, 242–44.

75. Ames v. Union Pac. Ry. Co. et al., 62 Federal Reporter (1894), 7–17.

76. Thomas v. Cinn. N.O. & T.P. Ry. Co., ibid., 17–24.

77. Eggert, *Railroad Labor Disputes*, 124–33.

78. Eggert, *Richard Olney*, 115–18.

79. Cooper, *The Army and Civil Disorder*, 101.

80. Eggert, *Richard Olney*, 132.

81. Eggert, *Railroad Labor Disputes*, 172.

82. U.S. v. Elliot et al., 62 Federal Reporter (1894), 801–3; Thomas v. Cinn., N.O. & T.P. Ry. Co., ibid., 803–23; U.S. v. Alger, ibid., 824–28; In re Charge to Grand Jury, ibid., 828–33; In re Charge to Grand Jury, ibid., 840–47, among other citations.

83. In re Charge to Grand Jury, ibid., 829.

84. Cooper, *The Army and Civil Disorder*, 115–25.

85. For the army's version of events, see U.S. Congress, Senate, *Federal Aid in Domestic Disturbances*, 228–38.

86. Salvatore, *Eugene V. Debs*, 133–34.

87. *CR*, 53d Cong., 2d sess., 1894, 7233–39, 7284, 7544–46.

88. Cooper, *The Army and Civil Disorder*, 210–11.

89. Eggert, *Railroad Labor Disputes*, 279 n. 27.

90. Eggert, *Richard Olney*, 168; In re Debs, 158 U.S. (1895), 564–600.

91. Arthur et al. v. Oakes et al., 63 Federal Reporter (1894), 310–29.

92. Eggert, *Richard Olney*, 153–57.

93. Leiby, *Carroll Wright and Labor Reform*, 168–70; U.S. Congress, Senate, U.S. Strike Commission, *Report*.

94. *CR*, 53d Cong., 2d sess., 1894. 2533–34, 2629; U.S. Congress, House, *Receivership of Northern Pacific Railway Company*, 17–19.

95. Eggert, *Richard Olney*, 161–64.

96. *CR*, 54th Cong., 2d sess., 1897, 2387–90, 55th Cong., 2d sess., 1898, 4640–49, 4858, 5048, 5053.

97. *CR*, 54th Cong., 2d sess., 1897, 2026–30, 2291–92, 2387–90, 2746, 2751, 2980.

98. American Steel & Wire Co. v. Wire Drawers' and Die Makers' Unions Nos. 1 & 3 et al., 90 Federal Reporter (1898), 598–622. For judges' fears and assumptions that strikes and violence were synonymous, see Avery, "Images of Violence in Labor Jurisprudence." A certain logic underlay the ruling of the judge in the Cleveland case. Assuming that the vast majority of American workers were nonunion and that many among that majority themselves believed in freedom of contract and the right to replace strikers, the judge found it easy to conclude that only coercion by the strikers denied the employer the ability to replace strikers.

99. Cooper, *The Army and Civil Disorder*, 195; Dubofsky, "Hawley and the Haywood Case," 25–27; and for the official army version, U.S. Congress, Senate, *Federal Aid in Domestic Disturbances*, 246–52.

100. U.S. Congress, House, U.S. Industrial Commission, *Final Report*, 19:801–5, 813–17.

101. Ibid., 947–55. For an interpretation that the economists who drew up the recommendations sought to replace the voluntarism of the late-nineteenth-century industrial relations regime with a form of corporatism based on representation from corporate interests, trade unions, and public administrators in order to distribute income more equitably, see Wunderlin, *Visions of New Industrial Order*, 27–71. Wunderlin also suggests that the recommendations of the commission presaged the reforms of the Wilson administration and the New Deal. For a strikingly similar interpretation, see Furner, "Knowing Capitalism."

Chapter 2

1. Ramirez, *When Workers Fight*.

2. See, for example, Ray Stannard Baker, "Parker and Theodore Roosevelt on Labor," *McClure's* 14 (November 1904): 41, part of a series on the labor question that Parker wrote for that muckraking magazine. Among other general works on these themes, see Wiebe, *Search for Order*, chaps. 5–7, and Wiebe, *Businessmen and Reform*; Gabriel Kolko, *Triumph of Conservatism*; James Weinstein, *The Corporate Ideal in the Liberal State*; Yellowitz, *Labor and the Progressive Movement in New York State*; Huthmacher, "Urban Liberalism and the Age of Reform." For a recent detailed examination of the subject that is more theoretical than the others and also more subtle in its analysis of the relationship

between capitalism and the state, one should read carefully Sklar, *Corporate Reconstruction of American Capitalism*.

3. Brody, *Workers in Industrial America*, 127. For the fullest treatment of the militancy of both radicals and moderates in the labor movement, see Montgomery, *The Fall of the House of Labor*, chap. 6.

4. Adams, *Age of Industrial Violence*; Montgomery, *Workers' Control in America*, 91–112.

5. Cited in Karson, *American Labor Unions and Politics*, 90.

6. For an interpretation of Roosevelt along precisely these lines, see Blum, *The Republican Roosevelt*. Sklar, in *Corporate Reconstruction of American Capitalism*, takes a similar, if more theoretical, approach to the subject; see esp. 334–65.

7. *Messages and Papers of the Presidents*, 13:6650.

8. Ibid., 14:6716, 6786.

9. Ibid., 14:7190–91.

10. Ibid., 14:6982–86.

11. Ibid., 14:6716.

12. Roosevelt to Knox, November 10, 1904, Knox Papers, cited in Mowry, *Era of Theodore Roosevelt*, 142.

13. Hanna, "Industrial Conciliation and Arbitration," 25; Croly, *Marcus A. Hanna*, 386–410.

14. For the years between 1894 and 1908 it is difficult to know with certainty how working people cast their ballots. We do know, however, that only a small proportion of workers belonged to trade unions (less than 10 percent) and also that a smaller proportion of eligible voters, especially among the working class, cast votes during that period. The two most famous labor leaders of the era, Samuel Gompers and John Mitchell, chose opposing political paths. Gompers refused to endorse any party, while Mitchell favored the Republicans. The best research that we have on electoral politics for the era suggests that the combination of the depression of the 1890s and the astute politics of McKinley republicanism as designed by Mark Hanna attracted increasing numbers of working-class voters in the northeastern and north central states to the Republican party. See, among other works, Kleppner, *Cross of Culture*, chaps. 6–9; Jensen, *Winning of the Midwest*, chaps. 8–10; and McSeveney, *Politics of Depression*, chaps. 4–7. For an analysis that also suggests the fragmentation of American working-class voters but is less convinced of their Republican proclivities between 1894 and 1912, see Oestreicher, "Urban Working-Class Political Behavior."

15. Hanna, "Industrial Conciliation and Arbitration," 26.

16. For the best brief summary of the dispute and Roosevelt's part in it, see Wiebe, "The Anthracite Strike of 1902."

17. On these points, see ibid., 243–44.

18. U.S. Bureau of Labor Statistics, *Report to the President on the Anthracite Coal Strike*.

19. Roosevelt, *Letters*, 3:330ff.

20. Wiebe, "The Anthracite Strike of 1902," 248; Berman, *Labor Disputes and the Presidents*, 46–59; Leiby, *Carroll Wright and Labor Reform*, 175.

21. Anthracite Coal Strike Commission, *Report to the President*; Blatz, "Work and Labor Relations in the Anthracite Coal Industry," chaps. 9–10.

22. For precisely that interpretation, see Wiebe, "The Anthracite Strike of 1902," and Gowaskie, "John Mitchell and the Anthracite Mine Workers"; Blatz, *Labor Relations in the Anthracite Coal Industry*, chap. 6, makes the same point.

23. For interpretations that stress labor's gains from federal intervention, see Leiby, *Carroll Wright and Labor Reform*, 175; Mowry, *Era of Theodore Roosevelt*, 139–40; Blum, *Republican Roosevelt*, 59.

24. Cited in Blum, *Republican Roosevelt*, 60.

25. Berman, *Labor Disputes and the Presidents*, 59–60.

26. U.S. Congress, Senate, *A Report on Labor Disturbances in the State of Colorado from 1880 to 1904, Inclusive*; see also Dubofsky, *We Shall Be All*, 47–55, 101–4.

27. U.S. Congress, House, *Papers Relative to Labor Troubles at Goldfield*; Dubofsky, *We Shall Be All*, 122–24; Berman, *Labor Disputes and the Presidents*, 64–69.

28. In everyday language, "union shop" and "closed shop" tended to be used interchangeably. In fact and at law, however, the two categories of union security differed. A closed shop, in effect, gave a trade union control of the labor market. Employers could hire only union members, and, as frequently was the case in the building and printing trades, unions operated hiring halls where employers came for workers. By contrast, the union shop allowed employers to hire workers without regard to union membership but required such new hires to become union members after a negotiated time; if they did not, they stood to lose their jobs.

29. Roosevelt to George B. Cortelyou, July 13 and 14, 1903, in *Messages and Papers of the Presidents*, 14:6783–84.

30. Mowry, *Era of Theodore Roosevelt*, 141. This was also, as we saw in Chapter 1 above, how the law operated in the realm of industrial relations. As Herbert Hovenkamp demonstrated so clearly, judges in treating employers and workers identically persistently favored the former. See Hovenkamp, *Enterprise and American Law*, chap. 18.

31. *Messages and Papers of the Presidents*, 14:6895–98.

32. Ibid., 13:6650, 14:6786, 15:7342–46.

33. 198 U.S. 45. The Supreme Court majority in its decision relied on the doctrine of the absolute inviolability of the right of individuals to contract for themselves and all the shibboleths of free market principles. For evidence of an alternative judicial tradition, which also derived from the doctrine of the late nineteenth century and which sanctioned the police power of the state in the spheres of safety and welfare legislation, see Hurvitz, "American Labor Law and the Doctrine of Entrepreneurial Property Rights." Cf. Urofsky, "State Courts and Progressive Legislation during the Progressive Era."

34. Muller v. Oregon, 208 U.S. 412 (1908); Bunting v. Oregon, 243 U.S. 426 (1917); Wilson v. New, 243 U.S. 332 (1917).

35. Frankfurter and N. Greene, *Labor Injunction*, 222. See also Avery, "Images of Violence in Labor Jurisprudence," esp. 53–70, and Hovenkamp, "Labor Conspiracies."

36. Frankfurter and N. Greene, *Labor Injunction*, 49–65; see Forbath, *Law and the Shaping of the American Labor Movement*, chap. 3.

37. Gordon, "The Labor Boycott in New York City"; Zieran, "The Boycott and Working-Class Solidarity."

38. Loewe et al. v. Lawlor et al. 148 Federal Reporter (1906), 924–26.

39. Loewe v. Lawlor, 208 U.S. 274 (1908).

40. Lawlor et al. v. Loewe et al., 187 Federal Reporter (1911), 522–29; Lawlor et al. v. Loewe et al., ibid., 209 (1913), 721–29.

41. Mandel, *Samuel Gompers*, 263–83; Barry F. Helfand, "Labor and the Courts"; Gompers v. Buck's Stove & Range Co., 221 U.S. 418 (1911).

42. Adair v. U.S., 208 U.S. 161 (1908).

43. Coppage v. Kansas, 236 U.S. 1 (1915).

44. Cited in Parrish, *Frankfurter*, 69.

45. Hitchman Coal & Coke Co. v. Mitchell et al., 172 Federal Reporter (1909), 963–70.

46. Hitchman Coal & Coke Co. v. Mitchell et al., ibid., 202 (1912), 512–56.

47. Mitchell et al. v. Hitchman Coal & Coke Co., ibid., 214 (1914), 685–716.

48. Parrish, *Frankfurter*, 75; Hitchman Coal & Coke Co. v. Mitchell, 245 U.S. 229.

49. For an analysis that emphasizes the AFL's commitment to "voluntarism," see Tomlins, *The State and the Unions*, Part 1. For approaches that stress the AFL's need to act politically, and frequently in a partisan manner, in the early twentieth century, see Montgomery, *The Fall of the House of Labor*; Sklar, *Corporate Reconstruction of American Capitalism*, esp. chaps. 4 and 6; and J. Greene, "The American Federation of Labor."

50. Laslett, *Labor and the Left*, chaps. 2–7; Montgomery, *Workers' Control in America*, 48–90; AFL Papers, Office of the President, File A, SHSW. Cf. J. Greene, "The American Federation of Labor."

51. See note 49 above and also Forbath, *Law and the Shaping of the American Labor Movement*, esp. chaps. 2 and 5, and Hattam, "Economic Visions and Political Strategies." For a view of labor politics more consonant with mine, one that stresses labor's central role in the construction of twentieth-century political liberalism, see Orren, "Organized Labor and the Invention of Modern Liberalism in the United States," and Orren, *Belated Feudalism*, chaps. 1 and 6.

52. *American Federationist* 12 (May 1906): 293–96; ibid. 12 (August 1906): 529–31; ibid. 15 (August 1908): 589, 598–605; Karson, *American Labor Unions and Politics*, 42–70; Mandel, *Samuel Gompers*, 284–95; J. Greene, "The American Federation of Labor," and "The Strike at the Ballot Box."

53. *Messages and Papers of the Presidents*, 14:6982–86, 7027–29, 7086.

54. Ibid., 7190–91.

55. Ibid., 7194–95.

56. Ibid., 15:7209–18, 7342–46.

57. Scheinberg, "Theodore Roosevelt and the A.F. of L.'s Entry into Politics."

58. For samples of this in congressional debates, see, *CR*, 56th Cong., 2d sess., 1902, 2589–98; *CR*, 60th Cong., 2d sess., 1908, 114–34; cf. Frankfurter and N. Greene, *Labor Injunction*, 140–41.

59. *CR*, 56th Cong., 2d sess., 1901, 2593.

60. Jones, "Wilson Administration," 1–33; Boemeke, "Wilson Administration," 34–41; J. Greene, "The American Federation of Labor," chaps. 6–7.

61. *Messages and Papers of the Presidents*, 15:7378, 7432, 7524–25, 7865–66.

62. Parrish, *Frankfurter*, 68–69.

63. *CR*, 61st Cong., 2d sess., 1910, 8847–53; 62d Cong., 2d sess., 1912, 6415–71.

64. *CR*, 62d Cong., 2d sess., 1912, 10,679–82.

65. Link, *Wilson: The Road to the White House*, 112, 127, 158–59; Boemeke, "Wilson Administration," 42–64.

66. Link, *Road to White House*, 470–71; Boemeke, "Wilson Administration," 64–82; Gompers, *Seventy Years of Life and Labor*, 2:282–83; AFL Papers, Office of the President, File A, Box 17, SHSW.

67. For interpretations that stress the influence of Louis Brandeis, see Jones, "Wilson Administration," 50; Boemeke, "Wilson Administration," 69–87.

68. Jones, "Wilson Administration," 312–20; Boemeke, "Wilson Administration," 89–

110; Smith, "Organized Labor and the Government," 267–68, 272; Gompers to John L. Lewis, November 19, 1916; Lewis to Gompers, November 20 and 21, 1916; and Gompers to W. B. Wilson, November 23, 1916; all in AFL Papers, Office of the President, File A, Box 23, SHSW.

69. For the letter to Gompers, see Jones, "Wilson Administration," 88; for the quotations, Lombardi, *Labor's Voice in the Cabinet*, 104–7. Also see pp. 75–95 for a sketch of William B. Wilson.

70. The files of the U.S. Mediation and Conciliation Service, RG 280, NA, show how Wilson used his former union colleagues. Boemeke, in "Wilson Administration," shows precisely how this worked in the Colorado coal miners' strike; see chaps. 3–5.

71. The best history of the CIR remains Adams, *Age of Industrial Violence*. A briefer, more tendentious version can be found in Weinstein, *The Corporate Ideal in the Liberal State*, chap. 7. For an extremely sympathetic treatment of Walsh, see Montgomery, *The Fall of the House of Labor*, 360–65.

72. U.S. Congress, Senate, Commission on Industrial Relations, *Final Report and Testimony Submitted to Congress*; more material can be found in the Frank P. Walsh Papers, NYPL, and the unpublished reports of the field investigators, Department of Labor, RG 1 and RG 174, NA. For an approach more sympathetic to Rockefeller and less so to Walsh and his allies on the CIR, see Gitelman, *Legacy of Ludlow*, chap. 6.

73. U.S. Congress, Senate, Commission on Industrial Relations, *Final Report and Testimony Submitted to Congress*, 1:1–91; Adams, *Age of Industrial Violence*, 215–17; Commons, *Myself*, 166–67, 172–73; cf. Weinstein, *The Corporate Ideal in the Liberal State*, 188, 190–91, 208–10; Gitelman, *Legacy of Ludlow*, chaps. 6–7. For interpretations more sympathetic to Commons's approach to industrial relations as a forerunner of New Deal–style corporatist polices, see Wunderlin, *Visions of New Industrial Order*, 113–29, and Furner, "Knowing Capitalism." 275–84.

74. Adams, *Age of Industrial Violence*, 219–20.

75. *CR*, 62d Cong. 1st sess., 1912, 1105–14, 1189–97.

76. *CR*, 63d Cong., 2d sess., 1914, 9262.

77. Link, *Wilson: The New Freedom*, 428–31, and Link, *Wilson and the Progressive Era*; Gompers, *Seventy Years of Life and Labor*, 2:298–99.

78. *CR*, 62d Cong., 1st sess., 1913, 1288.

79. *CR*, 63d Cong., 2d sess., 1914, 9567, 13,977; see also 9562–63, 14,585–610.

80. Ibid., 9542.

81. Frankfurter and Greene, *Labor Injunction*, 144–45, 163–64; Witte, *Government in Labor Disputes*, 67; Mason, *Organized Labor and the Law*, 180–81, 190–91. For a more recent interpretation, which suggests that the labor clause represented a shift in popular attitudes toward organized labor, see Ernst, "The Labor Exemption."

82. Kutler, "Labor, the Clayton Act, and the Supreme Court."

83. On Colorado, see Boemeke, "Wilson Administration," chaps. 3–5, showing how the president not only insisted on military neutrality but also pressured the companies to bargain with the UMW; and B. B. Jensen, "Woodrow Wilson's Intervention in the Coal Strike of 1914."

84. Link, *Wilson and the Progressive Era*, 235–37.

85. On this history, see Lecht, *Experience under Railway Labor Legislation*, 17–27.

86. *Messages and Papers of the Presidents*, 15:8144–49; Lecht, *Experience under Railway Labor Legislation*, 28–29.

87. *CR*, 64th Cong., 1st sess., 1916, 13,568–69, 13,580; K. A. Kerr, *American Railroad Politics*, 33–34; E. Berman, *Labor Disputes and the Presidents*, 106–25.

88. *American Federationist* 23 (November 1916): 1067–68; Karson, *American Labor Unions and Politics*, 85–89; Jones, "Wilson Administration," 315–20; Laslett, *Labor and the Left*, 168–69, 218–19, 302; Link, *Wilson, Campaigns for Progressivism and Peace*, 126–27; W. Thomas White, "Immigrants, Radicals, and Trade Unionists," 4.

89. Dowd v. United Mine Workers of America et al., 235 Federal Reporter (1916), 1–17.

Chapter 3

1. Hurvitz, "Meaning of Industrial Conflict," 98–99.

2. Montgomery, *The Fall of the House of Labor*, 320–21, and Montgomery, *Workers' Control in America*, 95–98; Dubofsky, *Industrialism and the American Worker*, 117–18.

3. Montgomery, *Workers' Control in America*, 95–98, and *The Fall of the House of Labor*, 360; Dubofsky, *Industrialism and the American Worker*, 120–21.

4. For Gompers's reiteration of such demands before the Council of National Defense, see Cronon, *Cabinet Diaries*, 176, 196, and passim.

5. On these developments, see Dubofsky, *We Shall Be All*, 358–75.

6. Cuff, *War Industries Board*.

7. Duplex v. Deering et al. 247 Federal Reporter (1917), 192–199, Duplex v. Deering et al. 252 Federal Reporter (1918), 727–48; on Hitchman, see chap. 2 above and Cronon, *Cabinet Diaries*, 277.

8. Robert Bruere, "Copper Camp Patriotism: An Interpretation," *Nation* 106 (February 1918): 236; on general war labor policies, see Cuff, "Politics of Labor Administration."

9. Kennedy, *Over Here*, 266–67.

10. Baruch to Wilson, June 30, 1917, U.S. Department of Labor, RG 280, File 33/493, NA; for more on Baruch's general disinterest in labor, see Schwarz, *The Speculator*, chap. 2.

11. Jones, "Wilson Administration," 343; Mandel, *Samuel Gompers*, 366–68.

12. Jones, "Wilson Administration," 350–51; Lombardi, *Labor's Voice in the Cabinet*, 238.

13. Cronon, *Cabinet Diaries*, 176.

14. For Wehle's beliefs and policies, see his three articles in the *Quarterly Journal of Economics*: "The Adjustments of Labor Disputes," "Labor Problems in the United States," and "War Labor Policies"; also see Wehle, *Hidden Threads in History*, 18–63, passim; and Kennedy, *Over Here*, 266–67.

15. *CR*, 68th Cong., 1st sess., 1917, 6104; *Literary Digest* 55 (July 28, 1917): 20–21; ibid. 55 (August 18, 1917): 12–13; and ibid. 55 (August 31, 1918): 14–15.

16. An enormous Department of Justice file details this antilabor campaign: File 186701, RG 60, NA.

17. Ibid., File 186813-13; Statement of George L. Bell to CND, File 20/77, RG 280, Department of Labor, NA.

18. On military repression, see Abraham Glasser mss., Department of Justice, RG 60, and File 33/438 et. seq., RG 280, File 20/473, RG 174, Department of Labor, NA.

19. Bernard Baruch to Newton Baker, July 3, 1917, War Department File AGO 370.6, cited in Glasser mss., "Arizona," 23; Wheeler to T. W. Gregory, December 8, 1917, File 186701-27-20, Justice Department, RG 60.

20. Hyman, *Soldiers and Spruce*; Dubofsky, *We Shall Be All*, 411–14.

21. Fitts to Fall, August 30, 1917, File 186701-27-16, RG 60, Justice Department, NA;

W. B. Wilson to Judge Harry Covington, August 7, 1917, File 20/77, RG 280, Labor Department, NA.

22. Francis F. Kane to Thomas W. Gregory, September 7, 1917, File 186701-39-4, RG 60, Justice Department, NA; Dubofsky, *We Shall Be All*, 404–10.

23. Gompers to Woodrow Wilson, August 10, 1917, Gompers Letterbooks, 5:237, LC; Newton D. Baker to William B. Wilson, August 1, 1917, and Wilson to Baker, August 3, 1917, both in File 33/574, RG 280, Department of Labor, NA.

24. Gompers to Baker, August 22, 1917, Gompers Letterbooks, 5:237; Gompers to W. B. Wilson, August 27, 1917; W. B. Wilson, memo to President Wilson, August 31, 1917; Woodrow Wilson to Baker, September 19, 1917; and Woodrow Wilson to W. B. Wilson, September 19, 1917; all in File 20/473, RG 280, Labor Department, NA.

25. Parrish, *Frankfurter*, 87–91; cf. Phillips, *Frankfurter Reminisces*, 117–21.

26. F. Frankfurter, memorandum to the commission, October 5, 1917, File 20/473, RG 174, Labor Department, NA.

27. President's Mediation Commission. *Report to the President of the United States*; the unpublished hearings and reports of the commission can be found in File 33/517, RG 280, Labor Department, NA.

28. See the sources cited above, Parrish, *Frankfurter*, 93–97, and Dubofsky, *We Shall Be All*, 417–22.

29. Jones, "Wilson Administration," 363–70; Brody, *Labor in Crisis*, 53.

30. For a detailed history of the NWLB, see Conner, *National War Labor Board*.

31. Ibid., 30–31.

32. Ibid., 185.

33. Records of the National War Labor Board, RG 2, NA; Frank P. Walsh Papers, Box 18, NYPL; Pringle, *William Howard Taft*, 2:916; U.S. Bureau of Labor Statistics, *National War Labor Board*. See also Montgomery, *The Fall of the House of Labor*, 416, 442–46, and McCartin, "Labor's Great War," for the most complete and informative study of the NWLB's impact on workers and their labor movement.

34. On these disputes, see the Western Union (Reel 16, Entry 4, Docket #3) and Bridgeport (Reel 17, Entry·4, Docket #132) case files in Papers of the National War Labor Board, University Publications of America Microfilm Series; Conner, *National War Labor Board*, 40–48, 133–34. For scholars who accuse the NWLB, and especially President Wilson, of antipathy to militant workers, see Montgomery, *The Fall of the House of Labor*, 411–19, and Bucki, "Dilution and Craft Tradition"; McCartin provides a more balanced account of the NWLB's intervention into those disputes in "Labor's Great War," chap. 6.

35. Cited in Jones, "Wilson Administration," 381.

36. Brody, *Labor in Crisis*, 58; Parrish, *Frankfurter*, 102–14; War Labor Policies Board Records, RG 1, NA.

37. Cited in Brody, *Labor in Crisis*, 61.

38. U.S. Bureau of the Census, *Historical Statistics of the United States*, Series D 735–740, p. 97; McCartin, "Labor's Great War"; Montgomery, *Workers' Control in America*, 95–101, and *The Fall of the House of Labor*, chap. 8; Brody, *Labor in Crisis*, 50–51; Shapiro, "The Great War and Reform."

39. Fraser, *Labor Will Rule*, chap. 5; Josephson, *Sidney Hillman*, 162–76.

40. *United Mine Workers' Journal*, June 21, 1917, p. 4; ibid., August 30, 1917, p. 6; Dubofsky and Van Tine, *John L. Lewis*, 35–37, 42.

41. K. A. Kerr, *American Railroad Politics*, 91–95; Lecht, *Experience under Railway Labor Legislation*, 31–37; Wolf, *Railroad Labor Board*, 32–69.

42. *Railway Carmen's Journal* 23 (June 1918): 347–48, cited in Freedman, "Organizing Workers in a Steel Company Town," 15.

43. Brody, *Butcher Workmen*, 76–83. For more critical analyses of the same developments, see Barrett, *Work and Community in the Jungle*, 188–202; and Montgomery, *The Fall of the House of Labor*, 383–85.

44. Brody, *Labor in Crisis*, 60–61, 63–77; McCartin, "Labor's Great War," chap. 7; see the Bethlehem Case File (Reel 16, Entry 4, Docket #22) in the NWLB microfilm records for federal efforts to gain steelworkers union recognition.

45. Cited in Shapiro, "The Great War and Reform," 340.

46. Josephson, *Sidney Hillman*, 190; Hurvitz, "Meaning of Industrial Conflict," 38.

47. Josephson, *Sidney Hillman*, 192–93; Ickes, cited in Kennedy, *Over Here*, 287.

48. Warren G. Harding to F. E. Scobey, October 25 and November 3, 1919, Warren G. Harding Papers (microfilm), Reel 21, Ohio Historical Society; Blum, *Joe Tumulty*, 206.

49. Conner, *National War Labor Board*, 158–59; Parrish, *Frankfurter*, 116–17; the files on reconversion planning in the microfilm records of the NWLB, Executive Session Minutes, November 21, 1918, to March 26, 1991, Reels 10–13; and War Labor Policies Board. The G. S. Arnold Folder and the Reconstruction Folder in Correspondence of the Chairman and of the Executive Secretary detail the failure of postwar planning.

50. Berman, *Labor Disputes and the Presidents*, 154–209; Lombardi, *Labor's Voice*, 306–15; Jones, "Wilson Administration," 436–40.

51. *Messages and Papers of the Presidents*, 16:8713–14.

52. Ibid., 8773–78; A. Mitchell Palmer to Chamber of Commerce, Moberly, Missouri, December 1, 1919, Box 207, RG 174, Labor Department, NA; Blum, *Joe Tumulty*, 148–49.

53. *Messages and Papers of the Presidents*, 16:8796; *CR*, 66th Cong., 1st sess., 1919, 3913, 4502–4, 4828–36, 5849–58.

54. On these points, see Brody, *Labor in Crisis*, 103–4, 127–28.

55. Brody, *Butcher Workmen*, 85–91; K. A. Kerr, *American Railroad Politics*, 97–100.

56. Brody, *Labor in Crisis*, 102–3, 147–78.

57. Dubofsky and Van Tine, *John L. Lewis*, 53–61; Cronon, *Cabinet Diaries*, 452–53.

58. Brody, *Workers in Industrial America*, 45.

59. Hurvitz, "Ideology and Industrial Conflict"; Hurvitz, "Meaning of Industrial Conflict," passim; for more benign views of the conference, see Brody, *Labor in Crisis*, 127–28, and Gitelman, *Legacy of Ludlow*, 313–19. For an interesting comparative perspective on the subject, see Gerber, "United States and Canadian National Industrial Conferences."

60. *Messages and Papers of the Presidents*, 16:8816–20.

61. Hurvitz, "Meaning of Industrial Conflict," passim; Best, "President Wilson's Second Industrial Conference"; Gitelman, *Legacy of Ludlow*, 325–28. Burner, *Herbert Hoover*, chaps. 1–4; Wilson, *Herbert Hoover*, chaps. 1–2; and for the most complete history of Hoover's years as an engineer and businessman, see G. H. Nash, *Herbert Hoover*.

62. *CR*, 67th Cong., 3d sess., 1920, 408–9, 568–69, 679.

63. K. A. Kerr, *American Railroad Politics*, 204–27; Lecht, *Experience under Railway Labor Legislation*, 38–40; Wolf, *Railroad Labor Board*, 32–69.

Chapter 4

1. Zieger, *Republicans and Labor*, chap. 2.

2. *Messages and Papers of the Presidents*, 16:9027–28.

3. Zieger, *Republicans and Labor*, passim; Murray, *The Harding Era*; and Hawley, *War and a Modern Order*, 66–71, 100–104, 173–80; Keller, *Regulating a New Economy*, chap. 6 and passim.

4. Hurvitz, "Meaning of Industrial Conflict," 242.

5. Ibid., 242, 250; Zieger, *Republicans and Labor*, chap. 5; Hawley, "Hoover and Economic Stabilization; Burner, *Herbert Hoover*, 143–46.

6. 247 Federal Reporter (1917), 192–99; 252 Federal Reporter (1918), 727–48.

7. Grin, "Unemployment Conference"; Zieger, *Republicans and Labor*, 90–97; Burner, *Herbert Hoover*, 164–66; Murray, *The Harding Era*, 231–34.

8. Hoover, *Memoirs*, 103–5; Zieger, *Republicans and Labor*, 97–107; Burner, *Herbert Hoover*, 174–75.

9. Murray, *The Harding Era*, 230–31.

10. Hoover, *Memoirs*, 101.

11. Ibid.; Zieger, *Republicans and Labor*, 57–59 and passim.

12. 254 U.S. 443 (1921).

13. Truax v. Corrigan, 257 U.S. 312 (1921).

14. 257 U.S. 184 (1921).

15. UMW v. Coronado Coal Co., 259 U.S. 344 (1922). Three years later, the court, citing new evidence in the case, found coal mining a part of interstate commerce; Coronado Coal Co. v. UMW, 268 U.S. 295 (1925).

16. For this diversity see, among other rulings, Herkert & Meisel et al. v. United Leatherworkers, 268 Federal Reporter (1920), 662–68; Gable et al. v. Vonnegut Machinery Co. et al., 274 Federal Reporter (1921), 66–74, 275; Borderland Coal Corp. v. International Organization of UMWA et al., 275 Federal Reporter (1921), 871–74; Gasaway et al. v. Borderland Coal Corp., 278 Federal Reporter (1921), 56–67.

17. For example, in one case four years passed between the issuance of the original injunction and the Supreme Court's decision overruling it. Herkert & Meisel et al. v. United Leatherworkers, 268 Federal Reporter (1920), 662–68; Herkert & Meisel et al. v. United Leatherworkers et al., 284 Federal Reporter (1922), 446–65; United Leather Workers v. Herkert & Meisel et al., 265 U.S. 457 (1924).

18. Edwin E. Witte, *Government in Labor Disputes*, 70–71, 152; Frankfurter and N. Greene, *Labor Injunction*, 49–50, 64–65. More recent treatments of the subject include Forbath, *Law and the Shaping of the American Labor Movement*, 158–59; and Avery, "Images of Violence in Labor Jurisprudence," 70–96.

19. Taft, as cited in Pringle, *William Howard Taft*, 2:967, 1030.

20. For the significance of these strikes, see Montgomery, *The Fall of the House of Labor*, 406–8.

21. Dubofsky and Van Tine, *John L. Lewis*, 80–83.

22. Herbert Hoover to John L. Lewis, June 11 and 14, 1922, Box 355, Pre-Presidential, Commerce, HCHL, West Branch, Iowa.

23. Dubofsky and Van Tine, *John L. Lewis*, 85–86; Warren G. Harding to John L. Lewis, June 28, 1922, and Lewis to Harding, June 29, 1922, Reel 184, Harding Papers (microfilm).

24. Memorandum on Bituminous Negotiations, July 26 (?), 1922, File 165/411, RG 280, NA; Dubofsky and Van Tine, *John L. Lewis*, 86.

25. *Messages and Papers of the Presidents*, 18:9137–47; Murray, *The Harding Era*, 250–52; Hoover, *Memoirs*, 101, 108.

26. Dubofsky and Van Tine, *John L. Lewis*, 87–89.

27. Ibid., 90–91; Zieger, *Republicans and Labor*, 218–20; Hunt, *What the Coal Commission Found.*

28. Montgomery, *The Fall of the House of Labor*, 408–10; see also his earlier essay, "The 'New Unionism.' "

29. Pennsylvania Railroad Co. v. Railroad Labor Board, 261 U.S. 72 (1923). All these developments can be followed best in C. Davis, "Bitter Storm," chap. 4.

30. Lecht, *Experience under Railway Labor Legislation*, 45; the best history of the RLB remains Wolf, *Railroad Labor Board.*

31. Wolf, *Railroad Labor Board*, 275–76.

32. Colin Davis's dissertation, "Bitter Storm," provides the fullest and most well-documented treatment of the emergence of unionism among the shopcraft workers and the creation of the Railway Employees Department and its subsequent history. See esp. chaps. 1–4.

33. C. Davis, "Bitter Storm," 187–94; Zieger, *Republicans and Labor*, 118.

34. Wolf, *Railroad Labor Board*, 239–41; Zieger, *Republicans and Labor*, 119; Berman, *Labor Disputes and the Presidents*, 229–30; C. Davis, "Bitter Storm," 198–241, passim.

35. Wolf, *Railroad Labor Board*, 328; C. Davis, "Bitter Storm," 265–66.

36. Zieger, *Republicans and Labor*, 130–34; Wolf, *Railroad Labor Board*, 244–46; C. Davis, "Bitter Storm," 232–64.

37. Hoover, *Memoirs*, 105–7.

38. *Messages and Papers of the Presidents*, 18:9144–47.

39. Murray, *The Harding Era*, 254–58; Zieger, *Republicans and Labor*, 138–39; C. Davis, "Bitter Storm," 273–77.

40. U.S. v. Railway Employees' Department, AFL et al. 283 Federal Reporter (1922), 479–96.

41. Berman, *Labor and the Sherman Act*, 145–46.

42. Great Northern Ry. Co. v. Local Great Falls Lodge of Int'l Assoc. of Mach., No. 287 et al., 283 Federal Reporter (1922), 557–65; Great Northern Ry. Co. v. Brosseau et al., 286 Federal Reporter (1922), 414–25.

43. U.S. v. Railway Employees' Department, AFL et al., 286 Federal Reporter (1922), 228–42. He ruled the injunction as still in force because some individual strikers had refused formally to surrender.

44. Colin Davis's "Bitter Storm" provides the best history of the end of the strike and the settlement grasped by the union leaders; see chap. 7.

45. Troy, "Labor Representation on American Railways," 299, 307; for these developments also see C. Davis, "Bitter Storm," chap. 7.

46. William M. Leiserson, *Right and Wrong in Labor Relations* (Berkeley, 1938), 24–27, cited in I. Bernstein, *The Lean Years*, 206.

47. Vadney, *Wayward Liberal*, 52.

48. I. Bernstein, *Lean Years*, remains the best general history of those aspects of the labor movement. A more critical treatment may be found in Montgomery, *The Fall of the House of Labor*, 452–64.

49. For the leading role of the railroad unions in all of this, see Olssen, "Making of a Political Machine." For general left-wing and labor politics during this period, consult Weinstein, *Decline of Socialism*, chaps. 6–8.

50. *Messages and Papers of the Presidents*, 17:9438.

51. For the administration's role, see Herbert Hoover to John L. Lewis, February 20,

1924, Box 355, Commerce-Coal, Hoover Papers; the correspondence in Series 1, Case 175, Reel 89, Calvin Coolidge Papers (microfilm); and *New York Times*, April 20, 1924, sec. 9, p. 7.

52. Herbert Hoover to Calvin Coolidge, November 25 and 27, 1925; Hoover to Andrew Mellon, November 25, 1925; both in Box 355, Commerce-Coal, Hoover Papers; Dubofsky and Van Tine, *John L. Lewis*, 140–42.

53. F. E. Taplin to James J. Davis, December 10 and 22, 1927; Morrow to Davis, December 12, 1927; Davis to John A. Topping, December 23, 1927; and Topping to Davis, December 28, 1927; all in RG 280, File 170/3918, 3918B, NA; Dubofsky and Van Tine, *John L. Lewis*, 145–47.

54. Vadney, *Wayward Liberal*, 52–56; Zieger, *Republicans and Labor*, 194–202; Wolf, *Railroad Labor Board*, 397–429.

55. *CR*, 68th Cong., 1st sess., 1924, 6383–90, 7701–22, 7875, 7880; Zieger, *Republicans and Labor*, 198–201.

56. For the negotiations between Richberg for the unions and the attorney Alfred Thom for the railroads, which led to the bill, see Vadney, *Wayward Liberal*, 56–65.

57. Zieger, *Republicans and Labor*, 207–15.

58. *CR*, 69th Cong., 1st sess., 1926, 4650.

59. Hoover, *Memoirs*, 108.

60. Brims et al. v. U.S., 6 Fed (2) (1925) 98–100; U.S. v. Brims, 272 U.S. 549 (1926).

61. UMWA et al. v. Red Jacket Consol Coal & Coke, 18 Fed (2) (1927) 839–50 ; Pitts. Terminal Coal Corp. v. UMWA et al., 22 Fed (2) (1927) 559–66. These cases also declared yellow-dog contracts legal and binding.

62. Bedford Stone Co. v. Journeymen Stone Cutters, 274 U.S. 37 (1927). Brandeis's dissent appears on pp. 57–65.

63. Dubofsky and Van Tine, *John L. Lewis*, 148; Zieger, *Republicans and Labor*, 271–75.

64. Romasco, *Poverty of Abundance*, chaps. 7–8, and Romasco, "Hoover's Policies for Dealing with the Great Depression"; Hawley, "Hoover and American Corporatism"; Fausold, *Presidency of Herbert C. Hoover*, 118–23.

65. Dubofsky and Van Tine, *John L. Lewis*, 156–57, 185; I. Bernstein, *Lean Years*, chaps. 12–15.

66. Memorandum, June 11, 1931, Box 565, PSF, Hoover Papers; F. E. Taplin to Hoover, June 27, 1931, RG 280, File 165/944, Labor Department; Dubofsky and Van Tine, *John L. Lewis*, 173–75.

67. Zieger, *Republicans and Labor*, 259–71; I. Bernstein, *Lean Years*, 394–412; Michael Johnson, "The Anti-Injunction Movement" (Unpublished seminar paper, Northern Illinois University, 1963).

68. The AFL refused at first to endorse the Norris Bill because its key actor in the movement to reform the judicial process since the opening years of the century, Andrew Furuseth, the crusty and idiosyncratic leader of the seamen's union, amalgamated syndicalism and voluntarism to demand that unions be liberated from all state regulation. During the 1920s Furuseth succeeded in influencing the maverick "progressive" senator from Minnesota, Hendrik Shipstead, to introduce a bill that, by narrowing the legal definition of property to encompass only tangible properties, allegedly would make it impossible for judges to issue antistrike injunctions. The consensus among legal experts considered the Shipstead Bill to be an inappropriate solution to the injunction problem. The majority of reformers in the legal community and their allies in the labor movement and Congress,

moreover, agreed. Yet the AFL Executive Council allowed Furuseth to set policy on the injunction question in an almost reflexive form of obedience to the principle of voluntarism. M. Johnson, "Anti-Injunction Movement"; I. Bernstein, *Lean Years*, 397–402; Frankfurter and Greene, *Labor Injunction*, 226. For a more recent analysis of the AFL's and Furuseth's position on the injunction, see Forbath, *Law and the Shaping of the American Labor Movement*, 154–56, 158–64. Cf. Gorman and Finkin, "Individual and 'Concert' under the National Labor Relations Act."

69. *CR*, 72d Cong., 1st. sess., 1932, 4502–10, 5019, 5511, 5950–52, 6327–29, 6334–37.

70. Lowitt, *George W. Norris*, 518–27; Vadney, *Wayward Liberal*, 91–92.

71. Lauck to Lewis, August 26, 1931; Lewis to Lauck, August 31, 1931; and Lauck to Lewis, September 4, 1931; all in Box 39, W. Jett Lauck Papers, Alderson Library, University of Virginia.

72. Memorandum #1 to Lewis *in re* Statement to Senate Finance Committee, February 17, 1933, Box 231, Lauck Papers; *United Mine Workers' Journal*, March 1, 1933, 3–4.

Chapter 5

1. Schlesinger, *Coming of the New Deal*, 2–3.

2. G. D. Nash, "F.D.R. and New Deal Labor Policy."

3. On this point, see the following general histories of the New Deal and labor: Leuchtenberg, *Roosevelt and the New Deal*, 60–62; Schlesinger, *Coming of the New Deal*, 299–301, and chaps. 32–35; I. Bernstein, *Turbulent Years*, 9–14; Perkins, *The Roosevelt I Knew*, 239–45, 302–27; and Martin, *Madame Secretary, Frances Perkins*, 3–4, 120–21, 327–29.

4. *United Mine Workers' Journal*, March 1, 1933, pp. 3–4; Leuchtenberg, "New Deal and Analogue of War."

5. On this point, see Leuchtenberg, "New Deal and Analogue of War."

6. Hawley, *New Deal and Monopoly*, chaps. 1–3; Bellush, *Failure of the NRA*; Raymond Moley to Marvin McIntyre, March 21, 1933, Roosevelt Papers, OF 75, FRDL; *New York Times*, March 28, 1933, p. 3.

7. *CR*, 73d Cong., 1st sess., 1933, 5279–84.

8. Ickes, cited in Schlesinger, *Coming of the New Deal*, 23; Dubofsky and Van Tine, *John L. Lewis*, 184.

9. H. S. Johnson, *Blue Eagle*, 238–39; Vadney, *Wayward Liberal*, 130–31; and Ohl, *Johnson and the New Deal*, 128–37, 194–217.

10. Van A. Bittner to William Mitch, June 23, 1933, Mitch Papers, PSULA; untitled, undated report on the UMW organizing campaign in Edward A. Wieck Collection, Box 12, ALHUA. WSU; John Brophy, COHC, 505–6.

11. See note 10 above.

12. Roosevelt Papers, OF 175, Coal, Box 1; William Taylor to John L. Lewis, September 19, 1933, UMW Archives, John L. Lewis Papers; Dubofsky and Van Tine, *John L. Lewis*, 186–92.

13. J. P. Johnson, *Politics of Soft-Coal*, chaps. 5–6; J. P. Johnson, "Drafting the NRA Code."

14. All the correspondence and negotiations can be found in the Roosevelt Papers, OF 175, Coal, Box 1, FDRL; Dubofsky and Van Tine, *John L. Lewis*, 192–96.

15. National Labor Board, Stenographic Report of Hearing in the Matter of Provisions of the Captive Mines of the H. C. Frick Company et al., January 4, 1934, National Recovery Administration, RG 9, File 702/45, NA; Dubofsky and Van Tine, *John L. Lewis*, 196.

16. E. Wieck's field reports in the ALUHA describe these company tactics in numbing detail.

17. Josephson, *Sidney Hillman*, 365–66; Fraser, *Labor Will Rule*, 290–304, and Fraser, "From the 'New Unionism' to the New Deal," 405–30, esp. 426–30.

18. H. Johnson, *Blue Eagle*, 238–39.

19. Three excellent books provide detailed information about the NLB: I. Bernstein, *The New Deal Collective Bargaining Policy*; Gross, *Making of the National Labor Relations Board*; and an older but classic study, Lorwin and Wubnig, *Labor Relations Boards*.

20. I. Bernstein, *New Deal Collective Bargaining*, and *Turbulent Years*, 173–77; Lorwin and Wubnig, *Labor Relations Boards*, 97–99.

21. I. Bernstein, *Turbulent Years*, 173–77.

22. Vadney, *Wayward Liberal*, 130–31; H. Johnson, *Blue Eagle*, 293–94.

23. Gross, *Making of the National Labor Relations Board*, 22–23.

24. Galambos, *Competition and Cooperation*, 230–31, 243–45. Hodges, *New Deal*, chap. 4.

25. Franklin D. Roosevelt, *Public Papers and Addresses of Roosevelt*, 2:385–87.

26. Gross, *Making of the National Labor Relations Board*, 42–51.

27. NLRB, *Legislative History of the National Labor Relations Act*, 1:430–31; I. Bernstein, *Turbulent Years*, 178–80.

28. Bellush, *Failure of the NRA*, chaps. 4–5.

29. *CR*, 73d Cong., 2d sess., 1934, 12,043.

30. Huthmacher, *Wagner and Urban Liberalism*, chaps. 9–11; Casebeer, "Holder of the Pen," and "Drafting Wagner's Act"; Keyserling, "Wagner Act" and "Why the Wagner Act?"

31. *CR*, 73d Cong., 2d sess., 1934, 3443–46.

32. NLRB, *Legislative History*, 1:40–41.

33. Ibid., 140–41, 186.

34. Fine, *Automobile under the Blue Eagle*, 200–27; I. Bernstein, *Turbulent Years*, 183–85; Taft, *The A. F. of L.*, 100–104.

35. Roosevelt, *Public Papers*, 3:165–69.

36. See "Hearings Before the Committee on Education and Labor, U.S. Senate, 73rd Cong., 2nd sess. on S. 2926," in NLRB, *Legislative History*, vol. 1.

37. "Hearings Before the Committee on Education and Labor," 1:383, 440–41.

38. Roosevelt, *Public Papers*, 3:260–62.

39. Senate Report No. 1184, "To Create a National Industrial Adjustment Board, Senate Education and Labor Committee Report on S. 2926," in NLRB, *Legislative History*, 1:1099–1106.

40. Roosevelt, *Public Papers*, 3:301.

41. *CR*, 73d Cong., 2d sess., 1934, 12,016–22, 12,044, 12,052.

42. Roosevelt, *Public Papers*, 3:310.

43. Ibid., 322–27.

44. A. H. Young to L. H. Corndorf, June 16, 1934, cited in NLRB, *Legislative History*, 2:2225.

45. I. Bernstein, *Turbulent Years*, chap. 6, is the best narrative history of labor's "Eruption." On California, see Daniel, *Bitter Harvest*, chaps 6–7.

46. I. Bernstein, *Turbulent Years*, chap. 6; Daniel, *Bitter Harvest*, chaps. 6–7; Hodges, *New Deal*, chaps. 6–7; D. Nelson, *Rubber Workers and Organized Labor*, 128–50.

47. I. Bernstein, *Turbulent Years*, chap. 6.

48. Galambos, *Competition and Cooperation*, 258–66; Hodges, *New Deal*, 112–18; Hall et al., *Like a Family*, 329–57; Daniel, *Bitter Harvest*, 167–77, 248–49.

49. Eisner, *Leiserson*; Shils et al., *Industrial Peacemaker*, chaps. 3, 5.

50. Gross, *Making of the National Labor Relations Board*, 91, 100.

51. Irons, *New Deal Lawyers*, 216–17.

52. Roosevelt, *Public Papers*, 4:57–58; Leab, *Union of Individuals*, 187–94; Biddle, *In Brief Authority*, 36–38.

53. Roosevelt, *Public Papers*, 4:70–76.

54. Irons, *New Deal Lawyers*, 220.

55. Gross, *Making of the National Labor Relations Board*, 94, 130; Irons, *New Deal Lawyers*, 225.

56. *CR*, 74th Cong., 1st sess., 1935, 2368–72.

57. The bill, as now drawn, provided for a presidentially appointed board that would consist solely of impartial members and that would be entirely quasi-judicial in function.

58. Casebeer, "Holder of the Pen," and "Drafting Wagner's Act"; Huthmacher, *Wagner and Urban Liberalism*, 189–91; Keyserling, "Wagner Act."

59. The full hearing record is republished in NLRB, *Legislative History*, vols. 1–2.

60. *CR*, 74th Cong., 1st sess., 1935, 7565–81.

61. Ibid., 9678–91.

62. Ibid., 10,259, 10,298–300.

63. For evidence of how some people on the left, especially those in the American Civil Liberties Union close to the Communist party, perceived the Wagner Act as a precursor of fascist-style corporatism, see Daniel, *The ACLU and the Wagner Act*.

64. See Weiss, *Farewell to the Party of Lincoln*, 163–66. Cf. Hill, "National Labor Relations Act," 305–8.

65. Numerous books and essays elaborate on the theme of the "corporate liberal" origins and purposes of the Wagner Act. The following are among the most important and most often cited: Radosh, "Corporate Ideology"; Radosh, "The Myth of the New Deal"; Weinstein, *Corporate Ideal*, ix–xv, 253–54; Domhoff, *Higher Circles*, 156–250; and the most scholarly and documented of such works, which stresses the theory and practice of the Wagner Act more than the motives of its supporters, Tomlins, "The State and the Unions," 140–67 and passim. For a terser and fairer treatment along the same lines, see Tomlins's book, *The State and the Unions*, chaps. 4–5. In his most recent publication, Domhoff concedes that business steadfastly opposed the enactment of the Wagner Act, yet he still asserts that a corporate capitalist power elite controlled public policy; see *Power Elite and State*, chap. 4. For a recent and more sophisticated interpretation of corporate influence on the drafting of the Wagner Act, an interpretation that credits farsighted labor leaders, Sidney Hillman in particular, and equally farsighted business leaders with developing a vision of a more corporate-based society that united functional interest groups to pursue Keynesian policies of demand management, see Fraser, *Labor Will Rule*, 330–33.

66. Leuchtenberg, *Roosevelt and the New Deal*, 151–52.

67. Among the literature that suggests the radical implications of the Wagner Act in origin and theory, the following are the best: Sipe, "A Moment of State"; Vittoz, "The Economic Foundations of Industrial Politics in the United States and the Emerging Structural Theory of the State in Capitalist Society," esp. 380–92, and the same author's unpublished doctoral dissertation, "The American Industrial Economy and the Political Origins of Federal Labor Policy between the World War"; Vittoz's dissertation has been

published under the title *New Deal Labor Policy and the American Industrial Economy*; Klare, "Judicial Deradicalization of the Wagner Act"; and Skocpol, "Political Response to Capitalist Crisis," esp. 187–92. For two recent essays that assert the transformative impact of New Deal labor legislation, see Goldfield, "Worker Insurgency, Radical Organization, and New Deal Labor Legislation," and Plotke, "The Wagner Act, Again."

68. For the case that the Wagner Act ended the private ordering of labor relations and diluted trade union power, see Tomlins, *The State and the Unions*, chaps. 6–7 and passim. For an analysis that also stresses how the Wagner Act enabled the state to regulate theretofore private transactions but magnified union power to the detriment of workers and employers, see Dickman, *Industrial Democracy*, esp. 257–86.

69. (October 1938), 52ff.

70. Gross, *Making of the National Labor Relations Board*, 205–11.

71. W. Jett Lauck to John L. Lewis, October 22, 1934, Lauck Papers.

72. AFL, Minutes of the Executive Council, January 29–February 14, 1935, pp. 56–58.

73. Dubofsky and Van Tine, *John L. Lewis*, 210–21.

74. *CR*, 74th Cong. 2d sess., 1936, 10,218–22, 10,476, 10,551.

75. Auerbach, *Labor and Liberty*, 72, 88–89.

76. Dubofsky and Van Tine, *John L. Lewis*, 249–50. For an interpretation that stresses Hillman's role rather than Lewis's in building the political alliance between the "new" unionism and the Roosevelt administration, see Fraser, *Labor Will Rule*, 355–70.

77. Dubofsky and Van Tine, *John L. Lewis*, 250–51.

78. Ibid., 251–52; Roosevelt, *Public Papers*, 5:546–50.

79. Dubofsky and Van Tine, *John L. Lewis*, 252–53.

Chapter 6

1. Leuchtenberg, *Roosevelt and the New Deal*, 252–72; Patterson, *Congressional Conservatives and the New Deal*, chaps. 4–9; Polenberg, *Reorganizing the Government*, chaps. 6–8.

2. *New York Times*, November 13, 1936, p. 22, and November 16, 1936, p. 18.

3. Fine, *Sit-Down*, is a masterful and indispensable history of the event.

4. Typescript of Speech, "Industrial Democracy," JLL Papers, SHSW.

5. Blankenhorn to John L. Lewis, January 4, 1937, Blankenhorn Papers, Series 1, Box 1, File 1–9, ALHUA; Auerbach, *Labor and Liberty*, 99, 207. Gall, "Blankenhorn."

6. Fine, *Murphy: New Deal Years*, 293–99.

7. *New York Times*, January 22, 1937, p. 1, January 23, 1937, p. 1, January 27, 1937, p. 1; Fine, *Sit-Down*, 256–59.

8. Settlement of General Motors Strike, February 10, 1937 (February 25, 1937), Blankenhorn Papers, Series I, Box 1, File 1–37. Cf. Fine, "Lewis Discusses Sit-Down Strike," and Fine, *Murphy: New Deal Years*, 315–19.

9. Memorandum for the President, February 5, 1937; Memorandum for President's Conversation with John Lewis and with Knudsen and Brown; Proposal for General Motors Agreement, Roosevelt Papers, PSF (Labor), Box 61, FDRL; Memorandum of Phone Conversation with Governor Murphy, February 8, 1937, ibid., OF 407B, Box 18; Fine, *Sit-Down*, 287–90, 302–5.

10. CIO Executive Board Minutes, March 9, 1937, Ellickson Papers, FDRL. Fine, *Sit-Down*, 317–31; Galenson, *CIO Challenge to the AFL*, 147–50.

11. For evidence of how the New Deal altered the political balance of power and the consciousness of mass-production workers newly drawn to participation in voting, see, among other books, Allswang, *New Deal and American Politics*; Anderson, *Creation of a Democratic Majority*; and especially, Lizabeth Cohen, *Making a New Deal*, chaps. 6–7. For evidence of how the New Deal simultaneously released and restrained radical political tendencies at the local and state levels, see Valelly, *Radicalism in the States*. For a different interpretation of the same events, see Haynes, *Dubious Alliance*. And for local histories that suggest perhaps a smaller impact on the consciousness and behavior of working-class voters, see Stave, *The New Deal and the Last Hurrah*; Trout, *Boston, the Great Depression, and the New Deal*; and Argensinger, *Toward a New Deal in Baltimore*. For studies that focus more specifically on labor and politics, see the following: Dembo, *Unions and Politics in Washington State*; Buffa, *Union Power and American Democracy*; Ozanne, *Labor Movement in Wisconsin*, 133–38; and Walzer, "Party and Polling Place."

12. Fine, *Sit-Down*, 317–31; Galenson, *CIO Challenge to the AFL*, 91–96.

13. Minutes, CIO Executive Board Meeting, March 9, 1937, Ellickson Papers; Dubofsky and Van Tine, *John L. Lewis*, 272–77; R. Brooks, *As Steel Goes*, 70–109; Galenson, *CIO Challenge to the AFL*, 193.

14. Gross, *Reshaping of the National Labor Relations Board*, 194–95.

15. Fraser, *Labor Will Rule*, 374–416; Dubofsky and Van Tine, *John L. Lewis*, 326–29.

16. The finest treatment of the NLRB's legal strategy can be found in Irons, *New Deal Lawyers*, chaps. 12–13. Cf. Cortner, *Wagner Act Cases*, chaps. 6–10, and Cortner, *Jones and Laughlin Case*, chaps. 4–6.

17. 301 U.S. 1. For Hughes's full opinion, see 22–77.

18. 301 U.S. 103–41, 142–47.

19. 301 U.S. 102. For the full dissent, 77–103.

20. 301 U.S. 141. For a recent scholarly interpretation of industrial relations policy asserting that since the passage of the Wagner Act, the state has put its power behind union monopolies that infringe upon an employer's right to hire whom he/she pleases and the individual worker's right to contract as he/she chooses, and that the Wagner Act indeed sacrificed customary constitutional liberties, see Dickman, *Industrial Democracy*, 3–22, 257–86.

21. Gross, *Making of the National Labor Relations Board*, 227.

22. Irons, *New Deal Lawyers*, 289.

23. Paul Senn v. Tile Layers, 301 U.S. 1937, 468–92. For Brandeis, see 473–83; for the dissent, 483–92.

24. For the fullest treatment of this development, one that, I think, exaggerates unionism's losses in the bargain, see Tomlins, "The State and the Unions: Federal Labor Relations Policy and the Organized Labor Movement in America, 1935–1955." For a less severe version of the same argument, see Tomlins, *The State and the Unions*, chap. 5. For arguments that this shift in jurisprudence wrested natural and constitutional rights from individual workers and gave them instead to corporate bodies — trade unions — which tyrannized individuals, see Dickman, *Industrial Democracy*.

25. On this point, see Cayton and Mitchell, *Black Workers and the New Unions*; Meier and Rudwick, *Black Detroit and the Rise of the UAW*, chaps. 1–2; Honey, "Industrial Unionism and Racial Justice in Memphis," Halpern, "Interracial Unionism in the Southwest," and Stein, "Southern Workers in National Unions," all in Zieger, *Organized Labor in the Twentieth-Century South*; Lizabeth Cohen, *Making a New Deal*, 334–37; and Karson

and Radosh, "The AFL and the Negro Worker," and Rosen, "The CIO Era," both in Jacobson, *The Negro and the American Labor Movement.*

26. *CR*, 75th Cong., 1st sess., 1937, 826, 2337, 2472.

27. Ibid., 3017–24, 3074–75, 3136, 3232–48; Auerbach, *Labor and Liberty,* 114–15.

28. Sofchalk, "Chicago Memorial Day Massacre." Cf. Galenson, *CIO Challenge to the AFL,* 101–3, and Lizabeth Cohen, *Making a New Deal,* 303–4.

29. FDR Press Conferences, Transcripts, 9:467, Roosevelt Papers; *New York Times,* June 22, 1937, pp. 1–2, June 30, 1937, pp. 1–2; Dubofsky and Van Tine, *John L. Lewis,* 314–15.

30. Harry Hopkins to Franklin D. Roosevelt, with enclosure, July 2, 1937, Roosevelt Papers, OF 407B, Box 27.

31. Leuchtenberg, *Roosevelt and the New Deal,* 249.

32. John Frey to W. A. Appleton, April 13 and August 1, 1938, John Frey Papers, Box 1, File 8, LC. On Keynesianism and the "politics of productivity," see Maier, "Two Postwar Eras and Conditions for Stability," and *In Search of Stability;* Fraser, *Labor Will Rule,* 262–65; and Renshaw, *American Labour and Consensus Capitalism,* chap. 2.

33. Gross, *Reshaping of the National Labor Relations Board,* 17, 5–41, passim, for the most complete history of the board's immediate postconstitutionality phase.

34. Ibid., 11, 43; Gross, *Making of the National Labor Relations Board,* 248.

35. Gross, *Reshaping of the National Labor Relations Board,* 42–45; for a defense of the AFL's position on the "Globe doctrine," see Tomlins, "The State and the Unions," 194–95; Tomlins reiterates the point as strongly in his book, *The State and the Unions,* 165–66, 216–18.

36. *CR*, 75th Cong., 1st. sess., 1937, 3215–16, 6347–48; 2d sess., 1129; 3d sess., 1938, 1853. Vandenberg's amendments defined certain union policies and tactics as illegal, promised company unions equal standing with independent unions, and granted employers more power to influence workers through oral and written communication.

37. For a remarkably fair-minded analysis of the NLRB and a rebuttal to most of the more extreme charges leveled against it, see, "The G—— D—— Labor Board," *Fortune,* October 1938, pp. 52ff.; on Communism and the NLRB, see Gross, *Reshaping of the National Labor Relations Board,* 131–50.

38. Dubofsky and Van Tine, *John L. Lewis,* 307–9.

39. Gross, *Reshaping of the National Labor Relations Board,* 61–68.

40. "The G—— D—— Labor Board," 52; Gross, *Reshaping of the National Labor Relations Board,* 64–68.

41. Dubofsky and Van Tine, *John L. Lewis,* 301–12; Galenson, *CIO Challenge to the AFL,* 41–43; I. Bernstein, *Turbulent Years,* 694–695.

42. Gross, *Reshaping of the National Labor Relations Board,* 68–74; Fine, *Murphy: New Deal Years,* 481–516; D. Nelson, "The CIO at Bay"; Valelly, *Radicalism in the States,* chap. 9.

43. *CR*, 76th Cong., 1st sess., 1939, 462, 741–42, 860, 1229–34, 1275, 1463–65, 1804–7, 1724, 1795, 1901, 2047, 2242, 2681, 3139, 4062.

44. Gross, *Reshaping of the National Labor Relations Board,* 74–76.

45. "Labor Board v. Labor Act" (February 1939), 79ff.; two months later, John L. Lewis responded with a ringing reaffirmation of the purposes of the Wagner Act and the work of the NLRB. "The Proposed NLRA Amendments" (April 1939), 76ff.

46. See esp. Fansteel Metallurgical Corp. v. NLRB, 306 U.S. (1939), 240–68, and NLRB v. Sands Mfg. Co., 306 U.S. (1939), 332–46.

47. *CR*, 76th Cong., 1st sess., 1939, 3376–77, 3840–42, 3857–58.

48. Ibid., 4063–69.

49. On Leiserson's life and career, see Eisner, *Leiserson*, esp. chap. 7, for the NLRB. Cf. Gross, *Reshaping of the National Labor Relations Board*, 89–91. For more on Witt's connections to the Communist party, see Gall, "Lee Pressman and the FBI."

50. On their alliance with conservatives, see Gross, *Reshaping of the National Labor Relations Board*, 96–102; on the growth of the AFL, see Tomlins, "AFL Unions in the 1930s."

51. Gross, *Reshaping of the National Labor Relations Board*, 109–50.

52. *CR*, 76th Cong., 1st sess., 1939, 7759, 8698–99, 8755, 9070, 9454, 9582–93, 11,210. Gall, "CIO Leaders and the Democratic Alliance."

53. Gross, *Reshaping of the National Labor Relations Board*, 102–8. For Roosevelt's intensifying concerns with world affairs, see Burns, *Roosevelt: The Lion and the Fox*, 383–404; Leuchtenberg, *Roosevelt and the New Deal*, chaps. 12–13; and Freidel, *Roosevelt: Rendezvous with Destiny*, chaps. 20–23.

54. For an excellent description and analysis of the committee's investigation and hearings, see Gross, *Reshaping of the National Labor Relations Board*, 151–86. Gall, "CIO Leaders and the Democratic Alliance," 13–20.

55. U.S. Congress, House, Special Committee of the House of Representatives Appointed Pursuant to H. Res. 258 to Investigate the National Labor Relations Board, *Intermediate Report*, Part 1.

56. Ibid., Part 2. Wagner had said almost the same thing in the Senate on March 13; *CR*, 76th Cong., 3d sess., 1940, 2774–82.

57. *CR*, 3615–32.

58. U.S. Congress, House, *Amendments to National Labor Relations Act*.

59. *CR*, 76th Cong., 3d sess., 1940, 6213–29, 6365–70, 6373–89, 6689–708, 6771–96, 6879–907; Auerbach, *Labor and Liberty*, 198–203.

60. *CR*, 76th Cong., 3d sess., 1940, 7506–18, 7706–39, 7775, 7800, 7805. Cf. Gall, "CIO Leaders and the Democratic Alliance," 20–23. For an example of how Howard Smith's defense of the rights of individual workers and their employers against union and state tyranny resonated down the decades even among many intellectuals, see Dickman, *Industrial Democracy*.

61. J. and Lillian Cohen, "The National Labor Relations Board in Retrospect."

62. U.S. Congress, House, Special Committee to Investigate the National Labor Relations Board, *Report*. Tomlins, *The State and the Unions*, 205–24.

63. Gross, *Reshaping of the National Labor Relations Board*, 229–40; Tomlins, *The State and the Unions*, 224–43.

64. *CR*, 76th Cong., 3d sess., 1940, 13,733–38, 13,873–79, 13,960–65.

65. The fullest case for this interpretation is Klare, "Judicial Deradicalization of the Wagner Act," 265–339.

66. Atleson, *Values and Assumptions*, 62–63.

67. Ibid., 21–24. Atleson asserts that the decision granted employers rights not specified in the Wagner Act while diluting those rights explicitly conferred on employees.

68. 92 Fed 2 (1937) 761–68. For the minority opinion, 767; 304 U.S. (1938) 333–51.

69. NLRB v. Sands Mfg. Co., 96 Fed 2 (1938) 721–27; Consolidated Edison Co. v. NLRB, 305 U.S. (1938) 197–250; NLRB v. Sands Mfg. Co., 306 U.S. (1939) 332–46.

70. 98 Fed 2 (1938) 375–89; 306 U.S. (1939) 240–68, at 252–53. Justices Stanley Reed

and Hugo Black dissented and approved the NLRB's action; see 265–68. For a critique of those "radical" legal scholars such as Karl Klare who perceive the decision as a step toward the "deradicalization" of the Wagner Act, see Finkin, "Revisionism in Labor Law."

71. NLRB v. Penn. Greyhound, 303 U.S. (1938) 261–72, 272–75; NLRB v. Pac. Greyhound, 308 U.S. (1938) 241–51; NLRB v. Newport News Shipbuilding & Dry Dock Co., 309 U.S. (1939) 350–70.

72. IAM v. NLRB, 311 U.S. (1940) 72–83; AFL v. NLRB, 308 U.S. (1940) 401–12, NLRB v. IBEW, 308 U.S. (1940) 413–15, Nat'l Licorice Co. v. NLRB, 309 U.S. (1940) 453–63.

73. Pitts. Plate Glass v. NLRB, and Crystal City Glass Workers v. NLRB, 313 U.S. (1941) 146–77, Phelps Dodge Corp. v. NLRB, 313 U.S. (1941) 177–212. Fine, *Murphy: Washington Years*, 179–81.

74. H.J. Heinz v. NLRB, 311 U.S. (1941) 514–26.

75. NLRB v. Ford Motor Co., 114 Fed. 2 (1940) 905–16.

76. NLRB v. Virg. Elect. & Power Co. and NLRB v. Ind. Org. of Employees of the Virg. Elect. & Power Co., 314 U.S. (1941) 469–80. The opinion sought simultaneously to uphold employers' constitutional right to noncoercive free speech and to relate abstract rights to economic and historical realities. See Fine, *Murphy: Washington Years*, 300–303.

77. Fine, *Murphy: Washington Years*, 168–79; Fine, "Murphy, Thornhill, and Picketing"; Thornhill v. Alabama, 310 U.S. (1940) 88–106; The opinion was worded in such a way as not to eliminate the power of the states to regulate truly coercive or violent picketing, and the court would subsequently uphold state restrictions on violent picketing.

78. Apex Hosiery Co. v. Leader, 310 U.S. (1940) 469–529.

79. U.S. v. Hutcheson, 312 U.S. (1941) 219–46.

80. Fahy, "NLRB and Courts," 49.

81. For further evidence of the links between the Wilson era labor reforms and those of the New Deal, see Steve Fraser's biography of Sidney Hillman, *Labor Will Rule*, passim, and Leon Fink's review of the biography, "Clearing It Up with Sidney."

Chapter 7

1. Not only were the AFL and CIO at odds politically but within the CIO until June 22, 1941, when Germany invaded the Soviet Union, the Communists, who were influential in several of the largest CIO mass-production unions, and John L. Lewis, then their political ally, refused to cooperate with defense planning or to offer no-strike pledges. Cochran, *Labor and Communism*, chap. 7; Klehr, *Heyday of American Communism*, chap. 20; Keeran, *Communist Party and Auto Workers Unions*, 205–25; and Dubofsky and Van Tine, *John L. Lewis*, 329–34, 339–64.

2. For the situation of the CIO unions on the eve of the war crisis, see Lichtenstein, *Labor's War*, 8–25.

3. Ibid., 44–45.

4. Dubofsky and Van Tine, *John L. Lewis*, 390–404.

5. U.S. Bureau of Labor Statistics, *Strikes in 1941 and Strikes affecting Defense Production*; Lichtenstein, *Labor's War*, 45–47; Seidman, *American Labor*, 41–54.

6. Galenson, *CIO Challenge to the AFL*; Zieger, *Rebuilding the Pulp and Paper Workers' Union*, esp. chaps. 6–9.

7. *CR*, 77th Cong., 1st sess., 1941, 2862–64.

8. Ibid., 4401, 4803, 7539–40.

9. *Fortune*, June 1941, pp. 70–71, 144–52.

10. *CR*, 77th Cong., 1st sess., 1941, 9300–9397.

11. Ibid., 9515–18, 9837.

12. See especially the following memoranda in the UMWA Archives, Correspondence File, 1930–39, Lee Pressman to Lewis, September 11 and October 27, 1939 and W. Jett Lauck to Lewis, September 13, 1939; CIO Executive Board Minutes, October 6, 1939, CIO Papers, Secretary-Treasurer's Office, Box 90, ALHUA.

13. UMWA, Proceedings 1940 Convention, 315.

14. FDR Press Conferences, Transcripts, 15:102, 120, Roosevelt Papers.

15. Lee Pressman, COHC, 317; Josephson, *Sidney Hillman*, 481–84; Fraser, *Labor Will Rule*, 453–54.

16. Minutes, CIO Executive Board Meeting, June 1940, John Brophy Papers, Box A5–8, CUA.

17. Sidney Hillman Papers, File, "John L. Lewis Correspondence and Executive Order, 1940," ACWA Papers, Catherwood Library. Cf. Fraser, *Labor Will Rule*, 454–56.

18. War Production Board, *Labor Policies of the National Defense Advisory Commission and the Office of Production Management, May 1940 to April 1942*, 46–49, 50–54, 63–64. Fraser, *Labor Will Rule*, 457–58.

19. Schatz, "Murray and Subordination of Industrial Unions," 248.

20. War Production Board, *Labor Policies*, passim; Fraser, *Labor Will Rule*, 460–61.

21. Catton, *War Lords*, 96–99.

22. Lichtenstein, *Labor's War*, 50–53; Seidman, *American Labor*, 45, 56–57.

23. U.S. Bureau of Labor Statistics, *Report on the Work of the National Defense Mediation Board*.

24. Lichtenstein, *Labor's War*, 57–63, 65–66, 74; Seidman, *American Labor*, 42–43, 48–49; Prickett, "Communist Conspiracy or Wage Dispute?"; and Keeran, *Communist Party and Auto Workers Unions*, 214–18.

25. Dubofsky and Van Tine, *John L. Lewis*, 390–94.

26. Taylor to Roosevelt, October 25, 1941, RG 202, Box 165, Bituminous Coal File, NA; Dubofsky and Van Tine, *John L. Lewis*, 397–398.

27. Roosevelt to Lewis, October 26, 1941, Taylor to Roosevelt, October 26, 1941, Lewis to Roosevelt, October 27, 1941, Roosevelt to Lewis, October 27, 1971, Roosevelt Papers, OF407B, FDRL.

28. Minton to Roosevelt, November 1941, Roosevelt Papers, PPF 2235.

29. Dubofsky and Van Tine, *John L. Lewis*, 400–402.

30. Ibid., 402–4.

31. Lichtenstein, *Labor's War*, 71; Dubofsky and Van Tine, *John L. Lewis*, 405.

32. *Termination Report of the National War Labor Board*, 1:1–80.

33. Gross, *Reshaping of the National Labor Relations Board*, 243.

34. Witney, *Wartime Experiences*, 30–61, esp. 38.

35. Ibid., 24–25; Gross, *Reshaping of the National Labor Relations Board*, 243–45.

36. U.S. Bureau of Labor Statistics, *Problems and Policies of Dispute Settlement and Wage Stabilization during World War II*, 81; *Termination Report of the National War Labor Board*, 1:81–86; Willard, "Labor and the National War Labor Board," 352. Cyrus Ching, a former chief executive of the U.S. Rubber Company and himself a member of the wartime federal labor mediation apparatus, referred to union security as the "most dramatic and

explosive problem" employers, unions, and the government had to solve; Ching, *Review and Reflections*, 51–61.

37. *Termination Report of the National War Labor Board*, 1:80.

38. On this point, see Lichtenstein, *Labor's War*, 72–76.

39. Ibid., chap. 5; *Termination Report of the National War Labor Board*, 1:81–86; Bureau of Labor Statistics, *Problems and Policies*, 81–84; Willard, "Labor and the National War Labor Board," 150–51; Ching, *Review and Reflections*, 51–61.

40. Bureau of Labor Statistics, *Problems and Policies*, 84.

41. Willard, "Labor and the National War Labor Board," 352–64; Lichtenstein, *Labor's War*, 80–81, 180–82.

42. The theme of voluntarism, which the public members of the NWLB took quite seriously and which was a favorite refrain of the industrial relations professionals who largely staffed the wartime labor production committees, was captured exceedingly well in the two reports that Milton Derber, a professor of industrial relations, supervised soon after the war: *Termination Report of the National War Labor Board*, and Bureau of Labor Statistics, *Problems and Policies*. For more jaundiced perspectives on the wartime system, which are less beguiled by the rhetoric of voluntarism, see Lichtenstein, *Labor's War*, chaps. 7–10, and Willard, "Labor and the National War Labor Board," whose thesis asserts that corporatism as a system of voluntary cooperation between labor and business failed because the private parties were fragmented actors unable to develop common programs of action.

43. Bureau of Labor Statistics, *Problems and Policies*, 90–91; Lichtenstein, *Labor's War*, 71–72.

44. As cited in Bureau of Labor Statistics, *Problems and Policies*, 90–91.

45. Willard, "Labor and the National War Labor Board," 151.

46. Fraser, *Labor Will Rule*, 483–86; War Production Board, *Labor Policies*, 30–31.

47. Catton, *War Lords*, 146–49; D. M. Nelson, *Arsenal of Democracy*, 318–19.

48. Sanford Jacoby, "Union-Management Cooperation in the United States, 1915–1945," Unpublished paper presented at the Third U.S.-U.S.S.R. Colloquium on World Labor and Social Change, State University of New York at Binghamton, November 18–20, 1982, 37–38.

49. Ibid., 49.

50. D. M. Nelson, *Arsenal of Democracy*, 321; cf. *Industrial Mobilization for War*, 1:748–50.

51. Reed, *Seedtime for the Modern Civil Rights Movement*, is now the most complete history of the subject. For the AFL's resistance to the FEPC, see esp. 37–38, 164–65. For the role of A. Philip Randolph, see Pfeffer, *A. Philip Randolph*, 45–101. Cf. W. H. Harris, "Federal Intervention in Union Discrimination."

52. UMWJ, March 15, 1943, p. 18.

53. Lichtenstein, *Labor's War*, chaps. 7–9.

54. UMWJ, April 1, 1943, p. 7; Dubofsky and Van Tine, *John L. Lewis*, 416–19.

55. Dubofsky and Van Tine, *John L. Lewis*, 420–26.

56. Ibid., 426–27; "Press Release," April 29, 1943, Roosevelt Papers, FDRL.

57. Dubofsky and Van Tine, *John L. Lewis*, 428–38; Memorandum, McIntyre to Tully, May 3, 1943, and Memorandum, McIntyre to Roosevelt, May 3, 1943, Of 407B, Box 29, FDRL.

58. Dubofsky and Van Tine, *John L. Lewis*, 432–34; Lichtenstein, *Labor's War*, 167–68.

59. As an editorial in *Business Week* observed and the rising rate of strikes proved, the act failed to create labor peace. This led a prolabor congressman from Illinois to insert the following editorial in the *Congressional Record*: "In the intensely practical but delicately balanced competition of labor relations, the concepts of politicians written into law may have unpredictable and intolerable results. The interests of business will best be served by leaving the details of collective bargaining and personnel policy to its industrial relations experts. Better than anyone else, they know what hazards inhere in further Government intervention of any sort." *CR*, 78th Cong., 1st sess., 1943, Appendix 4063–64.

60. Dubofsky and Van Tine, *John L. Lewis*, 435–39.

61. Willard, "Labor and the National War Labor Board," 150–51.

62. Ibid., 263–64, 335–36, 363–64.

63. Ibid., 439–40; Lichtenstein, *Labor's War*, 165–71, 177. A poll conducted by *Fortune* magazine in February 1944 showed a strong and rising antiunion sentiment among the public as expressed in the demand for new labor laws to place unions more firmly under government control and to curtail union or closed shop arrangements; *Fortune*, February 1944, pp. 94–112.

64. Fraser, *Labor Will Rule*, 560–562; Lichtenstein, *Labor's War*, 216–17; Dubofsky and Van Tine, *John L. Lewis*, 454–56; Hamby, *Beyond the New Deal*, 65–67, 76–79; Cochran, *Truman and the Crisis Presidency*, 203–8; Donovan, *Conflict and Crisis*, 208–18, 239–42.

65. D. M. Nelson, *Arsenal of Democracy*, 307.

66. For scholars who take "corporate liberals" at their word, see Lichtenstein, *Labor's War*, 217–18, and Fraser, *Labor Will Rule*, 563. For a more clearheaded view of corporate antipathy toward unionism, even among the sophisticated corporate leaders, see H. J. Harris, *Right to Manage*, chap. 3.

67. Johnston, *America Unlimited*, 176–77, 180–82.

68. On the history of the tendency of law in the United States to equate union and corporate monopolies and to seek to outlaw both, see Hovenkamp, *Enterprise and American Law*, chaps. 18–19. For an intellectual and jurisprudential critique of union monopoly's infringement on the constitutional rights of individual workers, see Dickman, *Industrial Democracy*.

69. H. J. Harris, *Right to Manage*, 111–18. The quotation is on p. 116.

70. UMWJ, November 15, 1945, p. 19.

71. For the general strikes of 1946, see Lipsitz, *Class and Culture in Cold War America*, chaps. 3–4; Fraser, *Labor Will Rule*, 566; Lichtenstein, *Labor's War*, 221–30; Dubofsky and Van Tine, *John L. Lewis*, 458.

72. Gross, *Reshaping of the National Labor Relations Board*, 252–53; Lichtenstein, *Labor's War*, 239; Fraser, *Labor Will Rule*, 567.

73. B. Bernstein, "Truman Administration and Steel Strike," and B. Bertstein, "Reuther and General Motors Strike"; Lichtenstein, *Labor's War*, 221–30; Fraser, *Labor Will Rule*, 566–567. Howell John Harris, *Right to Manage*, chap. 5, explains and analyzes the corporate campaign to secure management rights and its success in 1946 and after.

74. This dispute can be followed best in the following files in the Truman Library: Warner Gardner Papers, Box 4, File Coal (1946–47) and Clark M. Clifford Papers, Boxes 3 and 4, File Coal Case #1. See also Dubofsky and Van Tine, *John L. Lewis*, 458–68. For a somewhat different version of the coal dispute and also for a description of the threatening and red-baiting rhetoric Truman used to condemn the railroad strikers, whom he threatened to conscript into military service, see Donovan, *Conflict and Crisis*, 208–18, 239–42.

Chapter 8

1. Maier, "Politics of Productivity," and *In Search of Stability*, chaps. 3–4; Renshaw, *American Labour and Consensus Capitalism*, chaps. 4–6; Brinkley, "New Deal and the State," and Lichtenstein, "From Corporatism to Collective Bargaining," See also Lichtenstein, "Labor in the Truman Era," 128–55.

2. C. Kerr, *Labor and Management in Industrial Society*; C. Kerr et al., *Industrialism and Industrial Man*; Bok and Dunlop, *Labor and the American Community*, 7–12. Kassalow, *Trade Unions and Industrial Relations*; Galenson and Dunlop, *Labor in the Twentieth Century*. The annual reports and papers published by the Industrial Relations Research Association offer a good guide to the thinking of the experts dominant in the field during the 1950s and 1960s.

3. The term "industrial pluralism" comes from Christopher Tomlins, who uses it in his book, *The State and the Unions*, and more sharply and consistently in his essay "The New Deal, Collective Bargaining, and the Triumph of Industrial Pluralism." For statements by two of the leading theoreticians and practitioners of "industrial pluralism," see Cox, "Rights under a Labor Agreement," and Cox and Dunlop, "Regulation of Collective Bargaining," and "The Duty to Bargain Collectively"; and Feller, "General Theory of the Collective Bargaining Agreement."

4. Dubofsky, "Workers' Movements," 28–30; cf. Troy, *Trade Union Membership, 1897–1962* and *Distribution of Union Membership*; I. Bernstein, "Growth of American Unions," "Union Growth and Structural Cycles," and "Growth of American Unions, 1945–1960"; Solomon, "Dimensions of Union Growth"; and A. A. Blum, "Why Unions Grow."

5. Foster, *Union Politic*, chaps. 1–3; Greenstone, *Labor in American Politics*, chaps. 2, 8; and Gall, *Politics of Right to Work*, 9–10.

6. Brody, *Workers in Industrial America*, 173–83; Slichter, "Are We Becoming a Laboristic State?" 11; Chamberlain, *Union Challenge*; Lichtenstein, "From Corporatism to Collective Bargaining," 123–32; Fraser, *Labor Will Rule*, 559–71; and Mills, *New Men of Power*, in which he not only characterized labor leaders as "men of power" but also quite prophetically exposed the real limitations on their power.

7. Tomlins, *The State and the Unions*, for craft union resentment of NLRB rulings and resistance to aspects of federal industrial relations policy. Taft, *The A.F. of L.*, 303–23.

8. Dubofsky and Van Tine, *John L. Lewis*, 472–76; Zieger, *John L. Lewis*, 160–64.

9. Cochran, *Labor and Communism*, chaps. 10–11; Levenstein, *Communism, Anti-Communism, and the CIO*; Prickett, "Aspects of the Communist Controversy"; Schatz, *Electrical Workers*, chaps. 7–8; J. B. Freeman, *In Transit*, chap. 13; Renshaw, *American Labour and Consensus Capitalism*, chap. 5; and also see the new collection of essays edited by Steve Rosswurm, *The CIO's Left-Led Unions*, esp. the essays by Rosswurm (1–18, 119–38), Gerald Zahavi (159–82), and Mark McColloch (183–200).

10. B. S. Griffith, *Crisis of American Labor*; Zieger, "Textile Workers and Historians," and Honey, "Industrial Unionism and Racial Justice in Memphis," 147–51, and "Operation Dixie"; and Korstad and Lichtenstein, "Opportunities Found and Lost."

11. Chamberlain, *Union Challenge*, esp. chap. 6 for a call to oppose union infringement on management's rights. H. J. Harris, *Right to Manage*, chaps. 2–7, for big business antipathy to unionism and how managers designed a means to live with a reality that they disliked. Schatz, *Electrical Workers*, 144–60, 233–40; and Brody, *Workers in Industrial America*, chap. 5.

12. Jacoby, *Employing Bureaucracy*, for the early history of such policies. Most recently, Jacoby has been studying alternative nonunion industrial relations systems that predate the 1970s. See, for example, "Norms and Cycles," and "Reckoning with Company Unions."

13. Dubofsky, "Workers' Movements," 31–32; and Edwards, *Strikes in the United States*, 258, Table A-4.

14. Schnapper, *The Truman Program*, 121–24; Hartmann, *Truman*, 80–81; Lee, *Truman and Taft-Hartley*, 49–51.

15. For the chronology and calendar of the legislation, see National Labor Relations Board, *Legislative History of the Labor Management Relations Act 1947* 1:vii–x.

16. *Legislative History*, 1:657–58, 672–73; see Lee, *Truman and Taft-Hartley*, 53–71, and Hartmann, *Truman*, 81–87, for the political and legislative history of the legislation. See Patterson, *Mr. Republican*, 353–61, for the Ohio senator's role in the process.

17. The legislation also restructured the NLRB, allegedly to separate its judicial and prosecutory functions, bringing it more in accord with conventional judicial rules of procedure and evidence. The legislation sought also to dilute part of the Department of Labor's active role in the arena of industrial relations by removing the United States Conciliation Service from the department and establishing it as an independent federal agency. For the full details of the proposed amendments recommended by Hartley's and Taft's committees, see *Legislative History*, 1:591–600, 1000–1003; Lee, *Truman and Taft-Hartley*, 61–74; Hartmann, *Truman*, 82–86; Millis and Brown, *From Wagner to Taft-Hartley*, 366ff.

18. *Legislative History*, 1:864–65, 998–99.

19. Lee, *Truman and Taft-Hartley*, 75–79; Hartmann, *Truman*, p. 86; Tomlins, *The State and the Unions*, 284–95; for the assertion that the conference committee bill retained the most important provisions of the Hartley Bill, see Hartley, *Our New National Labor Policy*, 75–88.

20. *Legislative History*, 1:899–900, 2:1522. A little more than 70 percent of the members in both houses voted in favor of Taft-Hartley, giving it a veto-proof majority if no votes shifted in the event of a presidential rejection. As usual, the majority consisted of nearly all the Republicans and most of the Southern Democrats. In the House a number of border state Democrats and Southerners from heavily unionized districts, who had voted against the Hartley Bill, voted for Taft-Hartley. Jacob Javits, Republican from Manhattan, proved the great exception to Republican solidarity. In the Senate only ardent old New Dealers and Southern and border state loyalists, the latter of whom represented states with substantial union strength or held party leadership positions, voted in the negative. Wayne Morse, a former NWLB member, maverick politician from Oregon, and a senator soon to switch his party affiliation to the Democrats, was the great exception in the Senate to Republican solidarity.

21. For a postmortem critique of Taft-Hartley that reflects quite accurately the views of most industrial relations practitioners and experts, see Millis and Brown, *From Wagner to Taft-Hartley*, 664–65. For the politics of the veto, see Lee, *Truman and Taft-Hartley*, 80–96, and Hartmann, *Truman*, 87–90.

22. For the full texts of the veto message and the radio address, see *Public Papers of the Presidents of the United States, Harry S. Truman*, 1947, 289–301.

23. For Reynolds's testimony, see Gross, *Reshaping of the National Labor Relations Board*, 258–59.

24. *Legislative History*, 2;1206–7; Bernstein and Matusow, *Truman Administration*, 128–30. Cf. Patterson, *Mr. Republican*, 361–365.

25. That, to say the least, is the conclusion of Christopher Tomlins, who argues in *The State and the Unions* that Taft-Hartley simply legitimated the New Deal policy and practice of "industrial pluralism," in which managements and unions bargained to establish and maintain contractually ensured stability at the expense of workers' rights and democratic participation in industrial decision-making. In Tomlins's hyperbolic formulation of a union attorney's advice to his clients, workers should accept post-Taft-Hartley rulings by the NLRB as " 'advice from the Government' and take it and 'lie down like good dogs' " (315). For the full flavor of Tomlins's interpretation, see 247–314. A school of legal scholars shares Tomlins's perspective, believing that federal courts had already leached the Wagner Act of most of its potential liberatory power and handed down rulings that presaged Taft-Hartley policies. See especially Klare, "Judicial Deradicalization of the Wagner Act," 265–339, and "Labor Law as Ideology," 450–82; and Atleson, *Values and Assumptions*. For the distillation of the interpretation that managements and unions allied to secure their interests against the wishes of workers, see Serrin, *The Company and the Union*.

For sharp critiques of the Tomlins-Klare-Atleson Critical Legal Theory approach to labor relations law, see Finkin, "Revisionism in Labor Law," 25–33, and Rabban, "Has the NLRA Hurt Labor?"

26. For interpretations that stress the antiunion motivation of the sponsors of Taft-Hartley and how drastically the law revised New Deal industrial relations policy, see Gross, *Reshaping of the National Labor Relations Board*, 255–59; Lee, *Truman and Taft-Hartley*, 49–79; Hartmann, *Truman*, 85–87; and Millis and Brown, *From Wagner to Taft-Hartley*, 604–665, passim.

27. Freeman and Medoff, *What Do Unions Do?*, chaps. 3, 5, 10; Jacoby, "Reckoning with Company Unions"; Brody, *Workers in Industrial America*, chap. 5.

28. Lester, *As Unions Mature*.

29. Bell, *End of Ideology*, chap. 11.

30. Galbraith, *American Capitalism*.

31. Orren, "Union Politics and Postwar Liberalism" and "Organized Labor and Modern Liberalism." Greenstone, *Labor in American Politics*, chaps. 3–7; Foster, *Union Politic*, chaps. 6–9; Gall, *Politics of Right to Work*, chaps. 3–5; Brody, *Workers in Industrial America*, chap. 6.

32. David Plotke in his forthcoming book on the creation of the Democratic regime describes and analyzes this political situation with amazing acuity (chap. 5). Reuther quoted in Brody, *Workers in Industrial America*, 234; Lee, *Truman and Taft-Hartley*, 160–80, for the failed politics of repeal; Mike Davis characterizes the marriage between labor and the Democrats as "barren"; *Prisoners of the American Dream*, 83–101.

33. On the political campaigns against Taft-Hartley, see Pomper, "Labor and Congress"; Patterson, *Mr. Republican*, 358–371; and Foster, *Union Politic*, 185–95. For the amendment to Taft-Hartley, see Lee, *Truman and Taft-Hartley*, 180, and Patterson, *Mr. Republican*, 501.

34. Some wags derisively dismissed Durkin as the plumber in a cabinet of millionaires. For Eisenhower's early efforts to woo labor support, see Peters, "Taft-Hartley and Landrum-Griffin"; Lee, *Eisenhower and Landrum-Griffin*, 20–31; and Reichard, *Reaffirmation of Republicanism*, 4–5, 143–46.

35. R. Griffith, "Eisenhower and the Corporate Commonwealth"; there is an enormous theoretical literature on "corporatism" written largely by political scientists and sociologists (see, for example, Schmitter, *Trends toward Corporate Intermediation* and *Patterns of*

Corporatist Policy-Making), but by far the best historical work on the subject has been done by Charles Maier in his collection of essays, *In Search of Stability*, and his earlier book that examined the reconstruction of European polities, economies, and societies after World War I, *Recasting Bourgeois Europe*.

36. For Eisenhower's reference to Weeks's conservatism, see Ferrell, *Eisenhower Diaries*, 264; Peters, "Taft-Hartley and Landrum-Griffin"; Lee, *Eisenhower and Landrum-Griffin*, 29–32; Patterson, *Mr. Republican*, 584–585, 590.

37. Lee, *Eisenhower and Landrum-Griffin*, 30–32; Reichard, *Reaffirmation of Republicanism*, 143; and Peters, "Taft-Hartley and Landrum-Griffin."

38. *Public Papers of the Presidents of the United States, Dwight D. Eisenhower*, 1953, 609–10.

39. Ibid., 1954, 40–44; for Humphrey's resistance to amendments, see Ferrell, *Eisenhower Diaries*, 264; Peters, "Taft-Hartley and Landrum-Griffin"; and Lee, *Eisenhower and Landrum-Griffin*, 36–43.

40. Lee, *Eisenhower and Landrum-Griffin*, 37–42; Reichard, *Reaffirmation of Republicanism*, 145–47; Peters, "Taft-Hartley and Landrum-Griffin."

41. *Public Papers of Eisenhower*, 1955, 851–54.

42. The literature published on "industrial pluralism" and the common law of industrial relations during the 1950s and 1960s is absolutely enormous. The following essays and books include only the most notable of such publications. John T. Dunlop, *Industrial Relations Systems* (1958); C. Kerr, *Labor and Management in Industrial Society*; C. Kerr et al., *Industrialism and Industrial Man*; Feller, "General Theory of the Collective Bargaining Agreement"; Cox and Dunlop, "Regulation of Collective Bargaining"; Cox, "Rights under a Labor Agreement," and "The Legal Nature of Collective Bargaining Agreements," *Michigan Law Review*, 57 (November 1958), 1–36.

43. United Steelworkers of America v. Warrior & Gulf Navigation, 363 U.S. 574 (1960); cf. American Manufacturing Co. v. United Steelworkers, 363 U.S. 564 (1960), and Enterprise Wheel and Car Corp. v. United Steelworkers, 363 U.S. 593 (1960). For other landmark Supreme Court rulings that implemented the principles of "industrial pluralism," see Vaca v. Sipes, 386 U.S. 171 (1967); Lincoln Mills of Alabama v. Textile Workers' Union, 353 U.S. 448 (1957); NLRB v. Fibreboard Paper Products, 379 U.S. 203 (1964); and Boys Market, Inc. v. Retail Clerks Local 770, 398 U.S. 235 (1970).

44. Local 24, International Brotherhood of Teamsters v. Oliver, 358 U.S. 283 (1958).

45. For Brody's analysis of the system of contractual industrial relations, see *Workers in Industrial America*, 198–210. For critiques of industrial pluralism and its common law that take a more jaundiced view of how the system worked in practice and that suggest, in the words of Karl Klare, that "collective bargaining is a system for inducing workers to participate in their own domination by managers and those whom managers serve," see the following: Klare, "Labor Law as Ideology: Toward a New Historiography of Collective Bargaining Law," *Industrial Relations Law Journal*, 4 (1981), 450–82; Staughton Lynd, "Government without Rights: The Labor Law Vision of Archibald Cox," ibid., 483–95; Stone, "Post-War Paradigm"; Tomlins, "The New Deal, Collective Bargaining, and the Triumph of Industrial Pluralism"; Rogers, "Divide and Conquer"; Lynd, "Beyond 'Labor Relations' "; and Atleson, *Values and Assumptions*. All these critiques perceive post–New Deal labor law as a conscious attempt by corporate interests, their allies in the state, their friends in the academic-legal communities, and compliant labor leaders to strengthen capitalism at the expense of workers. So hostile are they to unionism as it functioned in the

era of American affluence and to the attitudes of most labor leaders that they extol the theoretical "natural" and individual rights of workers, at the expense of the collective power represented by unionism. For a sharp but brief critique of this interpretation, see Dubofsky, "Legal Theory and Workers' Rights."

46. *Legislative History*, 2:945.

47. On Truman's intervention in the coal disputes of 1948 and 1950, see Dubofsky and Van Tine, *John L. Lewis*, 478–79. For his intervention in the coal and other industrial disputes, see *Public Papers of Truman*, 1948, pp. 204–5, 212–13, 251–52, 379–81, 435–36, 455–56; 1949, pp. 367–369, 477–78, 482; 1950, pp. 138–39, 154, 176, 187–91, 519–20, 597; 1951, pp. 499–500, 570–71, 604–5; 1952, pp. 157–59.

48. *Public Papers of Truman*, 1948, 251–52.

49. Ibid., 1950, pp. 519–520. A month later with the war on, Truman ordered the Secretary of Defense to take control of the nation's railroads in order to avert a national railroad strike; ibid., 597.

50. See Blackman, *Presidential Seizure*; Cochran, *Truman and the Crisis Presidency*, 341–43; Hamby, *Beyond the New Deal*, 449–53.

51. Truman's intervention in the dispute culminating in federal seizure can be followed in a series of papers, orders, and speeches published in *Public Papers of Truman*, 1951, pp. 652–53; 1952, pp. 246–51, 299–301, 309–10, 315–18, 410–14. The best history of the steel seizure case remains Marcus, *Truman and the Steel Seizure Case*; cf. Hamby, *Beyond the New Deal*, 454–58; Cochran, *Truman and the Crisis Presidency*, 343–46; and for a briefer, more recent treatment, McCoy, *Presidency of Harry S. Truman*, 290–93. For Truman's own version of what happened, see Truman, *Memoirs, Volume Two*, 465–77.

52. *Public Papers of Eisenhower*, 1954, pp. 193–94; 1959, pp. 708–709.

53. For his friendship with MacDonald, see Ferrell, *Eisenhower Diaries*, 277–78, 321–22.

54. Ibid., 366–68; *Public Papers of Eisenhower*, 1959, 482–83, 520–21, 643–44, 705, 711–12, 730–31, 741–42.

55. On the history of the committee and the extent of corruption in the labor movement, see R. F. Kennedy, *The Enemy Within*; and Hutcheson, *The Imperfect Union*. For the politics of the committee and its relation to labor legislation, see McAdams, *Power and Politics*, 36–40, and Lee, *Eisenhower and Landrum-Griffin*, chap. 3. For the durability of the image of organized labor as corrupt and coercive, see Thieblot and Haggard, *Union Violence*.

56. *Public Papers of Eisenhower*, 1958, 118–24.

57. McAdams, *Power and Politics*, 40–48; Lee, *Eisenhower and Landrum-Griffin*, 77–90. Congress did enact legislation to regulate union-management welfare and pension funds; ibid., 78–79.

58. McAdams, *Power and Politics*, 2–3; Lee, *Eisenhower and Landrum-Griffin*, 91–96; Gall, *Politics of Right to Work*, 130–32.

59. McAdams, *Power and Politics*, chaps. 3–4; Lee, *Eisenhower and Landrum-Griffin*, chap. 5.

60. This paragraph and what follows are drawn largely from McAdams, *Power and Politics*, 113–266, and Lee, *Eisenhower and Landrum-Griffin*, 117–59. The former, although written twenty-six years before the latter, is more complete and superior in nearly every way.

61. McAdams, *Power and Politics*, 202–5, 215–16, 221–23.

62. *Public Papers of Eisenhower*, 1959, 567–71.

63. C. Kerr et al., *Industrialism and Industrial Man*, 282–84, 290–91. Ten years later, some of the same authorities wrote an equally celebratory set of essays. Somers, *Essays in Industrial Relations Theory*.

64. For background on the corruption in the United Mine Workers and the murder of Yablonski, see Armbrister, *Act of Vengeance*; Finley, *Corrupt Kingdom*; and Hume, *Death in the Mines*; for the mine workers' insurgency and the labor department supervised election, see Clark, *Miners' Fight for Democracy*, and Geoghegan, *Which Side Are You On?*, 9–39.

65. The events in the Teamsters' union that culminated in Ron Carey's victory can be best followed in the pages of *Labor Notes* between 1988 and 1992, especially in the reports written by Kim Moody and Dan LaBotz.

66. Galbraith, *The Affluent Society* and *The New Industrial State*.

67. Maier, "Politics of Productivity," and also the essays in *In Search of Stability*.

68. On the NAACP-UAW alliance, see Meier and Rudwick, *Black Detroit and the Rise of the UAW*. For the premodern civil rights history of labor, federal law, and discriminatory hiring practices, see Hill, "Black Labor," and "National Labor Relations Act"; for labor's role in forging a political coalition in favor of civil rights legislation, see Orren, "Union Politics and Postwar Liberalism" and "Organized Labor and Modern Liberalism," as well as Brody, *Workers in Industrial America*, 231–34.

69. Hill, "National Labor Relations Act," 335–60, "Black Labor," 216–23, "Equal Employment Opportunity Acts," and *Black Labor and the American Legal System*. Cf. Gould, *Black Workers in White Unions*.

70. Clearly, the primary purpose of the craft union exclusionary traditions had always been to control (monopolize) the labor market, not to discriminate against workers on the basis of race. Yet the members of those unions had a long history of racist sentiments and practices, and by creating exclusively white organizations, they did more easily monopolize labor markets. On this score, see Roediger, *Wages of Whiteness*; P. S. Foner, *Organized Labor and the Black Worker*; Marshall, *Negro and Organized Labor*; Gould, *Black Workers in White Unions*; and the Hill works cited above.

71. For the quotation, see Hill, "Equal Employment Opportunity Acts," 91, and 35–36, 90–91, for union and AFL-CIO opposition to enforcement of Title VII. Cf. Hill, *Black Labor and the American Legal System*, and Gould, *Black Workers in White Unions*.

72. For the role played by the mass-production unions, especially the automobile workers, steelworkers, packinghouse workers, electrical workers, and West Coast maritime workers, in the promotion of civil rights and the advancement of minority workers, see Meier and Rudwick, *Black Detroit and the Rise of the UAW*; Stein, "Southern Workers in National Unions"; also see Honey, "Industrial Unionism and Racial Justice in Memphis," and Halpern, "Interracial Unionism in the Southwest; Street, "Working in the Yards," chaps. 4, 7; "Breaking Up Old Hatreds and Breaking through the Fear"; and "Packinghouse Blues"; Kimeldorf, *Reds or Rackets?*, 144–51, 165; Schatz, *Electrical Workers*, 129–31. For the classic study of how CIO at its origins promoted the interests of African-American workers, see Cayton and Mitchell, *Black Workers and the New Unions*.

73. On the race-based splits in the labor movement especially in the mass-production unions, see Geschwender, *Class, Race and Worker Insurgency*; Leggett, *Class, Race, and Labor*; and T. Brooks, "Negro Militants, Jewish Liberals, and the Unions," and "Black Upsurge in the Unions."

74. For the overall differences between the earning prospects and promotion oppor-

tunities for women and men employees, see Goldin, *Understanding the Gender Gap*; and Bergmann, *Economic Emergence of Women*, chap. 6.

75. For the increasing numbers of women entering the labor force on a fulltime basis and their growing importance and permanence in the labor market, see Kessler-Harris, *Out to Work*, chap. 11; Wiener, *From Working Girl to Working Mother*. For some of the history of the relationship between unions and women's rights as workers, see Milkman, *Gender at Work*, and "Women Workers, Feminism, and the Labor Movement"; Gabin, *Feminism in the Labor Movement*; Baron, "Gender and Labor History," and Gabin, "Time Out of Mind."

76. Orren, "Union Politics and Postwar Liberalism," 219, 251. Cf. Lowi, *End of Liberalism*, 80. For background on labor's influence on the "Great Society" reforms see I. Bernstein, *Promises Kept*.

77. Maier, "Response," for the exceptional character of the post–World War II order and why the 1980s proved to be a more conventional historical epoch.

78. Goldfield, *Decline of Labor*, chaps. 1, 3, 4–5, spells out the extent and gravity of the decline; Weiler, "Promises to Keep," provides further insight on the decline; M. Davis, *Prisoners of the American Dream*, 127–53; and K. Moody, *Injury to All*, chaps. 6–9.

79. For the collapse of the New Deal coalition and labor's political influence, Jonathan Rieder, "The Rise of the 'Silent Majority'," and Thomas Byrne Edsall, "The Changing Shape of Power: A Realignment in Public Policy," in S. Fraser and G. Gerstle, *Rise and Fall of New Deal*, 243–93; Edsall, *Chain Reaction*; M. Davis, *Prisoners of the American Dream*, chaps. 4–5; K. Moody, *An Injury to All*, chap. 7; D. Brody, *Workers in Industrial America*, 238–51; Dubofsky, "Gli operai," 226–30; for the use of federal law against unions and their inability to respond, see Goldfield, *Decline of Labor*, chap. 9; and Weiler, "Promises to Keep," 1769–1827.

80. On the failure of labor law reform, Brody, *Workers in Industrial America*, 246–49; M. Davis, *Prisoners of the Dream*, 132–35 ; K. Moody, *An Injury to All*, 134–35; for Douglas Fraser's open letter, see *Radical History Review* 18 (Fall 1978): 117–22.

81. May 31, 1981, 3:1.

82. For Reagan's speech to the carpenters (which, by the way, the president's speechwriters discussed with me by phone), see the *New York Times*, September 4, 1981. On Reagan and the PATCO strike, see K. Moody, *Injury to All*, 139–41, and Shostak, *Air Controllers' Controversy*; Northrup, *The Federal Government as Employer*.

83. *New York Times*, May 31, 1983, pp. 1, 16; January 20, 1985, sec. 3, p. 2; February 8, 1985; March 24, 1985, sec. E, p. 24; May 4, 1986, sec. F, pp. 1, 8; October 5, 1986, sec. F, p. 2; March 3, 1991, sec. F, p. 8.

84. Ibid., February 5, 1984, sec. F, p. 8; for the failure of the NLRB to expedite action on complaints about management's antiunion practices and for its more sympathetic response to management tactics, see Geoghegan, *Which Side Are You On?*, and Weiler, "Promises to Keep"; for the inability of unions to respond effectively to the changed federal policies, see Goldfield, *Decline of Labor*, chaps. 8–11, passim.

85. *New York Times*, January 28, 1992, p. 12; April 12, 1992, pp. 1, 34; *International Herald-Tribune*, March 1, 1989, p. 5.

86. Edsall, *Chain Reaction*, and "The Changing Shape of Power" and Dubofsky, "Gli operai," 228–30; and M. Davis, *Prisoners of the American Dream*, 256–300. Cf. Juravich, "Beyond the Myths of '84."

87. *New York Times*, June 12, 1992, p. 13; September 7, 1992, p. 27; for sharp critiques of

labor's political failures during the 1980s, see M. Davis, *Prisoners of the American Dream*, 256–314, and K. Moody, *An Injury to All*, 156–64. For other essays that explore the subject from a variety of perspectives, see Lipset, *Unions in Transition*.

88. Kochan, Katz, and McKersie, *Transformation of American Industrial Relations*; Hecksher, *The New Unionism*; Piore and Sabel, *Second Industrial Divide*; Shaiken, *Work Transformed*; Weiler, *Governing the Workplace*, for how an advocate of trade unionism suggests that the law might be used in place of unions to protect individual workers' rights on the job and that European forms of workplace codetermination might be substituted for traditional collective bargaining practices. For other perspectives on the sad state of trade unionism and suggested proposals for the revival of a healthy labor movement, see the volume published by the Industrial Relations Research Association in 1991 and edited by George Strauss et al., *The State of the Unions*, esp. the contributions by David Brody ("Labor's Crisis in Historical Perspective," 277–311), Thomas Kochan and Kirsten Wever, ("American Unions and the Future of Worker Representation," 363–86), and Michael J. Piore ("The Future of Unionism," 387–410).

Conclusion

1. Block, "The Ruling Class Does Not Rule," and *Revising State Theory*.

2. Korpi, *Democratic Class Struggle*; Shalev, "Social Democratic Model and Beyond"; Korpi and Shalev, "Strikes, Power, and Conflict"; Przeworski, *Capitalism and Social Democracy* and *Paper Stones*; Fraser, *Labor Will Rule*, chaps. 13–17, and "The 'Labor Question' "; Lizabeth Cohen, *Making a New Deal*, chaps. 6–8; Gerstle, *Working-Class Americanism*.

3. Skocpol, "Bringing the State Back In"; Weir and Theda Skocpol, "State Structures and the Possibilities for 'Keynesian' Responses"; Weir, Orloff, and Skocpol, "Introduction," and "Epilogue"; and Skocpol, "Political Response to Capitalist Crisis"; Skocpol and Finegold, "State Capacity and Economic Intervention"; Finegold and Skocpol, "Explaining New Deal Labor Policy."

4. For the role of the South in weakening unionism and collective bargaining by weakening the NLRB and amending the Wagner Act, see Gross, *Reshaping of the National Labor Relations Board*, chap. 5. For Southern congressional influence and the passage of the Landrum-Griffin Act, see McAdams, *Power and Politics*.

5. Glendon, *Rights Talk*.

6. Katznelson, "Working-Class Formation."

7. Lizabeth Cohen, *Making a New Deal*, chaps. 1–4; Gerstle, *Working-Class Americanism*, Part 1; and Goldberg, *Tale of Three Cities*.

8. Atleson, *Values and Assumptions*; Stone, "Post-War Paradigm"; Klare "Traditional Labor Law Scholarship and Collective Bargaining," and the following responses stimulated by it: Finkin, "Does Karl Klare Protest Too Much?" and Klare, "Lost Opportunity"; and Atleson, "Reflections on Labor, Power and Society"; and Stone, "Re-Envisioning Labor Law." Also see the papers by Klare and Staughton Lynd in the *Industrial Relations Law Journal* 4 (1981): 450–90. For analysis and argument from the conservative, libertarian perspective, see Dickman, *Industrial Democracy*, and Thieblot and Haggard, *Union Violence*.

9. Dubofsky, "Legal Theory and Workers' Rights," 502.

10. Ibid., 501; Thompson, *Whigs and Hunters*, 266.

Cases Cited

Adair v. U.S., 208 U.S. 161 (1908).
AFL v. NLRB, 308 U.S. 401 (1940).
American Manufacturing Co. v. United Steelworkers, 363 U.S. 564 (1960).
American Steel & Wire Co. v. Wire Drawers' and Die Makers' Unions Nos. 1 & 3 et al., 90 Federal Reporter 598 (1898).
American Steel Foundries v. Tri-Cities Central Trade Council, 257 U.S. 184 (1921).
Ames v. Union Pac. Ry. Co. et al., 62 Federal Reporter 7 (1894).
Apex Hosiery Co. v. Leader, 310 U.S. 469 (1940).
Arthur et al. v. Oakes et al., 63 Federal Reporter 310 (1894).
Bedford Stone Co. v. Journeymen Stone Cutters, 274 U.S. 37 (1927).
Borderland Coal Corp. v. International Organization of UMWA et al., 275 Federal Reporter 871 (1921).
Boys Market, Inc. v. Retail Clerks Local 770, 398 U.S. 235 (1970).
Brims et al. v. U.S., 6 Fed (2) 98 (1925).
Bunting v. Oregon, 243 U.S. 426 (1917).
Casey v. Cincinnati Typographical Union, No. 3., et al., 45 Federal Reporter 135 (1891).
Chicago, Burlington, & Quincy Railway Co. et al. v. Burlington, C.R. & N. Railway Co. et al., 34 Federal Reporter 481 (1888).
Coeur d'Alene Consolidated Mining Co. v. Miners' Union of Wardner et al., 51 Federal Reporter 260 (1892).
Consolidated Edison Co. v. NLRB, 305 U.S. 197 (1938).
Coppage v. Kansas, 236 U.S. 1 (1915).
Coronado Coal Co. v. UMW, 268 U.S. 295 (1925).
Dowd v. United Mine Workers of America et al., 235 Federal Reporter 1 (1916).
Duplex v. Deering et al., 247 Federal Reporter 192 (1917).
Duplex v. Deering et al., 252 Federal Reporter 727 (1918).
Duplex v. Deering et al., 254 U.S. 443 (1921).
Enterprise Wheel and Car Corp. v. United Steelworkers, 363 U.S. 593 (1960).
Fansteel Metallurgical Co. v. NLRB, 98 Federal Reporter (2) 375 (1938).
Fansteel Metallurgical Corp. v. NLRB, 306 U.S. 240 (1939).
Farmers' Loan & Trust Co. v. Northern Pac. Ry. Co. et al., 60 Federal Reporter 803 (1894).
Gable et al. v. Vonnegut Machinery Co. et al., 274 Federal Reporter 66 (1921).
Gasaway et al. v. Borderland Coal Corp., 278 Federal Reporter 56 (1921).
Gompers v. Buck's Stove & Range Co., 221 U.S. 418 (1911).
Great Northern Ry. Co. v. Local Great Falls Lodge of Int'l Assoc. of Mach., No. 287 et al., 283 Federal Reporter 557 (1922).

Great Northern Ry. Co. v. Brosseau et al., 286 Federal Reporter 414 (1922).

H.J. Heinz v. NLRB, 311 U.S. 514 (1941).

Herkert & Meisel v. United Leatherworkers et al., 268 Federal Reporter 662 (1920).

Herkert & Meisel v. United Leatherworkers et al., 284 Federal Reporter 446 (1922).

Hitchman Coal & Coke Co. v. Mitchell et al., 172 Federal Reporter 963 (1909).

Hitchman Coal & Coke Co. v. Mitchell et al., 202 Federal Reporter 512 (1912).

Hitchman Coal and Coke Co. v. Mitchell, 245 U.S. 229 (1917).

IAM v. NLRB, 311 U.S. 72 (1940).

In re Charge to Grand Jury, 62 Federal Reporter 828 (1894).

In re Debs, 158 U.S. 564 (1895).

In re Wabash Railway Co., 24 Federal Reporter 217 (1885).

Lawlor et al. v. Loewe et al., 187 Federal Reporter 522 (1911).

Lawlor et al. v. Loewe et al., 209 Federal Reporter 721 (1913).

Lincoln Mills of Alabama v. Textile Workers' Union, 353 U.S. 448 (1957).

Local 24, International Brotherhood of Teamsters v. Oliver, 358 U.S. 283 (1958).

Lochner v. N.Y., 198 U.S. 45 (1905).

Loewe et al. v. Lawlor et al., 148 Federal Reporter 924 (1906).

Loewe v. Lawlor, 208 U.S. 274 (1908).

Mitchell et al. v. Hitchman Coal & Coke Co., 214 Federal Reporter 685 (1914).

Muller v. Oregon, 208 U.S. 412 (1908).

Nat'l Licorice Co. v. NLRB, 309 U.S. 453 (1940).

NLRB v. Fibreboard Paper Products, 379 U.S. 203 (1964).

NLRB v. Ford Motor Co., 114 Federal Reporter (2) 905 (1940).

NLRB v. IBEW, 308 U.S. 413 (1940).

NLRB v. Jones and Laughlin, 301 U.S. 1 (1937).

NLRB v. Mackay Radio and Telegraph, 92 Federal Reporter (2) 761 (1937).

NLRB v. Mackay Radio and Telegraph, 304 U.S. 333 (1938).

NLRB v. Newport News Shipbuilding & Dry Dock Co., 309 U.S. 350 (1939).

NLRB v. Pac. Greyhound, 303 U.S. 271 (1938).

NLRB v. Penn. Greyhound, 303 U.S. 261 (1938).

NLRB v. Sands Mfg. Co., 96 Federal Reporter (2) 721 (1938).

NLRB v. Sands Mfg. Co., 306 U.S. 332 (1939).

NLRB v. Virg. Elect. & Power Co. and NLRB v. Ind. Org. of Employees of the Virg. Elect. & Power Co., 314 U.S. 469 (1941).

Paul Senn v. Tile Layers, 301 U.S. 468 (1937).

Pennsylvania Railroad Co. v. Railroad Labor Board, 261 U.S. 72 (1923).

Phelps Dodge Corp. v. NLRB, 313 U.S. 177 (1941).

Pitts. Plate Glass v. NLRB, and Crystal City Glass Workers v. NLRB, 313 U.S. 146 (1941).

Pitts. Terminal Coal Corp. v. UMWA et al., 22 Federal Reporter (2) 559 (1927).

Thomas v. Cinn. N.O. & T.P. Ry. Co., 62 Federal Reporter 17 (1894).

Thomas v. Cinn. N.O. & T.P. Ry. Co., 62 Federal Reporter 803 (1894).

Thornhill v. Alabama, 310 U.S. 88 (1940).

Toledo, A.A. & N.M. Railway Co. v. Penn. Co. et al., 54 Federal Reporter 730 (1893).

Truax v. Corrigan, 257 U.S. 312 (1921).

UMW v. Coronado Coal Co., 259 U.S. 344 (1922).

UMWA et al. v. Red Jacket Consol. Coal & Coke, 18 Federal Reporter (2) 839 (1927).

United Leather Workers v. Herkert & Meisel, 265 U.S. 457 (1924).
United Steelworkers of America v. Warrior & Gulf Navigation, 363 U.S. 574 (1960).
U.S. v. Alger, 62 Federal Reporter 824 (1894).
U.S. v. Brims, 272 U.S. 549 (1926).
U.S. v. Elliot et al., 62 Federal Reporter 801 (1894).
U.S. v. Hutcheson, 312 U.S. 219 (1941).
U.S. v. Railway Employees' Department, AFL et al. 283 Federal Reporter 479 (1922).
U.S. v. Railway Employees' Department, AFL et al., 286 Federal Reporter 228 (1922).
U.S. v. Workingmen's Amalgamated Council of New Orleans et al., 54 Federal Reporter 994 (1893).
Vaca v. Sipes, 386 U.S. 171 (1967).
Waterhouse et al. v. Comer, 55 Federal Reporter 149 (1893).
Wilson v. New, 243 U.S. 332 (1917).

Bibliography

The research for this book flows from work in scattered archives and depositories, undertaken when I wrote histories of the Industrial Workers of the World and John L. Lewis. I also did extensive archival research specifically for this project. In my capacity as general editor for the University Publications of America microfilm series, Research Collections in Labor Studies, I examined numerous collections around the country as well. The quantity of materials on the subject of labor relations in the holdings of the National Archives alone is so enormous that an individual scholar might devote an entire lifetime of research to examining them and never approach closure on the project. Hence, the bibliography that follows scarcely pretends to cite every archival collection or published piece that deals with the state and labor in modern America. Instead, it simply lists all the documents, books, and articles cited either in this text or in the notes to the text.

Manuscript and Archival Sources

Boise, Idaho
  Idaho State Historical Society
    Telegrams and Correspondence, Idaho Congressional Delegation, Pertaining to
      Coeur d'Alenes (microfilm copy)
    Norman H. Willey Papers (microfilm copy)
Charlottesville, Virginia
  University of Virginia Alderson Library
    W. Jett Lauck Papers
Columbus, Ohio
  Ohio Historical Society
    Warren G. Harding Papers (microfilm)
Detroit, Michigan
  Wayne State University Archives of Labor History and Urban Affairs
    Heber Blankenhorn Papers
    Congress of Industrial Organizations Papers
    Edward A. Wieck Papers
Frederick, Maryland
  University Publications of America Microfilm Series 1985
    Papers of the National War Labor Board
Hyde Park, New York
  Franklin D. Roosevelt Library
    Katherine Pollack Ellickson Papers
    Franklin D. Roosevelt Papers

Independence, Missouri
  Harry S. Truman Library
    Clark M. Clifford Papers
    Warner Gardner Papers
Ithaca, New York
  Cornell University Catherwood Library, Labor-Management Documentation Center,
    New York State School of Industrial and Labor Relations
    Sidney Hillman Papers, Amalgamated Clothing Workers of America Papers
Madison, Wisconsin
  State Historical Society of Wisconsin
    American Federation of Labor Papers
New York, New York
  Columbia University
    Oral History Collection
  New York Public Library
    Frank P. Walsh Papers
State College, Pennsylvania
  Pennsylvania State University Labor Archives
    William Mitch Papers
Washington, D.C.
  Catholic University of America
    John Brophy Papers
  Library of Congress
    Calvin Coolidge Papers (microfilm)
    John Frey Papers
    Samuel Gompers Letterbooks
  National Archives
    Department of Justice, Record Group 60
    Department of Labor Papers, Record Groups 1 and 174
    National Recovery Administration, Record Group 9
    Records of the National War Labor Board, Record Group 2
    United Mine Workers of America, John L. Lewis Papers (originally at Union Head-
      quarters, Washington, D.C.; now in storage, Alexandria, Virginia)
    U.S. Mediation and Conciliation Service Files, Record Group 280
    War Labor Policies Board Records, Record Group 1
West Branch, Iowa
  Herbert C. Hoover Library
    Herbert C. Hoover Papers

Government Documents

Anthracite Coal Strike Commission. *Report to the President on the Anthracite Coal
  Strike of May–October, 1902*. Washington, D.C.: Government Printing Office, 1903.
*Industrial Mobilization for War: History of the War Production Board and Predecessor
  Agencies, 1940–1945. The Story of American War Production*. Washington, D.C.:
  Government Printing Office, 1947. Reprint. New York: Greenwood Press, 1969.
Messages and Papers of the Presidents. 1794–1902. 20 vols. plus supplement. New
  York: Bureau of National Literature, 1912–25.

National Labor Relations Board. *Legislative History of the Labor Management Relations Act 1947.* 2 vols. Washington, D.C.: Government Printing Office, 1948.

———. *Legislative History of the National Labor Relations Act.* 2 vols. Washington, D.C.: Government Printing Office, 1949.

President's Mediation Commission. *Report to the President of the United States, January 9, 1918.* Washington, D.C.: Government Printing Office, 1918.

Public Papers of the Presidents of the United States. Dwight D. Eisenhower. 8 vols. Washington, D.C.: Government Printing Office, n.d.

Public Papers of the Presidents of the United States. Harry S. Truman. 9 vols. Washington, D.C.: Government Printing Office, 1961–66.

The Termination Report of the National War Labor Board: Industrial Disputes and Wage Stabilization in Wartime, January 12, 1942–December 31, 1945. 6 vols. Washington, D.C.: Government Printing Office, n.d.

U.S. Bureau of the Census. *Historical Statistics of the United States, Colonial Times to 1957.* Washington, D.C.: Government Printing Office, 1960.

U.S. Bureau of Labor Statistics. *National War Labor Board.* Bulletin no. 287. Washington, D.C.: Government Printing Office, 1922.

———. *Problems and Policies of Dispute Settlement and Wage Stabilization during World War II.* Bulletin no. 1009. Washington, D.C.: Government Printing Office, 1950.

———. *Report on the Work of the National Defense Mediation Board, March 19, 1941– January 12, 1942.* Bulletin no. 714. Washington, D.C.: Government Printing Office, 1942.

———. *Report to the President on the Anthracite Coal Strike.* Bulletin no. 43. Prepared by Carroll D. Wright. Washington, D.C.: Government Printing Office, 1902.

———. *Strikes in 1941 and Strikes affecting Defense Production.* Bulletin no. 711. Washington, D.C.: Government Printing Office, 1942.

U.S. Commission on Industrial Relations. *Final Report and Testimony Submitted to Congress.* 11 vols. 64th Cong., 1st Sess., 1916. S. Doc. 415. Washington, D.C.: Government Printing Office.

U.S. Congress. House. *Amendments to National Labor Relations Act.* 76th Cong., 3d Sess., 1940. H. Rept. 1928, pts. 1, 2, and 3.

U.S. Congress. House. *Employment of Pinkerton Detectives.* 52d Cong., 2d Sess., 1893. H. Rept. 2447.

U.S. Congress. House. *Investigation of Labor Troubles in Missouri, Arkansas, Kansas, Texas, and Illinois.* 49th Cong., 2d Sess., 1887. H. Rept. 4174.

U.S. Congress. House. *Papers Relative to Labor Troubles at Goldfield.* 60th Cong., 1st Sess., 1908. H. Doc. 607.

U.S. Congress. House. *Receivership of Northern Pacific Railway Company.* 53d Cong., 2d Sess., 1894. H. Rept. 1049.

U.S. Congress. House. *Report on Labor Troubles in the Anthracite Regions of Pennsylvania.* 50th Cong., 2d Sess., 1889. H. Rept. 4147.

U.S. Congress. House. Special Committee of the House of Representatives Appointed Pursuant to H. Res. 258 to Investigate the National Labor Relations Board. *Intermediate Report.* 76th Cong. 3d Sess., 1940. H. Rept. 1902, pt. 1.

U.S. Congress. House. Special Committee to Investigate the National Labor Relations Board. *Report.* 76th Cong., 3d Sess., 1941. H. Rept. 3109.

U.S. Congress. House. U.S. Industrial Commission. 19 vols. *Final Report.* 57th Cong., 1st Sess., 1902. H. Doc. 380.

U.S. Congress. Senate. *Federal Aid in Domestic Disturbances, 1787–1903*. Report prepared by Frederick T. Wilson. 57th Cong., 2d Sess., 1903. S. Doc. 209.

U.S. Congress. Senate. *Investigation of Labor Troubles*. 52d Cong., 2d Sess., 1893. S. Rept. 1280.

U.S. Congress. Senate. *A Report on Labor Disturbances in the State of Colorado from 1880 to 1904, Inclusive*. 58th Cong., 3d Sess., 1905. S. Doc. 122.

U.S. Congress. Senate. U.S. Strike Commission. *Report*. 53d Cong., 3d Sess., 1895. S. Exec. Doc. 7.

War Production Board. *Labor Policies of the National Defense Advisory Commission and the Office of Production Management, May 1940 to April 1942*. Historical Reports on War Administration. Special Study no. 23. Prepared by Richard J. Purcell. Washington, D.C.: Government Printing Office, 1946.

Books

Adams, Jr., Graham. *Age of Industrial Violence, 1910–1915*. New York: Columbia University Press, 1966.

Allswang, John. *The New Deal and American Politics: A Study in Political Change*. New York: Wiley, 1978.

Anderson, Kristi. *The Creation of a Democratic Majority, 1928–1936*. Chicago: University of Chicago Press, 1979.

Argensinger, Jo Ann E. *Toward a New Deal in Baltimore: People and Government in the Great Depression*. Chapel Hill: University of North Carolina Press, 1988.

Armbrister, Trevor. *Act of Vengeance: The Yablonski Murders and Their Solution*. New York: Saturday Review Press/Dutton, 1975.

Asher, Robert, and Charles Stephenson, eds. *Life and Labor*. Albany: State University of New York Press, 1986.

Atleson, James. *Values and Assumptions in American Labor Law*. Amherst: University of Massachusetts Press, 1983.

Auerbach, Jerold S. *Labor and Liberty: The LaFollette Committee and the New Deal*. Indianapolis: Bobbs Merrill, 1966.

Baron, Ava, ed. *Work Engendered: Toward a New History of American Labor*. Ithaca: Cornell University Press, 1991.

Barrett, James R. *Work and Community in the Jungle: Chicago's Packinghouse Workers, 1894–1922*. Urbana: University of Illinois Press, 1987.

Bell, Daniel. *The End of Ideology*. Glencoe, Ill.: Free Press, 1960.

Bellush, Bernard. *The Failure of the NRA*. New York: W. W. Norton, 1975.

Bennett, Sari, and Carville Earle. *The Geography of American Labor and Industrialization, 1865–1908: An Atlas*. Baltimore, 1980.

Bergmann, Barbara R. *The Economic Emergence of Women*. New York: Basic Books, 1986.

Berman, Edward. *Labor and the Sherman Act*. New York: Harper, 1930.

———. *Labor Disputes and the Presidents of the United States*. New York: Columbia University Press, 1924.

Bernstein, Barton J., and Allen J. Matusow, eds. *The Truman Administration: A Documentary History*. New York: Harper and Row, 1966.

Bernstein, Irving. *The Lean Years: A History of the American Worker, 1920–1933*. Boston: Houghton Mifflin, 1960.

———. *The New Deal Collective Bargaining Policy.* Berkeley: University of California Press, 1950.

———. *Promises Kept: John F. Kennedy's New Frontier.* New York: Oxford University Press, 1991.

———. *Turbulent Years: A History of American Workers, 1933–1939.* Boston: Houghton Mifflin, 1969.

Biddle, Francis, *In Brief Authority.* Garden City, N.Y.: Doubleday, 1962.

Blackman, John L. *Presidential Seizure in Labor Disputes.* Cambridge: Harvard University Press, 1967.

Blatz, Perry K. *Labor Relations in the Anthracite Coal Industry, 1875–1925: Managing the Ebb and Flow of Rank-and-File Militancy.* Albany: State University of New York Press, forthcoming.

Block, Fred. *Revising State Theory: Essays on Politics and Postindustrialism.* Philadelphia: Temple University Press, 1987.

Blum, John Morton. *Joe Tumulty and the Wilson Era.* Boston: Houghton Mifflin, 1951.

———. *The Republican Roosevelt.* New York: Atheneum, 1962.

Bok, Derek C., and John T. Dunlop. *Labor and the American Community.* New York: Simon and Schuster, 1970.

Braeman, John, David Brody, and Robert Bremner, eds. *Change and Continuity in Twentieth-Century America.* Columbus: Ohio State University Press, 1964.

Brody, David. *The Butcher Workmen: A Study of Unionization.* Cambridge: Harvard University Press, 1964.

———. *Labor in Crisis: The Steel Strike of 1919.* Philadelphia: J. B. Lippincott, 1965.

———. *Steelworkers in America: The Nonunion Era.* Cambridge: Harvard University Press, 1960.

———. *Workers in Industrial America.* New York: Oxford University Press, 1980.

Brooks, Robert R. *As Steel Goes: Unionism in a Basic Industry.* New Haven: Yale University Press, 1940.

Bruce, Robert V. *1877: Year of Violence.* Reprint. Chicago: Quadrangle Books, 1970.

Buffa, Dudley W. *Union Power and American Democracy: The UAW and the Democratic Party, 1935–1972.* Ann Arbor: University of Michigan Press, 1984.

Burner, David. *Herbert Hoover: A Public Life.* New York: Alfred A. Knopf, 1979.

Burns, James MacGregor. *Roosevelt: The Lion and the Fox.* New York: Harcourt, Brace, 1956.

Burt, Robert A. *The Constitution in Conflict.* Cambridge: Harvard University Press, 1992.

Catton, Bruce. *The War Lords of Washington.* New York: Harcourt, Brace, 1948.

Cayton, Horace, and George S. Mitchell. *Black Workers and the New Unions.* Chapel Hill: University of North Carolina Press, 1939.

Chamberlain, Neil W. *The Union Challenge to Management Control.* New York: Harper, 1948.

Chandler, Jr., Alfred D. *Scale and Scope: The Dynamics of Industrial Capitalism.* Cambridge: Harvard University Press, 1990.

———. *The Visible Hand: The Managerial Revolution in American Business.* Cambridge: Harvard University Press, 1977.

Ching, Cyrus. *Review and Reflections: A Half-Century of Labor Relations.* New York: B. C. Forbes and Sons, 1953.

Clark, Paul F. *The Miners' Fight for Democracy: Arnold Miller and the Reform of the United Mine Workers.* Ithaca: New York State School of Industrial and Labor Relations, Cornell University Press, 1981.

Cochran, Bert. *Harry Truman and the Crisis Presidency.* New York: Funk and Wagnalls, 1973.

——. *Labor and Communism: The Conflict That Shaped American Unions.* Princeton: Princeton University Press, 1977.

Cohen, Lizabeth. *Making a New Deal: Industrial Workers in Chicago, 1919–1939.* New York: Oxford University Press, 1990.

Commons, John R. *Myself.* Madison: University of Wisconsin Press, 1964.

Conner, Valerie Jean. *The National War Labor Board: Stability, Social Justice, and the Voluntary State in World War I.* Chapel Hill: University of North Carolina Press, 1983.

Cooper, Jerry M. *The Army and Civil Disorder: Federal Military Intervention in Labor Disputes, 1870–1900.* Westport, Conn.: Greenwood Press, 1980.

Cortner, Richard C. *The Jones and Laughlin Case.* New York: A. A. Knopf, 1970.

——. *The Wagner Act Cases.* Knoxville: University of Tennessee Press, 1964.

Croly, Herbert. *Marcus A. Hanna.* New York, 1912.

Cronon, E. David, ed. *The Cabinet Diaries of Josephus Daniels, 1913–1921.* Lincoln: University of Nebraska Press, 1963.

Cuff, Robert D. *The War Industries Board.* Baltimore: Johns Hopkins University Press, 1973.

Daniel, Cletus E. *The ACLU and the Wagner Act.* Ithaca: New York State School of Industrial and Labor Relations, Cornell University Press, 1980.

——. *Bitter Harvest: A History of California Farmworkers, 1870–1941.* Ithaca: Cornell University Press, 1981.

Davis, Mike. *Prisoners of the American Dream.* New York: Verso, 1986.

Dawley, Allan. *Struggles for Justice: Social Responsibility and the Liberal State.* Cambridge: Harvard University Press, 1991.

Dembo, Jonathan. *Unions and Politics in Washington State, 1885–1935.* New York: Garland, 1983.

Dickman, Howard. *Industrial Democracy in America: Ideological Origins of National Labor Policy.* LaSalle, Ill.: Open Court, 1987.

Domhoff, G. William. *The Higher Circles: The Governing Class in America.* New York: Random House, 1970.

——. *The Power Elite and the State: How Policy Is Made in America.* New York: A. deGruyter, 1990.

Donovan, Robert J. *Conflict and Crisis: The Presidency of Harry S Truman, 1945–1948.* New York: W. W. Norton, 1977.

Dubofsky, Melvyn. *Industrialism and the American Worker, 1865–1920.* 2d ed. Arlington Heights, Ill.: Harlan Davidson, 1985.

——. *We Shall Be All: A History of the IWW.* Chicago: Quadrangle Books, 1969.

Dubofsky, Melvyn, and Warren Van Tine. *John L. Lewis: A Biography.* New York: Times Books, 1977.

——, eds. *Labor Leaders in America.* Urbana: University of Illinois Press, 1987.

Dulles, Foster Rhea, and Melvyn Dubofsky. *Labor in America: A History.* Arlington Heights, Ill.: Harlan Davidson, 1984.

Dunlop, John T. *Industrial Relations Systems.* New York: Holt, 1958.

Edsall, Thomas Byrne. *Chain Reaction: The Impact of Race, Rights, and Taxes on American Politics.* New York: W. W. Norton, 1991.

Edwards, Paul K. *Strikes in the United States, 1881–1974.* New York: St. Martin's Press, 1981.

Eggert, Gerald G. *Railroad Labor Disputes: The Beginnings of Federal Strike Policy.* Ann Arbor: University of Michigan Press, 1967.

———. *Richard Olney, Evolution of a Statesman.* University Park: Pennsylvania State University Press, 1974.

Eisner, J. Michael. *William Morris Leiserson: A Biography.* Madison: University of Wisconsin Press, 1967.

Evans, Peter B., Dietrich Rueschmeyer, and Theda Skocpol. *Bringing the State Back In.* New York: Cambridge University Press, 1985.

Fausold, Martin L. *The Presidency of Herbert C. Hoover.* Lawrence: University of Kansas Press, 1985.

———, ed. *The Hoover Presidency: A Reappraisal.* Albany: State University of New York Press, 1974.

Ferrell, Robert H., ed. *The Eisenhower Diaries.* New York: W. W. Norton, 1981.

Fine, Sidney. *The Automobile under the Blue Eagle.* Ann Arbor: University of Michigan Press, 1963.

———. *Frank Murphy: The New Deal Years.* Chicago: University of Chicago Press, 1979.

———. *Frank Murphy: The Washington Years.* Ann Arbor: University of Michigan Press, 1984.

———. *Sit-Down: The General Motors Strike of 1936–1937.* Ann Arbor: University of Michigan Press, 1969.

Fink, Leon. *Workingmen's Democracy: The Knights of Labor and American Politics.* Urbana: University of Illinois Press, 1983.

Finley, Joseph I. *The Corrupt Kingdom: The Rise and Fall of the United Mine Workers.* New York: Simon and Schuster, 1972.

Foner, Eric. *Politics and Ideology in the Age of the Civil War.* New York: Oxford University Press, 1980.

Foner, Philip S. *Organized Labor and the Black Worker, 1619–1973.* New York: Praeger, 1974.

Forbath, William E. *Law and the Shaping of the American Labor Movement.* Cambridge: Harvard University Press, 1991.

Foster, James C. *The Union Politic: The CIO Political Action Committee.* Columbia: University of Missouri Press, 1975.

Fox-Genovese, Elizabeth, and Eugene Genovese. *Fruits of Merchant Capital.* New York: Cambridge University Press, 1983.

Frankfurter, Felix, and Nathan Greene. *The Labor Injunction.* Reprint. Gloucester, Mass.: Peter Smith, 1963.

Fraser, Steven. *Labor Will Rule: Sidney Hillman and the Rise of American Labor.* New York: Free Press, 1991.

Fraser, Steve, and Gary Gerstle, eds. *The Rise and Fall of the New Deal Order, 1930–1980.* Princeton: Princeton University Press, 1989.

Freeman, James, and Richard Medoff. *What Do Unions Do?* New York: Basic Books, 1984.

Freeman, Joshua B. *In Transit: The Transport Workers Union in New York City, 1933–1966*. New York: Oxford University Press, 1989.

Freidel, Frank. *Franklin D. Roosevelt: A Rendezvous with Destiny*. Boston: Little, Brown, 1990.

Furner, Mary O., and Barry Supple. *The State and Economic Knowledge: The American and British Experiences*. New York: Cambridge University Press, 1990.

Gabin, Nancy. *Feminism in the Labor Movement: Women and the United Auto Workers, 1935–1975*. Ithaca: Cornell University Press, 1990.

Galambos, Louis. *Competition and Cooperation: The Emergence of a National Trade Association*. Baltimore: Johns Hopkins University Press, 1966.

Galbraith, John Kenneth. *The Affluent Society*. Boston: Houghton Mifflin, 1958.

——. *American Capitalism: The Concept of Countervailing Power*. Boston: Houghton Mifflin, 1952.

——. *The New Industrial State*. Boston: Houghton Mifflin, 1967.

Galenson, Walter. *The CIO Challenge to the AFL: A History of the American Labor Movement, 1935–1941*. Cambridge: Harvard University Press, 1960.

Galenson, Walter, and John T. Dunlop, eds. *Labor in the Twentieth Century*. New York: Academic Press, 1978.

Gall, Gilbert J. *The Politics of Right to Work, The Labor Federations as Special Interests, 1943–1979*. New York: Greenwood Press, 1988.

Garraty, John A. *Labor and Capital in the Gilded Age*. Boston: Little, Brown, 1968.

Geoghegan, Thomas. *Which Side Are You On? Trying to Be for Labor When It's Flat on Its Back*. New York: Farrar, Straus, and Giroux, 1991.

Gerstle, Gary. *Working-Class Americanism: The Politics of Labor in a Textile City, 1914–1969*. New York: Cambridge University Press, 1989.

Geschwender, James. *Class, Race, and Worker Insurgency: The League of Revolutionary Black Workers*. New York: Cambridge University Press, 1977.

Gitelman, Howard M. *Legacy of the Ludlow Massacre: A Chapter in American Industrial Relations*. Philadelphia: Temple University Press, 1988.

Glendon, Mary Ann. *Rights Talk: The Impoverishment of Political Discourse*. New York: Free Press, 1991.

Goldberg, David J. *A Tale of Three Cities: Labor Organizations and Protest in Paterson, Passaic, and Lawrence, 1916–1921*. New Brunswick, N.J.: Rutgers University Press, 1989.

Goldfield, Michael. *The Decline of Organized Labor in the United States*. Chicago: University of Chicago Press. 1987.

Goldin, Claudia. *Understanding the Gender Gap: An Economic History of American Women*. New York: Oxford University Press, 1990.

Gompers, Samuel. *Seventy Years of Life and Labor*. 2 vols. New York: E. P. Dutton, 1925.

Gould, William. *Black Workers in White Unions: Job Discrimination in the United States*. Ithaca: Cornell University Press, 1977.

Greenstone, J. David. *Labor in American Politics*. Chicago: University of Chicago Press, 1977.

Griffith, Barbara S. *The Crisis of American Labor: Operation Dixie and the Defeat of the CIO*. Philadelphia: Temple University Press, 1988.

Gross, James A. *The Making of the National Labor Relations Board*. Albany: State University of New York Press, 1974.

———. *The Reshaping of the National Labor Relations Board, 1937–1941*. Albany: State University of New York Press, 1981.

Gutman, Herbert. *Work, Culture, and Society in Industrializing America*. New York: Alfred A. Knopf, 1976.

Hall, Jacquelyn Dowd, James Leloudis, Robert Korstad, Mary Murphy, Lu Ann Jones, and Christopher B. Daly. *Like a Family: The Making of a Southern Cotton Mill World*. Chapel Hill: University of North Carolina Press, 1987.

Hamby, Alonzo. *Beyond the New Deal: Harry S. Truman and American Liberalism*. New York: Columbia University Press, 1973.

Harris, Howell John. *The Right to Manage: Industrial Relations Policies of American Business in the 1940s*. Madison: University of Wisconsin Press, 1982.

Hartley, Jr., Fred A. *Our New National Labor Policy, The Taft-Hartley Act, and the Next Steps*. New York: Funk and Wagnalls, 1948.

Hartmann, Susan M. *Truman and the 80th Congress*. Columbia: University of Missouri Press, 1971.

Hattam, Victoria C. *Labor Visions and State Power: The Origins of Business Unionism in the United States*. Princeton: Princeton University Press, 1993.

Hawley, Ellis. *The Great War and the Search for a Modern Order: A History of the American People and Their Institutions, 1917–1933*. 2d ed. New York: St. Martin's Press, 1979.

———. *Herbert Hoover as Secretary of Commerce: Studies in New Era Thought and Practice*. Iowa City: University of Iowa Press, 1981.

———. *The New Deal and the Problem of Monopoly*. Princeton: Princeton University Press, 1966.

Haynes, John. *Dubious Alliance: The Making of Minnesota's DFL Party*. Minneapolis: University of Minnesota Press, 1984.

Hecksher, Charles C. *The New Unionism: Employee Involvement in the Changing Corporation*. New York: Basic Books, 1988.

Hill, Herbert. *Black Labor and the American Legal System*. Washington, D.C.: Bureau of National Affairs, 1977.

Hodges, James A. *New Deal Labor Policy and the Southern Textile Industry, 1933–1941*. Knoxville: University of Tennessee Press, 1988.

Hoover, Herbert C. *Memoirs: The Cabinet and the Presidency, 1920–1933*. New York: Macmillan, 1952.

Hovenkamp, Herbert. *Enterprise and American Law, 1836–1937*. Cambridge: Harvard University Press, 1991.

Hume, Britt. *Death in the Mines: Rebellion and Murder in the United Mine Workers*. New York: Grossman, 1971.

Hunt, E. E. *What the Coal Commission Found*. Baltimore: Johns Hopkins University Press, 1925.

Hutcheson, John P. *The Imperfect Union: A History of Corruption in American Trade Unions*. New York: E. P. Dutton, 1970.

Huthmacher, J. Joseph. *Senator Robert F. Wagner and the Rise of Urban Liberalism*. New York: Atheneum, 1968.

Hyman, Harold M. *Soldiers and Spruce: Origins of the Loyal Legion of Loggers and Lumbermen*. Los Angeles: Institute of Industrial Relations, University of California at Los Angeles, 1963.

Irons, Peter H. *The New Deal Lawyers*. Princeton: Princeton University Press, 1982.
Jackson, Robert M. *The Formation of Craft Labor Markets*. Orlando: Academic Press, 1984.
Jacobson, Julius, ed. *The Negro and the American Labor Movement*. Garden City, N.Y.: Doubleday, 1968.
Jacoby, Sanford. *Employing Bureaucracy: Managers, Unions, and the Transformation of Work in American Industry, 1900–1945*. New York: Columbia University Press, 1985.
Jensen, Richard J. *The Winning of the Midwest: Social and Political Conflict, 1888–96*. Chicago: University of Chicago Press, 1971.
Johnson, Hugh S. *The Blue Eagle from Egg to Earth*. New York: Doubleday, Doran, 1935.
Johnson, James P. *The Politics of Soft-Coal: The Bituminous Industry from World War I through the New Deal*. Urbana: University of Illinois Press, 1979.
Johnston, Eric. *America Unlimited*. Garden City, N.Y.: Doubleday, 1944.
Josephson, Matthew. *Sidney Hillman: Statesman of American Labor*. New York: Doubleday, 1952.
Karson, Marc. *American Labor Unions and Politics, 1900–1918*. Reprint. Boston: Beacon Press, 1965.
Kassalow, Everett M. *Trade Unions and Industrial Relations: An International Comparison*. New York: Random House, 1969.
Katznelson, Ira, and Aristide Zolberg, eds. *Working-Class Formation: Nineteenth-Century Patterns in Western Europe and the United States*. Princeton: Princeton University Press, 1986.
Keeran, Roger. *The Communist Party and the Auto Workers Unions*. Bloomington: Indiana University Press, 1980.
Keller, Morton. *Affairs of State*. Cambridge: Harvard University Press, 1977.
———. *Regulating a New Economy: Public Policy and Economic Change in America, 1919–1933*. Cambridge: Harvard University Press, 1990.
Kennedy, David. *Over Here: The First World War and American Society*. New York: Oxford University Press, 1980.
Kennedy, Robert F. *The Enemy Within*. New York: Harper, 1960.
Kerr, Clark. *Labor and Management in Industrial Society*. Garden City, N.Y.: Doubleday, 1964.
Kerr, Clark, John T. Dunlop, Frederick H. Harbison, and Charles A. Myers. *Industrialism and Industrial Man: The Problems of Labor and Management in Economic Growth*. London: Heinemann, 1962.
Kerr, K. Austin. *American Railroad Politics, 1914–1920*. Pittsburgh: University of Pittsburgh Press, 1968.
Kessler-Harris, Alice. *Out to Work: A History of Wage-Earning Women in the United States*. New York: Oxford University Press, 1982.
———. *A Woman's Wage: Historical Meanings and Social Consequences*. Lexington: University of Kentucky Press, 1990.
Kimeldorf, Howard. *Reds or Rackets? The Making of Radical and Conservative Unions on the Waterfront*. Berkeley: University of California Press, 1988.
Klehr, Harvey. *The Heyday of American Communism*. New York: Basic Books, 1984.
Kleppner, Paul. *The Cross of Culture: A Social Analysis of Midwestern Politics, 1850–1900*. New York: Free Press, 1970.

Kochan, Thomas A., Harry Katz, and Robert McKersie. *The Transformation of American Industrial Relations*. New York: Basic Books, 1986.

Kolko, Gabriel. *Main Currents in American History*. New York: Harper and Row, 1976.

——. *The Triumph of Conservatism: A Reinterpretation of American History, 1900–1916*. New York: Free Press, 1963.

Korpi, Walter. *The Democratic Class Struggle*. London: Routledge, Kegan, and Paul, 1983.

Krause, Paul. *The Battle for Homestead, 1880–1892: Politics, Culture, and Steel*. Pittsburgh: University of Pittsburgh Press, 1992.

Lacey, Michael J., ed. *The Truman Presidency*. New York: Cambridge University Press, 1991.

Laslett, John H. M. *Labor and the Left*. New York: Basic Books, 1970.

Leab, Daniel J. *A Union of Individuals: The Formation of the American Newspaper Guild*. New York: Columbia University Press, 1970.

Lecht, Leonard A. *Experience under Railway Labor Legislation*. New York: Columbia University Press, 1955.

Lee, R. Alton. *Eisenhower and Landrum-Griffin, A Study in Labor-Management Politics*. Lexington: University of Kentucky Press, 1990.

——. *Truman and Taft-Hartley: A Question of Mandate*. Lexington: University of Kentucky Press, 1966.

Leggett, John C. *Class, Race, and Labor: Working-Class Consciousness in Detroit*. New York: Oxford University Press, 1968.

Leiby, James. *Carroll Wright and Labor Reform: The Origins of Labor Statistics*. Cambridge: Harvard University Press, 1960.

Lester, Richard A. *As Unions Mature*. Princeton: Princeton University Press, 1958.

Leuchtenberg, William E. *Franklin D. Roosevelt and the New Deal, 1932–1940*. New York: Harper, 1963.

Levenstein, Harvey A. *Communism, Anti-Communism, and the CIO*. Westport, Conn.: Greenwood Press, 1981.

Lichtenstein, Nelson. *Labor's War at Home: The CIO in World War II*. New York: Cambridge University Press, 1982.

Lincoln, Abraham. *The Collected Works of Abraham Lincoln*. Edited by Roy F. Basler. 4 vols. New Brunswick, N.J.: Rutgers University Press, 1953.

Link, Arthur S. *Wilson: Campaigns for Progressivism and Peace, 1916–1917*. Princeton: Princeton University Press, 1965.

——. *Wilson: The New Freedom*. Princeton: Princeton University Press, 1956.

——. *Wilson: The Road to the White House*. Princeton: Princeton University Press, 1947.

——. *Woodrow Wilson and the Progressive Era, 1910–1917*. New York: Harper, 1954.

Lipset, Seymour Martin. *Consensus and Conflict: Essays in Political Sociology*. New Brunswick, N.J.: Transaction Books, 1986.

——, ed. *Unions in Transition: Entering the Second Century*. San Francisco: Institute for Contemporary Studies, 1986.

Lipsitz, George. *Class and Culture in Cold War America: A Rainbow at Midnight*. New York: Praeger, 1982.

Lombardi, John. *Labor's Voice in the Cabinet*. Reprint. New York: AMS Press, 1968.

Lorwin, Lewis L., and Arthur Wubnig. *Labor Relations Boards: The Regulation of Col-*

lective Bargaining under the National Industrial Recovery Act. Washington: Brookings Institution, 1935.

Lowi, Theodore J. *The End of Liberalism: The Second Republic of the United States*. 2d ed. New York: W. W. Norton, 1979.

Lowitt, Richard. *George W. Norris: The Persistence of a Progressive, 1913–1933*. Urbana: University of Illinois Press, 1971.

McAdams, Alan K. *Power and Politics in Labor Legislation*. New York: Columbia University Press, 1964.

McCoy, Donald R. *The Presidency of Harry S. Truman*. Lawrence: University of Kansas Press, 1984.

McMurry, Donald L. *The Great Burlington Strike of 1888*. Cambridge: Harvard University Press, 1956.

McSeveney, Samuel. *The Politics of Depression: Political Behavior in the Northeast, 1893–1896*. New York: Oxford University Press, 1972.

Maier, Charles. *In Search of Stability: Explorations in Historical Political Economy*. New York: Cambridge University Press, 1987.

———. *Recasting Bourgeois Europe: Stabilization in France, Germany, and Italy after World War I*. Princeton: Princeton University Press, 1975.

Mandel, Bernard. *Samuel Gompers*. Yellow Springs, Ohio: Antioch University Press, 1963.

Marcus, Maeva. *Truman and the Steel Seizure Case: The Limits of Presidential Power*. New York: Columbia University Press, 1977.

Marshall, F. Ray. *The Negro and Organized Labor*. New York: Wiley, 1965.

Martin, George. *Madame Secretary, Frances Perkins*. Boston: Houghton Mifflin, 1976.

Mason, Alpheus T. *Organized Labor and the Law*. Reprint. New York: Arno Press, 1969.

Meier, August, and Elliott Rudwick. *Black Detroit and the Rise of the UAW*. New York: Oxford University Press, 1979.

Miliband, Ralph. *The State in Capitalist Society*. New York: Basic Books, 1969.

Milkman, Ruth. *Gender at Work: The Dynamics of Job Segregation by Sex during World War II*. Urbana: University of Illinois Press, 1987.

———. *Women, Work, and Protest*. New York: Routledge, Kegan, and Paul, 1985.

Millis, Harry A., and Emily Clark Brown. *From the Wagner Act to Taft-Hartley: A Study of National Labor Policy and Labor Relations*. Chicago: University of Chicago Press, 1950.

Mills, C. Wright. *The New Men of Power: America's Labor Leaders*. New York: Harcourt, Brace, 1948.

Montgomery, David. *Beyond Equality: Labor and the Radical Republicans, 1862–1872*. New York: Alfred A. Knopf, 1967.

———. *The Fall of the House of Labor*. New York: Cambridge University Press, 1987.

———. *Workers' Control in America*. New York: Cambridge University Press, 1979.

Moody, J. Carroll, and Alice Kessler-Harris, eds. *Perspectives on American Labor History: The Problems of Synthesis*. De Kalb: Northern Illinois University Press, 1989.

Moody, Kim. *An Injury to All: The Decline of American Unionism*. New York: Verso, 1988.

Morgan, H. Wayne. *From Hayes to McKinley: National Party Politics, 1877–1896*. Syracuse: Syracuse University Press, 1969.

Mowry, George E. *The Era of Theodore Roosevelt, 1900–1912*. New York: Harper, 1958.

Murray, Robert K. *The Harding Era*. Minneapolis: University of Minnesota Press, 1969.

Nash, George H. *The Life of Herbert Hoover: The Engineer, 1874–1914*. New York: W. W. Norton, 1983.

National Civic Federation. *Industrial Conciliation: Reports of the Proceedings of the Conference, December 16 and 17, 1901*. New York, 1902.

Nelson, Daniel. *American Rubber Workers and Organized Labor, 1900–1941*. Princeton: Princeton University Press, 1988.

——. *Managers and Workers: Origins of the New Factory System*. Madison: University of Wisconsin Press, 1975.

Nelson, Donald M. *Arsenal of Democracy: The Story of American War Production*. New York: Harcourt, Brace, 1946.

Northrup, Herbert R. *The Federal Government as Employer: The Federal Labor Relations Authority and the PATCO Challenge*. Philadelphia: Wharton School, 1988.

Ohl, John K. *Hugh S. Johnson and the New Deal*. De Kalb: Northern Illinois University Press, 1985.

Orren, Karen. *Belated Feudalism: Labor, the Law, and Liberal Development in the United States*. New York: Cambridge University Press, 1991.

Ozanne, Robert. *The Labor Movement in Wisconsin*. Madison: University of Wisconsin Press, 1984.

Palladino, Grace. *Another Civil War: Labor, Capital, and the State in the Anthracite Regions of Pennsylvania, 1840–1868*. Urbana: University of Illinois Press, 1990.

Palmer, Bryan. *Descent into Discourse: The Reification of Language and the Writing of Social History*. Philadelphia: Temple University Press, 1990.

Parrish, Michael E. *Felix Frankfurter and His Times: The Reform Years*. New York: Free Press, 1982.

Patterson, James T. *Congressional Conservatives and the New Deal: The Growth of the Conservative Coalition in Congress, 1933–1939*. Lexington: University of Kentucky Press, 1967.

——. *Mr. Republican: A Biography of Robert A. Taft*. Boston: Houghton Mifflin, 1972.

Paul, Arnold M. *Conservative Crisis and the Rule of Law*. New York: Harper and Row, 1969.

Perkins, Frances. *The Roosevelt I Knew*. New York: Harper and Row, 1964.

Pfeffer, Paula. *A. Philip Randolph, Pioneer of the Civil Rights Movement*. Baton Rouge: Louisiana State University Press, 1990.

Phillips, Harlan B. *Felix Frankfurter Reminisces*. New York: Reynal, 1960.

Piore, Michael J., and Charles F. Sabel. *The Second Industrial Divide: Possibilities for Prosperity*. New York: Basic Books, 1984.

Polenberg, Richard. *Reorganizing the Government: The Controversy over Executive Reorganization*. Cambridge: Harvard University Press, 1966.

Pringle, Henry F. *The Life and Times of William Howard Taft*. 2 vols. New York: Farrar and Rinehart, 1939.

Przeworski, Adam. *Capitalism and Social Democracy*. New York: Cambridge University Press, 1985.

——. *Paper Stones: A History of Electoral Socialism*. Chicago: University of Chicago Press, 1986.

Radosh, Ronald. *American Labor and United States Foreign Policy*. New York: Random House, 1969.

Radosh, Ronald, and Murray Rothbard, eds. *A New History of Leviathan: Essays on the Rise of the American Corporate State*. New York: E. P. Dutton, 1972.

Ramirez, Bruno. *When Workers Fight: The Politics of Industrial Relations in the Progressive Era, 1898–1916*. Westport, Conn.: Greenwood Press, 1978.

Randall, James G. *Lincoln the Liberal Statesman*. London: Eyre and Spottiswoode, n.d.

Reed, Merl E. *Seedtime for the Modern Civil Rights Movement: The President's Committee on Fair Employment Practices, 1941–1946*. Baton Rouge: Louisiana State University Press, 1991.

Reichard, Gary W. *The Reaffirmation of Republicanism: Eisenhower and the Eighty-third Congress*. Knoxville: University of Tennessee Press, 1975.

Renshaw, Patrick. *American Labour and Consensus Capitalism, 1935–1990*. London: Macmillan, 1991.

Roediger, David. *The Wages of Whiteness: Race and the Making of the American Working Class*. New York: Verso, 1991.

Romasco, Albert U. *The Poverty of Abundance: Hoover, the Nation, and the Depression*. New York: Oxford University Press, 1965.

Roosevelt, Franklin D. *The Public Papers and Addresses of Franklin D. Roosevelt*. Edited by Samuel I. Rosenman. 13 vols. New York: Random House, 1938–50.

Roosevelt, Theodore. *The Letters of Theodore Roosevelt*. Edited by Elting Morison. 8 vols. Cambridge: Harvard University Press, 1951–54.

Rosswurm, Steve, ed. *The CIO's Left-Led Unions*. New Brunswick, N.J.: Rutgers University Press, 1992.

Salvatore, Nick. *Eugene V. Debs: Citizen and Socialist*. Urbana: University of Illinois Press, 1982.

Schatz, Ronald W. *The Electrical Workers: A History of Labor at General Electric and Westinghouse, 1923–1960*. Urbana: University of Illinois Press, 1983.

Schlesinger, Jr., Arthur M. *The Coming of the New Deal*. Boston: Houghton Mifflin, 1959.

Schmitter, Phillipe C. *Patterns of Corporatist Policy-making*. Beverly Hills: Sage Publications, 1982.

———. *Trends toward Corporate Intermediation*. Beverly Hills: Sage Publications, 1979.

Schnapper, M. B., ed. *The Truman Program: Addresses and Messages by President Harry S. Truman*. Washington, D.C.: Public Affairs Press, 1949.

Schwarz, Jordan. *The Speculator: Bernard Baruch in Washington, 1917–1965*. Chapel Hill: University of North Carolina Press, 1981.

Scott, Joan. *Gender and the Politics of History*. New York: Columbia University Press, 1988.

Seidman, Joel. *American Labor from Defense to Reconversion*. Chicago: University of Chicago Press, 1953.

Serrin, William. *The Company and the Union: The "Civilized Relationship" of the General Motors Corporation and the United Automobile Workers*. New York: A. A. Knopf, 1973.

Shaiken, Harley. *Work Transformed: Automation and Labor in the Computer Age*. New York: Holt, Rinehart, Winston, 1984.

Shils, Edward B., Walter J. Gershenfeld, Bernard Ingster, and William W. Weinberg. *Industrial Peacemaker: George W. Taylor's Contributions to Collective Bargaining*. Philadelphia: University of Pennsylvania Press, 1979.

Shostak, Arthur B. *The Air Controllers' Controversy: Lessons from the PATCO Strike.* New York: Human Sciences Press, 1981.

Silverberg, Louis G., ed. *The Wagner Act: After Ten Years.* Washington, D.C.: Bureau of National Affairs, 1945.

Sklar, Martin. *The Corporate Reconstruction of American Capitalism, 1890–1916: The Market, the Law, and Politics*: New York: Cambridge University Press, 1988.

Skowronek, Stephen. *Building A New American State: The Expansion of National Administrative Capacities, 1877–1920.* New York: Cambridge University Press, 1982.

Somers, Gerald G., ed. *Essays in Industrial Relations Theory.* Ames: Iowa State University Press, 1969.

Stave, Bruce. *The New Deal and the Last Hurrah: Pittsburgh Machine Politics.* Pittsburgh: University of Pittsburgh Press, 1970.

Strauss, George, Daniel G. Gallagher, and Jack Fiorito. *The State of the Unions.* Madison, Wis.: Industrial Relations Research Association, 1991.

Taft, Philip S. *The A. F. of L. from the Death of Gompers to the Merger.* New York: Harper, 1959.

Thieblot, Jr., Armand J., and Thomas R. Haggard. *Union Violence: The Record and the Response by Courts, Legislatures, and the NLRB.* Philadelphia: Wharton School, 1983.

Thompson, E. P. *Whigs and Hunters: The Origins of the Black Act.* New York: Pantheon, 1975.

Tomlins, Christopher L. *The State and the Unions: Labor Relations, Law, and the Organized Labor Movement in America, 1880–1960.* New York: Cambridge University Press, 1986.

Trout, Charles. *Boston, the Great Depression, and the New Deal.* New York: Oxford University Press, 1977.

Troy, Leo. *Distribution of Union Membership among the States, 1939 and 1953.* New York: National Bureau of Economic Research, 1957.

———. *Trade Union Membership, 1897–1962.* New York: National Bureau of Economic Research, 1965.

Truman, Harry S. *Memoirs, Volume Two: Years of Trial and Hope.* Garden City, N.Y.: Doubleday, 1956.

Twiss, Benjamin R. *Lawyers and the Constitution.* Princeton: Princeton University Press, 1942.

Ulman, Lloyd D. *The Rise of the National Trade Union.* Cambridge: Harvard University Press, 1955.

Vadney, Thomas E. *The Wayward Liberal: A Political Biography of Donald Richberg.* Lexington: University of Kentucky Press, 1970.

Valelly, Richard M. *Radicalism in the States: the Minnesota-Farmer Labor Party and the American Political Economy.* Chicago: University of Chicago Press, 1989.

Vittoz, Stanley. *New Deal Labor Policy and the American Industrial Economy.* Chapel Hill: University of North Carolina Press, 1987.

Wall, Joseph F. *Andrew Carnegie.* New York: Oxford University Press, 1970.

Wallerstein, Immanuel, ed. *Labor in the World Social Structure.* Beverly Hills: Sage Publications, 1983.

Wehle, Louis. *Hidden Threads in History.* New York: Macmillan, 1953.

Weiler, Paul C. *Governing the Workplace: The Future of Labor and Employment Law.* Cambridge: Harvard University Press, 1990.

Weinstein, James. *The Corporate Ideal in the Liberal State*. Boston: Beacon Press, 1968.
———. *The Decline of Socialism in America, 1912–1925*. New York: Monthly Review Press, 1967.
Weinstein, James, and David Eakins, eds. *For a New America: Essays in History and Politics from "Studies on the Left" 1959–1967*. New York: Random House, 1970.
Weir, Margaret, Ann Shola Orloff, and Theda Skocpol, eds. *The Politics of Social Policy in the United States*. Princeton: Princeton University Press, 1988.
Weiss, Nancy J. *Farewell to the Party of Lincoln: Black Politics in the Age of FDR*. Princeton: Princeton University Press, 1983.
Wiebe, Robert. *Businessmen and Reform: A Study of the Progressive Movement*. Cambridge: Harvard University Press, 1962.
———. *The Search for Order, 1877–1920*. New York: Hill and Wang, 1977.
Wiener, Lynn. *From Working Girl to Working Mother: The Female Labor Force in the United States*. Chapel Hill: University of North Carolina Press, 1985.
Wilentz, Sean. *Chants Democratic: New York City and the Rise of the American Working Class, 1788–1850*. New York: Princeton University Press, 1984.
Wilson, Joan Hoff. *Herbert Hoover, Forgotten Progressive*. Boston: Little, Brown, 1975.
Witney, Fred. *Wartime Experiences of the National Labor Relations Board, 1941–1945*. Urbana: University of Illinois Press, 1949.
Witte, Edwin E. *The Government in Labor Disputes*. Reprint. New York: Arno, 1969.
Wolf, Harry D. *The Railroad Labor Board*. Chicago: University of Chicago Press, 1927.
Wolff, Leon. *Lockout*. New York: Harper and Row, 1965.
Wunderlin, Jr., Clarence E. *Visions of New Industrial Order: Social Science and Labor Theory in America's Progressive Era*. New York: Cambridge University Press, 1992.
Yellowitz, Irwin. *Labor and the Progressive Movement in New York State, 1897–1916*. Ithaca: Cornell University Press, 1965.
Zieger, Robert H. *John L. Lewis, Labor Leader*. Boston: Twayne, 1988.
———. *Organized Labor in the Twentieth-Century South*. Knoxville: University of Tennessee Press, 1991.
———. *Rebuilding the Pulp and Paper Workers' Union, 1933–1941*. Knoxville: University of Tennessee Press, 1984.
———. *Republicans and Labor, 1919–1929*. Lexington: University of Kentucky Press, 1969.

Articles and Essays

Atleson, James. "Reflections on Labor, Power, and Society." *Maryland Law Review* 45 (1986): 841–72.
Avery, Dianne. "Images of Violence in Labor Jurisprudence: The Regulation of Picketing and Boycotts, 1894–1921." *Buffalo Law Review* 37 (Winter 1988–89): 3–117.
Baron, Ava. "Gender and Labor History: Learning from the Past, Looking to the Future." In *Work Engendered: Toward a New History of American Labor*, edited by Ava Baron, 1946. Ithaca, N.Y.: Cornell University Press, 1991.
Bernstein, Barton. "The Truman Administration and the Steel Strike of 1946." *Journal of American History* 52 (1966): 791–803.
———. "Walter Reuther and the General Motors Strike of 1945–1946." *Michigan History* 49 (1965): 260–77.

Bernstein, Irving. "The Growth of American Unions." *American Economic Review* 44 (June 1954): 301–18.

———. "The Growth of American Unions, 1945–1960." *Labor History* 2 (Spring 1961): 131–57.

———. "Union Growth and Structural Cycles." In Industrial Relations Research Association, *Annual Proceedings* (1954): 202–246.

Best, Gary Dean. "President Wilson's Second Industrial Conference, 1919–1920." *Labor History* 16 (Fall 1975): 505–20.

Block, Fred. "The Ruling Class Does Not Rule: Notes on the Marxist Theory of the State." *Socialist Revolution*, no. 33 (May–June 1977): 6–28.

Blum, Albert A. "Why Unions Grow." *Labor History* 9 (Winter 1968): 39–72.

Brinkley, Alan. "The New Deal and the Idea of the State." In *The Rise and Fall of the New Deal Order, 1930–1980*, edited by Steve Fraser and Gary Gerstle, 85–121. Princeton: Princeton University Press, 1989.

Brooks, Tom. "Black Upsurge in the Unions." *Dissent* (March–April 1970): 124–34.

———. "Negro Militants, Jewish Liberals, and the Unions." *Commentary* (September 1961): 209–16.

Bucki, Cecilia. "Dilution and Craft Tradition: Bridgeport, Connecticut Munitions Workers, 1915–1919." *Social Science History* 4 (February 1980): 105–24.

Buhle, Mari Jo. "Gender and Labor History." In *Perspectives on American Labor History: The Problems of Synthesis*, edited by J. Carroll Moody and Alice Kessler-Harris, 55–79. De Kalb: Northern Illinois University Press, 1989.

Casebeer, Kenneth M. "Drafting Wagner's Act: Leon Keyserling and the Precommittee Drafts of the Labor Disputes Act and the National Labor Relations Act." *Industrial Relations Law Journal* 11 (1989): 73–131.

———. "Holder of the Pen: An Interview with Leon Keyserling on Drafting the Wagner Act." *University of Miami Law Review* 42 (November 1987): 285–363.

Cohen, Julius, and Lillian Cohen. "The National Labor Relations Board in Retrospect." *Industrial and Labor Relations Review* 1 (1948): 649–50.

Cox, Archibald. "The Legal Nature of Collective Bargaining Agreements." *Michigan Law Review* 57 (November 1958): 1–36.

———. "Rights under a Labor Agreement." *Harvard Law Review* 69 (February 1956): 601–57.

Cox, Archibald, and John T. Dunlop. "The Duty to Bargain Collectively during the Term of an Existing Agreement." *Harvard Law Review* 63 (May 1950): 1097–1133.

———. "Regulation of Collective Bargaining by the National Labor Relations Board." *Harvard Law Review* 63 (January 1950): 389–432.

Cuff, Robert D. "The Politics of Labor Administration in World War I." *Labor History* 21 (Fall 1980): 546–69.

Dawley, Allan. "Workers, Capital, and the State in the Twentieth Century." In *Perspectives on American Labor History: The Problems of Synthesis*, edited by J. Carroll Moody and Alice Kessler-Harris, 152–200. De Kalb: Northern Illinois University Press, 1989.

Dubofsky, Melvyn. "Gli operai dell'industria statunitense e i partiti politici da Roosevelt a Reagan." In *Il partito americano e l'Europa*, edited by Maurizio Vaudagna, 211–35. Milan: Feltrinelli, 1991.

———. "James H. Hawley and the Origins of the Haywood Case, 1892–1899." *Pacific Northwest Quarterly* 58 (January 1967): 23–27.

———. "Legal Theory and Workers' Rights: A Historian's Critique." *Industrial Relations Law Journal* 4 (1981): 496–502.

———. "Workers' Movements in North America, 1873–1970: A Preliminary Analysis." In *Labor in the World Social Structure*, edited by Immanuel Wallerstein, 22–43. Beverly Hills: Sage Publications, 1983.

Edsall, Thomas Byrne. "The Changing Shape of Power: A Realignment in Public Policy." In *The Rise and Fall of the New Deal Order, 1930–1980*, edited by Steve Fraser and Gary Gerstle, 269–93. Princeton: Princeton University Press, 1989.

Ernst, Daniel R. "The Labor Exemption, 1908–1914." *Iowa Law Review* 74 (July 1989): 1151–73.

Fahy, Charles. "The NLRB and the Courts," In *The Wagner Act: After Ten Years*, edited by Louis G. Silverberg, 43–60. Washington, D.C.: Bureau of National Affairs, 1945.

Feller, David. "A General Theory of the Collective Bargaining Agreement." *California Law Review* 61 (1973): 663–856.

Ferguson, Thomas. "From Normalcy to the New Deal: Industrial Structure, Party Competition, and American Public Policy in the Great Depression." *International Organization* 38 (Winter 1984): 41–94.

Fine, Sidney. "Frank Murphy, the Thornhill Doctrine, and Picketing as Free Speech." *Labor History* 6 (Spring 1965): 99–120.

———. "John L. Lewis Discusses the General Motors Sit-Down Strike: A Document." *Labor History* 15 (Fall 1974): 562–70.

Finegold, Kenneth, and Theda Skocpol. "Explaining New Deal Labor Policy." *The American Political Science Review* 84 (December 1990): 1298–1304.

Fink, Leon. "Clearing It Up with Sidney: A New Labor-Political Synthesis for the Twentieth Century." *Reviews in American History* 20 (September 1992): 366–71.

Finkin, Matthew W. "Does Karl Klare Protest Too Much?" *Maryland Law Review* 44 (1985) 1100–23.

———. "Revisionism in Labor Law." *The Maryland Law Review* 43 (1984): 23–92.

Fox-Genovese, Elizabeth, and Eugene Genovese. "The Political Crisis of Social History: Class Struggle as Subject and Object." In Elizabeth Fox-Genovese and Eugene Genovese, *Fruits of Merchant Capital*, 179–212. New York: Cambridge University Press, 1983.

Fraser, Steven. "From the 'New Unionism' to the New Deal." *Labor History* 25 (Summer 1984): 405–30.

———. "The 'Labor Question.' " In *The Rise and Fall of the New Deal Order, 1930–1980*, edited by Steve Fraser and Gary Gerstle, 55–84. Princeton: Princeton University Press, 1989.

Freedman, Stephen. "Organizing Workers in a Steel Company Town: The Union Movement in Joliet, Illinois, 1870–1920." *Illinois Historical Journal* 79 (Spring 1986): 2–18.

Friedman, Gerald. "Strike Success and Union Ideology: The United States and France, 1880–1914." *Journal of Economic History* 48 (March 1988) 1–26.

———. "Worker Militancy and Its Consequences: Political Responses to Labor Unrest in the United States, 1877–1914." *International Labor and Working-Class History*, no. 40 (Fall 1991): 5–17.

Furner, Mary O. "Knowing Capitalism: Public Investigation and the Labor Question in the Long Progressive Era." In *The State and Economic Knowledge: The American and British Experiences*, edited by Mary O. Furner and Barry Supple, 241–86. New York: Cambridge University Press, 1990.

Gabin, Nancy. "Time Out of Mind: The UAW's Response to Female Labor Laws and Mandatory Overtime in the 1960s." In *Work Engendered: Toward a New History of American Labor*, edited by Ava Baron, 351–374. Ithaca, N.Y.: Cornell University Press, 1991.

Gall, Gilbert J. "CIO Leaders and the Democratic Alliance: The Case of the Smith Committee and the NLRB." *Labor Studies Journal* 14 (Summer 1989): 3–27.

———. "Heber Blankenhorn: The Publicist as Reformer." *The Historian* 45 (August 1983): 513–28.

———. "A Note on Lee Pressman and the FBI." *Labor History* 32 (Fall 1991): 551–61.

Gerber, Larry G. "The United States and Canadian National Industrial Conferences of 1919: A Comparative Analysis." *Labor History* 32 (Winter 1991): 42–65.

Gold, David, Clarence Y. H. Lo, and Erik Olin Wright, "Recent Developments in Marxist Theories of the Capitalist State." *Monthly Review* 27 (October 1975): 29–43, and 27 (November 1975): 36–51.

Goldfield, Michael. "Worker Insurgency, Radical Organization, and New Deal Labor Legislation." *American Political Science Review* 83 (December 1989): 1257–82.

Gordon, Michael. "The Labor Boycott in New York City, 1880–1886." *Labor History* 16 (1975): 184–229.

Gorman, Robert A., and Matthew W. Finkin. "The Individual and the Requirement of 'Concert' under the National Labor Relations Act." *University of Pennsylvania Law Review* 130 (December 1981): 332–36.

Gowaskie, Joseph. "John Mitchell and the Anthracite Mine Workers: Leadership Conservatism and Rank-and-File Militancy." *Labor History* 27 (Winter 1985–86): 54–83.

Greene, Julia. " 'The Strike at the Ballot Box': The American Federation of Labor's Entrance into Election Politics, 1906–1909." *Labor History* 32 (Spring 1991) 165–92.

Griffith, Robert. "Dwight D. Eisenhower and the Corporate Commonwealth." *American Historical Review* 87 (February 1982): 87–122.

Grin, Carolyn. "The Unemployment Conference of 1921." *Mid-America* 55 (April 1973): 83–107.

Halpern, Rick. "Interracial Unionism in the Southwest: Fort Worth's Packinghouse Workers, 1937–1954." In *Organized Labor in the Twentieth-Century South*, edited by Robert H. Zieger, 158–82. Knoxville: University of Tennessee Press, 1991.

Hanna, Marcus A. "Industrial Conciliation and Arbitration." *Annals of the American Academy of Political and Social Science* 20 (July 1902): 21–26.

Harris, William H. "Federal Intervention in Union Discrimination: FEPC and West Coast Shipyards during World War II." *Labor History* 22 (1981): 325–47.

Hattam, Victoria. "Economic Visions and Political Strategies: American Labor and the State, 1865–1896." *Studies in American Political Development* 4 (1990): 82–129.

Hawley, Ellis. "Herbert Hoover and American Corporatism, 1929–1933," In *The Hoover Presidency: A Reappraisal*, edited by Martin L. Fausold, 101–19. Albany: State University of New York Press, 1974.

———. "Herbert Hoover and Economic Stabilization, 1921–1922." In *Herbert Hoover as Secretary of Commerce: Studies in New Era Thought and Practice*, edited by Ellis Hawley, 43–60. Iowa City: University of Iowa Press, 1981.

Helfand, Barry F. "Labor and the Courts: The Common Law Doctrine of Criminal Conspiracy and Its Application in the Buck's Stove Case." *Labor History* 18 (Winter 1977): 91–114.

Hill, Herbert. "Black Labor, the NLRB, and the Developing Law of Equal Employment Opportunity." *Labor Law Journal* (April 1975): 207–10.

———. "The Equal Employment Opportunity Acts of 1964 and 1972: A Critical Analysis of the Legislative History and Administration of the Law." *Industrial Relations Law Journal* 2 (Spring 1977): 1–96.

———. "The National Labor Relations Act and the Emergence of Civil Rights Law: A New Priority in Federal Labor Policy." *Harvard Civil Rights–Civil Liberties Law Review* 11 (Spring 1976): 299–334.

Honey, Michael. "Industrial Unionism and Racial Justice in Memphis." In *Organized Labor in the Twentieth-Century South*, edited by Robert H. Zieger, 135–57. Knoxville: University of Tennessee Press, 1991.

———. "Operation Dixie." *Labor History* 31 (Summer 1990): 373–78.

Hovenkamp, Herbert. "Labor Conspiracies in American Law, 1880–1930." *Texas Law Review* 66 (April 1988): 919–65.

Hurvitz, Haggai. "American Labor Law and the Doctrine of Entrepreneurial Property Rights: Boycotts, Courts, and the Juridical Reorientation of 1886–1895." *Industrial Relations Law Journal* 8 (1986): 307–61.

———. "Ideology and Industrial Conflict: President Wilson's First Industrial Conference of October 1919." *Labor History* 18 (Fall 1977): 516–22.

Huthmacher, J. Joseph. "Urban Liberalism and the Age of Reform." *Mississippi Valley Historical Review* 49 (September 1962): 231–41.

Jacoby, Sanford. "Norms and Cycles: The Dynamics of Nonunion Industrial Relations in the United States, 1897–1985." In *New Developments in Human Resources and Labor Markets*, edited by Katherine Abraham and Robert McKersie. Cambridge, Mass., forthcoming.

———. "Reckoning with Company Unions: The Case of Thompson Products, 1934– 1964." Paper presented at the conference "Historical Perspectives on American Labor: An Interdisciplinary Approach," New York State School of Industrial and Labor Relations, Cornell University, Ithaca, April 1988.

———. "Union-Management Cooperation in the United States, 1915–1945." Paper presented at the Third U.S.-U.S.S.R. Colloquium on World Labor and Social Change, State University of New York at Binghamton, November 18–20, 1982.

Jensen, Billie Barnes. "Woodrow Wilson's Intervention in the Coal Strike of 1914." *Labor History* 15 (Winter 1974): 63–77.

Jessop, Bob. "Recent Theories of the Capitalist State." *Cambridge Journal of Economics* 1 (December 1977): 352–73.

Johnson, James P. "Drafting the NRA Code of Fair Competition for the Bituminous Coal Industry." *Journal of American History* 53 (December 1966): 521–41.

Juravich, Tom. "Beyond the Myths of '84: Union Members and the Presidential Election." *Labor Studies Journal* 11 (Fall 1986): 135–48.

Karson, Marc, and Ronald Radosh. "The AFL and the Negro Worker." In *The Negro and the American Labor Movement*, edited by Julius Jacobson, 163–73. Garden City, N.Y.: Doubleday, 1968.

Katznelson, Ira. "Working-Class Formation: Constructing Cases and Comparisons." In *Working-Class Formation: Nineteenth-Century Patterns in Western Europe and the United States*, edited by Ira Katznelson and Aristide Zolberg, 1–21. Princeton: Princeton University Press, 1986.

Kessler-Harris, Alice. "A New Agenda for American Labor History: A Gendered Analysis and the Question of Class." In *Perspectives on American Labor History: The Problems of Synthesis*, edited by J. Carroll Moody and Alice Kessler-Harris, 217–34. De Kalb: Northern Illinois University Press, 1989.

Keyserling, Leon. "The Wagner Act: Its Origins and Current Significance." *George Washington Law Review* 29 (December 1960): 199–233.

———. "Why the Wagner Act?" In *The Wagner Act: After Ten Years*, edited by Louis G. Silverberg, 5–33. Washington, D.C.: Bureau of National Affairs, 1945.

Klare, Karl. "Judicial Deradicalization of the Wagner Act and the Origins of Modern Legal Consciousness." *Minnesota Law Review* 62 (1978): 265–339.

———. "Labor Law as Ideology: Toward a New Historiography of Collective Bargaining Law." *Industrial Relations Law Journal* 4 (1981): 450–82.

———. "Lost Opportunity: Concluding Thoughts on the Finkin Critique." *Maryland Law Review* 44 (1985): 1100–23.

———. "Traditional Labor Law Scholarship and the Crisis of Collective Bargaining." *Maryland Law Review* 44 (1985): 731–840.

Korpi, Walter, and Michael Shalev. "Strikes, Power, and Conflict in the Western Nations, 1900–1976." *Political Power and Social Theory* 1 (1980): 309–16.

Korstad, Robert, and Nelson Lichtenstein. "Opportunities Found and Lost: Labor, Radicals, and the Early Civil Rights Movement." *Journal of American History* 75 (December 1988): 801–6.

Kutler, Stanley I. "Labor, the Clayton Act, and the Supreme Court." *Labor History* 3 (Winter 1962): 19–38.

Leuchtenberg, William E. "The New Deal and the Analogue of War." In *Change and Continuity in Twentieth-Century America*, edited by John Braeman, David Brody, and Robert Bremner, 81–144. Columbus, O.: Ohio State University Press, 1964.

———. "The Persistence of Political History: Reflections on the Significance of the State in America." *Journal of American History* 73 (December 1986): 585–600.

Lichtenstein, Nelson. "From Corporatism to Collective Bargaining: Organized Labor and the Eclipse of Social Democracy in the Postwar Era." In *The Rise and Fall of the New Deal Order, 1930–1980*, edited by Steve Fraser and Gary Gerstle, 122–52. Princeton: Princeton University Press, 1989.

———. "Labor in the Truman Era: Origins of the 'Private Welfare State.' " In *The Truman Presidency*, edited by Michael J. Lacey, 128–55. New York: Cambridge University Press, 1991.

Lipset, Seymour Martin. "North American Labor Movements: A Comparative Perspective." In *Unions in Transition: Entering the Second Century*, edited by Seymour Martin Lipset, 421–51. San Francisco: Institute for Contemporary Studies, 1986.

Lynd, Staughton. "Beyond 'Labor Relations': 14 Theses on the History of the N.L.R.A. and the Future of the Labor Movement." Paper delivered at the Workshop on Critical Perspectives on the History of American Labor Law, Georgetown Law School, Washington, D.C., June 10, 1987.

———. "Government without Rights: The Labor Law Vision of Archibald Cox." *Industrial Relations Law Journal* 4 (1981): 483–95.

McDonnell, Lawrence. " 'You Are Too Sentimental': Problems and Suggestions for a New Labor History." *Journal of Social History* 17 (Summer 1984): 629–54.

McMurry, Donald L. "The Legal Ancestry of the Pullman Strike Injunctions." *Industrial and Labor Relations Review* 14 (January 1961): 235–56.

Maier, Charles. "The Politics of Productivity: Foundations of American International Economic Policy after World War II." *International Organization* 31 (Autumn 1977): 607–34.

———. "Response." *International Labor and Working-Class History* 32 (Fall 1987): 25–30.

———. "The Two Postwar Eras and the Conditions for Stability in Twentieth-Century Western Europe." *American Historical Review* 86 (April 1981): 327–52.

Milkman, Ruth. "Women Workers, Feminism, and the Labor Movement since the 1960s." In *Women, Work, and Protest*, edited by Ruth Milkman, 300–322. New York: Routledge, Kegan, and Paul, 1985),

Montgomery, David. "The 'New Unionism' and the Transformation of Workers' Consciousness in America, 1909–1922." *Journal of Social History* 7 (1974): 509–29.

———. "Strikes in Nineteenth-Century America." *Social Science History* 4 (February 1980): 81–103.

Nash, Gerald D. "F.D.R. and the World War I Origins of Early New Deal Labor Policy." *Labor History* 1 (Winter 1960): 39–52.

Nelson, Daniel. "The CIO at Bay: Labor Militancy and Politics in Akron, 1936–1938." *Journal of American History* 71 (December 1984): 565–86.

Oestreicher, Richard. "Urban Working-Class Political Behavior and Theories of American Electoral Politics, 1870–1940." *Journal of American History* 74 (March 1988): 1257–86.

Olssen, Erik. "The Making of a Political Machine: The Railroad Unions Enter Politics." *Labor History* 19 (Summer 1978): 373–96.

Orren, Karen. "Liberalism, Money, and the Situation of Organized Labor." In *Public Values and Private Power in American Politics*, edited by J. David Greenstone, 173–206. Chicago: University of Chicago Press, 1982.

———. "Organized Labor and the Invention of Modern Liberalism in the United States." *Studies in American Political Development* 2 (1987): 317–36.

———. "Union Politics and Postwar Liberalism in the United States." *Studies in American Political Development* 1 (1986): 215–52.

Panitch, Leo, and Donald Swartz. "Towards Permanent Exceptionalism: Coercion and Consent in Canadian Industrial Relations." *Labour/Le Travail* 13 (Spring 1984): 133–57.

Peters, Daniel. "Taft-Hartley and the Origins of Landrum-Griffin in the Early Eisenhower Years." Paper presented at the North American Labor History Conference, Toronto, October 24, 1986.

Plotke, David. "The Wagner Act, Again: Politics and Labor, 1935–37." *Studies in American Political Development* 3 (1989): 105–56.

Pomper, Gerald D. "Labor and Congress: The Repeal of Taft-Hartley." *Labor History* 2 (Fall 1961): 323–43.

Prickett, James. "Communist Conspiracy or Wage Dispute? The 1941 Strike at North American Aviation." *Pacific Historical Review* 50 (1981): 215–33.

———. "Some Aspects of the Communist Controversy in the CIO." *Science and Society* 33 (1969): 299–321.

Rabban, David M. "Has the NLRA Hurt Labor? *The State and the Unions*, Christopher L. Tomlins." *University of Chicago Law Review* 54 (Winter 1987): 407–31.

Radosh, Ronald. "The Corporate Ideology of American Labor Leaders from Gompers to Hillman." In *For a New America: Essays in History and Politics from "Studies on the Left" 1959–1967*, edited by James Weinstein and David Eakins, 125–52. New York: Random House, 1970.

———. "The Myth of the New Deal." In *A New History of Leviathan: Essays on the Rise of the American Corporate State*, edited by Ronald Radosh and Murray Rothbard, 146–87. New York: E. P. Dutton, 1972.

Rieder, Jonathan. "The Rise of the 'Silent Majority.' " In *The Rise and Fall of the New Deal Order, 1930–1980*, edited by Steve Fraser and Gary Gerstle, 243–68.

Rodgers, Daniel T. "Republicanism: The Career of a Concept." *Journal of American History* 79 (June 1992): 11–38.

Rogers, Joel. "Divide and Conquer: Further Reflections on the Distinctive Character of American Labor Laws." Paper delivered at the Workshop on Critical Perspectives on the History of American Labor Law, Georgetown Law School, Washington, D.C., June 10, 1987.

Romasco, Albert U. "Herbert Hoover's Policies for Dealing with the Great Depression: The End of the Old Order or the Beginning of the New?" In *The Hoover Presidency: A Reappraisal*, edited by Martin L. Fausold, 69–86. Albany: State University of New York Press, 1974.

Rosen, Sumner. "The CIO Era, 1935–1955." In *The Negro and the American Labor Movement*, edited by Julius Jacobson, 188–208. Garden City, N.Y.: Doubleday, 1968.

Schatz, Ronald. "Philip Murray and the Subordination of the Industrial Unions to the United States Government." In *Labor Leaders in America*, edited by Melvyn Dubofsky and Warren Van Tine, 234–57. Champaign: University of Illinois Press, 1987.

Scheinberg, Stephen J. "Theodore Roosevelt and the A.F. of L.'s Entry into Politics, 1906–1908." *Labor History* 3 (1962): 131–48.

Scott, Joan. "On Language, Gender, and Working-Class History" and the responses by Bryan Palmer, Christine Stansell, and Anson Rabinbach in *International Labor and Working-Class History*, no. 31 (Spring 1987): 1–36.

Shalev, Michael. "The Social Democratic Model and Beyond: Two Generations of Comparative Research on the Welfare State." *Comparative Social Research* 6 (1983): 87–148.

Shapiro, Stanley. "The Great War and Reform." *Labor History* 12 (Summer 1971): 334–35.

Skocpol, Theda. "Bringing the State Back In: Strategies of Analysis in Current Research." In *Bringing the State Back In*, edited by Peter B. Evans, Dietrich Rueschmeyer, and Theda Skocpol, 3–37. New York: Cambridge University Press, 1985.

———. "Political Response to Capitalist Crisis: Neo-Marxist Theories of the State and the New Deal." *Politics and Society* 10 (1980): 155–201.

Skocpol, Theda, and Kenneth Finegold. "State Capacity and Economic Intervention in the Early New Deal." *Political Science Quarterly* 97 (1982): 255–78.

Smith, John S. "Organized Labor and the Government in the Wilson Era, 1913–1921." *Labor History* 3 (Fall 1962): 265–86.

Sofchalk, Donald G. "The Chicago Memorial Day Massacre: An Episode of Mass Action." *Labor History* 6 (1965): 3–43.

Solomon, Benjamin. "Dimensions of Union Growth." *Industrial and Labor Relations Review* 9 (July 1956): 544–61.

Stein, Judith. "Southern Workers in National Unions: Birmingham Steelworkers, 1936–1951." In *Organized Labor in the Twentieth-Century South*, edited by Robert H. Zieger, 183–222. Knoxville: University of Tennessee Press, 1991.

Stone, Katherine. "The Post-War Paradigm in American Labor Law." *Yale Law Journal* 90 (June 1981): 1509–80.

———. "Re-Envisioning Labor Law: A Reply to Finkin." *Maryland Law Review* 44 (1985) 978–1013.

Street, Paul, "Breaking Up Old Hatreds and Breaking through the Fear: The Emergence of the Packinghouse Workers Organizing Committee in Chicago, 1933–1940." *Studies in History and Politics* 5 (1986): 63–82.

———. "Packinghouse Blues." *Chicago History* 16 (Fall 1989): 69–85.

Stromquist, Shelton. "Looking Both Ways: Ideological Crisis and Working Class Recomposition in the 1890s." Paper delivered at the conference "The Future of American Labor History—Toward a Synthesis." Northern Illinois University, 1984.

———. "The Politics of Class: Urban Reform and Working Class Mobilization in Cleveland and Milwaukee, 1890–1910." Paper presented at the annual meeting of the Organization of American Historians, Reno, Nevada, April 1988.

Tomlins, Christopher L. "AFL Unions in the 1930s: Their Performance in Historical Perspective." *Journal of American History* 65 (March 1979): 1021–42.

———. "The New Deal, Collective Bargaining, and the Triumph of Industrial Pluralism." *Industrial and Labor Relations Review* 39 (1985): 19–34.

Troy, Leo. "Labor Representation on American Railways." *Labor History* 2 (Fall 1961): 295–322.

Urofsky, Melvin I. "State Courts and Progressive Legislation during the Progressive Era: A Reevaluation." *Journal of American History* 72 (June 1985): 63–91.

Vittoz, Stanley. "The Economic Foundations of Industrial Politics in the United States and the Emerging Structural Theory of the State in Capitalist Society: The Case of New Deal Labor Policy." *Amerikiastudien* 27 (1987): 365–412.

Walzer, Kenneth. "The Party and the Polling Place: American Communism and an American Labor Party in the 1930s." *Radical History Review* 23 (Spring 1980): 104–35.

Wehle, Louis. "The Adjustments of Labor Disputes." *Quarterly Journal of Economics* 32 (1917–18): 122–41.

———. "Labor Problems in the United States," *Quarterly Journal of Economics* 32 (1917–18): 333–92.

———. "War Labor Policies." *Quarterly Journal of Economics* 33 (1919): 321–43.

Weiler, Paul C. "Promises to Keep: Securing Workers' Rights to Self-Organization under the NLRA." *Harvard Law Review* 96 (June 1983): 1768–1827.

Weir, Margaret, and Theda Skocpol. "State Structures and the Possibilities for 'Keynesian' Responses to the Great Depression in Sweden, Britain, and the United States." In *Bringing the State Back In*, edited by Peter B. Evans, Dietrich Rueschmeyer, and Theda Skocpol, 107–63. New York: Cambridge University Press, 1985.

Weir, Margaret, Ann Shola Orloff, and Theda Skocpol. "Introduction: Understanding American Social Politics" and "Epilogue: The Future of Social Policy in the United

States: Political Constraints and Possibilities." In *The Politics of Social Policy in the United States*, edited by Margaret Weir, Ann Shola Orloff, and Theda Skocpol, 3–27, 421–45. Princeton: Princeton University Press, 1988.

White, W. Thomas. "Immigrants, Radicals, and Trade Unionists: The Railway Workers' Search for Order in the Pacific Northwest, 1895–1916." Unpublished paper.

Wiebe, Robert. "The Anthracite Strike of 1902: A Record of Confusion." *Mississippi Valley Historical Review* 48 (September 1961): 229–51.

Wilentz, Sean. "The Rise of the American Working Class, 1776–1877: A Survey." In *Perspectives on American Labor History: The Problems of Synthesis*, edited by J. Carroll Moody and Alice Kessler-Harris, 83–151. De Kalb: Northern Illinois University Press, 1989.

Zieger, Robert H. "Textile Workers and Historians." In *Organized Labor in the Twentieth-Century South*, edited by Robert H. Zieger, 35–59. Knoxville: University of Tennessee Press, 1991.

Zieran, Gregory. "The Boycott and Working-Class Solidarity in Toledo, Ohio in the 1890s." In *Life and Labor*, edited by Robert Asher and Charles Stephenson, 131–49. Albany: State University of New York Press, 1986.

Dissertations

Blatz, Perry. "Work and Labor Relations in the Anthracite Coal Industry, 1863–1903." Ph.D. diss., Princeton University, 1987.

Boemeke, Manfred F. "The Wilson Administration, Organized Labor, and the Colorado Coal Strike, 1913–1914." Ph.D. diss., Princeton University, 1984.

Davis, Colin. "Bitter Storm: The 1922 National Railroad Shopmen's Strike." Ph.D. diss., State University of New York at Binghamton, 1989.

Greene, Julia. "The Strike at the Ballot Box: The American Federation of Labor, Local Trade Union Leadership, and Political Action." Ph.D. diss., Yale University, 1990.

Hurvitz, Haggai. "The Meaning of Industrial Conflict in Some Ideologies of the Early 1920s: The AFL, Organized Employers, and Herbert Hoover." Ph.D. diss., Columbia University, 1971.

Jones, Dallas Lee. "The Wilson Administration and Organized Labor, 1912–1919." Ph.D. diss., Cornell University, 1954.

McCartin, Joseph. "Labor's Great War: American Workers, Unions, and the State, 1916–1920." Ph.D. diss., State University of New York at Binghamton, 1990.

Sipe, Daniel A. "A Moment of State: The Enactment of the National Labor Relations Act, 1935." Ph.D. diss., University of Pennsylvania, 1981.

Street, Paul. "Working in the Yards: Workers, Managers, and Militants in Chicago's Meatpacking Industry, 1900–1943." Ph.D. diss., State University of New York at Binghamton, 1993.

Tomlins, Christopher L. "The State and the Unions: Federal Labor Relations Policy and the Organized Labor Movement in America, 1935–1955." Ph.D. diss., Johns Hopkins University, 1980.

Vittoz, Stanley. "The American Industrial Economy and the Political Origins of Federal Labor Policy between the World War." Ph.D. diss., York University, Toronto, 1979.

Willard, Timothy A. "Labor and the National War Labor Board, 1942–1945: An Experiment in Corporate Wage Stabilization." Ph.D. diss., University of Toledo, 1984.

Index

Adair v. U.S. (1908), 47

Adams, Graham, Jr., 38

Adamson Act of 1916, 59–60, 61, 110

Advisory Council on Labor, 61

African Americans, 129, 187–88, 198, 221

Agricultural implements industry, 2

Agriculture, U.S. Department of, 234; view of labor, 64

Airplane industry, 172

Allis Chalmers, 172

Alschuler, Samuel, 75

Altgeld, John, 30

Amalgamated Association of Iron, Steel, and Tin Workers, 75

Amalgamated Clothing Workers of America (ACWA), 70, 74, 97, 116

Amalgamated Meat Cutters, 75

American Arbitration Association, 198

American Civil Liberties Union (ACLU), 129

American Communist parties, 77

American Federation of Government Employees, 225

American Federation of Labor (AFL), 31, 38, 78, 84, 121, 133, 151, 156, 167, 204; and voluntarism, xvi, 49; and Erdman Act, 32; and "We Don't Patronize" list, 46; and Democratic party, 49–60, 166, 197; and World War I, 61–76; and First Industrial Conference (1919), 80; and Plumb Plan, 81; and election of 1920, 83; Railway Employee Department (RED), 93–95; losses during the 1920s, 97; and Norris Bill, 104, 255–56 (n. 68); and election of 1932, 107; and appointment of Francis Perkins as secretary of labor, 108; and Black Bill, 111; Franklin Roosevelt's view of, 111; and NIRA Section 7a, 111–12, 123; and strike wave of 1934, 124; protest against automobile code, 126; and Wagner Act, 129, 131, 154–56, 202; and racial discrimination, 129, 187; and John L. Lewis's call for mass-production organizing campaign, 133; and 1935 convention, 133; and rise of CIO, 137–38; criticisms of NLRB and CIO, 146; and Globe doctrine, 150–51; attack on New Deal, 152–53; conflict with CIO, 152–53, 156–57, 163, 199; and election of 1938, 153–54; and Smith Committee investigation, 159; repudiation of sit-down tactic, 164; impact of New Deal reforms on, 166; and World War II, 170–73, 176–79, 182–83; and Labor-Management Charter of 1945, 192; and election of 1946, 195; and Republican party, 199, 210–12; and Taft-Hartley Act, 204, 206, 207, 210, 212; merger with CIO, 208, 212, 217; and election of 1952, 210; and McClellan Committee, 218; and civil rights, 223

American Federation of Labor–Congress of Industrial Organizations (AFL-CIO), 217; and Taft-Hartley Act, 217; and McClellan Committee, 218–19; and election of 1958, 219; and regulation of corruption, 219–20; and civil rights, 223; and Civil Rights Act of 1964, 223–25; and conflict with EEOC, 224; and Great Society reforms, 226; and elections of 1984 and 1988, 230. See also American Federation of Labor; Congress of Industrial Organizations; Trade unionism; *and individual unions*

American Federation of State, County, and Municipal Employees, 225

American Federation of Teachers, 225

American Newspaper Guild, 126

American Railway Union, 28–31

American Steel and Wire Company, 33

American Steel & Wire Co. v. Wire Drawers' and Die Makers' Unions Nos. 1 & 3 et al. (1898), 33

American Steel Foundries v. Tri-Cities Central Trade Council (1921), 88, 144

American Workers' party, 124

Amidon, Charles F., 96

Anarchism, 41, 43

Anthracite coal region of northeastern Pennsylvania, 8, 10–12, 21, 40–44, 189–91

Anthracite Coal Strike Commission of 1902, 42, 44

Anthracite strike of 1902, 40–44

Anticommunists, 200

Antiprofessional strikebreaker bill of 1936, 134

Appeal to Reason, 55–56

Arbitration, 17–19, 32, 42, 75, 78, 213

Armaments industry, 62, 72

Army, U.S., 1, 7, 9–10, 21–22, 28, 30, 34, 41, 43, 57, 79, 90–91, 179, 215

Arthur, Chester A., 13

Arthur, P. M., 26

Ashurst, Henry, 67

Associated Press, 144, 145

Atomic Energy Commission, 216

Automobile Labor Board, 121

Baer, George, 41

Baker, Newton, 64, 65, 66, 68, 69, 70

Baltimore and Ohio Railroad (B&O), 8–9, 95, 101

Barkley, Alben, 100

Baruch, Bernard, 64, 109, 117

Beck, David, 218

Bell, Daniel, 208, 222

Berman, Edward, 95

Bethlehem Steel, 72, 172, 175, 179

Biddle, Francis, 125, 126

Billings, Mont., 62

Bittner, Van, 113

Bituminous Coal Code, 114

Black, Hugo, 111

Blacklist, 56

Blair, Henry W., 12

Blair, John, 14

Blair Committee, 12–13

Blankenhorn, Heber, 134, 138, 141, 145

Block, Fred, xiv, xv

Board of Arbitration and Conciliation, 58

Bolshevik Revolution, 76

Bourquin, George M., 96

Boycotts, 4, 20, 21, 26, 29, 45–47, 52, 56, 218

Boyle, Anthony "Tony," 222

Brandeis, Louis, 58, 70, 101, 145

Brennan, William, 213

Brewer, David J., 26–27

Bridgeport, Conn., 72

Bridges, Harry, 124

Brody, David, xvii, 38, 75, 214

Brotherhood of Locomotive Engineers, 20, 25–26, 38, 44. *See also* Railroad brotherhoods

Brotherhood of Railway Carmen, 74, 96. *See also* Railroad brotherhoods

Brotherhood of Sleeping Car Porters, 187. *See also* Railroad brotherhoods

Bruce, Robert, 8

Bryan, William Jennings, 51

Buck's Stove and Range Company, 46–47

Budd Company, 118

Bureau of Labor: federal, 13, 17, 19; state, 13–14

Burke, Edward R., 151

Burleson, Albert S., 64

Business cycles, xvi, 226

Business depressions, 2, 8, 27–28, 86, 87, 102–5, 138

Business-Labor Advisory Council, 227

Byrd, Harry, 173, 174

Byrnes, James, 134, 147

Canadian labor, xiii, xv–xvi

Canal workers, 7, 10

Cantonments, 66, 72
Carey, Ron, 223
Carnegie, Andrew, 24, 28–29
Carnegie Company, 22
Carter, Jimmy, 227, 228
Carter Coal case (1936), 132, 142
Case, Francis, 194
Catton, Bruce, 178, 186
Central Competitive Field (CCF), 89, 98
Central Railroad of Georgia, 25
Century Magazine, 30
Chandler, Alfred D., Jr., 2
Chicago, Burlington, and Quincy Railroad (CB&Q), 20
Child labor, 44, 58, 78, 111
Children's Bureau, 52
Christian Socialist, 46
Cincinnati Typographical Union No. 3, 21
Civil Rights Act of 1964, 223–25
Clark, Champ, 53
Clarke, E. E., 42
Class consciousness, 40, 50, 51, 207, 233–37
Clayton Antitrust Act of 1914, 56–57, 60, 85, 87–88, 96, 101, 103, 110, 127, 165
Clerks and Maintenance of Way workers, 93, 96
Cleveland, Grover: call for railroad arbitration commission, 17–19; and election of 1892, 21–24; and labor, 27–31; and Pullman Boycott of 1894, 29–32, 94
Clifford, Clark, 195
Closed-shop agreements, 16, 21–22, 34, 38, 43, 48, 62, 65, 72, 73, 127, 173, 179, 247 (n. 28)
Coal industry, xvii, 38, 40, 74, 79, 89, 103, 113
Coeur d'Alenes, 21–24, 34
Collective bargaining, xiii, xv, 1, 32, 38, 55, 75, 185, 198, 203, 212–13
Colorado Fuel and Iron Company, 55
Commerce, U.S. Department of: view of labor, 64
Commission on Industrial Relations (CIR), 54–55, 109, 119, 130–31, 156, 166
Committee for Industrial Organization, 133–35

Common law conspiracy, 7, 15–16, 20, 29, 45, 48
Common law of labor relations, 117, 124–25, 212–13
Commons, John R., 55, 109, 124, 131, 156
Common situs picketing, 206
Communist party, 129, 156, 161, 203
Communists, 124, 200
Company unions, 55, 101, 117. *See also* Employee representation plans
Conference for Progressive Political Action (CPPA), 98
Congress, U.S., 28, 29, 234; agrarian and republican heritage, 4; and military appropriations, 12; and labor, 14, 57, 110, 164; and upheaval of 1886, 16–19; and Sherman Antitrust Act, 25; and Pullman Boycott of 1894, 30–31; and Erdman Act, 32; and Industrial Commission Bill, 33; Theodore Roosevelt's messages to, 39–40, 44, 50; and AFL, 49; and Clayton Act, 56; and Adamson Act, 59–60; denunciation of IWW, 67; and mandatory arbitration, 78; and Transportation Act, 81; and election of 1922, 98; and Railway Labor Act, 100–101; and election of 1932, 103; and Norris-LaGuardia Act, 104; and NIRA, 112; and election of 1934, 127; and antiprofessional strikebreaker bill of 1936, 134; and election of 1936, 135; rejection of Roosevelt's reforms of 1937, 138; and antistrike bills, 147–48, 183; opposition to New Deal labor policies, 151, 154–58, 167; and charges of Communist influence in unions, 161; denunciation of sit-down strikes as a violation of public policy, 163–64; differences with Supreme Court, 164; stalled antilabor initiatives, 169; and labor during World War II, 173–75; dilutes authority of NLRB, 183; and UMW strike of 1943, 190; and Smith-Connally Act, 190; and antilabor amendments to NLRA, 191–92, 194, 201; denunciations of labor and radicalism, 194; and election of 1946, 195,

201; and Full Employment Act, 197–98; and Taft-Hartley Act, 202–8, 209, 268 (n. 20); and election of 1953, 210; and 1951 seizure of steel industry, 215; and McClellan Committee, 218–19; and election of 1958, 219; and end of labor regulation, 222; and Great Society reforms, 226; and election of 1976, 227

Congress of Industrial Organizations (CIO), 146–49, 156, 167; and organization of General Motors and United States Steel, 137; support of New Deal Democrats, 137; connections with LaFollette Committee, 139; legitimated by UAW triumph over General Motors, 141; and United States Steel–SWOC settlement, 141–42; support for Roosevelt's reform efforts, 143; and African Americans, 146, 188; and recession of 1937, 149; and Roosevelt's withdrawal of support, 149; NLRB's view of, 150–51; and House Committee on Un-American Activities, 152; conflict with AFL, 152–53, 156–57, 163, 199; and election of 1938, 153–54; and Smith Committee investigation, 158, 160; repudiation of sit-down tactic, 164; impact of New Deal reforms on, 166; and Democratic party, 166, 197; and World War II, 169–70, 171–73, 176–79, 182–88; and maintenance of membership clauses, 184; and tripartite committees, 186–87; and FEPC, 187–88; and Labor-Management Charter of 1945, 192; and PAC, 192–93, 199; and Truman's 1945 labor-management conference, 193; and election of 1946, 195; internal wars of, 199, 200; and Democratic party, 199, 216; and Operation Dixie, 200, 206–7; and Taft-Hartley Act, 204, 206, 207, 212; merger with AFL, 208, 212, 217; and Dwight D. Eisenhower, 216

Connery, William, 147

Connery Bill of 1935, 128

Constitution, U.S., 17, 20, 25, 30–31, 48, 101, 132, 143

Construction industry, 66

Contract labor, 14

Coolidge, Calvin, 98, 103; appeals to workers, 98; and John L. Lewis, 99; and Jacksonville Agreement of 1924, 99; and railroad labor reform, 100–101

Cooper, Jerry, 23

Copper industry, 67, 70

Copper miners, 62, 63

Corporate liberalism, xiv, 55, 192, 240 (n. 13); and AFL, 80

Corporatism, 192, 210, 245 (n. 101)

Costigan, Edward, 110, 130

Council on National Defense (CND), 61, 64–65, 67, 69

Cox, Archibald, 212, 219

Coxey's industrial army, 28

Craft unionism, xvi, 272 (n. 70)

Cummings, Homer, 125

Cummins, Albert, 56

Cutting, Bronson, 110, 123

Danbury Hatters, 47, 60

Daniel, Price, 174

Daniels, Josephus, 64

Daugherty, Harry, 94, 95

David, William H., 178, 181

Davis, James J., 86, 87, 90, 94, 95, 99

Davis, John, 52, 98

Davis, William H., 178, 183

Dayton, Alston G., 47–48

Debs, Eugene V., 29–32, 53

Debs case, 95

Democratic party: and tariffs, 6; and free trade, 19; and election of 1892, 22–23; and AFL, 49–60, 61, 166, 197; Democratic National Committee, 51, 53; and elections of 1918 and 1920, 83; and election of 1922, 98; and election of 1932, 103; and labor, 110, 197, 199, 207, 208–10; and election of 1934, 127; and election of 1936, 135; defeat of New Deal Democrats, 138; criticism of sit-down strikes, 147; and election of 1938, 153–54; alliance with organized labor, 166; and labor during World War II, 174; and PAC of CIO, 192–93; and Operation Dixie, 200; and Taft-Hartley

Act, 202–3; New Deal–Fair Deal wing of, 208, 209–10; and election of 1948, 209; and union corruption, 218–19; and election of 1958, 219; and Landrum-Griffin Act, 220; and election of 1976, 227
Dies, Martin, 152, 158, 167
Disque, Brice P., 68, 71
Doak, William, 103
Dotson, Donald, xiii, 229
Douglas, William, 213
Downsizing, 229
Drummond, Thomas, 11
Dues checkoff, 185
Dunlop, John, 212
Duplex v. Deering et al. (1917), 85–86, 87
Durkin, Martin P., 210–12

Eisenhower, Dwight D.: appointees to NLRB, 210; elected president, 210; modern republicanism of, 210; and labor, 210–12, 216, 217; and Taft-Hartley Act, 210–12, 216, 218; and union corruption, 218; and Landrum-Griffin Act, 221
Emerson, Thomas, 126
Emery, James, 122
Employee representation plans (ERPs), 117. See also Company unions
Employers' liability laws, 44
Equal Employment Opportunity Commission (EEOC), 224–25
Erdman, Constantine, 32
Erdman Act of 1898, 32, 47, 58, 104
E. W. Loewe, 46
Executive branch, U.S.: and industrial disputes, 1, 4, 29, 41; and capital, 11; cooperation with federal judges, 16; power of, 37

Fair Employment Practices Committee (FEPC), 187–88
Fair Labor Standards Act of 1938, 166
Fairless, Benjamin, 181
Fall, Albert, 69
Fansteel Metallurgical Co. v. NLRB (1938), 163–64

Farm workers, 62, 63
Federal Drydock, 179
Federal employees, 7
Federal government, 30–31, 67; and industrial disputes, 1, 7, 51; and free labor doctrine, 22; and interstate commerce, 32; and 1902 Industrial Commission report, 35; and labor policies, 64, 101; and union growth, 74–76; contradictory war labor policies of, 171
Federal mail statutes, 31
Federal Mediation and Conciliation Service, 54, 84, 120
Federal Railroad Administration, 74
Federal Trade Commission (FTC), 120
Feller, David, 212
Field, Stephen, 30
Fink, Leon, xi
First Industrial Conference (1919), 76, 79–80, 83, 85
Fitts, William C., 69
Fitzpatrick, John, 75, 78–79
Foner, Eric, 5
Foran, Martin, 19
Forbath, William, xvi
Ford, Henry, 165
Ford Motor Company, 165, 171, 172, 175, 179
Fortune, 132, 154, 174
Foster, William Z., 74, 75
Fox-Genovese, Elizabeth, xi
Frankfurter, Felix, 47–48, 68, 70, 71, 72, 73, 77, 103, 109, 165
Fraser, Douglas, 227
Frayne, Hugh, 66
Freedom of contract, 16
Free labor ideology, 22
Frey, John, 149, 152, 183
Friedman-Harry Marks, 143, 144
Fruehauf Trailer, 143, 144
Full Employment Act of 1946, 197–98
Furuseth, Andrew, 255–56 (n. 68)

Galbraith, John Kenneth, 208, 210, 222, 223
Garment industry, 38
Garment workers, 62, 97

Garrison, Lloyd K., 124, 125, 183
Gary, Elbert, 75, 78
General Electric, 72
General Managers Association, 29
General Motors, 137–42, 143, 144, 177, 193, 194
Genovese, Eugene, xi
George, Walter, 147
Gilder, Richard, 30
Glendon, Mary Ann, 235
Globe doctrine, 150–51
Goldberg, Arthur, 219
Golden, Clint, 186–87
Gompers, Samuel, 38, 176; applauded by Mark A. Hanna, 41; and political action, 49–50; and election of 1908, 51; and election of 1912, 53; and Woodrow Wilson, 54, 57; and election of 1916, 60; and World War I, 61–72; and First Industrial Conference (1919), 76; and Herbert Hoover, 85; antipathy toward Warren G. Harding, 86–87; last two years as president of AFL, 97
Gompers v. Buck's Stove & Range Co. (1911), 46–47
Gould, Jay, 15–17
Graham, Frank, 183–84
Grant, Ulysses S., 6–7
Great Depression, 102–5, 107, 109–10, 194
Great Northern Railroad, 28
Great Society, xvii
Great upheaval of 1885–86, 13
Green, William, 97, 111, 120–21, 127, 152, 154–57, 160, 176
Gregory, Thomas, 64
Gresham, Walter Q., 11–12, 24
Griffin, Robert, 220
Guffey Bituminous Coal Act of 1935, 132, 144
Guffey-Snyder Bituminous Coal Act of 1936, 134
Guffey-Vinson Coal Act of 1937, 147
Gutman, Herbert, xi

Halleck, Charles, 157, 158
Hancock, Winfield, 10–11, 34

Hand, Learned, 86
Hanna, Mark A., 40–42
Harding, Warren G., 77; and labor, 83–87, 89; appeals to working people, 84; appointment of William Howard Taft as chief justice, 86; and unemployment conference of 1921, 86; and Samuel Gompers, 86–87; and coal and railroad strikes of 1922, 89–97; defense of RLB's "outlaw resolution," 93–94
Hard-rock miners, 22, 43
Harlan, John Marshall, 31
Harriman, J. Borden, 55
Harris, Howell, 193
Harrison, Pat, 112
Harrison, William Henry, 23, 34, 41
Hartley, Fred, 199, 202–3
Hartley Bill of 1947, 202
Hattam, Victoria, xvi
Hay, John, 8
Hayes, Rutherford B., 9–11
Haymarket tragedy, 16
Haywood, William D. "Big Bill," 43, 55
Health and safety regulations, 13, 35, 44
Healy, Arthur, 157, 159
Hillman, Sidney, 70, 74, 76, 111, 132, 176–77, 186
Hillquit, Morris, 55
Hitchman Coal and Coke Company, 47–48, 64
H. J. Heinz v. NLRB (1941), 164
Hoffa, James R., 218
Homestead, Pa., 21–24
Hooper, Ben, 93
Hoover, Herbert, 86, 98, 100, 103, 107, 113; and Second Industrial Conference (1920), 80; and labor, 85, 86, 87, 101; and coal and railroad strikes of 1922, 89–97; and Jacksonville Agreement of 1924, 98–99; and election of 1928, 102; and panic of October 1929, 102; and Reconstruction Finance Corporation, 102; and Great Depression, 102–4; and Norris-LaGuardia Act, 104
Hopkins, Harry, 148–49
Houde case (1934), 125, 126

Houde Company, 125

Hough, Charles, 86

Hours regulation: and state laws, 13;
eight-hour-day movement, 16; and railroad workers, 35, 45, 59; and government employees, 52; and World War I,
63, 65, 68, 71–76; and Woodrow Wilson, 78; and NIRA, 111

House of Representatives, U.S.: and
Grover Cleveland's arbitration bill, 17–
18; and 1892 Homestead strike, 22; and
Pullman Boycott of 1894, 30; and Erdman Act, 32; and Industrial Commission Bill, 33; election of trade unionists
to, 51; and Wagner Act, 127–28, 159,
160; and House Committee on Un-
American Activities, 152; Labor Committee, 155; Smith Committee investigation of NLRB, 157–61; and labor
during World War II, 174; and Vinson
Bill, 174; and Case Bill, 194; Committee on Education and Labor, 202; and
Landrum-Griffin Act, 220; and union
regulation, 220

Houston, David, 64

Howe, Louis, 126

Howell, Robert, 100

Hughes, Charles Evans, 60, 144–45, 162,
163, 165

Humphrey, George, 211

Hurvitz, Haggai, 80

Hutcheson, William, 62, 66, 83, 98, 153

Ickes, Harold, 76, 112, 189–90

Illinois Central Railroad, 93

Immigration, 22, 62, 84, 98

Imperial Germany, 67

Indian Territory, 28

Industrial Commission, 34–35, 71

Industrial Commission Bill of 1898, 33

Industrial pluralism, 198, 207, 212–14,
219, 222, 223, 226–31, 234, 267 (n. 3),
270–71 (n. 45)

Industrial Relations Act of 1948 (Canada),
xv–xvi

Industrial Workers of the World (IWW),
xii, 43, 55, 63, 67–71

Injunctions, 1, 11, 20–23, 26–29, 33–35,
45–46, 49–52, 56–57, 85, 87, 104

Interior, U.S. Department of: establishment of Bureau of Labor in, 13; supervision of mines in Indian Territory, 28

International Association of Machinists
(IAM), 49, 60, 85, 93, 97

International Harvester, 172

International Ladies Garment Workers'
Union (ILGWU), 97, 101, 116

International Typographical Union, 44, 97

Interstate commerce, 29, 32, 46–47, 60,
85, 88

Interstate Commerce Commission (ICC),
17, 20, 92, 120

Interstate Commerce Commission Act of
1887, 20, 25, 29–31

Interstate railroads, 14, 17, 20, 28–29, 32,
59

Involuntary servitude, 16, 31, 32

Iron and steel industry, 2–3, 38, 40, 72, 74,
75, 79, 114–15, 215

Iron Molders' International Union, 5–6,
46

Irons, Martin, 18

Ives, Irving, 219

Jackson, Andrew, 4–5, 6, 39

Jacksonville Agreement of 1924, 98–99

Jacobstein, Meyer, 101

Jefferson, Thomas, 60

Jewell, Bert, 93, 95, 97

Johnson, Hiram, 147

Johnson, Hugh, 109, 112, 116, 117–18,
125

Johnson, Lyndon B., xvii, 216, 226

Johnston, Eric, 192–93

Jones and Laughlin Steel, 142, 143, 144,
145

Judiciary, U.S.: and industrial disputes, 1,
4, 7, 11, 13, 15, 20, 34, 67; and strike
injunctions, 1, 11, 20–23, 26–29, 33–
35, 45–46, 49–50, 51–52, 56–57, 85,
87, 88–89, 95; and law of conspiracy,
16, 48; and boycotts, 20–21, 45–47,
88–89; and 1892 Coeur d'Alenes strike,
22–23; and labor, 24–27, 44–48, 162–

66, 198, 227, 241 (n. 20), 243 (n. 40),
244 (n. 67); and Pullman Boycott of
1894, 29; and legality of unions, 31,
101; and picketing, 33–34, 88; and
national labor policy, 37, 64, 234; and
yellow-dog contracts, 47; and the closed
shop, 48; and Congress, 50; and Clayton
Act, 60, 85, 87–89, 96, 101; and investigation of IWW, 69; Duplex v. Deering
et al. (1917, 1918, 1921), 85–86, 87–88;
during Harding administration, 86–89;
American Steel Foundries v. Tri-Cities
Central Trade Council (1921), 88; and
interstate commerce, 88; and state laws,
88; and RLB ruling, 92; declares RLB
orders unenforceable, 93–94; and Wilkerson injunction of 1922, 95–96,
103; and Railway Labor Act, 101; and
Houde case (1934), 125–26; Weirton
Steel Company ruling of 1935, 126,
128; and Wagner Act, 132; and AFL/
CIO conflict, 163; Fansteel Metallurgical Co. v. NLRB (1938), 163; and strike
violence, 163, 245 (n. 98); and NLRB v.
Ford Motor Co. (1940), 165; and industrial pluralism, 213; and judicial trusteeship, 223; and civil rights, 225; and
women's rights, 225; recent rulings of,
229–30. *See also* Supreme Court, U.S.
Justice, U.S. Department of, 52; labor policy of, 28, 64; and IWW, 69; and disdain for NLRB, 125–26

Katznelson, Ira, 235–36
Keating-Owens Act of 1916, 58
Keenan, John, 176
Kelley's industrial army, 28
Kennedy, John F., 203, 216, 217, 219, 225
Kennedy, Robert F., 217–18
Kennedy, Tom, 115, 148, 181
Kerr, Clark, 212, 219
Keynesian economics, 149, 183, 198
Keyserling, Leon, 127, 129
Kirkland, Lane, 227
Klare, Karl, xv
Knights of Labor, xi, xvi, 14–17
Knox, Philander C., 40

Knudsen, William, 177, 178, 186
Korean War, xvii, 206, 215

Labor, U.S. Department of, 107, 109, 121,
127, 218; establishment of, 19; on cabi-
net, 52; and labor, 54, 64, 68–69, 84;
and Landrum-Griffin Act, 222–23
Labor-Management Reporting and Disclo-
sure Act of 1959. *See* Landrum-Griffin
Act of 1959
Labor movement, xvi, 23–24, 63, 120,
131, 207, 210, 217. *See also* Trade
unionism
Labor Representation Committee, 49
Labor's Bill of Grievances, 49, 51
Labour party (Britain), 49, 76
LaFollette, Robert, 84, 98
LaFollette, Robert, Jr., 110, 123, 134, 147,
159
LaFollette Committee, 134, 139, 159
LaFollette Seamen's Act of 1915, 58
LaGuardia, Fiorello, 84
Laissez-faire, 1, 19
Lamont, Robert P., 103
Landon, Alfred M., 107
Landrum, Philip, 220
Landrum-Griffin Act of 1959, 220–23
Lane, Franklin K., 64
Lapham, Roger, 183, 184
Lauck, W. Jett, 104–5, 133
Law of contract implementation, 212–14
Leiserson, William M., 96–97, 156–57,
158, 159, 161, 164
Lester, Richard, 208, 217
Leuchtenberg, William E., xiv
Lewis, John L., xii, 83, 103, 104–5, 108–9,
111, 113, 115, 133, 138, 143, 146, 152,
199, 201, 202, 215; and election of
1912, 53; and Herbert Hoover, 85, 90,
98–99; and 1922 coal strike, 90; en-
dorsement of Republican party in 1924
and 1928, 98–99; and Jacksonville
Agreement of 1924, 98–99; and Calvin
Coolidge, 99; and election of 1928, 102;
and election of 1932, 108; and NIRA
Section 7a, 112; and New Deal, 112–13;
and Wagner Labor Relations Bill, 120–

21; and Wagner Act, 127; demands
mass-production organizing campaign,
133; forms CIO, 133; makes CIO part
of New Deal coalition, 133–34; forms
Labor's Nonpartisan League, 134; and
political alliance with Roosevelt, 134–
35; and election of 1936, 135; launches
CIO organizing campaign in steel, 135;
and General Motors sit-down strike
of 1937, 138–42; and United States
Steel–SWOC settlement, 142; support
for Roosevelt's reform efforts, 143; and
Little Steel campaign of 1937, 148–49;
and World War II, 172, 174, 175, 176,
177, 180–81, 189–90; and 1941 captive
mines dispute, 180–81; and Little Steel
decision, 189; and 1943 anthracite
strike, 189–91; attacks CIO conferees,
193; and 1946 UMW strike, 195; criti-
cizes federal labor policy, 199–200
Liberty League, 132, 140, 153
Lincoln, Abraham, 4–5, 40
Lippmann, Walter, 68, 77
Lipset, Seymour Martin, xiii
Little Steel companies, 148–49, 171, 172,
179, 184
Little Steel decision, 188–89, 191
Lochner v. N.Y. (1905), 45
Locomotive Engineers' union rule no. 12,
25–26
Loewe et al. v. Lawlor et al. (1906), 46, 60
Longshoremen, 62, 216
Los Angeles Times building bombing, 38
Lowi, Theodore, 226
Loyal Legion of Loggers and Lumbermen,
68, 71
Ludlow, Colo.: site of massacre of 1914,
55, 57
Lumber industry, 67, 68, 70, 179
Lumber industry workers, 62, 63

McAdoo, William Gibbs, 72, 74
McClellan, John, 217, 220
McClellan Committee, 217–19, 220, 221,
222
MacDonald, David, 216, 220
Machinists, 62, 73

McKinley, William, 33, 34, 41, 71, 98
McNamara, James B., 38
McNamara, John J., 38
McReynolds, James, 145
Madden, Warren, 157, 160
Maier, Charles, 198, 223
Manly, Basil, 54–56
March on Washington Movement
(MOWM), 187
Marshall Plan, 205
Marx, Karl, 60, 212
Marxism: theories of the state, xiv
Masses, 56
Mathews, H. M., 9
Meany, George, 223, 227
Meatpacking industry, 2, 3, 38, 70, 71, 72,
74, 75, 172, 179
Membership maintenance clauses, 179,
184–85
Memorial Day Massacre, 148
Metalworkers, 62
Mexico, 59
Miliband, Ralph, xi, xiii
Miller, Arnold, 222
Millis, Harry A., 124, 160–61, 164
Mills, C. Wright, 199
Mine workers, 10, 34, 40–42, 48, 62,
79, 188–89, 194–95. *See also* Copper
miners
Minton, Sherman, 181
Mitchell, James P., 211
Mitchell, John, 38–39, 41, 46–47
Montague, Gilbert, 154
Montgomery, David, xi, 5
Morgan, J. P., 42
Morgan, John T., 12
Morrison, Frank, 46–47
Morse, Wayne, 214
Murdock, Abe, 157, 159
Murphy, Frank P., 138–42, 154, 165
Murray, Philip, 115, 172, 176, 177, 181,
186
Murray Plan, 186

National Association for the Advancement
of Colored People (NAACP), 129, 131,
223

National Association of Manufacturers
(NAM), 118, 122, 125, 152, 153, 154,
204
National Defense Advisory Commission
(NDAC), 176
National Defense Mediation Board
(NDMB), 178–82
National Industrial Adjustment Act of
1934 (Public Resolution 44), 123, 124
National Industrial Conference Board, 72
National Industrial Recovery Act (NIRA)
of 1933, 111–21, 126, 144; Section 7a,
111–12, 124, 126, 127
National Labor Board (NLB), 115–19,
126; and common labor law, 117; employer resistance to, 117–18; and executive orders 6511 and 6580, 118; removal
of automobile industry from, 121
National Labor Relations Act (NLRA) of
1935. *See* Wagner Act of 1935
National Labor Relations Board (NLRB),
xiii, 123–67 passim, 172, 175, 177, 182,
197, 200, 210, 224, 227, 234; common
law concept of, 124–25; *Houde* case
(1934), 125–26; Weirton Steel Company ruling of 1935, 126; and Wagner
Act, 130–31; and employer resistance,
131–32; and connection to LaFollette
Committee, 139; and legality under
Wagner Act, 142–46, 164; crusaders on,
149–51; and Globe doctrine, 150–51;
under siege, 151–54; and AFL/CIO
conflict, 152–53, 161, 199; and election
of 1938, 154; congressional attacks on,
154–58; Smith Committee investigation
of, 157, 158–61; cutting of appropriations to, 159; appointment of Harry Millis as chair of, 160; end of radical, pro-
CIO phase, 161; appointment of Gerard
Reilly to, 161; dismissal of Nathan Witt
from, 161; coercive power of, 166; and
strikes of 1941, 178; Congress dilutes
authority of, 183; and Case Bill, 194;
and Taft-Hartley Act, 202–5, 209; and
industrial pluralism, 213; and civil
rights, 224; conservative appointments
to, 229

National railroad strike of 1877, xvii,
8–12
National Recovery Administration (NRA),
109, 112, 118, 120–21, 126
National Right to Work Committee, 229
National Wage Stabilization Board
(NWSB), 188, 215
National War Labor Board (NWLB): dur-
ing World War I, 71–75, 77, 86, 109,
116, 121, 166; during World War II,
182–91, 192, 204
Navy, U.S.: view of labor, 64
Nazi-Soviet Non-aggression Pact of 1939,
161
Nelson, Daniel, 3
Nelson, Donald, 186–87
Neo-Marxism, 235–36; theories of the
state, xiv–xv
Neo-voluntarism, 198
New Deal, xvi–xvii, 107–67 passim, 226;
compared to crisis model of World War
I, 108; and labor policy, 108–9, 111,
125, 137, 166, 167, 197, 199, 205, 210,
228, 233; distinguished from Wilson
administration, 110; and NIRA, 111–19;
and strike wave of 1934, 123–24; and
Wagner Act, 129; conservative opposi-
tion to, 133, 146–49, 152; undermining
of coalition with militant labor, 149; and
Keynesian economics, 149, 183; and
election of 1938, 153–54; judicial revo-
lution of, 198, 199; death of, 226–31
New Dealers, 207, 208; links to Wilson
administration, 109; views of state
action, 110–11; defeated in Congress,
138; and trade unionism, 166; and Taft-
Hartley Act, 203, 205, 207
New Freedom, 58
Newlands Act of 1913, 58
New Left: and the state, xiv; and Wagner
Act, 129
New Republic, 76
Nields, John P., 126, 128
Nixon, Richard, 227
NLRB v. Ford Motor Co. (1940), 165
NLRB v. Mackay Radio and Telegraph
(1937), 162

Nonoperating railroad workers, 74, 93, 96, 101
Norris, George, 84, 103, 104, 110, 112
Norris Bill of 1928, 103–4, 255–56 (n. 68)
Norris-LaGuardia Act of 1932, 104, 112, 127, 165, 204, 213, 222
North American Aviation Company, 179
Northern Pacific Railroad, 26, 31–32
Norton, Mary, 155, 157
No-strike pledges, 63, 170

Office of Production Management (OPM), 178, 186
Oil-refinery workers, 62
Oil-refining industry, 38
Olney, Richard, 28–32
Open shop, 174, 181. *See also* Right-to-work laws
Operating trainmen, 15
Operation Dixie, 200, 206–7
Order of Railway Conductors, 42
Orren, Karen, 226, 227
Owens, John, 176

Packinghouse workers, 62
Padway, Joseph, 153, 154
Palmer, A. Mitchell, 78
Panic of 1893, 27–28
Panitch, Leo, xv, xvi
Parker, Carleton, 68
Parker, James, 100
Pearl Berghoff agency, 134
Pearl Harbor, 169, 175
Pennsylvania Railroad, 9
People's party, 28
Pepper, George Wharton, 103, 104
Perkins, Charles E., 20
Perkins, Frances, 108, 127, 140
Perlman, Selig, 156
Picketing, 16, 33, 45, 68
Pinkertons, 22
Pittsburgh, Pa., 8–10
Platt, Thomas, 33
Plumb Plan, 81
Pluralist model of the state, xiv. *See also* Industrial pluralism
Poindexter, Miles, 80

Political Action Committee (PAC), 192–93, 199
Populism, xvi, 28–29
Populist-Democratic coalition, 23
Positive state, xvi, 61
Post Office, U.S. Department of the: view of labor, 64
Poulantzas, Nikos, xiv
President's Mediation Commission. *See* Wilson, Woodrow: and Special Mediation Commission
Pressman, Lee, 176
Professional Air Traffic Controllers Organization (PATCO), xiii, 228
Progressive Era, xii, 35
Progressive party, 44, 53, 56
Progressivism, 35, 68
Prohibition, 97
Protective legislation, 44–45, 55, 58. *See also* Health and safety regulations; Hours regulation
Public Resolution 44. *See* National Industrial Adjustment Act of 1934
Public utilities, 67
Public works projects, 6–7
Pullman, George M., 29
Pullman Boycott of 1894, 29–33, 58, 94

Race riots of 1919, 77
Radical Republicanism, 5
Railroad Arbitration Commission, 19
Railroad brotherhoods, 31–32, 38, 54, 55, 58, 59, 60, 83, 84, 92–93, 97, 98, 99, 101, 201
Railroad Labor Board (RLB), 84, 92–94, 99–101
Railroad shopmen, 15, 91–97
Railroad workers, 8–12, 14–15, 35, 45, 58, 93, 194
Railway Employee Department (RED), 93–95, 97
Railway Labor Act of 1926, 100–101, 104, 112, 127, 222
Randolph, A. Philip, 187
Reading Formula, 116–17, 118
Reagan, Ronald, xiii, 228–29
Reconstruction Finance Corporation, 102

Reed, Earl F., 142

Reilly, Gerard, 161, 202

Replacement workers. *See* Strikebreakers

Republicanism, xi–xii, 4–7, 9, 16–18, 21, 27, 39, 40, 210, 238, 240 (n. 7)

Republican party, 19, 101, 234; and trade protection, 6, 84, 98; and labor, 23, 40–43, 50, 56–57, 59, 60, 83, 84–102 passim, 166, 201, 207, 209, 210, 212, 218, 220, 227, 228; and populism, 28; and Industrial Commission Bill, 33; targeted for defeat by AFL, 49; and injunction reform, 51; and election of 1910, 52; and "progressive" Republicans, 52, 84, 98, 103, 110; and election of 1912, 53; and election of 1916, 58, 60; and election of 1918, 77; and election of 1920, 83; and equity jurisdiction of federal courts, 83; and immigration restriction, 84, 98; and election of 1922, 98; and election of 1924, 98; working-class votes in 1924 and after, 98; opposition to railroad labor reform, 100; and Railway Labor Act, 101; and election of 1928, 102; and election of 1932, 103; and Wagner Act, 128, 159, 161; attack on New Deal, 146–48, 166; and anti-strike bills, 147; and election of 1938, 153–54; attack on CIO and NLRB, 161; and labor during World War II, 174; and antilabor amendments to NLRA, 191–92, 194, 201–2; and election of 1946, 195, 201; and AFL leaders, 199, 210; and Taft-Hartley Act, 202–3, 212; accommodation with New Deal, 210; and elections of 1952 and 1953, 210; and union corruption, 218, 220; and election of 1958, 219; and Landrum-Griffin Act, 220–21; and civil rights, 221; and election of 1968, 227; and election of 1980, 227–28

Republic Steel mill, 148

Restraint of trade, 7, 15, 20, 45, 46, 60, 88

Reuther, Walter, 209, 212, 220

Reuther Plan, 186

Reynolds, James, 205

Richberg, Donald, 97, 103, 112, 117–18, 125, 126

Right-to-work laws, 173, 203, 219

Roberts, Owen, 144–45, 162, 165

Robinson, Joseph, 123

Rockefeller, John D., Jr., 55

Rock Island Railroad, 215

Roosevelt, Franklin Delano, 105, 107–67 passim; labor policy experience, 107–8; campaign of 1932, 108; appointment of Frances Perkins as secretary of labor, 108; and Wilson administration, 108–10; view of AFL, 111–12; and UMW organizing drive of 1933, 113–15; and captive mines dispute, 114–15; establishment of NLB, 116; comparison of Depression to Great War, 118; and executive orders 6511 and 6580, 118; deference to employers, 119; creation of Automobile Labor Board, 121; and Wagner Labor Relations Bill, 121–23; and strikes of 1934, 122, 124; creation of Steel Labor Relations Board, 123; creation of first NLRB with Executive Order 6763, 123; and *Houde* case (1934), 125–26; curtails authority of NLRB, 126; two minds on labor policy, 126; signs Wagner Act, 128; appointments to NLRB, 132; looks to labor for support, 133; and CIO–New Deal coalition, 133–35; and election of 1936, 134–35; political alliance with John L. Lewis, 134–35; endorsement of UMW, CIO, and collective bargaining, 135; rejection by Congress of reforms of 1937, 138; and recession of 1937, 138, 149; and General Motors sit-down strike of 1937, 139–42; opposition to, 143; looks to Lewis, Hillman, and CIO for support, 143; Republican and Southern Democratic critics of, 147; and Little Steel campaign of 1937, 148–49; and AFL/CIO conflict, 152–53; and election of 1938, 153–54; appointment of William Leiserson to NLRB, 156; appointment of Harry Millis as chair of NLRB, 160; appointment of Gerard Reilly to

NLRB, 161; judiciary appointments, 162; Roosevelt Court, 163, 165; repudiates sit-down tactic, 164; and labor during World War II, 169, 171, 175–91 passim; and 1941 emergency industry-labor conference, 175; appeals to Hillman and Murray, 176; appointment of Hillman to NDAC, 176; establishment of NDAC, 176; establishment of NDMB, 178; establishment of OPM, 178; and 1941 North American Aviation strike, 179; and seizure of Federal Drydock, 179; and Southern Appalachian mine operators, 179–80; and 1941 captive mines dispute, 180–81; abolition of OPM and creation of WPB, 186; establishment of FEPC, 187–88; and 1943 anthracite strike, 189–91; veto of Smith-Connally Act, 190; death of, 191

Roosevelt, Theodore, 35, 37–44, 51, 103, 205; and labor, 39, 43–44; and 1902 anthracite strike, 40–44; and equity process reforms, 50; and election of 1912, 53

Roper, Elmo, 174

Rostow, Walt Whitman, 198

Routzohn, Harry, 157, 158

Rubber industry, 38

Ryan, John, 117

St. John, Vincent, 55

Saposs, David, 132

Schurz, Carl, 11

Scientific management, 2–3, 98

Secondary boycotts, 20, 201, 218. *See also* Boycotts

Second Industrial Conference (1920), 79–80, 85

Senate, U.S.: Committee on Education and Labor, 12, 120–22, 128, 155, 160, 173; Committee upon the Relations between Labor and Capital (Blair Committee), 12–13; and interstate commerce, 17; and 1892 Homestead strike, 22; and Sherman Antitrust Act, 25; and Pullman Boycott of 1894, 30; and Erdman Act, 32; and Industrial Commission Bill, 33;

and antistrike bill of 1920, 80–81; and Transportation Act, 81; Finance Committee, 108; opposition to NIRA Section 7a, 112; and Wagner Labor Relations Bill, 119–23; and Wagner Act, 127–28; and Carter Coal case (1936), 132, 142; and LaFollette Committee investigation, 134, 138–39, 147; attempts to amend NLRA, 151, 154–55, 160; and Smith Committee, 160; Committee on Labor and Public Welfare, 201–2; McClellan Committee on labor racketeering, 217–19; and Landrum-Griffin Act, 220

Sherman Antitrust Act of 1890, 24–25, 29, 31, 45–48, 50–52, 56, 85, 88, 101, 165

Shipbuilding industry, 66, 72, 172

Skocpol, Theda, xiv, xv

Skowronek, Stephen, xiv, xv

Slichter, Sumner, 199

Smith, Donald Wakefield, 155

Smith, Edwin S., 124, 155, 160, 161

Smith, Howard, 152, 157, 158, 160, 167, 174, 204

Smith and Wesson Gun Company, 73

Smith Committee, 157–61, 202

Smith-Connally Act of 1943, 190

Socialism, 41, 43, 49, 50, 55–56

Socialist party, 49, 53, 55, 56

Socialists, 37, 97, 98

Social Security Act of 1935, 166

Social Security Administration, 234

Soft-coal mining, 8

Sombart question, xvi

Southern Democrats, 13, 17, 18, 28, 51–52, 110, 112, 128, 146–48, 152–54, 155, 159–60, 161, 167, 169, 173, 174, 175, 191–92, 194, 195, 200, 201, 203, 218, 219, 220–21, 227, 234

Special Mediation Commission, 70

Spruce Production Division, 68

State, the, 233–35; Marxist models of, xiv; pluralist model of, xiv; neo-Marxist theories of, xiv–xv; and school of critical legal history, xv; positive intervention of, xvi, 61; the national state and labor, 4–8; and the judiciary, 44; and capital, 233; unintended policy consequences,

233; autonomy of, 233–34, 236–37; and
class, 233–37; administrative capacities
of, 234; and federal system, 234, 237;
and separation of power, 234, 237; and
civil society, 237; and labor historians,
240–41 (n. 14)

State courts: and legality of unions, 7; and
the closed shop, 43; and yellow-dog
contracts, 47; right-to-work laws, 219

State militias, 8, 38, 43

States' rights, 35, 51

Steel Labor Relations Board, 123

Steelman, John, 181

Steelworkers, 22, 62

Steel Workers Organizing Committee
(SWOC)–CIO, 141–42, 148–49, 171,
179

Steelworkers Trilogy rulings (1960), 213

Steunenberg, Frank, 34

Stevenson, Adlai E., 210

Stockyards Labor Council, 75

Stone, Harlan F., 162, 164

Stone, Katherine, xv

Strikebreakers, 10, 15–16, 20, 22, 33, 38,
57, 68, 93, 124, 134, 162, 228–29, 230

Strikes: in the nineteenth century, 4, 7,
8–12, 14–15, 28; legality of, 7, 31–32,
45, 56–57; 1877 railroad strikes, 8–12;
1892 Homestead strike, 21–22, 24;
1892 Coeur d'Alenes strike, 22–24; era
of the mass strike, 38; 1902 anthracite
strike, 40–44; during World War I,
62–63, 67–68, 70; in 1919, 76–79; 1922
coal strike, 89–91; 1922 railroad shopmen's strike, 91–97; decline of, after
1922, 97, 101–2; and New Deal, 113;
wave of 1933, 115–16; wave of 1934,
123–24, 126–27; General Motors sit-
down strike of 1937, 138–42; Fansteel
sit-down strike of 1937, 163; wave of
1941, 178; 1943 wildcat strikes, 188–
91; general strikes of 1946, 193, 199;
wave of 1946, 193–94; and Wagner Act,
201; and industrial pluralism, 213–14;
1951 steel strike, 215; 1981 PATCO
strike, 228

Structural Iron Workers' Union, 38

Suffrage, 12

Supreme Court, U.S., 17, 30, 44–48, 52,
53, 57, 58, 64, 86, 87–88, 92, 93–94,
162; declares Railway Act unconstitutional, 101; and Wagner Act, 127;
declares NIRA unconstitutional, 128;
declares Guffey Bituminous Coal Act
unconstitutional, 132; and 1936 Democratic party platform, 134; approves
New Deal labor laws and policies, 137;
and legality of Wagner Act, 142–46,
164; upholds peaceful picketing and
closed shop, 145; and NLRB, 149–50,
155, 162–66; impact of Roosevelt's
appointees to, 162; NLRB v. Mackay
Radio and Telegraph (1937), 162; and
differences with Congress, 164; H. J.
Heinz v. NLRB (1941), 164; and free
speech and picketing, 165; and Sherman
Act applicability to strikes, 165; U.S. v.
Hutcheson (1941), 165; and industrial
pluralism, 213; Steelworkers Trilogy
(1960), 213; and 1951 seizure of steel
industry, 215; recent rulings of, 229–30.
See also Judiciary, U.S.

Sutherland, George, 145

Suzzalo, Henry, 68

Swartz, Donald, xv–xvi

Syndicalism, 37

System-bargaining, 100

Taft, Robert A., 202–11 passim

Taft, William Howard, 26, 54, 144; and
antistrike injunctions, 27, 45; and labor,
51–52, 86, 89; and Supreme Court, 57,
87–88; and NWLB, 72, 73

Taft Bill of 1947, 202

Taft-Hartley Act of 1947, xv, xvii, 202–
22 passim, 234, 268 (nn. 17, 20), 269
(n. 25)

Tariffs, 6, 22

Taylor, Myron, 114, 142, 180, 181

Teamsters, 24, 38, 85, 124, 218, 220,
222–23

Technology, 3

Telephone industry, 70, 71

Telephone operators, 62

Teller, Henry M., 18–19
Textile industry, 1, 38, 117
Thomas, Elbert, 155, 157, 160, 174
Thompson, E. P., xi, 238
Tobacco industry, 3
Tomlins, Christopher, xv, 260 (n. 24), 269 (n. 25)
Trade unionism, xv, 13–14, 42, 45–47, 62, 76; decline of, xii–xiii, 226–28, 231; growth of, xvi–xvii, 3, 38–39, 48–49, 66–67, 71, 74–76, 79, 87, 97, 112, 115–19, 137–38, 141, 166, 169–70, 206, 225–28, 231; and local market competition, 2; legality of, 7, 15, 32; and local politics, 13–14; and Department of Labor, 19–20, 64; and election of 1892, 23–24; politics of, 31, 33, 37–39, 97–102, 246 (n. 14); and 1902 Industrial Commission report, 34–35; and Republican party, 40–41, 59–60, 209, 216, 218, 219; and federal courts, 45, 87, 88–89; and election of 1908, 49–52; and election of 1910, 51–53; and election of 1912, 53; and Democratic party, 53–60, 61, 197, 199, 207, 209, 210, 216, 219, 226, 230; and election of 1916, 58–60; and World War I, 61–67; after World War I, 79; and Transportation Act, 81, 84; and election of 1920, 83; and Congress, 84, 86, 87, 208–9; and appointment of William Howard Taft as chief justice, 86; and depression of 1920–21, 87; disdain of leadership for James J. Davis, 87; and election of 1922, 97, 98; and political action during the 1920s, 97–102; and Conference for Progressive Political Action, 98; and election of 1924, 98; and railroad labor reform efforts, 100; and election of 1928, 102; and Great Depression, 102–3; and election of 1932, 103, 107; and support for NIRA, 112; and New Deal, 113–19, 124, 135, 166; and NRA, 118–19; impact of 1934 strikes on, 124; and Wagner Act, 131–35, 207; gains and losses of 1937, 137–38; and recession of 1937, 138, 149; and UAW triumph over General Motors, 141; and NLRB, 149–51; and election of 1938, 153–54; popular attitudes toward, 166; and World War II, 169–70; congressional attacks during World War II, 173–75; position of, after World War II, 192–93, 199; and Truman's 1945 labor-management conference, 193; and election of 1946, 195; and postwar managerial counterattack, 200–201; and Taft-Hartley Act, 202–8, 212; and Korean War, 206; and creation of modern American liberalism, 208–9; campaign to repeal Taft-Hartley Act, 209; and election of 1948, 209; and election of 1952, 210; and Dwight D. Eisenhower, 210–12, 216, 217, 218; and corruption, 217–23; and election of 1958, 219; political weaknesses of, 219–20; and civil rights movement, 223–25; and women's rights, 225; and public-sector unions, 225–26; and economic contractions of the 1970s, 226, 227–28; and election of 1968, 227; and election of 1980, 227–28; and elections of 1984 and 1988, 230. *See also* American Federation of Labor; American Federation of Labor–Congress of Industrial Organizations; Congress of Industrial Organizations; Labor movement; *and individual unions*
Transit workers, 73
Transport and communications industries, 1, 2, 8, 11, 58, 59, 67, 70, 72, 74
Transportation Act of 1920, 81, 84, 92
Tripartite commissions, 55, 66, 71, 72, 192–93
Truman, Harry S., 191, 193, 205, 208, 209; labor policies of, 194–95, 201, 204–8, 214–17
Tumulty, Joe, 77, 78, 79
Tydings, Millard, 128

Unemployment, 62, 86, 102, 107
Union Pacific Railroad, 27, 30
Unions. *See* American Federation of Labor; American Federation of Labor–Congress of Industrial Organizations;

Congress of Industrial Organizations;
Trade unionism; *and individual unions*
Union-shop agreements, 65, 66, 67, 71,
71, 172, 181, 247 (n. 28)
United Automobile Workers (UAW),
138–42, 144, 171, 172, 179, 193, 194,
223, 225
United Brewery Workers, 49, 97
United Brotherhood of Carpenters, 62, 66,
97
United Electrical Workers, 171
United Hatters' Union, 46–47
United Mine Workers (UMW), 38, 41–42,
47–49, 54, 55, 60, 74, 79, 84, 88, 89–
91, 97, 98–99, 101, 102, 103, 113–15,
134, 135, 180, 189–91, 195, 220, 222,
223
United States Chamber of Commerce,
151, 152, 192
United States Coal Commission, 91
U.S. Law Week, 126
United States Steel, 75, 114, 137, 141–42,
143, 180–81
U.S. v. Hutcheson (1941), 165
United Steelworkers of America (USWA),
184
Upheaval of 1877. *See* National railroad
strike of 1877

Vandenberg, Arthur, 151
Vinson, Carl, 174
Voluntarism, xvi, 19, 49, 111, 182, 185,
188, 199, 214–17, 219, 245 (n. 101),
265 (n. 42). *See also* Neo-voluntarism

Wabash Railroad, 15
Wagner, Robert, 110, 112, 116, 118, 119–
20, 122, 123, 126–31, 144, 155, 164,
192, 203
Wagner Act of 1935, xv, 128–31, 139,
154–66, 175, 177, 182, 183, 222; drafting of, 126–27, 207; debated in Congress, 127–28; political and historical
controversy over, 128–29; provisions
of, 129–31; conservative opposition to,
130; liberal and radical support for,
130–31; employer resistance to, 131–

32; legality of, 142–46, 164; attempts
to amend, 151, 154–55, 159, 161, 173,
174, 190, 191, 194, 201–2, 227; and
NWLB, 184–85; and Smith-Connally
Act, 190; and Case Bill, 194; and
strikes, 201; and Taft-Hartley Act,
202–4
Wagner Labor Relations Bill of 1934,
119–23, 125
Wall Street Journal, 67
Walsh, David I., 110, 120–23, 151, 154
Walsh, Frank P., 54–55, 72–73, 75, 77, 86,
109, 116, 119, 156, 166
Walsh report, 55–56, 130
War, U.S. Department of: and labor, 64,
67–69, 234
War Industries Board (WIB), 63–64, 109,
117
War Labor Conference Board (WLCB),
71
War Labor Disputes Act of 1943. *See*
Smith-Connally Act of 1943
War Labor Policies Board (WLPB), 72,
73, 77
War Production Board (WPB), 186–88
Watson, James E., 100
Weeks, Sinclair, 211
Wehle, Louis B., 66, 67, 72, 109
Weiler, Paul, xiii
Welfare capitalism, xiv, xvii, 192
Welfare state, xvii
Western Federation of Miners, 38, 43
Western Union Company, 72, 73
Westinghouse, 171
Wheeler, Burton K., 68, 98, 112
Wierton Steel Company, 118, 126
Wilentz, Sean, xi
Wilkerson, James, 95
Wilkerson injunction, 95
Willard, Daniel, 95
Williams, William Appleman, xiv
Wilson, William B., 52, 54, 64, 65, 69, 70,
71, 72, 79, 87, 108
Wilson, Woodrow, 35, 37, 107, 108, 109,
110, 166, 167, 176; and labor, 52–60,
61–65, 69–71, 166, 167; appointments
to CIR, 54; and Clayton Act, 57; and

election of 1916, 58, 60; and railroad strike threat of 1916, 58–59; and Adamson Act, 59–60; and appointment of Samuel Gompers to Advisory Council on Labor, 61; and World War I, 62–65, 69–71; and Special Mediation Commission, 64, 70–72; and NWLB, 72–74, 166; and First and Second Industrial Conferences, 76, 79–81; two minds on labor question, 77–78; and Boston police strike of 1919, 78; and steel strike of 1919, 79

Witt, Nathan, 156, 157, 158
Witte, E. E., 103
Woll, Matthew, 152
Wolman, Leo, 121

Women workers, 73, 198. *See also* Protective legislation
Wood, Leonard, 79
Woodworkers' union, 68
World War I, xvi, 59, 60, 61–63, 197, 233
World War II, xvii, 161, 169–91 passim, 194, 197, 215, 216
Wright, Carroll, 13, 14, 19, 20, 31, 42
Wyzanski, Charles, 125, 126, 145

Yablonski, Joseph, 222
Yellow-dog contracts, 32, 35, 45, 47, 65, 104, 130
Young, A. H., 123

Zolberg, Aristide, 235–36